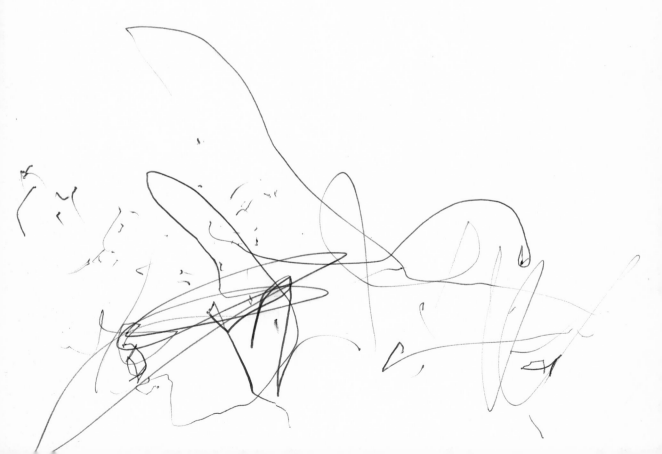

Once Upon a
Christmastime

Once Upon a Christmastime

Short Stories for the Season

Deseret Book Company
Salt Lake City, Utah

Library of Congress Cataloging-in-Publication Data

Once upon a Christmastime.
     p.   cm.
   ISBN 1-57345-287-4 (hardcover)
   1. Christmas stories. 2. Inspiration—Religious aspects—
Christianity—Fiction.
PS648.C45053   1997
813'.0108334—dc21   97-26741
                                                                          CIP

Printed in the United States of America   18961
10 9   8   7   6   5   4   3   2   1

CONTENTS

Thanks to the following, who helped make this book possible:

Sheri L. Dew, vice-president of publishing at Deseret Book
Jay A. Parry, editor and project manager
Elsha L. Ulberg, administrative assistant
Jennifer Pritchett, editorial assistant
Daniel B. Hogan, copy editor
Richard Erickson, designer
Patricia J. Parkinson, typographer
Christine Y. Neilson, proofreader
Vicki L. Parry, proofreader
Kathryn L. Poulter, proofreader

And special thanks to the dozens of authors
who shared their talent in creating memorable short stories
of the wonderful season of Christmas.

SHOP WITH A COP

Jack Weyland

DUTTON WAS ON HIS WAY home after working all night and most of the afternoon, investigating a string of convenience-store holdups that had been plaguing the metropolitan area since late November. He was five blocks from his run-down flat on the eighth floor of a soon-to-be condemned building when Rita, the police dispatcher, contacted him by radio and reminded him of the Shop with a Cop program, taking place at that very moment at a shopping mall on the other side of town.

"They need you there, Dutton. More kids showed up this year than they had planned on."

"Get someone else," he muttered.

"There isn't anybody else to get. C'mon, Dutton, this is for kids. It won't kill you to help out for once, will it? They're expecting you."

"How can they be expecting me when I never signed up?"

"I just talked to them down at the mall and told 'em you were on your way."

"You had no right to do that."

"I know, but I figured you could use some Christmas spirit. Get over there and spread some cheer. I'll tell 'em you're on your way. Report at the main office at the mall. Actually, you're late already. If you want to use your siren, be my guest."

Dutton didn't use the siren. That would have been against regulations. Dutton never did anything against regulations. That's why he was such a good cop.

When he first stepped into the main office at the mall, he saw a girl about ten years old and a boy around two or three. They both had blond hair and blue eyes.

"Have you come to take these two away?" the secretary asked hopefully.

"That's right. I'm Dutton."

The boy took one look at Dutton and started to cry.

"Termi—nator," the boy whispered to the girl.

"He thinks you're the Terminator," the girl said. "You know, like in the movies."

"I'm not the Terminator," Dutton said to the boy, with a slight European accent and deep voice thrown in just to keep the boy in check.

"He's a nice man," the girl explained to her brother. "He's come to take us shopping."

As they left the mall office, Dutton couldn't help himself. He turned to the secretary and said in his lowest voice, "I'll be back."

They left the mall office and headed for the discount store sponsoring the Shop with a Cop program. "You got a name?" Dutton asked the girl.

"Jamie Jordan. Elliott here is my brother."

"Elliott?"

"You don't like the name?"

"It just seems like an awfully big name for such a little boy."

"My mom wants him to grow up and be a lawyer," Jamie said.

Dutton cringed. To him lawyers were the ones who got the people he arrested off on a technicality.

"What's your name?" Jamie asked.

"Dutton."

"What's your last name?" she asked.

"That is my last name."

"What's your first name then?" she asked.

"I just go by my last name."

"How come?"

"I just do, that's all."

"You've never done Shop with a Cop before, have you?" she asked.

"No."

"Do you want me to explain the program to you?" she asked. "This is my fifth time."

"All right, go ahead."

"You're supposed to tag along with Elliott and me and help us pick out presents. Oh, also, you're supposed to act like you want to be our friend. My first year, the cop who took me around told me he'd take me fishing sometime when it got warmer. I waited all summer, but he never called. Finally in August I called the police station and left a message, but he never called back." She sighed. "But that's all right. I probably wouldn't have had any fun anyway."

"Give me his name," Dutton said. "I'll go remind him."

"I wouldn't want you to beat him up."

"Is that what you think I'd do?"

"I don't know. I can't tell much about you. Don't you ever smile?"

"Not much."

"I didn't think so. Well, let's see, that's about all I need to tell you. Oh, except for one thing—in a little while a TV news team will show up, and they'll get a couple of great shots to show on the ten o'clock news. I was interviewed on TV my first year. I was really a cute little kid then, and I smiled real big for the camera, and when they talked to me I told 'em how, because of Shop with a Cop, this was going to be my best Christmas ever. I watched myself that night on the news; it was so good it probably brought tears to everybody's eyes. But now I'm too old. I could never give the same performance. It's hard to fake sincerity, you know what I mean? I'm eleven now. This is my last year on the program. They stop when a kid quits being cute. I'm past that stage."

"I see."

"Actually, you're supposed to say, 'C'mon, Jamie, don't be so hard on yourself. Why, you're as cute as a button.' I heard somebody say that once on TV. It's so stupid. I mean buttons aren't that cute, right?"

Dutton nearly smiled. He used to have a grandmother who told children they were as cute as a button.

They were walking aimlessly through the aisles. Dutton could see other cops and the kids assigned to them finishing up and leaving. He wished he were done. "Can I ask a question?" Dutton said. "What are we doing in this aisle? Are you and little Elliott really that interested in a crock pot?"

"Not really, but this is my last year on the program and I want the full treatment. And that means we've got to walk down every aisle. Why don't you tell Elliott and me how we're going to be best buddies and you'll take us fishing this summer. See, Elliott has never had a real dad."

"How come?"

"Our dad left when Elliott was just a baby. He's never been back."

"I guess I could take you fishing sometime."

"Thanks for saying it. You don't actually have to do it though. It'll just be something I can tell Elliott during the summer. It'll give him something to look forward to."

Dutton looked around. "By the way, where is Elliott?"

They found him standing in front of a ten-foot-tall pyramid made from canned potato chips. He pulled one can from the bottom of the stack.

"Elliott," Dutton called out, sounding like a cop. "Just slowly back away from the stack . . . and nobody'll get hurt."

Elliott reached out and pulled another one out, and the rest came tumbling down around him. He started crying. Dutton rushed in and picked him up in his arms. "How come you didn't listen to me?"

Elliott was crying as cans continued to roll down the aisle.

"Let's get out of here before someone comes," Jamie said quickly.

"No, we're staying here."

"How come? We'll get in trouble."

"We're going to tell 'em what Elliott did and then we're going to offer to help clean up."

"We don't have to do that."

"We have to do it. Go get a shopping cart. We can put some of the cans in there so people won't trip on 'em."

"Did you see who did this?" a bald, cheerless man who worked for the store asked.

Dutton had Elliott in his arms. "This little guy did it. But he's willing to help clean up. I sent . . . my . . . daughter, uh, to go get a shopping cart." Dutton wasn't sure why he said Jamie was his daughter. Maybe just to cut down on having to explain everything. Also, the way Elliott was hugging him made it believable that he was a father.

The clerk nodded his head. "Look, I appreciate you taking responsibility for this. Most people don't. They just run away. I know what it's like though. I had kids of my own once. They're all gone now though. They grow up so fast—enjoy them while you can."

"I'll do that. Thanks."

Jamie returned with a shopping cart.

"You don't really have to clean up," the clerk said.

"No, we'll do it." He caught Jamie's eye. "When you mess up, it's best to own up to it, and try to make things better. Elliott, you need to help too."

Elliott got down and started to pick up the cans.

"I can't believe he's helping," Jamie said to Dutton. "He never helps out around home. It's probably because you're a man."

Dutton was on his knees picking things up when Jamie came to him. At this level she was his height. She came up to him and looked him in the eye and said, "You know what? I wish you could be our dad . . . at least for Christmas Day."

Dutton cleared his throat. "I'm afraid I'm not much good at Christmas."

"What do you usually do on Christmas?"

"I usually take two shifts," he said.

"How come?"

"So someone on the force with a family won't have to work."

"So you never get a Christmas?" she asked.

"Somebody usually brings by a plate of cookies, so it's not too bad."

"You know what I'd like to do sometime on Christmas?"

"No, what?"

"I'd like to go fishing."

"I've never heard of anyone doing that before," Dutton said.

"I know, but it'd be fun, I know it would. If you took us, then we'd both have something to do on Christmas."

Dutton had picked up the last can of potato chips. He was on his way up when Jamie whispered, "Maybe you'd like to meet our mom sometime. She's real nice . . . most of the time. And she can be pretty if she has a reason to—

like if you wanted to come over for Christmas dinner . . . or something."

Dutton felt bad the way this was going. "Look, Jamie, one thing I've learned is that things don't usually work out the way you'd like 'em to."

"I know—you don't have to tell me that."

"Now, I'm sure your mom's real nice, but the truth is that I'm not much good for anything, except for being a cop. That's about the only thing I really do well."

"You could change."

Dutton shook his head. "That's the thing though—I'm not sure I can change. Actually, I'm not sure anybody can change."

"Not even for Christmas?"

"What's Christmas got to do with changing?"

"Don't you ever watch the Christmas specials? Scrooge changed because of Christmas. The Grinch who stole Christmas changed because of Christmas. The other reindeer quit picking on Rudolph. Christmas helps people change."

He hesitated saying what was on his mind. "Jamie, those are just made-up stories. They're not necessarily true."

"What about Jesus then? That's not a made-up story, is it?"

"No, I guess it isn't."

"Didn't angels come and say 'Peace on earth, good will to men'?"

Dutton didn't know what to say. He had worked too long on the force to believe there was much peace on earth. If there was, it wasn't in midtown.

"That was a long time ago, Jamie."

"I know. You don't think people can change?"

He hated to say it. "Maybe for a few days, they can, but not for good."

"Then why do we even have a Christmas?" she asked.

"I don't know. Tradition I guess."

"The hardest thing for me is to think that nothing will ever change, that we'll always live in our dumpy trailer on Pole Line Road, that my mom will always be working as a waitress, and that things will just always stay the same. And that all you'll ever be is a cop, and nobody will ever know what's inside you."

He shook his head. She was sounding much older than eleven. Maybe that's what being on your own so much did to a person. For whatever reason, he felt like he could answer and she might just understand. Or maybe by answering he himself would understand. "There isn't anything inside me—not anymore."

"I don't believe that. My mom could bring it out. She's a nice person. I think you'd like her. And Elliott and I wouldn't stand in your way. I mean like if you wanted to go out with her sometime to a movie, we'd be good while you were gone."

"I know you'd be good, Jamie, I know that. You're a good girl. I could see that the minute I saw you. And I think it's great the way you look out for Elliott and you think about your mom all the time. There's not many like you, that's for sure."

She threw her arms around him. People walked past them, not wishing to say anything. "I've tried so hard," she said through her tears.

"I know you have, Jamie."

He held her because she was sobbing, and then Elliott came to him too and wanted to be held. Dutton did the best he could. He'd never been good at things like this.

Finally Jamie's embarrassment of knowing that people were staring at them got to be too much for her and she moved away. She wiped her tears with the sleeve of her shirt.

"We'd better find something to buy," Dutton said. "The store's almost ready to open for regular customers, and I'll bet your mom will be coming for you real soon."

Jamie didn't really shop around for anything but, instead, just picked the first thing she saw in the toy department. It was yellow and made from plastic and had parts that you put together. Dutton knew it would be broken by the end of Christmas Day.

Dutton held Elliott's hand as they approached the checkout counter, but Jamie stayed her distance.

He walked them outside and waited with them until their mom drove up. Jamie grabbed Elliott's hand and ran with him to the car, and then they got in and drove off.

Dutton didn't get a good look at their mom. He did notice, though, that she was driving an '84 Ford. Because of the black smoke pouring out of the exhaust, he knew he could cite them for violating the state's clean air act. Also, her inspection sticker had expired. But he decided to let it go this time.

Dutton went home. He hadn't realized how empty it was there. He couldn't get Jamie and Elliott out of his mind.

Don't you ever smile? he heard her say in his mind.

No, I never do, he thought.

You don't think people can change?

Maybe for a few days, they can, but not for good.

Then why do we even have a Christmas?

Good question, Dutton thought.

* * *

On Christmas morning, Dutton knocked on the door of a trailer in a sea of other trailers. It was seven o'clock in the morning. He had to knock several times before a woman came to the door wearing a tattered gown.

Dutton showed her his badge. "I'd like to have a word with you. Could you come outside for a minute?"

"Is anything wrong?"

"No, ma'am, I just need to talk to you, that's all."

"All right. Let me get dressed first, okay?"

"Yes, of course."

Five minutes later, when she got in his car, he tried not to stare. She *was* a pretty woman— short blonde hair, pale features, nice eyes.

"Ma'am, my name is Officer Dutton. I was the one who did the Shop with a Cop program with Jamie and Elliott."

"Yes?"

Dutton was embarrassed, realizing how stupid this was going to sound, especially coming from the one everyone on the force called Ice Man. He cleared his throat. "I was wondering if I could spend Christmas Day with you and Jamie and Elliott."

Her mouth dropped open. "Well . . . I don't know."

"Actually, Jamie . . . sort of . . . invited me."

"Oh. Well, in that case, I guess so. It's just that I didn't plan for company, that's all."

"That's all right. I brought some things— food and some presents for Jamie and Elliott . . . and even you." He started to blush. "Not much for you though because we really don't know each other, and I certainly don't want you to worry . . . you know . . . about me. You have nothing to worry about. I'll be out of your life after today. This is just for Christmas. One thing, though, I'd kind of like to take the kids fishing this afternoon. I bought fishing poles and bait and everything. You could come too if you want. Of course I realize that not everyone likes to fish. Actually, to tell you the truth, I'm not sure I even like to fish."

Jamie's mom ran her hand nervously through her hair. "I'm sorry. This is so confusing. And I just woke up. Who did you say you were again?"

"Dutton. I can show you my badge if you'd like."

"What's your last name?"

"That is my last name. I go by Dutton."

"I see. Come to think of it, I do remember Jamie saying something about you. Are you the one Elliott thought was the Terminator?"

"Yes ma'am, that's me. I have a plan, actually, if I could go over that with you."

"All right."

"First thing we do is carry in the presents and the food I got, and then we go wake up Jamie and Elliott, and then we sit around the tree—"

"I should warn you about the tree. It's only plastic and it's missing about half of its branches."

"It'll be okay. Like I said, we sit around the tree, and we watch the kids open their presents, and then we have cinnamon buns and orange juice."

"I don't have any cinnamon buns, and orange juice is very expensive."

"It's in the trunk, ma'am."

"Oh."

"And then after breakfast, we play some of the games I got 'em for Christmas, and then, if it'd be all right, we put the turkey in the oven, and then we go fishing. And then when we come back, we eat the turkey and maybe we sing some Christmas songs, and then I was thinking maybe you could talk to the children about the true meaning of Christmas."

She cleared her throat. "You want me to do that?"

"Yes, ma'am. I was hoping you would."

"I'm not sure I even know what the true meaning of Christmas is."

"I know what you mean, but, actually, I think Jamie knows what it is. At least she was talking about it at the mall."

"What did she say?"

"Something about the fact that we can change. To me that seems about as good an explanation as any. Actually, if you think about it, I guess that's why I'm here. I must have believed her."

"We can change?"

"Yes, ma'am, it looks that way."

She looked over at him and, for the first time, smiled. "If you're so fired up about changing, then maybe you can learn to call me by my first name."

"What's your first name, ma'am?"

"Melissa, but the people down at the diner call me Mel."

"I'll stick with Melissa, if that'd be all right. It's a pretty name, ma'am." He corrected himself. "Melissa, that is."

"Thank you."

It took them ten minutes to lug everything into the trailer, what with the presents and all the food. And then they crept into the room where Jamie and Elliott were sleeping.

Dutton knelt down and whispered. "Jamie? It's Christmas. Time to get up."

She opened her eyes. "You came for Christmas, didn't you?"

"I did. And we're going fishing later on."

She smiled. "This will be my best Christmas ever."

And it was . . . for that year. But it got better year after year.

JACK WEYLAND is the author of twenty books for LDS youth. In addition, more than fifty of his short stories have been published in the *New Era*. He and his wife, Sheryl, have five children and two grandchildren. They both teach at Ricks College in Rexburg, Idaho.

THE SECOND NOEL

Lael Littke

WHEN MY SISTER, Ardis, made up her mind about something, nothing could change her direction. That's why I knew we were in for trouble when she said she was going to play "The First Noel" for Sister Burton's Christmas piano recital.

"But that's what *I'm* going to play," I protested. "Sister Burton told me I could play 'The First Noel' because it's my favorite."

Ardis shrugged. "It's *my* favorite, too."

"But I spoke for it first," I said.

"I spoke for it second," Ardis said implacably.

"But-but-but," I sputtered, "you can't list it twice on the program. Everyone will get bored if they see 'The First Noel' played by Sharlene Renquist and then 'The First Noel' played by Ardis Renquist. They won't stay to listen to you."

"Yes, they will," Ardis said. "They'll know I'll play it *better* than you do, so they'll want to wait and hear it."

"Won't," I said.

"Will," Ardis said.

I wasn't too worried that Ardis would play it better than I did. Ardis didn't practice. We hadn't had the piano very long, but I was into a second book of music while Ardis, although she was eleven and I was only nine, was still only halfway through the first book. She hated to work on scales and said she was too old to play "Birds in the Treetops" and "Happy Little Breezes."

On the other hand, she *might* play it better

because Ardis had a flair for the piano. When *she* played "Ponies in the Pasture," you could almost see those little horses prance across the grass. When *I* played it, the ponies had sore knees.

"Besides, if you're going to make all this fuss, I'll change the title," Ardis said. "I'll call it 'The Second Noel' when I play it."

It was no use arguing. "Mo-om," I yelled. "Ardis is being mean to me."

"Ardis," Mom yelled back. "Don't be mean to your little sister."

It was something she said five or six times a day. It never did any good. Today wasn't any different.

Not that Ardis *meant* to be mean. It's just that, like I said, when she set her mind to something you might as well move out of her way or be steamrollered.

I wasn't moving out of her way, though, about "The First Noel." It was the only piano piece I could play that wasn't a baby thing like "Frogs in the Pond." I could play "Silent Night," but that was so easy it wasn't much better than "Frogs."

I don't know what Ardis said to Sister Burton, but she agreed to let her play the same thing as I'd be playing.

I didn't dare protest—I guess I was more than a little afraid of Sister Burton. She was a big woman who moved around the room like a mobile grand piano whenever she taught piano lessons. "Count, Sharlene," she'd bellow when I messed up on the timing of a tune. Or, "Watch the fingering. You're allowed to use the same fingers more than once, you know."

So was I going to whimper about Ardis playing the same Christmas carol as I did on the recital?

Not to Sister Burton, I wasn't.

But as time went on, I wished I had. I could play "The First Noel" okay, but it was just a pounding out of notes. A simplified version, too. It just sort of thudded steadily along the way I played it.

Our little brother, Herbie, sang with me. "The FIRTHT NoEL," he'd sing, "the ANGelth did THAY . . . " Herbie had some teeth missing.

But he couldn't sing along so well when Ardis played her rendition of "The First Noel," because it was hard to figure out just what she was going to do next.

Ardis played "The First Noel" like nobody had ever played it before. Her best friend, Molly, was one of those people who was born knowing how to play the piano. Molly could toss off a Beethoven sonata with three fingers and a couple of toes. And Ardis was learning fancy stuff from her, stuff like chords and trills and glissandos.

I thought Mom would get sick of hearing "The First Noel" all day long—my plodding version plus Ardis's prancing one. Sometimes she'd stand in the doorway of the living room when Ardis was playing and listen with a puzzled smile. But she didn't say anything.

Dad was profuse with his praises. "And how is my little concert pianist today?" he'd say if Ardis was practicing when he came home from work. Then he'd remember I was there, too, and he'd amend that to, "My *two* little concert pianists?"

Even Sister Burton was dazzled. "Ardis," she'd say, "your possibilities are limitless. But you must build on a foundation. You must do your scales and exercises, dear."

In answer Ardis would launch into yet another version of "The First Noel," this time with little twinkles in an upper octave, which made you think of bright, warm stars shining over the manger scene.

And Sister Burton would smile with pleasure.

I continued to tramp through the scales as well as practicing my simplified rendition of "The First Noel." I considered playing "Silent Night" instead since nobody else was doing that. I even memorized it after Sister Burton told us to have an encore number ready. "Just in case," she said.

But "Silent Night" was just not impressive enough to be my main offering. So I'd hurry each day to pound out my practice before Ardis did hers. Otherwise the comparison was too depressing.

Actually, it wasn't hard to beat Ardis to the piano, because she didn't practice every day. She said she already knew her piece. In fact, she said, she usually changed it each time she played it anyway, so why practice?

One day she said to me, "Sharlene, if you'll give me some blank audiotapes for Christmas, I'll make a tape for you to keep."

I knew what she meant, but I said, "A tape of what?"

She knew I knew what she meant, and I knew she knew I knew. "We can tape your version, too," she said. "Then we can remember everything. Maybe we will want to make a time capsule and put the tape in it. Then we can open it as a Christmas present in twenty years and remember how things were before . . ."

She didn't finish the sentence, but I knew she meant before she became rich and famous as a concert pianist.

"Forget it," I said. "I don't want to remember any of this."

No way was I going to give Ardis blank audiotapes for Christmas.

In fact, I didn't think I'd give her anything.

One day Sister Harkness, who plans the sacrament meeting music for our ward, was at our house when Ardis was practicing. She listened, astounded.

"Ardis," she said, "I had no idea you were such a piano virtuoso."

Ardis smiled indulgently and did a rapid arpeggio with her right hand.

"We'd really love to have you play a solo in sacrament meeting soon," Sister Harkness said. "And some of the other wards would probably like to have you play for them, too."

"I think that can be arranged," Ardis said grandly, as if she were a queen granting a favor to a peasant.

Sister Harkness didn't seem to notice. "I had no idea," she marveled as Ardis did some fancy descending chords with her left hand while her right hand stuttered on one high note like a chicken pecking corn.

And Herbie, playing with his toy cars in a corner, broke into, "The FIRTHt NoEL, the ANGelth did THAY-AY-AY-AY-AY-AY."

In past years Christmas had been fun at our house, and Ardis and I had always done a lot of giggling and guessing about what we'd got for each other. But this year everything was focused on the coming Christmas recital. And Ardis.

I think Mom and Dad looked forward to showing off as the parents of the newest piano prodigy.

And Herbie bragged to his friends that his sister could play the piano like a whole army marching on tiptoes.

The night of the recital came. Sister Burton had arranged for it to be held in the formal meeting room of the public library because of the grand piano there.

"It's good for the children to experience a grand piano," she always said. "And it looks so professional."

Not all of us sounded professional, though.

Jamie Marsh, five years old, played "Jolly Old St. Nicholas" with his hands on the wrong keys.

People applauded anyway. Maybe they were just glad that he was through.

Rhonda Stratton, age seven, forgot her music altogether and broke into tears.

The audience didn't seem to know what to do. A few applauded. A few murmured, "It's all right, Rhonda," and reached out to pat her back as she slunk to her seat.

I plodded stolidly through "The First Noel," simplified version. I made only one mistake and that was because I hadn't really worked out the fingering. There was a patter of polite applause when I finished.

Mom and Dad hugged me when I went back to sit with them, and Herbie whispered, "That was nithe, Tharlene."

Ardis smiled a little but didn't say anything.

Nine other students played their pieces before it was Ardis's turn. She was last on the program.

Then Sister Burton stood up and said, "You've probably wondered why the Renquist sisters are both playing 'The First Noel' tonight. They thought it would be interesting to show you a contrast of the standard version, the way we all sing it, and a concert version."

That was news to me. Had Ardis told her to say that?

"So," Sister Burton continued, "here is Ardis Renquist."

There was some applause as Ardis stood up. Apparently people had already heard about the treat that was in store for them.

She walked up to the piano, stood for just a moment with her hand on its curve, nodded to the audience, then drifted gracefully onto the bench, carefully arranging her skirt as she sat down.

Where had she learned to do all that? It made the rest of us seem like geeks.

The audience was silent as she flexed her hands. Then she bent over the keys.

She started off softly. "The first Noel, the angels did say . . ." It was an appropriate mood for angels—gentle and reverent.

She did an arpeggio when she got to the sheep, as if to remind us that there were a lot of them. The part about the cold winter night she played in an upper octave, with notes as brittle as icicles.

It wasn't until she got to the stars shining in the east that the music got really exciting. She did a long glissando then, and you could see the light spilling down to the earth. The amazed shepherds trudged (soft, trudging chords) to the manger to worship, and the angel choir triumphantly emphasized, "Born . . . is . . . the . . . king . . . of . . . Israel."

But she wasn't finished. Now church bells chimed out joyfully as she swooped into a bonus verse. A thousand angel choirs sang. I wouldn't have been surprised to have heard cannons blasting out the good news.

But no. As she came back to the Noels, she suddenly softened down to a worshipful and reverent "Born is the king of Israel."

It made you feel full of awe.

I could see several people wipe their eyes.

Even I joined in the thunderous applause.

People smacked their hands together so hard you'd think they'd hurt.

One father even yelled, "Brava!"

Ardis's face was flushed as she enjoyed her

triumph. She stood up and bowed to the audience as if she'd been doing it all her life.

Again and again she bowed. The audience continued to applaud.

"They're clapping her on," Herbie whispered. His own hands spatted together so hard his cheeks jiggled.

He was right. The audience wanted an encore. They *demanded* an encore.

So what was she going to play? "Ponies in the Pasture?" It was the only other piece she knew.

But how could she play that for an audience whose ears still vibrated with the majesty of her "First Noel"?

Ardis had stopped bowing and stood there by the piano, her face now flushed not with triumph but with embarrassment.

I watched with something close to glee filling my heart. Smug, arrogant Ardis, who had sneered at practicing scales and had taken over *my* recital piece, was getting what she deserved. Ardis, who was right now in the process of learning that you can't be a concert pianist if you only know one piece of music.

But my glee turned sour as the audience continued to clap and Ardis continued to stand there.

I thought of all the giggles we'd shared and how she always helped me with my math homework. I thought of the times she'd rescued me at school when some older kid teased me.

I thought of Christmas. What was Christmas all about, anyway?

I stood up. She'd been wrong, but it was Christmas and I had a gift I could give her.

She looked at me, bewildered, as I approached the piano. "Sit down," I told her. "We're going to do a duet of 'Silent Night.'"

She sat, turning terrified eyes on me. I took my place beside her.

"Just do some twinkles and arpeggios," I whispered. "Key of C."

I began playing softly. "Silent night. Holy night."

After a couple of hesitant plinks, Ardis got into it. As softly as falling snow, she touched the treble keys, counterpointing the melody I was playing, as if I were accompanied by a heavenly harp.

We played it through twice, then Ardis stood up and asked the audience to join in singing the third verse.

It was a perfect ending to the Christmas concert. There was no clapping when it was over, just a reverent silence.

People congratulated us as we headed out to the parking lot, but Ardis was quiet. She was worried about finding Sister Harkness and telling her she couldn't play a solo in sacrament meeting after all. "I can't play 'The First Noel' in January," she said.

In the car Mom and Dad told us how proud they were of both of us, and Ardis squeezed my hand.

"I learned a lot tonight," she whispered. "You don't need to give me those audiotapes for Christmas."

I hadn't planned to.

But maybe I would anyway. Maybe I needed to remember this night and the way it felt so good to realize what Christmas really was and what being part of a family meant.

"We can learn some duets," Ardis was saying, and I knew I might as well start practicing the bass part because her mind was made up.

"We can be a sister act," I said.

"We already are," Ardis said.

And Herbie sang, "Thleep in heavenly peathe."

LAEL LITTKE frequently uses impressions from her childhood in her books for national publishers as well as for Deseret Book. *The Second Noel* is fiction, but Lael says her younger brother was the model for Ardis since he could play the showy *Robin's Return* after a year of piano lessons while she was still plodding through *The Merry Farmer.* Her Bee There series with Deseret Book won the Independent LDS Booksellers Award for the Best Youth/Children's Book in 1995. She is the widow of George C. Littke and has one married daughter, Lori Silfen, as well as too many cats and a couple of dogs.

CHRISTMAS DAY IN THE MORNING

Susan Evans McCloud

CHRISTMAS IN THE COUNTRY—something I had never thought to experience. I rubbed my sleeve along the frosted windowpane and pressed my nose, childlike, against the cold glass.

It had been beautiful the first time the snow blew across the brown cornfields, frosting every inch of the landscape with a generous layer of white. Hugh built a fire in the deep, blackened hearth. I brewed hot chocolate and placed candles on saucers, and we cuddled on the couch together, the room around us pulsing with a soft, cordial light.

We were still playacting then: a newly married couple with our first teaching job. I grew up in a busy Chicago suburb, and Hugh in a typical, midsized American city in the heart of Missouri. We took the position in the little community of a thousand because it was the best one offered us, and because we were drawn in by the romance of, well, face it, of beauty—the beauty of love and our new life together; of the unhurried, uncrowded countryside; of brisk, fresh mornings and slow sunsets; of the faces of eager children and of strangers who would soon become friends.

That was four months ago. Today I did not want to think about any of those things we had shaded with such sweet idealism. Today I wanted to feel sorry for myself, and even a little bit angry. Today was Christmas Eve.

I drew back from the window, where the swirls of snow obscured everything, and felt my eye drawn toward the long wooden table piled high with presents—presents I had selected so carefully and wrapped with such care. I was proud of them—proud of how much of myself went into the selection or creation of every one. For days now my excitement had been building, and I could scarcely wait to place each offering into the hands of its intended and see pleasure and appreciation spill from their eyes, from their hearts into my heart.

A cold draft shivered along my skin like a sudden douse of ice water.

"Oh, shut the door, Hugh!" I cried. "You're sucking all the heat out! It will take us a week to warm these cavernous rooms up again."

My husband managed to grimace and grin at the same time.

"Has the snow let up—even a little?" I asked.

He shook his head. "Worse, if anything." He pulled his thermal gloves from his fingers and placed his cold hands against my cheeks. I started at the tingling touch, then covered them with my own, and Hugh moaned in appreciation. "I'm not used to being out in weather like this," he said, "except to dash from a heated house to a heated car."

We smiled weakly at one another. I could feel his reluctance, like an apology, before he even started to speak again. "I plowed a path to the barn," he said, "and another out to the road . . ." I saw the hesitation in his eyes.

"It's just past noon," I said. "There's still time for the plows to come. If we leave before dark—"

His shaking head cut off my words midsentence.

"It's just over three hours to Chicago!"

"Double in this weather—even if the roads were plowed, and the blizzard let up."

I knew what he was saying; I shouldn't have made him spell it out for me. But he did so, kindly, as his eyes searched the misery of my face.

"I think you'd best call your folks, Audrey, and let them know we can't make it."

Stop it! I told myself, sucking my bottom lip in. *You're a married woman now. You can't stand here and blubber like a spoiled child.*

I walked to the wall where the phone hung and dialed the familiar number, then waited. "Nothing's happening," I said dully, at length. Hugh took the receiver from my hand. "The line's dead," he said.

I grabbed it back again, having to listen to the mute silence myself. "I don't believe it," I moaned. "This is our first Christmas together. You know how hard I've worked—the sewing and baking, not to speak of the shopping. Julie and Rob will be expecting us . . ."

Julie and Rob were our oldest friends—we four had met our first year at Northwestern. We were going to celebrate in the city, then they planned to drive back here with us—a retreat in the country for a few days, immersing ourselves in music and poetry, before going back to the real world again. We had planned and arranged and anticipated together for weeks—the perfect holiday.

"Audrey?"

Hugh had his hands on my shoulders. He was bending close to me, his eyes intent upon mine. "That's it, sweetie. It's still our first year together. I know you're disappointed, but we can find some way to make it memorable, despite—everything."

He finished the sentence lamely, halfheartedly. I knew the thoughts that sprang up in me were both petty and ungrateful, and I had not really meant to voice them until I heard myself speaking out loud.

"Nice as they are, that's all we've had, Hugh, is nights by the fire together. I'm lonely—I miss my friends, my little brothers and sisters—" I choked on tears that constricted my throat. "Christmas, more than any other time, is for people, for fellowship, for celebration."

"I know, Audrey . . . I'm so sorry."

We looked at each other more than a bit mournfully, tenderness struggling against disappointment. Then a sudden thought startled me into life: "My parents will worry about us! We have to get in touch with them somehow!"

Hugh glanced toward the white, sightless window. "This blizzard is all over the news, sweetie. They'll figure we didn't even start— they'll try to call us, and put two and two together."

"We're stranded!" I blurted.

"Snowbound—that word has a nicer connotation, somehow."

"What's the difference!" I pouted, turning away from him, suddenly unwilling to have his big, sorrowful eyes gazing into my soul. Long hours stretched before me, and they seemed limp and colorless. "We don't have anything for supper," I realized out loud, "except sugar cookies, a pumpkin pie, and a huge pan of kuchen."

The German ladies who cooked in the lunchroom at my husband's school had taught me the art of kuchen, with a light, moist dough that baked up much like my mother's sweet rolls but was smothered in sweet, sticky fruit instead. I had been anxious to show it off— after eating my father's turkey and dressing, my mother's famous fruit salad, and Aunt Betty's cooked yams.

"Have we anything at all?" Hugh asked. "Something in the freezer?"

He had already crossed the kitchen to check for himself. "A big package of pork chops," he said, with relief. "I'll get them out to thaw." He whistled under his breath as he unwrapped the white butcher paper. "I'll help you cook them. We can scare up some potatoes and carrots and maybe—" He stopped himself short. "I'd better feed the stock first and check on Millie, like I told Mr. Shephard." He flashed me a smile of encouragement. "Then it will all be taken care of, and we can relax."

I watched him don his boots and coat, pull the flaps of his cap down over his ears, and stomp out into the snow again. It would be dark in a couple of hours; the sky was already a gloomy, glowering gray. He disappeared from my sight long before he reached the barn. "This can't be happening!" I cried aloud to the impartial stillness. Then I wandered back into the house, whose rooms seemed stark, cheerless, and unconcerned with the distress in my heart.

Hugh burst in the back door, much sooner than I had expected him, breathing frost and a tense excitement he could scarcely contain.

"Merciful heavens, Audrey!" he cried. "I think Millie's getting ready to have her calf!"

"That can't be!" I rose, feeling his sense of panic rush into me. "He said it shouldn't be before Christmas, unless she came early—he said that he'd call—and come back at once. If anything happ—"

Hugh shrugged his shoulders in a helpless gesture. *Of course Mr. Shephard could not call. What had I been thinking?* "Is there a vet near here?"

"I'm sure there are several; in fact, I think I have the number of one somewhere. But—"

Bill Shephard was our landlord. He owned the place we lived in, playing at being farmers like we seemed to be playing at everything else. "What can we do?" My voice came out little and thin, and the sound of it annoyed me.

"Jimmy Boswell's our nearest neighbor. I don't think it's half a mile to his place. I'll walk down and see if he'll come help us."

"Oh, Hugh, not the Boswells!" I groaned. "Aren't they the ones with all the dirty, anemic-looking children?"

"I s'pose they are, but what does that matter here, Audrey?" Hugh scowled.

My words had offended and probably disappointed him. He never spoke of other people disparagingly. In fact, he seemed to notice something good in everyone, often when I could not.

"I'll be off then," Hugh said, watching me intently from under the brim of his hat.

I flew at him suddenly, kissing his cold cheek, then his lips. "Be careful!" I whispered. I could feel him relax.

"Oh, I'll be all right." He pressed his lips to my forehead. "I'll be back with help before you can miss me."

I missed him as soon as the door closed behind him, closed me in with the empty silence of this strange Christmas Eve.

I turned on a recording of my favorite carols. *It's too early to cut up vegetables to go with the pork chops,* I thought, realizing vaguely that, if a calf was really on its way, dinner would wait until after the event—and who could say how long that might be?

The music did not have its usual, warming effect upon me. I could hear the keen of the wind above the words of the song. I picked up a book of Christmas stories and poems and attempted to read. But nothing on the pages seemed real. I wondered how Hugh was doing, if he had found his way to the Boswells', if they had agreed to help. I could picture him wandering off the snow-obscured road, breaking his leg as he stumbled into one of the ditches that lined these country roads. I could envision him lying there frozen the following morning when I went out to look for him, after a long night of terror and longing . . . and I knew, with a clarity I had never experienced before, how much I loved him, how much a part of my own self he had become. *Nothing else is essential,* I thought. *Nothing else is even important, as long as we have each other, and this love that can carry us anywhere . . .*

Heavy pounding outside the door made me start—it was loud and urgent. I jumped to my feet as half a dozen people poured through the open portal—different shapes and sizes of snowmen, shaking the cold, wet weight onto the kitchen floor. I saw no one but Hugh until his eyes met mine and he smiled at me.

"Audrey, let me introduce you to the Boswell clan! Jimmy, and his son of the same name, and over here, Abe." The two Jimmies were of medium height and slightly stocky, but Abe fit his name—tall and lanky, with thick, disheveled black hair and pensive, watchful eyes.

"The girls—they came along to keep you company, honey, and in case we needed extra hands. Their names are Emma and Alicia."

"Lovely names," I murmured

"Oh, and the little one here is Annie."

I looked down into a cherub's face, not more than five years old.

"She won't be any trouble, ma'am," Emma said shyly. "But we didn't dare leave her alone. She has asthma, you see, and if one of her attacks came upon her—"

The men had opened the door to a rush of dark, icy air. I shivered. "Are you going out there already?"

Jimmy the younger grinned. "Millie won't wait for us to warm our hands, missus! We'll be all right!"

I felt foolish. The door closed upon myself and my visitors, and I wondered what in the world we should do. "Would you like some cocoa to warm you up?" I ventured. *Of course they would!* I put on the kettle and measured the chocolate into large mugs, then remembered the plate of sugar cookies and brought those out, too. We sat around the fire, cups on our knees or a table beside us.

"You're nearly as good a cook as Emma," Annie said.

I smiled at the older girl. "Do you do a lot of the cooking?" I asked. "Your mother must appreciate that."

"Mother's been dead these three years," Alicia said softly. "Emma does all the cooking because she enjoys it, and she's so good at it. I do the sewing and mending, and usually the dishes, 'cause I don't mind."

"I help with dishes," Annie chirped, "and I keep our room clean."

"Do you three share a room," I asked, trying to take all this in.

"Yes," Emma answered. "We like it that way."

"I have a sister," I answered "but, being the oldest, I always wanted a room of my own. When Mother finally gave in to my whining and fussing and had my dad fix up a little corner of the basement, I was miserable—though it took me half a year to admit it and ask Sarah if I could come back."

They relaxed because I had been open with them, because they saw me, at least in a small way, to be like themselves. We talked nonstop then, unaware of time, of wind and snow, of hunger—"Oh, dear!" I said suddenly. "I'd better put the pork chops on to cook. If the men should come in now, half frozen and starving—"

"Let me help you." Emma rose to her feet and followed me out to the kitchen, the other two trailing behind. Actually, it happened the other way round; I helped Emma, who worked with an assurance and efficiency I had not yet come near to experiencing. She found a turnip in the fridge that she added to the potatoes and pulled jars of herbs from my cupboard that I'd never used before. Once the fragrant concoction was bubbling in the oven she asked, a little shyly, if she might stir up a quick batch of bread. Hiding my astonishment, I went in search of yeast and flour and watched with appreciation as she kneaded the dough and the loaves took form.

"Emma sells twenty loaves of bread a week," Annie said proudly. Emma looked down, her fair cheeks blushing, and Alicia gave her sister a gentle poke in the ribs.

"That is admirable," I cried. "No, it's downright amazing."

"She does it for us," Alicia said, determined to defend her sister, now that I knew anyway. "I want to go to college and study music, so we put part of the bread money away each week."

"Some goes for my medicine," Annie added, with an air of importance.

Emma, resigned, looked up from her loaves. "When Mother died there were lots of hospital bills the insurance didn't cover. And farming has been slow these past few years . . ."

Her voice trailed off. I realized I was trembling. I wanted to gather them into my arms—all at once.

"Let's go see if the calf's born yet!" Annie cried, jumping up and down.

"We might take some hot chocolate and cookies to the men," Emma suggested hesitantly.

"Of course! Why didn't I think of that?"

We moved quickly, anxious now that we had made the decision. When I walked out into the cold, it hit me with a force that pierced all the way through me. I gasped, and Annie giggled and reached a gloved hand for mine.

"It won't be so bad once you get used to it," she soothed.

"Look at the stars," Alicia breathed, her face lifted upward.

I raised my eyes—I had never before seen such splendor, so many glittering points of light, so many clumps of glowing, pulsing stars sweeping across a sky that was more of a soft, plum-stained blue than it was black.

"O holy night . . ." Alicia whispered.

"Sing it for us," I asked, my eyes entreating hers. "Just the first verse."

The notes, crystalline-pure, floated into the blue night, encircling us, spiraling up to the silent, watching stars. *A thrill of hope, the weary world rejoices*—I had forgotten altogether the real meaning of Christmas. Even in my giving there had always remained a sense of myself, of pride, and of all the trappings that money can buy. *For yonder breaks a new and glorious morn*—I looked into the beautiful, solemn faces of the three motherless girls. *Can a new dawn break within the soul? Isn't that what the Christ child intended?*

We walked the remainder of the way to the barn clothed in the splendor of those heavenly notes and that young, heavenly voice.

At first I could see nothing in the dusty, steamy interior of the barn. Someone glanced in our direction and spoke—I think it was Abe.

"We've been havin' a bit of trouble with her. But the calf's on his way now."

I could just make out Hugh's grin. "Would you like to help us pull him out, Audrey?"

I realized that a rope was tied about the unborn animal's forelegs. Hugh and the two boys pulled it taut when the cow pushed, and eased when she stopped. Annie leaned close, her eyes wide. "Will he make it?" she whispered.

Just then Mr. Boswell, his hand inside the cow, felt the calf's head—and it came, in one gentle pull, sliding forward, dropping against the soft straw on the floor.

I realized I was holding my breath. The calf did not appear to be breathing. Abe picked him up in his long arms and poked a length of straw into his nostrils, freeing them so the air could pass through, then lifted him by his hind legs and held him upwards—until we could see the lungs start to move.

Someone cheered. I could hear Annie let her breath out in a sigh. The next time I looked over, the calf was beneath his mother, who had begun to lick him slowly and methodically.

"That'll do it," Jimmy Boswell said, rising stiffly.

I looked down at the tray of cookies I had set in the straw at my feet. "We have pork chops and potatoes inside," I assured the tired men, "and some of Emma's bread rising and ready to bake."

Everyone moved toward the door and the crisp outside air. I lingered a little, and Hugh moved up close to me. "I've never been part of a miracle before," he said, his breath against my cheek. "Except when I married you."

I nestled my head against his shoulder. "Not

a bad way to spend Christmas Eve," I murmured, feeling the sudden gathering of tears in my throat.

Hugh pushed back the sleeve of his shirt and glanced at his wristwatch. "It's nearly half past twelve," he said. "Merry Christmas, my love."

The first thing I did on the first Christmas of my married life was to kiss my husband and wrap my whole soul in the warm joy of his love. We walked out of the dim barn hand in hand together, but we were not alone. The spirit of love, the wonder of life moved with us—like a shield, like a glow, like the soft prayer I whispered to One I knew would be listening.

Christmas Day in the morning! my heart sang. "Annie!" I called out; she turned and ran into my arms.

"The baby calf was born in a stable on Christmas morning—just like the baby Jesus," she said, the wonder of it all coursing through her still, lighting her eyes.

"I know." My voice was hoarse now with tears.

I thought of the warm meal that waited, of the gifts—precious belongings of my own—that I was anxious to wrap for the girls. I thought of how wonderful it would be sharing Christmas with this family I had thought—in my ignorance and pride—to reject.

I had spoken of love and giving, but I had not understood my own words. "So much has been born this day, Annie," I whispered. And she looked up at me, as if she knew what I meant.

"Wait up, Emma!" I cried. "Wait for me and Annie."

I took Annie's hand, and Hugh grabbed hold of the other, and the three of us ran—ran through the dark of a Christmas morning, with the stars soaring and singing above our heads—ran to the gentle hearts that waited for us.

Susan Evans McCloud is the mother of five daughters and one son and has five grandchildren (to date). She has published extensively in a variety of media: biography, historical fiction, film, poetry, children's literature. She is the author of the lyrics to the well-loved hymn "Lord, I Would Follow Thee."

SOMETHING FOR MYSELF

Dean Hughes

As he often did these days, Dennis was listening to the radio and reading the war news in the *Ogden Standard-Examiner*. "I can go to the store for you," he told his mother when he saw her putting her coat on.

She smiled. "That's all right. I have a little Santa shopping to do." It was Saturday afternoon, but Christmas was on Monday, so there would be no chance for last-minute shopping on Christmas Eve.

"Are you okay, Mom?"

She hesitated and her smile faded. "I'm worried, Dennis. I can't help it. But I don't want to ruin Christmas—especially for Linda and Sharon."

"I know," Dennis said. "But I don't think they really understand."

Mom touched Dennis's shoulder. "I'm glad I have you to lean on a little," she said, and her eyes filled with tears.

"Glen is smart, Mom. He got through Normandy and Holland all right. He'll get through this."

She patted his shoulder, but she didn't say anything. And then she left. A few minutes later, Dennis was listening to Lowell Thomas on the early news when he heard his dad on the front porch, home earlier than usual. As Dad stepped through the door, he noticed the news and stopped to listen. He was holding his lunch bucket under his arm, and he was wearing a burly wool P-coat over his coveralls.

"Have they talked about Bastogne already?" Dad asked.

Dennis nodded, still listening, but Lowell Thomas began to talk about the battle in the Philippines. "Bastogne is surrounded now," Dennis said. "All the supply lines are cut."

Dad nodded, his face solemn. "Anything about casualties?"

"No. But he said they're living in foxholes, out in the snow, and the temperatures are down around zero at night."

Dennis hated to think of the misery his brother had to be going through. When Glen had first gone to war almost three years ago, Dennis had pictured him single-handedly winning battles, but Dennis was fifteen now, and the romance had gone out of the war. He knew far too many boys his age whose big brothers had been killed. Since he had first heard about Glen being pulled into the German counterattack in the Ardennes—what the papers were now calling the Battle of the Bulge—he had felt an almost constant quivering in his stomach.

"Where's your mother?"

"She walked over to the market. I think she wanted to get some Christmas candy."

"Look, I need you to do something for me. I ain't bought her a thing yet. Could you run downtown and find something?"

"Me?"

"Sure. You'll do better than I would. Maybe some perfume or something. I don't know. You know what your mom likes."

Dad set his lunch bucket on a little end table by the living room couch and pulled his wallet from his back pocket. He took out a five-dollar bill and held it in front of Dennis, who had gotten up from the floor. Dennis took the money, but he said, "She needs a church dress more than anything. But that would cost more than five dollars."

"Wouldn't Penney's have a nice enough dress for that price?"

"I don't think so."

Dad rolled his eyes. "Here's another five," he said. "But don't spend all of it."

So Dennis got his coat, but he was rather annoyed. Mom worked hard to make Christmas nice, and Dad never gave it a thought until the last second.

Dennis walked briskly down the Twenty-sixth Street hill and then turned north along Washington Boulevard. There was no fancy lighting downtown—not with the war on—but Christmas decorations were strung across the wide street: green pine boughs and bright red bells.

As Dennis passed by the Egyptian Theater on his way to Penney's, habit and curiosity caused him to glance over to see what was playing at the theater. As if he could afford to go anyway. But then his eyes shifted, drawn by fate—or something higher—to the display window next door, to the display window that contained perhaps the most beautiful dress he had ever seen: dark blue and elegant, with a white-lace collar. Even the petite mannequin reminded him of his mother. But this was L. R. Samuel's, probably the most expensive store in Ogden. Mom would never shop there. And ten dollars was certainly not enough for a dress like that.

Dennis stood and looked all the same. He knew his mom had never had anything that nice. She always "made do." She didn't work full-time, but she did seasonal work at a cannery and then spent the money on fabric to sew for the girls, or on something special for each of the kids on Christmas.

Dennis started to walk away, but a thought struck him. Maybe the store would let him pay ten dollars now, and a dollar a month or so after Christmas. Surely it was worth the trouble to ask in any case. He pushed his way through the glass doors, but he was immediately conscious of his old corduroy coat, which was frayed around the wrists and collar. Everything looked so fancy in this place.

Dennis slipped down an aisle and glanced about, looking to see where the dresses were. A saleslady with sleek black hair and red lipstick smiled at him and said, "Could I help you?"

Dennis was impressed that she would bother to wait on him. "I'm looking for something for my mother, and I saw that blue dress in the window," he said. "I wondered how much it is."

"I'm not sure," she said. But then she asked, "How much can you afford to spend?" The words, in another tone, might have sounded snooty, but Dennis didn't hear them that way.

"I only have ten dollars, but I was wondering whether I could make payments on it—you know, after Christmas."

The woman crossed her arms and considered. "We only do that on layaways," she said. "But you can't very well give it to your mother for Christmas if it's on layaway."

Dennis nodded. He wanted to leave—it was time to go to Penney's, where he belonged.

"Have you thought about something else? You might want to get her a—"

"No. That's all right," Dennis said. "I want to get her a dress."

"Well, let's take a look. That blue one is probably too expensive, but we have other dresses for around that price."

The woman led him down the aisle to the dresses, pulled one out, and draped it in front of her. But each one she chose seemed more like a housedress, not nearly so classy as the one he had seen in the window. Though his head told him that these dresses were more in his price range, his heart just could not let go of the image in the window.

"What was it you liked about the blue dress?" the woman finally but kindly asked. "Was it the color, or was it the style?"

"Both," Dennis said. "When I saw it on the mannequin, it made me think of my mom."

"She must be pretty then—that's such a beautiful dress."

Dennis nodded. "She's slim, like that." And then Dennis admitted more than he had intended. "But she doesn't have any really pretty dresses."

The woman nodded. "Do you think—if you hurried home—your father would be willing to make up the difference?"

"No. He gave me the ten dollars. It's really his present, not mine."

The woman nodded slowly, as though she were understanding more than Dennis had said. "I'm curious," she said. "Why did he send you rather than coming himself?"

"He thinks I know better what she likes."

The saleslady was holding a dress in her arms, a green one spread across the red dress she was wearing. Dennis felt self-conscious at how closely she was studying his face. "Are you and your mom quite close?" she asked.

"I guess so. We talk a lot."

"That's nice. Are you the oldest?"

Dennis glanced away from her steady gaze. "No. I have a brother in the army." Then, for some reason, he told her the rest. "He's in Bastogne. The city in Belgium that's surrounded by the Germans right now."

"Oh, dear," the woman said. "I've been reading about that. You must be worried."

"I am. My whole family is."

"How's your mom holding up?"

"Okay. She's trying to make Christmas as nice as she can. I have two little sisters who are only eleven and nine."

"The whole country is praying for the boys in Bastogne."

Dennis was stunned when he realized that the woman had tears in her eyes. "I know," he said. "Thanks."

"Do you miss your brother?"

"Sure. But I was only twelve when he left. I can't remember him that well. I wish . . ." But Dennis didn't know how to finish the sentence. There were so many things he wished.

The woman seemed to sense that she had asked enough. She straightened a little and said, "Do you know what size your mother is?"

"I'm not sure. I think eight, or something like that. She's little."

"You say the mannequin looks about right?"

"Yes."

"Well, I have a thought. After a dress has been in the window, we sometimes discount it. Let me see what that one would cost. Wait right here for just a minute."

The woman was gone for quite some time, and Dennis allowed himself to hope. He stood and watched all the well-dressed people, mostly men now, looking for something for their wives. Maybe they had waited until the last minute, but at least they were doing their own shopping. Dennis wished so much that his dad were more like that. He told himself that when he got married he would do more to make Christmas nice for his wife. And he would go to church with his family; he wouldn't let them go by themselves every week.

And then Dennis saw the saleslady walking toward him, the blue dress draped over her arm. She smiled at him, softly, and said, "I worked it out with my manager. You can have it for ten dollars, on the button. Would you like it in a Christmas box?"

Dennis nodded, too amazed to know what to say.

The store was busy, but the woman took the time to tie the box with a ribbon. Dennis watched her long fingers, her bright nail polish, as she tied the bow. He couldn't bring himself to look in her eyes.

But when she was finished, she put the package in his arms and said, "What's your mother's name? I'm wondering if I know her."

"Norma Hayes."

"No. I guess I don't."

"She doesn't ever come in here," Dennis said.

The woman nodded. "I understand. But someday I would like to meet her. I'd like to see her in that pretty dress."

"Maybe I could have her come in," Dennis said, and then he added, "Thanks a lot. I didn't think I would be able to get it."

"I'm just glad I thought of the discount," the woman said, and she gave Dennis's shoulder a little pat.

Dennis started to walk away, but he turned back. "What's your name?" he asked.

She smiled. "Helen Cliff."

"I'll tell my mom."

Strangely, her eyes filled with tears again. "Gosh, you're a handsome boy. I'll bet your mother is proud of you."

"I guess," he said, and he ducked away.

On Christmas morning, Mom tried to keep things bright and fun. Dennis had received much more than he expected: dress slacks for church, a new shirt and sweater, and a winter coat. He was going to feel so much better about going to high school with a nice-looking coat. What he couldn't wait for, though, was for Mom to open the package with the dress in it.

Dad was sitting on the couch, and he had turned the radio on. The news story of the morning was that the Germans had offered to let the Americans in Bastogne surrender, and General McAuliffe had returned a one-word answer to the German commander: "Nuts!"

Dennis watched Mom. The color was draining from her face. "What's going to happen then?" she asked.

"I don't know," Dad said. "Patton is supposed to be marching his troops up there. If the boys can hold out a day or two, maybe everything will be all right."

There were other questions, but Mom clearly didn't want to say any more in front of Linda and Sharon, who were still excited about the gifts they had found under the tree.

Mom turned and nodded to Dennis. "Why don't you play Santa and pass out the rest of the presents."

Dennis was glad to be in control. The gifts that were still under the tree were the wrapped ones, the ones family members had bought for each other. Dennis handed out everything, including the stationery he had gotten for his mom, but he made everyone wait and take turns, and then finally, he gave the last package—the bright red box—to his mother. "This is from Dad," he said.

Mom smiled and said, "Thank you, Hal." Dennis had told Dad that it was a dress, but nothing more. Dad had fussed about spending

the entire ten dollars, but he had finally let it go.

When Mom opened the box and pulled the dress out, she looked stunned. She stared at it, breathlessly, and then looked at her husband.

"Oh, Mom," Linda said, "It's beautiful. Look, it's from *Samuel's!*"

Mom continued to stare at Dad, as though she couldn't believe he had done such a thing. Dad looked confused. He was about to say something when Dennis said, "You'd better check to see if Dad knows what size you are. Try it on."

Mom stood up and held it against her. Dennis thought of the way Helen Cliff, at L. R. Samuel's, had done that.

"I think it's just right," Mom said, and then she hurried off to the bedroom.

Dennis was quick to laugh and say, "Dad, you made a good choice." But when his father tried to ask the obvious question, he ended up saying instead, "You must have gotten it on discount or something. Dresses at Samuel's cost a lot of money."

When Mom came back, she was glowing. The dress did fit, and it was amazing what had happened to her. She looked so classy, so vitalized. "Hal, it's perfect," she said. "Almost too nice." And she went to him, bent over, and kissed him.

But Dad had let this go far enough. "I didn't pick it out," he admitted. "Dennis did."

"That's what I thought," Linda said.

But all Dennis saw was the way his mom turned and looked at him. He thought she would be disappointed, but maybe she had already guessed. In any case, she was crying, and she said, "Oh, Dennis, it's the loveliest dress I've ever owned. Thank you so much."

"Dad bought it. I just picked it out."

"Well, thanks to both of you," and she walked over to Dennis, pulled him to his feet, and hugged him.

The following day was the big after-Christmas half-price sale at L. R. Samuel's. It was also the day when so many people came in to exchange gifts. Helen always dreaded all the fuss. But this year it seemed better to work than to be at home, where she would think too much.

Before the doors opened, Helen was trying to finish arranging some sale items when Dorothy, her manager, walked over to her. "Was your Christmas nice?" Dorothy asked.

"Well, better than I expected. We were careful what we talked about, and the kids did their best to keep me laughing."

"The first Christmas is the hardest one, don't you think?"

"Yes, I'm sure it is."

"How long has it been now?"

"Over six months. He was wounded on the morning of D day, and he died on the tenth of June."

"He was such a good kid. I'm sure you miss him every day."

Helen only nodded.

Dorothy put her arm around Helen's shoulder. "I'm sorry. It doesn't help for me to bring it all up again."

"It's okay."

"I was glad to see one thing," Dorothy said. "I noticed that you bought that pretty dress in the window. Was that for you?"

"Well . . . yes."

"Good. I hoped it was."

"I just felt like doing something for myself," Helen said.

"Good. Sometimes that's what it takes to

get through a hard time like this." Dorothy walked away.

Helen thought of Dennis. What a lovely young man he had been. What a treasure for a mother!

DEAN HUGHES, a full-time writer, has published more than seventy books for children, young adults, and adults. He is currently working on a series of historical novels about World War II. The series is titled "Children of the Promise," and the first volume, *Rumors of War*, was published in the spring of 1997 by Deseret Book. The second is soon to be released.

Dean received his B.A. from Weber State College in Ogden, Utah, and his M.A and Ph.D. from the University of Washington. He spent eight years at Central Missouri State University as an English professor. He has served in many LDS callings, including that of a bishop. He and his wife, Kathleen Hurst Hughes, live in Provo, Utah. They have three children and two grandsons.

UNTO YOU A CHILD IS BORN

Janene Wolsey Baadsgaard

THOMAS WINCHELL WATCHED his daughter's hands trembling, fingers grasping, knuckles turning white. Another hospital room. More pain. Why? Tom longed to race to Jane's bedside, take her in his arms, and rock her back and forth like he did forty years ago when she was a child. He could comfort her then, in the overstuffed rocker, stroke her forehead, and whisper quiet assurances in her ear.

Now he played the quiet observer in the corner of the hospital room—his daughter was having a baby. Jane's husband, Michael, stood at the side of the bed. Tom could only sit quietly in the corner of the birthing room and watch as the large round clock on the wall hummed. Waiting for the pain to return . . . waiting.

Suddenly his daughter cried out. Her contraction peaked, then slowly began to retreat.

What if something goes wrong? Tom thought. *I can't bear another loss.*

As the contraction subsided, Jane opened her eyes.

"Dad?" Jane said, quietly wiping away tears. "Are you still here? Would you like to see my baby born?"

"I'm here, Jane," Tom answered. "I'd like to stay if it's all right with you. I don't want to get in the way—distract you or anything."

Seventy-five years old, Tom had experienced his own children's births in the post–World War II, sterile, hands-off era of fatherhood. He'd paced the floor alone in the hospital waiting room while May gave birth—never seeing, never knowing, never touching. He suddenly felt cheated. He longed to go back, but the years had taught him there is no going back, not ever—only the moment is real. Tom watched his daughter's arms shake as another contraction began. Jane reached for Michael. Tom felt his body tighten at the peak of Jane's pain, his heart race.

"I'd like you to stay," Jane whispered after the pain slowly faded away. Michael nodded silently in agreement.

I don't know how to help her, Tom thought. *What would May do?* During his fifty-one years of married life, Tom had carefully filtered his relationship with his children through his wife. Now he was alone. May was gone. There was no one there to tell him what to do any more.

Tom heard the unborn baby's rapid heartbeat through a machine's sound system at the side of his daughter's bed. Contraction monitoring equipment attached to a belt around Jane's belly slowly released a long white roll of paper draping to the floor, on which the contractions that periodically racked Jane's body appeared like black ink mountains followed by equally black valleys on white tape. If he watched carefully, Tom could tell when the next contraction was about to begin. Then he'd turn his gaze from the paper to his daughter's face.

Tom wondered if God knew of his valleys, of his steep mountains; wondered if his Father in Heaven was near, knowing when the next one was coming, ready to offer aid and comfort as he did now for Jane. Need he only ask?

Jane breathed deeply from her chest, grasping then gripping Michael's forearm until another contraction peaked and slowly faded.

Tom noticed Michael gently rubbing Jane's lower back.

If I'd only known, Tom thought, *I would have been there for May. I could have helped her through this anguish like Michael helps Jane there. A team. May and me, we should have been a team . . .*

Their marriage had been troubled. Tom knew that. The disease that finally took May a week ago had taken her mind years before. Tom inwardly chilled as he thought of his overreactions to May's past mistakes and desperate accusations.

Wasted time, so much time, Tom thought. *Defending me . . . should have tried to understand her sadness. She needed my help, not my judgment.*

Tom heard the automatic blood pressure cuff attached to Jane's arm inflate, then tick slowly as it released the trapped air and gave a reading on the machine. The clock hummed. The baby's heart rate increased with each contraction.

Pressure, Tom thought. *Pressure weighs us down. Forget how to live, how to forgive. Never know how much time we have left.*

For over a year he'd known May was dying; he just didn't want to face it. As May's health gradually deteriorated day after day, Tom found himself slowly, almost indiscernibly, transforming inside. Caring for May's every need—bathing, feeding, diapering, combing—had seemed a baptism into love he'd long forgotten. The pain of past mistakes and accusations fell away, moment by moment, day by day, month by month, and finally year by year—until he stood naked before God, all his smallness revealed to himself.

"Progressive supranuclear palsy," the doctor had said. "No hope of recovery."

But Tom had learned this past year—experience had been his teacher—that there's always hope when there's love; it's never too late.

"How does he do it?" people at church or the grocery store had said as Tom pushed May in the wheelchair or lifted her into the car. "She always looks so beautiful. I hope my husband takes such good care of me if I ever get like that."

Tom didn't know how to tell them, for it surprised even him. In all their fifty years together, this was the best time. It was not hard to take care of May; it had become his whole life, his reason for breathing, his joy. May's suffering had awakened him from a long sleep full of himself to something far greater than his own needs. He didn't have the words to explain his gratitude to those people, for it astonished even himself.

"Heavenly Father, please give me the strength so I won't have to take May to a rest home," Tom pleaded. Yet sometimes late at night alone on his bed in the hall so he could be near May, doubts came. "Can I do it? My son's half a continent away, my daughter's pregnant. If I get sick, who'll take care of May?"

The day before she died, Tom almost dropped May as he carried her from the bed to the wheelchair to take her to the front room window. His strength alone was not adequate any more. Then precisely at that moment when all he had was not enough, something or someone had instantly empowered him, giving him the ability to carry her frail body one more time. May loved the mountains. She wanted to look at the snowcapped peaks surrounding their country home one more time.

May passed away in the middle of the night a little more than a week before Christmas.

Tom couldn't understand the timing. He didn't want to face Christmas morning without her. The day before May died, she told Tom she was happy, she was ready to go. Tom was not ready. But when the time came and May left peacefully in her sleep, Tom felt calm, overwhelmingly peaceful. A ward Relief Society president three times, May had trained Tom about the details of dying. After their last kiss before her skin felt cold, Tom gently removed the pillow from under May's head, squared her shoulders, folded her hands, and straightened out her legs.

"I love you, May," Tom had said, brushing his cheek next to hers for their last touch.

Suddenly Jane cried out, her anguished plea filling the birthing room.

"Oh . . . help me!" Jane pleaded, grabbing the air in her clenched hands.

The nurse checked her, ran to the door, and yelled, "Get Doctor Wood here, *stat!*" The nurse ran back to Jane's bed. "Don't push, Jane!" she said.

Jane panted between groans.

"Dear Father, help her now," Tom silently prayed. "Her own strength is not enough. Please give her the power to bear one moment longer."

Quickly, several hospital personnel from the hall, at the command of Jane's labor and delivery nurse, made the birthing room ready for delivery. In the flurry of activity, Tom watched Jane, her face straining and pale.

With the funeral just days past, Tom had expected a rest. But when he'd called Jane's house that Christmas Eve and found she was in the hospital, he couldn't stay away. Tom was surprised no one had asked him to leave the labor room, no one had moved his daughter's bed into a sterile delivery room. The nurse quickly dropped the end of the birthing room bed and attached two padded saddles for Jane's legs.

The door flew open suddenly as the obstetrician ran huffing into the room. He washed, gowned, and gloved in seconds, then braced himself on a stool at the end of Jane's bed.

"One nice long push here," the doctor said. "Take a deep breath and hold it as long as you can. Good, Jane. Wonderful. Take another breath and keep pushing."

Jane blindly searched for and gripped the two handholds at each side of the bed and lunged forward, pushing with all her might through the pain. All at once Tom saw the baby's head crown. In moments the corners of the old man's mouth softened into a broad smile as he spied two tiny eyes, then a nose, and finally an opened mouth gasping for breath. Tom looked up. Michael leaned over the bed straining, supporting Jane's back and neck as she lunged forward. There was no turning back now. Only pushing forward through the pain.

"Oh, look, Jane, there he is," Michael whispered reverently.

Tom could not utter a sound. He watched his tiny grandson's shoulders rotate and the small arms and legs slip through from the darkness into the light.

The clock struck twelve as the doctor glanced up. "A Christmas gift," the doctor said. "Mark this one down for 12:01 A.M., December 25th."

Tom stood in silent awe. He had never seen a child born before. He did not know how luminous it was. In a few short days, he'd witnessed his wife's exit and his grandson's entrance. Clothed in pain and parting, Tom had been there to witness both the end and the

beginning. A feeling of calm reverence filled him.

After the doctor cut the umbilical cord, Jane cradled her infant son on her breast in a warm flannel blanket. The tiny child turned his head and opened his mouth eager for life. Jane looked up and saw her father wiping his eyes in the darkened corner of the room.

"Michael, look. He wants to eat already." Jane put the child to her breast and stroked his head. "Oh, he's so beautiful. I love you, son."

As Tom watched Jane cradle her child, Michael's broad arm surrounding them both, a swelling came to his chest. Then, as suddenly as sunrise over the mountains, Tom's vision saw another family—another father, mother, and child—long years ago in a stable far away. He felt light spread all about him and through him.

Tom knew that Babe in the manger was the light and life of the world, that because of him, he would become new again, see May again. There was no final parting, no death, only a moving from life to life. Despair melted into the light of hope. Tom knew instantaneously the gift of joy.

"Dad? Would you like to hold your new grandson?" Michael said, smiling.

Tom walked slowly to Jane's bedside, bent down, and kissed his daughter on her moist forehead. Then he reached out and Michael placed his newborn son in Tom's waiting arms. Tom felt the baby's cheek with his curved palm, their first touch.

Is pain also God's gift? Tom wondered. *Only after pain have I come to understand that there is no way to go but through—the cross comes before the crown.*

Tom drew his infant grandson closer. He was astonished to realize that his aging eyes still had so much yet to see, his heart so much yet to feel.

Janene Wolsey Baadsgaard, a homemaker and freelance writer, is the author of many books about families. She has been a columnist for the *Deseret News* and several other newspapers, written articles for the *New Era* and the *Ensign*, and taught English and literature classes at Utah Valley State College. She and her husband, Ross, are the parents of nine children.

Maria's Poinsettia

Brad Wilcox

"Idaho is different from California," Maria's little brother said as he looked out of the car window across acres of snow-covered farmland.

"Idaho is different from Mexico too," Maria's mama added, pulling her jacket tightly around her neck against the cold that seemed to penetrate even the closed windows of their old car.

Ten-year-old Maria remained silent. Her family had moved from Mexico when she was small, so she didn't remember it at all, but she did remember California where she had lived most of her life. She remembered her friends in the Spanish-speaking ward her family had attended, even though they all spoke English now. Maria thought of her friends Rosa, Juliana, and Lupe. By now they would be practicing for the Primary Christmas program—singing songs and learning parts. Maria had been given a solo, but now she had to say good-bye to her friends, California, the Spanish ward, the solo, everything.

Maria shivered—not from the cold, but rather from the thought of having to start in a new school this late in the year. Her father said, "Don't worry. You'll find lots of friends at church." But Maria was worried because in Idaho they would be attending an English-speaking ward where she knew she would be different.

"The next exit should be ours," Maria's father said, trying to concentrate on the map

and the freeway ahead at the same time. Maria looked out of the window at this strange place soon to be her new home. Her brother and mother were right—Idaho was different than anywhere she had ever known.

The following week was full of activity— moving in, getting settled in school. On the first day, Maria's family met one of the counselors in the bishopric of their new ward because he worked at the store where they were buying some necessities for their apartment. Later the Relief Society president came by with cinnamon rolls and a ward list. Maria's brothers and sisters attacked the sweet rolls, while Maria picked up the ward list and searched hopefully for a familiar name like Garcia, Martinez, or Gomez, but all she found were names like Anderson, Berry, Smith, and Warner.

On Sunday the Primary president asked Maria and her younger brothers and sisters to sit in front and introduce themselves. Maria squirmed uncomfortably in her seat through the entire opening song and prayer. The Primary president then stood and said, "Before we have our talks today, I want you to meet some new Primary friends who have moved into our ward." She motioned for Maria and her brothers and sisters to stand.

Later, when the older classes were dismissed, the Primary president pointed out which class was to be Maria's. Maria recognized two girls from her class at school. They also seemed to recognize her and even smiled.

Maria's teacher was Sister Larsen, an older woman who reminded Maria of her grandmother who used to visit each year from Mexico—they had the same kind eyes, huggable size, and simple way of wearing their hair. "Welcome, Maria," Sister Larsen said.

"You're here just in time for Christmas and just in time to help with our class service project. We are each going to bring a gift to the church on Wednesday after school and then take them to a needy family that lives close by."

Sister Larsen turned to the rest of the class. "How are you all coming on your gifts?" she asked.

"My mother and I are painting a big wooden Santa with a bag full of toys," reported one girl.

Another said, "I am buying a doll with lots of extra clothes."

One of the boys said, "My mom gave me money to buy a huge stuffed animal for one of the little kids in the family."

Sister Larsen clapped her hands happily. "This will be better than I ever imagined," she said smiling broadly. "I can hardly wait until Wednesday!"

When church was over, Maria found her younger brothers and sisters and led them to the car. They all began talking at once, telling their parents about new friends and teachers. Maria took her usual place in the back seat and said nothing. Her father noticed her silence. "What about you, Maria?" he asked. "Did you like your new teacher?"

"*Sí, Papa,*" Maria answered, "but I have to bring a gift to the church on Wednesday for a needy family, and I don't know what to buy."

Her father and mother glanced at each other in the front seat. Maria knew they would. They always looked at each other like that when any of the children mentioned money. There had never been a lot of extra money in their family, and now with the move Maria knew that any list she or her brothers and sisters would make for Santa this year would have to be pretty short.

Maria's mother asked, "What kind of gift are you to bring for the family? Can it be food?"

Maria said, "Well, one girl is bringing a doll with extra clothes, and one boy is going to buy a giant teddy bear."

"Could you give one of your old toys?" Father asked, knowing full well that the family had just sold everything that would have been considered extra when they had their moving sale in California.

"Don't worry," said Maria's mother as their apartment building came into view. "We'll come up with something."

It was easy for Maria to put the whole matter out of her mind because she had so many other things to think about as she adjusted to her new school. But at school on Wednesday one of the girls from her Primary class reminded her that they were to meet at the church that afternoon. Maria's face darkened. She still had no gift to take.

"*Mamita*," Maria called as she arrived at the apartment. Her mother hurried in from the back bedroom. Before Maria could even ask about the gift, her mother pointed to a single artificial poinsettia flower sitting on the kitchen counter.

"Look, Maria!" her mother said excitedly. "I was so worried that you would not have a gift to take, and then like a miracle a neighbor brought this by today to welcome us, and now you can take it to the needy family."

"What?" Maria was shocked. "Take that? No way! I'm supposed to bring a nice gift."

"This is a nice gift, a very nice gift."

"No," Maria complained, "It's fake and it's not even a big poinsettia plant like the ones in the stores. It's just a single flower. I can't take this. All the kids will laugh."

"But, Maria," her mother tried to reason with her. "It's a beautiful flower, a Christmas flower, *La Flor de la Nochebuena*—the Flower of the Holy Night."

"But *Mamita*," Maria argued.

"Take it," her mother interrupted abruptly. "It is all we have to offer. I wish we could afford something else, but we can't." Her voice sounded firm. Her eyes looked weary. It was difficult for her to admit what she just had.

"Everyone will laugh," Maria grumbled as she snatched the fake flower and headed out through the door. She knew all along she would be walking to the chapel since her father had the car, but now Maria was glad she was walking. Perhaps if she went slowly enough she would arrive late and the other children would already have gone to deliver their wooden Santas, store-bought dolls, and giant stuffed animals. Maybe she could tell Sister Larsen that she had gotten lost because she was new and didn't remember her way.

Just then a van pulled over in front of her. Sister Larsen rolled down the window and waved at Maria. "Climb in and I'll give you a ride," she offered. "You're lucky I saw you."

"Yeah, lucky," Maria said quietly to herself as she opened the passenger door and stepped up into her teacher's van.

"Did you remember to bring a gift?" Sister Larsen asked. Maria debated whether she should show her teacher the flower she was hiding beneath her thin coat. Sister Larsen saw her hesitating and said, "It's okay if you didn't."

Maria said nothing, but pulled the plastic flower out and showed it halfheartedly to her Primary teacher. Sister Larsen looked at the flower and then in the rearview mirror. "That's lovely," she said driving out into traffic.

"Not really," said Maria. "I don't think my

mother understood what I was supposed to get."

Sister Larsen disagreed, "Oh, I think your mother and you chose a perfect gift for this family. They just moved here from Mexico to work on the farms, and I'm sure they'll be glad to see a flower from their homeland."

"But it's not even a real one," Maria lowered her eyes.

"That doesn't matter," Sister Larsen said. "Surely you know the legend of the Poinsettia."

Maria knew the flower was from Mexico. Her father and mother proudly told her that each Christmas, but Maria knew nothing of any legend.

Sister Larsen glanced out of the window behind her, signaled, and began changing lanes. "You see," she began, "the flower was first brought to the United States from Mexico by a Doctor Poinsett in 1830. So we call it the poinsettia after him, and since the year was 1830 it should have an extra special meaning for Latter-day Saints."

Maria didn't quite understand what her teacher was saying, but she wasn't about to ask a question—especially since the chapel was now in sight. Sister Larsen continued, "Well, legend has it that the flower first came to be many years ago in Mexico at Christmastime when a young girl was trying to find a gift to place at the manger in the church of her small mountain village."

Sister Larsen pulled into the church parking lot. "So," she went on. "The girl and her mother started weaving a blanket to place beneath the statue of the Baby Jesus in the manger, but the mother became ill and the girl could not finish the weaving alone. She tried and only made a tangled mess."

Sister Larsen parked, turned off the van, but instead of opening her door she leaned toward Maria to finish the story. "Now the girl felt as though she had ruined Christmas because she had nothing to take to the Baby Jesus. But then she saw a clump of green weeds growing near the church."

"She took weeds to the church?" Maria interrupted. She wondered if this story was real, or if Sister Larsen was just making it up to help her feel better.

"Yes," said the Primary teacher. "According to the legend the girl took weeds into the church and placed them around the manger as her gift. Then as she knelt to pray, the people in the church were astonished because the weeds were suddenly tipped with beautiful red flowers like flaming stars. The manger glowed and shimmered as if lit by hundreds of candles and every Christmas since that day the red flower stars shine on top of green branches in Mexico and all over the world."*

"She's here!" came a voice from outside. Maria couldn't see who was yelling because the windows had fogged over after Sister Larsen turned off the van, but from inside the chapel the other Primary children had recognized their teacher's vehicle and now came running toward the parking lot.

Maria cleared a peephole on the window with her hand and watched her classmates. They carried large boxes, beautifully wrapped with expensive paper and ribbons. Maria quickly sat back and hid her flower beneath her coat again.

"Maria," Sister Larsen said quietly. "In the legend even weeds became beautiful because

---

* See *The Legend of the Poinsettia,* as retold and illustrated by Tomie dePaola (New York: G.P. Putnam's Sons, 1994).

they were given with love." She rolled down the driver's window and called out to the class, "Open the side door and climb in, but be sure to shake off your boots. Is everyone here?"

"Yes!" shouted all the children as they opened the door and found places to sit.

"Buckle your seat belts," directed Sister Larsen as she began counting heads. The van that had been so quiet only a moment ago was now humming at full volume. The open door reminded Maria how cold it was outside.

"Let's go," shouted one of the girls, slamming the door shut. Sister Larsen backed up and started out of the parking lot. The noise level in the van became louder and louder as the Christmas travelers bubbled over with excitement. One boy was telling Rudolph-the-Red-Nosed-Reindeer jokes and everyone was laughing. Maria couldn't hear him clearly since he was in the very back, but she still probably wouldn't have joined in the laughter. She was thinking about her poinsettia flower and what her teacher had said about the Mexican legend.

Sister Larsen finally arrived at the farm of one of the members of the ward. She stopped the van on a dirt road in front of a small house that the farmer provided for his workers. The children piled out and knocked on the door before Sister Larsen even had a chance to give last-minute instructions or lead them in a Christmas carol.

Maria kept her flower under her coat and stayed close to her teacher. The father in the home motioned for all of them to come in. In Spanish—and a few words of broken English—he attempted to welcome them, but none of the children could understand him except Maria. Suddenly, the man's children saw the brightly wrapped packages, and all began speaking and calling out at once—whirling around the room like snowflakes in a winter storm.

"Merry Christmas!" Sister Larsen said loudly over the buzz of the children, "Or I suppose I should say *feliz Navidad*." Maria had to smile at Sister Larsen's attempt at Spanish with her heavy North American accent.

The father of the family nodded gratefully and replied, "*Gracias, gracias.*" He then said something more in Spanish, and Sister Larsen turned quickly to Maria for help.

Maria translated, "He can't believe everyone is being so nice to his family. He says this is the best Christmas they have ever had and that he hopes God will bless you."

Sister Larsen answered with, "Gracias, gracias," complete with accent.

While the rest of the Primary class helped the children open packages, Maria looked at the mother of the family, holding a baby in her arms. She was almost hidden behind her husband and seemed frightened of the roomful of visitors. Maria imagined that perhaps the mother was feeling the same way she had felt when she arrived at her new school and had to stand up in front of everyone at Primary. Maria stepped toward her, forgetting for a moment that she herself was also a newcomer, and offered the mother her simple flower.

The woman tucked a stray strand of black hair behind her ear and then smiled—first at Maria and then at her husband. "*La Flor de la Nochebuena*," she whispered. Maria understood—the Flower of the Holy Night.

Slowly, the mother stepped away from the safety of her husband's side and reached to take the artificial flower. Maria watched in silence as the mother held it to her almost as tenderly as she held her baby. Sister Larsen bent close to Maria and whispered, "It's probably the first familiar thing she has seen since leaving Mexico."

Maria smiled. Her heart felt like a bursting *piñata* scattering happiness like candy. Sister Larsen was right. Even the simplest gift can be made beautiful when it is given with love.

BRAD WILCOX is an assistant professor in the Department of Teacher Education at Brigham Young University, where he teaches graduate and undergraduate courses in literacy and directs the Mexico Student Teaching Program. He enjoys writing for Church magazines and has also served on the National Executive Board of the Boy Scouts of America.

Brad was born right on December 25th and spent his childhood years in Ethiopia, Africa, later serving a mission in Chile. He and his wife, Debi, have four children.

Brad loves pepperoni pizza, peanut M&M's, and singing along with his car stereo. He serves as first counselor in the bishopric of his ward and loves working with the youth.

ELDER NELSON FINDS JERUSALEM

Janette Rallison

IF BAD LUCK FOLLOWED some people, then it stalked Elder Nelson. His flight into Lima was changed three times. He was finally routed to Peru through Panama City, but his luggage went to La Paz, Bolivia. He ended up spending thirty-six hours in an assortment of airports—all in the same suit. And when he finally made it to Juliaca for the first real day of his mission, he tripped while getting off the train and sprained his ankle. He had been my companion for only a week when I decided the only person less fortunate than Elder Nelson was anyone who was forced to be with him: Elder Nelson complained so much, he could have been the mouthpiece for all human suffering and woe.

Every day he gave me another running commentary on the shortcomings of Peru. It was too hot. It was too dusty. The old woman who lived in a shoe had roomier accommodations than we did in our apartment. And the food, well, the rats in the United States ate better than we did, because at least the rats occasionally found a discarded Big Mac or package of potato chips. All we ever got was beans and rice, and beans and rice—except for when the members fed us, and then the food rated even worse than beans and rice.

One day we were barely out of a member's house before he started in on his review.

"What was that meat we just choked down? Was it beef, chicken, or free-ranging tractor tires?"

I didn't say anything.

"I mean, Elder Randall, did they seriously expect us to eat that, or were they just playing a joke on us because we're a couple of American gringos?"

I kept my eyes on the street, not wanting to misstep in the darkness. "Elder Nelson," I said, "did you look around at the home during dinner?"

"Darn straight, I did. Any civilized country would have condemned that house years ago. The whole time I ate, I was afraid the roof would collapse on us, which at least would have saved me from having to swallow that roast of tire treads I just consumed."

"My point is," I said firmly, "the Montoyas don't have meat for dinner very often. They gave us their best, and you ought to be grateful."

"Do you think they boiled the water before they gave it to us?" Elder Nelson touched his stomach apprehensively. "What does it feel like to get parasites?"

The next P-day Elder Nelson wrote home and begged for a carton of peanut butter and a review of his mission papers. "I'm sure there was a mistake. I just know the Lord didn't mean to send me here," he told me as he sealed up the envelope.

I was hanging up my white shirts, which we had sent out to be cleaned by a local member. Our wash, like everyone else's, got cleaned in the river on the rocks. This considerably shortened the life span of our clothing, and I was constantly looking for holes. "Oh? Where exactly was the Lord supposed to send you?"

"Someplace with paved roads, indoor plumbing, and insects smaller than house pets."

I said, "The people here are humble and genuine. They're eager to learn and quick to love. Give Juliaca a chance. You'll start to love it like I do."

He looked at me skeptically. "Come on. You can't tell me you actually love it here. I mean, all of the time when you were growing up and thinking about your mission, I'll bet not once did you think you'd live in a place where the people and the dogs have the same toilet habits."

"We serve where we're called."

"But why couldn't I serve in Europe, or Australia, maybe the Fiji Islands . . ."

"Because you got called here." I put away the last of my clothes and got out a pad of paper to write a letter to my folks.

"So really," Nelson said, "where did you want to go?"

I tried to pretend I didn't hear him, but when he asked again I looked up at him and said, "Jerusalem. I wanted to go to Jerusalem."

"But they don't send missionaries to Jerusalem."

"I know. So I wasn't disappointed when I opened my mission papers and didn't see Israel listed as the country I was going to."

Elder Nelson lay down on his bed and surveyed the ceiling of our apartment. I went back to my letter.

"Why Jerusalem?" he asked.

I tapped my pen against the paper. "I don't know. I guess I would have liked to walk the places the Savior walked, to serve the people He loved—you know, to teach like the ancient apostles taught."

"Well, at least that part of your wish came true," Nelson said. "Peru is about as advanced as the world during A.D. 32. Except, of course, the apostles probably got fed better."

I picked up my pillow and threw it at him.

"Do you mind? I only have one day to write home."

He put his hands underneath his head. "Jerusalem," he said. "Yeah, it would have been neat to see the temple mount, Gethsemane, maybe walk the shores of the Dead Sea. And at Christmastime you could visit Bethlehem on your P-day. You're right. Jerusalem would have been a cool place to go to. I wish I'd been called to Jerusalem."

*   *   *

Elder Nelson's calling didn't get reviewed, and the care package his parents sent, peanut butter included, never made it to our apartment. Packages larger than a check box had a way of mysteriously disappearing out of the mail system in Peru. I had hoped his attitude would improve once the culture shock wore off, but by the end of our second month together he was no better. It was December, and every day he made a point of telling me about all of the Christmas traditions they had back in Utah, and about how the missionaries there were treated like veritable icons, receiving a never-ending stream of Christmas goodies. "Fudge," he'd mumble over and over again. "Peanut brittle. Gingerbread cookies . . ."

He insisted we stop by the post office every day to see if a box had arrived for him. "Mom promised she'd send me a canned ham and hot chocolate mix along with my Christmas presents. It's bad enough not to have snow, a tree, or Christmas lights. At least I'll be able to have a regular meal."

But day after day our post office box stood empty.

*   *   *

On the day before Christmas, Elder Nelson was in a particularly surly mood. It was P-day, and we'd just been down at the collegio playing a game of soccer with the students. Not only were we soundly beaten, but Nelson had managed to get kicked in both shins. It wasn't on purpose. It was just another manifestation of his lousy luck.

We made the daily pilgrimage to our vacant post office box, then headed to our apartment to pick up clean clothes to take with us to the bathhouse. As we trudged down the dirt road, Nelson kicked a lot of rocks. "My parents have sent me two care packages, packages I know contained Snickers bars, and I have yet to see either one. I think our postman took them. I say next time we're in the post office we check his breath for chocolate."

"Snap out of it, Elder," I told him. "You're a servant of the Lord, not the candy bar police."

He kicked another rock. It went bouncing across the street into a ditch.

We'd almost reached our apartment, so I hurried ahead of him and went into the doorway. I was still gaping at the sight of our room when Elder Nelson caught up with me.

It was empty. Completely empty. I would have expected thieves to make a mess of things, to throw the less valuable things on the ground, but apparently they thought everything was valuable. Our clothes, our suitcases, our beds, even our scriptures were gone. The only things remaining were our flip charts and missionary tracts. They were stacked neatly on the floor in the corner where we'd left them.

Elder Nelson went to the middle of the room and turned slowly in circles, as though if he looked hard enough he'd notice our possessions stashed somewhere we'd overlooked before.

"I guess we'd better go call the zone leaders," I said.

We trekked back outside and headed across town to a phone station. All the way there Elder Nelson repeated over and over, "How could somebody do that? How could somebody steal all of our stuff on Christmas Eve day?"

"I guess crooks don't take holidays," I said.

Elder Nelson peered into every window we passed by, as if trying to get a glimpse of our belongings. "Our beds are gone. Even the Grinch who stole Christmas left the beds. What are we going to sleep on tonight?"

The zone leaders didn't pick up the phone when I called. Next I tried the mission president. He was there but wasn't encouraging about our situation. "The banks are all closed till after Christmas," he told me. "I'll send you money then. Why don't you see if you can borrow some clothes and things from the other elders in the district until you have a chance to go shopping."

Nelson didn't take the news well. In fact, he lifted his face towards the sky and let out a primal scream. Perhaps he was hoping the missionary board in Salt Lake City would hear him and reconsider reviewing his calling.

"We're not going to be able to get hold of the other elders tonight, and even if we do, whose clothes am I going to wear? Benion is four inches taller than I am. Smith is as thin as a beanpole. None of the stores around here carry long sleeve white shirts, and anything sent in the mail is stolen. I'm going to go through the rest of my mission looking like Bozo the Elder. I'll never be able to take more pictures to send home, because my mother will think I've contracted some strange Peruvian disease that makes people shrink and swell, although I guess it doesn't matter anyway, because someone stole my camera, *and it's Christmas Eve and I'm going to have to sleep on the floor!*"

"Elder," I said, "get ahold of yourself. We'll get through this." But even I wasn't truly optimistic. How could I be? It was the biggest holiday of the year, the very worst time to feel homesick, and I had to spend the night in an empty apartment with a rabid greenie.

I jingled the few coins I had left in my sweat-pants pocket. They were what we'd planned to buy our showers with.

"Well, Elder Nelson, since we don't have any clothes to change into, and this is the last of our money, do you still want to take a shower?"

He put his hand on his forehead. "Let's see. I can get clean and then get into dirty clothes, or I can take a shower with my clothes on to get them clean, but then I'll have to walk around in wet clothing until they dry." He thought about this for a moment. "It's Christmas Eve and I'm going to have to sleep on a bare floor either *wet* or *dirty.*"

"Actually, we can't be wet. We've got to go to the Condoris," I said.

P-day officially ended at five, and we'd managed to schedule a discussion after dinner.

"What's the point in taking a shower then," Nelson said with resignation. "We'll still smell better than most of the people in town." And he was right. Only the rich in Juliaca could afford the luxury of the bathhouse.

At 7:00, still dressed in sweats and T-shirts, we walked over to the Condori home. Like most of the people, they didn't have a living room. If it was too dark to talk to us outside they brought us into the family bedroom. It was a room no bigger than my bedroom at home, but had three beds and a table shoved inside. These were the sole sleeping accommodations for the entire family of six.

We took our place with the flip charts and pamphlets on one bed while Señor Condori assembled the children on another. In Spanish he asked, "Elders, where are your ties and tags?"

"We had a little problem with our clothes," I said.

"Someone broke into our room and stole them," Nelson clarified.

Señora Condori's eyes widened. "Someone stole your clothes?"

I said, "We'll be all right. The mission president will take care of us."

Señor Condori stood up and pulled a box from underneath one of the beds. Inside, neatly folded, were all the clothes he owned. Without hesitation he pulled out two shirts and handed one to each of us. "These are my biggest shirts. I think they will fit you. I'm just sorry I have no trousers to give you."

My first impulse was to refuse the gift. Señor Condori certainly needed the shirt more than I did. But how could I turn away such generosity? It would have been like refusing the widow's mite. I looked over at Nelson with a prayer in my heart that for once he would be gracious, be tactful, or at least be silent. He was staring down at the not-quite-white shirt with complete astonishment.

"Thank you," he said, and then again, "Thank you."

Nelson stayed quiet while I gave the discussion. His gaze hardly left the shirt in his hands.

Brother Condori closed with prayer. It was simple but pure of heart. He said, "We thank thee for the birth of the Savior, and everything the Savior has given us." And it struck me that he didn't ask—like we so often ask back in the States—that we remember the real meaning of Christmas. He went on to say he was thankful for the elders who had come to teach the words of God. "Help us to live these words. Help us to be worthy of baptism. And bless the elders that their needs will be met."

As we left the Condoris I glanced over at Elder Nelson and his eyes were moist—though to tell the truth I wasn't sure whether he had been moved by what happened, or whether he was just considering the fact that now we'd have to go spend Christmas Eve dirty, on the floor, and with used shirts as our only Christmas presents.

"Elder Randall," he said, "give me the shower money."

I reached into my pocket and handed him the coins. He counted them out in his hand. "All the shops are closed, but there will still be some street vendors out. I think we have just enough to buy the Condoris a Christmas cake."

I smiled over at him. "When the mission president gives us money for clothes, I'd like to keep these shirts and buy Señor Condori a couple of new ones."

"Yeah," he said, "that would be a good idea."

We walked in silence toward the main part of town, and even though there was no snow, decorated trees, or colored lights, it seemed very much like Christmas Eve. Nelson hummed half a verse of "Silent Night," then said, "Hey, Randall, the Savior came to ancient America. Maybe He could have even walked where we're walking."

"I guess He could have," I said.

"And the Lord loves these people," Elder Nelson said.

"He loves them a lot," I agreed.

"We're teaching pretty much like the early apostles did, don't you think?"

"Sure," I said.

He smiled over at me. "Congratulations. It looks like we got called to Jerusalem after all."

JANETTE RALLISON is the author of *Deep Blue Eyes and Other Lies*. She never went on a mission, but her husband, Guy, served in the Peru Arequipa Mission. He says he didn't complain about the conditions there, and Janette believes him, because in their ten years of marriage he has never once complained about her cooking, which at times rivals that from a third-world country. The couple have four children, all of whom have seen Guy's mission slides several times.

WESLEY'S CAROL

Benson Y. Parkinson

WESLEY'S MY BOY, and looked like me, of course. He has Jenny's face, but otherwise it could have been me standing there, only thirty years before. I remember him being tall for a seven-year-old, skinny, with protruding ears, shoulder blades poking back like wings, and a fuzzy blond head of hair. My own went dark long ago, though I was off my mission before I stopped thinking of myself as blond.

Wes and I are the lone men in the family, unless you count Bob, the yellow Manx cat. Wesley and Bob have four sisters, who never cease to amaze me with their capacity for chatter. I enjoy it now, unlike when I was Wes's age with four sisters (and two brothers) of my own. At seven, Wes's mouth was always open too, but in grunts and inhaled *oh*'s and squeals of laughter. He'd tumble in from school with a story about his addition test. "Oh, it was so hard—I couldn't believe—I was—" he'd stammer boyishly. "She just—passed 'em out, and I—" he'd finally scribble in the air, then hand in his imaginary quiz. "Easy!" he'd top off his brief tale, shining in triumph, by which I'd know he'd gotten another perfect score.

My parents warned me about kids and trouble. You couldn't guess, looking at Wes's twinkling, huge green eyes, that raising him would be as harrowing as sledding on the hill on Grandpa's dry farm at Christmastime. Dad would have five or six of us squeeze in front and behind him on the Flexible Flyer. All you could do when you came whipping down, dodging cedars and cinder boulders, was close your eyes, hang on, and hope Dad somehow had his feet still on the crossbar and could steer the thing.

I liked those Christmases well enough—playing Fox and Geese with the cousins, skating on the pond, tearing open presents while Dad bunched the paper and poked it in the roaring fire. I also remember the after-present boredom, with nothing to look forward to and the sense that what you'd given wasn't good enough, and that what you got didn't make you as happy as you thought it would. Jenny likes Christmas and baking and decorating and tucking away little gifts in the pantry and cellar starting in about June. I let her boss me out the door with ladder and staple gun in hand to get the lights on the house or to collect and mount the tree after she's scouted every lot in town. I don't mean to be a grump about it. I find it stressful is all—the shopping, the crowds, the appearances at parties, the worry over whether to spend five dollars on gifts for acquaintances, for fear that they might spend ten, or just as embarrassing, that they might spend nothing. I've heard that a lot of folks find the holidays depressing. I guess it's people's expectations we find so trying. They mass up at that time of year. The way I see it, there's no sense passing my anxieties to my children, so when Jenny and I started our own traditions, I thought we'd better stress the parts I do like. So we do carols—not Santa or reindeer songs so much as simple, old, worshipful, honest-to-goodness carols.

Wesley had two modes—fast and studious—and when he was one, he was anything but the other. So we'd see him in flits, chasing with the girls over the furniture, or storming after Bob through the pfitzers or corn, up pine

trees, around the fence, and into every backyard in the neighborhood. Or he'd slip into the living room with paper and sit making math problems for himself, tracing away with his pencil, counting and carrying out loud, seemingly for hours on end. Sometimes during family night he'd romp and dance to the singing and screech out the tune. Generally at church he'd spend half of sacrament meeting finding the hymns in the hymnbooks for all seven members of the family, but he couldn't be coaxed to sing. At Christmas Jenny tied strings one inch apart around a stick candle in an old cast-iron holder, and we'd turn out the lights and sing until the candle burned down enough that the string caught fire. The girls took to it. Tanna, twelve, was fascinated with the harmony of "Lo, How a Rose," which she never could quite master those first years. Carmen, nine, seemed almost ecstatic over the angels singing in "Ding, Dong, Merrily on High." Melanie, a blank-faced five, aped the French to "Jeanette Isabelle," which I had learned in the mission field, while Eve, two and a half, scooted behind chairs and through our legs, trying to grab Bob's stump of a tail. Wes, who could have gone either way, sulked in the background most days because we let Carmen go before him, or he didn't know the words and wouldn't follow along, or Melanie swung her legs and accidentally kicked him.

I talked it over with Jenny in bed after prayers. (I have always loved the sound of her voice in the dark.) I said it seemed like he was acting out a lot lately. She said, "You've got to remember he's the lone boy in a family of girls. I think he feels left out." I got the idea of making him a virtual piano on the computer. I did enough programming at work that it wasn't particularly hard. This was before sound cards, and the old PC speakers could only squawk one note at a time, but I managed to lay out a little menu with a dozen carols. The keyboard was made of white rectangles that changed colors when that note was played. He spent hours at the program and fought off his little sisters, who were nearly as fascinated as he was. He still sulked through most of our evenings of caroling, but then would pester me and the girls to follow him to the office, where he led a second session of singing, manning the computer, giving each child a turn, laughing and singing now at the top of his lungs.

I was raised in Utah, but we were fourteen years in Buffalo, ten of those at Kellman-Graham Corporation. I did everything from presentations to support to software testing. We liked where we were, liked our house and the ward—lots of good people and lots of opportunity to serve. Everyone I knew from college had left Utah. I didn't think we'd ever be back except to visit the folks in Kaysville, but we began toying with the idea when a friend told us about a position at Evans & Sutherland. The pay wasn't as good, but the cost of living was so much lower that we thought we might come out ahead. I went so far as to fly out to Salt Lake City to interview. They told us in business class you should do that every few years to maintain your interviewing skills. Maybe I sensed what was coming—I don't know—but I hadn't yet accepted their offer when the pink slips went out at Kellman-Graham the day after the office Christmas party. Within a week we were on the road with all our possessions in a Ryder truck. We lost the equity in our house plus ten thousand dollars. We lived in a damp, drafty apartment in the farthest corner of Magna, and even

then didn't have enough after rent for groceries, because the real estate market in Salt Lake was heating up. Six other men in my elders quorum had moved back to Utah after years away as well.

Jenny made the most of it, borrowing sugar for cookies and making decorations from newspaper ads. The girls got on all right, helped their mother, and Carmen somehow landed a solo on the ward Christmas program. Wesley, eleven now, had spent the last weeks in Buffalo in flit mode, charging in to thaw out from a snowball fight, eyes as big and mouth as round as when he was seven as he described some ambush he and his friends worked on the boys across the street. Or his friends would stand by the bushes, secretly catching his eye through the window, pointing with their noses at their sleds, and he'd go charging off again, forgetting he was cold. If we told him he had to clean his room first, he'd whimper on the way, "Aoww, aoww," sounding just like Bob the cat meowing at the door. Once in the Salt Lake valley, however, he converted to studious mode and spent hours with his comics locked up in his room. He wanted to see a movie on family night, but we just didn't have the money. Jenny proposed the lights on Temple Square—even then I wasn't sure we could afford the gas. "It's not fair, it's not fair," Wes blurted and stomped off.

"Wesley, come back here," I called, and he did, looking to one side, face scrunched in tears. "Listen," I urged, "we're having a rough time here, and this kind of thing just makes it harder." When his face bunched up all the tighter, I decided not to press him, just slugged his shoulder and said, "Go cheer up, huh?"

He stomped to his room, shouted, "This is the worst Christmas ever," then slammed the door. We waited till the next night to go to Temple Square, but when Wes was still in a snit, we let him stay home. I, quivering from the various stresses, could hardly make the delicate lights strewn on the ground and through all the trees hold still. Jenny rode herd, while Tanna and Carmen used their chatter to keep their little sisters in awe. "Oh, those look like sprinkles on a magic cake. Oh, those look like rainbow drippings." Eve, the one with the blank face now, opened her mouth and gazed as though she believed them utterly, then smiled smugly and looked around as though that were nothing unusual at all. I poked in on Wes when we got home and was surprised to see he had dragged the music keyboard and a stack of hymn- and songbooks into his room. No one could really play the keyboard, but the kids sometimes danced to the canned rhythms, and Wes had learned to program in a few rudimentary tunes.

"All right," I told him, mock serious. "File out here and we'll have some popcorn."

"Dad, can we leave this on all the time?" he asked, as eager as I had seen him since Buffalo.

"It'd get hot after a while. Why, you wanna play it in your sleep?"

"No-o-o! I got 'The Holly and the Ivy' on it, and a little bit of 'The First Noel.'"

"Is that what you've been doing? It's got a tape interface. I'd have to find the cable." We dug it out, together with my missionary tape recorder, and I showed him how to space the data files out on a cassette and keep track of them with the counter. When we loaded "The First Noel" again, it came out garbled, so I had him save two copies after that. "That's the redundancy principle."

"What?" he said, blond head tilted.

"First rule of engineering—always keep a spare." He spent the next three nights on it and got eight more carols hacked out and ready to go. He still sulked through our family singing, but then would troop off with Bob and from one to four of his sisters and hold his own sing-along after, bossing them around, making them wait while he fussed with the recorder.

"Why do they make it so impossible to use?" Jenny marveled as she passed by in the hall while I watched from the doorway.

I pointed to Wes. "To keep the power in the hands of the one who can think like the machine."

"You suppose he gets any pleasure out of the actual music?" she said, smiling.

"Well, there's 'Hark! the Herald Angels Sing,'" I reminded her, and she nodded and said that was true. He'd been eight when he noticed it was written by Charles Wesley, and ever after, that was his song.

The girls got on well, particularly when we moved into our house in West Valley that summer. Tanna and Carmen didn't even need to change schools. Tanna took an interest in dramatics and landed the lead in the play at Cyprus High her senior year. Carmen, who had always been a gentle thing, surprised us by making the Brockbank Junior High varsity basketball team and also sang with the choir. Melanie and Eve, ever adaptable, quickly made new friends. Buffalo styles were about a year ahead of Utah's, which helped us that fall when we had so little money for clothes. We had let Wesley grow a tail and shave the sides of his hair, which looked pretty goofy to us, but we figured we'd save the argument with him for something that mattered more. But unlike the girls, who waited for their classmates to catch up, Wesley still had the most extreme hair of any student in his class in the ninth grade four years later. Maybe we should have been stricter. I'd tease him about it, but I'd also tell him, "What you look like isn't what makes you who you are. What you believe in and stand up for, that's what makes you who you are."

Wes still had bright green eyes underneath his square mop, and pursued a variety of enthusiasms: math and programming, rappelling with the Scouts, X-men comics (which he said he thought were stupid), and skateboarding at twilight with his friends. They had a route they'd follow—over sidewalks and parking lots and playgrounds. I spotted them at the elementary once when Jenny sent me out for bread. They'd come down a little rise, flip up on a metal bike rack they'd moved into position, and skid along its ridge on the underbellies of their boards. They tumbled one after the other, but Wes managed to ride it out and land on his wheels when his turn came. I didn't know whether to go over and scold him or take him for a milk shake. They didn't see me, and they had the bike rack back in place before I returned, so I didn't say anything. We worried a little about those friends, who seemed slovenly and perhaps a little dissolute to us, though we could hardly fault them when Wes was the most wild-looking of any of them. Then suddenly he had a new batch of friends, including some girls and a couple of older boys who could drive. "Hey, Ma, can I go to the mall?" he'd holler, and before Jenny could say, "It depends—what time would you be back?" he'd be out the door.

I scolded him harshly the third time he got home after midnight. "Now you listen to me. As long as you're living in my house, I expect you to abide by the rules." It was a little funny to hear my father speaking through my mouth that way. Wes was an expert glowerer—goes with his talent for programming, I suppose. He folded his arms, jutted his lower lip, and spent the next three days hiding out in his room. Then he took to staying late at school; then to missing dinner. A month later he was out past midnight again on a night that one of Jenny's friends had warned us there was a beer party going on. I told Jenny while we waited up in bed in the dark that I hardly knew what to do with him, and that it seemed that there was an awful lot at stake. She said, "Once they get in ninth grade, they're like a horse in a new pasture." (Jenny's folks were horse people from Mantua.) "First thing they do is test every post and gate."

I drove him out to the desert the next day in our little pickup and let him take the wheel. He'd get off the track, thrashing down sagebrush, flushing out rabbits, stalling finally, both of us laughing till we were red. I'd talk him through starting it up and steering back onto the road. I picked a quiet moment to ask if he'd gone to the kegger, and he said yes in a relaxed if somewhat embarrassed voice.

"You drink any?"

"A little."

"You know we don't approve of that," I told him, in as stern a tone as I allowed myself all day.

"I know."

My heart was pounding in my ears, to where I could hardly hear my voice. "Just a sip, huh?"

"Yeah."

I waited for him to steer around a rut. "You know, I never did that."

"I just wanted to know how it tasted," he

explained, watching the road, leaning forward, wearing a sheepish grin. "I didn't like it."

I shut my eyes and nodded. That much was good.

We got a sound card for the computer, which played about as well as the music keyboard had. It came with notation software, and I entered two or three carols when we first got it, after which Wes took control. He said it was no harder than typing in hexadecimal program listings from computer magazines, which he did all the time. Bob the cat would perch like a puff-necked rooster in the window, craning as though reading over Wes's shoulder. We pulled the computer into the living room and did carols by computer light. After a few initial foul-ups, Wes got it all worked out and set up a menu with all our favorite carols, transposed where necessary, with the proper amount of lead in. Tanna finally got us through "Lo, How a Rose" by taking tenor, with Carmen on alto, and Melanie and Eve coaxing along their mother on soprano. It was heavenly, and Tanna had tears in her eyes.

The next year I was elders quorum president, Tanna was working at the Dairy Queen, and Jenny was taking classes, and I remember thinking the carols would be the only thing holding us together. Wes pestered about going ice skating with his friends, but I insisted, "Not till carols are done," and ignored him when he whined he'd miss the session. Jenny made spiced tomato juice and celery and crackers spread with cheese. Carmen wanted a fire, which gave me the idea of adapting the fireplace video clip from one of my screen savers so the computer's glow would be extra cheery and warm. All was in place for the first session when Jenny called the kids for dinner and Wes wasn't home. We waited till 7:30, then left the

kids to do homework and drove out to look for him. Sure enough, there he was in line at the rink, wrestling with a pair of floppy-haired girls over a carton of french fries.

I drove up opposite the sidewalk, pondered a moment, scratched my head, and decided on a stern "Wes, get in the car."

"Uh, Dad, what you doin' here?" he mumbled.

"Come on, let's go."

"Dad," he whispered, exasperated, "I'm with my friends."

"Wes," I pleaded, "Everybody's gone to a lot of trouble. What were you thinking, taking off like that?"

"Dad, come o-on," he whined.

"Get in the car!" I snapped. He twisted up his face in aggravation, almost like when he was little, stomped once, but then to my surprise got in, without so much as saying good-bye to his friends. He sat for carols but wouldn't sing with us or work the computer and spent the rest of the evening in his room. I thought he'd be angry at me for a month for humiliating him. He was late for school the next morning, but otherwise showed no sign of resentment. A few days later he asked permission to go skating after carols, and we let him. He even helped Jenny with the dishes that night. She told me later that she asked him why he'd done it, and he'd told her plainly, "To see if you would come."

Tanna did well in college, married Randy her sophomore year, and had our first grandbaby. Carmen kept her grades up and followed her sister to the "Y." Melanie and Eve ran Thanksgiving that year, helped with the turkey and pies, then when it snowed ran off and left me the dishes (fair enough) while they made a row of snowmen, all lined up with scarves and caps and choir books, facing the picture window to sing us a song. We rarely saw Wesley after he got his job bussing at the downtown Denny's. He ate at work and slept late and in the evenings and seemingly all weekend. He missed Thanksgiving with the family to get in the holiday time.

Wes wore an old, green trench coat now, indoors and out. His fully brown hair reached down between his two broad shoulder blades. Loud music buzzed from his ever-present earphones. His complexion had gone bad. His eyes were always dim and bloodshot, I hoped from lack of sleep. We teased, nagged, scolded, cajoled, anything we could think of, first to get him to go to church, then to get him to go to school. *How you gonna be a missionary?* "I dowanna be a missionary." *Why sure you do. How you gonna be a programmer?* "I hate programming." *But Wes, that's the definition of a programmer—someone who hates programming.*

I smelled tobacco on him sometimes. He claimed it was from work, but there's a difference when it's coming from your clothes as opposed to coming from your skin. Partly from things we heard about his friends, partly from his erratic hours and occasional all-nights out, we suspected he'd been experimenting with drugs. He wouldn't see the bishop. We got a recommend for LDS Social Services, but Wesley wouldn't come. We felt shame at first, but you can't let that get you. Some of the folks at church would whisper, but when we were open about it, they were mostly understanding. We had some horrible arguments with Wesley, and I said some things I'm not proud of. They always ended with him shouting some obscenity and telling us to leave him alone. What a harrowing sleigh ride; what a horrendous mix of anxiety and bewilderment and anger and pain. It scares you to death, so you shut your eyes and hang on all the tighter and hope someone is steering.

Then in mid-December, when I was swamped and working late at home with three proposals due, Eve wanted the Pentium to type up a report. "Why don't you do it on the old 386 in Wesley's room?"

"Yeah, like, sure, if you can find it under all the trash."

"I just can't spare this one now."

She shook her head urgently—"I'm not going in there." Jenny said Wes didn't really deserve the old computer, that he had hardly turned it on in months. So we sent Eve to clear a space on her study table, and I got Jenny to help me heft it up from Wes's room. The floor was knee-deep in blankets, clothes, potato chips, crumpled magazines, and greasy aluminum tins with blackened chicken bones. "No wonder Eve didn't want to come down here," I groaned. I brushed things aside gingerly to make a path to the desk. Bob, lumpy and lethargic now, was sprawled out on the monitor. "Shoo," I said, brushing him aside. "He doesn't do that on the Pentium, does he?"

Jenny, gathering up some of the more mildewy refuse, said, "Not since I took the flyswatter to him."

Strange, after all our arguments with Wes, that picking up a few things would have been what precipitated a crisis, but a half-hour later, the moment he tromped in the door and down to his room, he flew up again, stammering in falsetto.

"What did you—I can't believe you—I can't—Don't I get any privacy?"

Jenny protested, "Wesley, it was filthy!"

Wes was tongue-tied still, "I—I—That was

my stuff, that was my—What did you—I'm going! I'm moving out, and I'm never coming back here!"

"Wes," I urged, "be calm."

"I don't know who the blank blank you think you blank blank are. You blanking treat me like your blank blank whipping boy. Why don't you go take your blanking blank and go blank it, you blank blankity blank." I know, it doesn't sound like much if I write it that way, but if you just imagine an explosion, with percussion that shakes your frame, and brief, searing flame, then charred, black splinters raining down around you, for each of those thirteen blanks, you'll get the idea.

Out he stormed into the night. We watched the door a long time. I thought I'd turned into an old, arthritic man. But I couldn't stay there forever, so I hobbled up with Eve to help her finish setting up the 386. Jenny went silently to the kitchen with Melanie to finish some Christmas cookies they'd begun.

We didn't see him again that night, or the next day either. Jenny, lying awake in bed that second night, said, "You don't suppose we should report him as a runaway?"

I reminded her he'd be eighteen in a few months and would doubtless leave again. "If we haven't already lost him, we'll surely lose him then." When he didn't come home the second day, I wondered whether to search his room. Maybe that was what he was mad about—it gave me the shivers to think just what I'd do if I found anything. I put the tree and outside lights up. The girls didn't want to help. I don't remember ever feeling so bitter cold as on the ladder that year.

On the third day Wesley called me at work—said he had found a place with some friends in Rose Park, that he still had his job

and was going to buy a car, and wondered if I'd help him move. I swallowed a lump the size of an egg and said I would. I told him to stay in school as long as he could, and we'd help him if he got in trouble, and to come see us.

You try to do good things for your children, to make some happy times, so maybe when they start to drift away, home still has some hold on them. Tanna, Carmen, and Tanna's baby arrived that day for the holiday. Randy's army reserve unit had been called up for a couple of months in Bosnia, and Carmen was just finishing the semester, so we kicked Melanie back in with Eve to make room for them. I said our prayer at dinner, and thanked the Lord for all our family and their safe arrival here, and asked him to protect Randy and to please remember Wesley. We visited some. I went through the TV listings for a movie—in spite of our noble declarations in priesthood and Relief Society, sometimes one is grateful for the mindlessness of television. But Tanna and Carmen wanted to do carols, so Jenny made eggnog and we all sang a turn. A little into the second round, I saw a dark, trench-coated figure through the picture window, tromping up the walk. I looked hard but couldn't quite tell, so I went quickly to the door and got there just after him—it was Wes. He lifted a finger to ring the bell, but then hesitated, twisted the knob instead, and pushed the door open. I looked over my boy standing in the cold. All the anger and relief I felt, I held inside.

"I came to get some things," he said. The girls, who hadn't seen him yet, happened to be singing "Hark! the Herald Angels Sing."

"Come in, come in," I urged softly. "Tanna and Carmen are home, and the baby." I exchanged glances with Jenny, who appeared worried, perhaps that there would be a fight. Wes stepped tentatively past me.

"You're singin'."

"Yeah," I nodded. The girls saw him and brightened but kept going, maybe a little louder because this was Wesley's song.

"Where's the computer?"

"That's your job," I told him. He'd always done it, always set up the files and menu, always directed things from his chair, back to the others, facing the computer's dim flicker.

"We could get it," he said.

I don't know how I kept from bawling. "Sure," I said, treading light-footed toward the office, and he followed. I glanced at Jenny again, who through her worry seemed to say, *I'm with you.*

Wes hesitated in the doorway while I gathered cables. "Dad?" he said, ever so tentatively.

"Yeah?"

"It's hard out there."

I looked at him, then at the cables. "Welcome to the club," I joked. "Here, grab the monitor."

"Dad?"

"Yeah?"

"I wanna be part of the family again for a little while." His green eyes sparked like I hadn't seen in months, and he made a little half-embarrassed smile. We had a rough ride ahead of us, I knew, and trouble enough that we'd probably wish him gone before he was through, but none of that mattered that minute.

I whispered, "Sure. You come on home."

BENSON Y. PARKINSON was born in Provo, Utah, in 1960, served a French mission, and graduated from Brigham Young University in 1985. He and his wife, Robin, have five children and live in South Ogden, Utah, where he works full time as a writer. He is the author of a biography, *S. Dilworth Young,* and an LDS novel, *The MTC: Set Apart.* He moderates AML-List, an Internet mailing list devoted to the discussion of Mormon literature. He serves as membership clerk in the South Ogden 5th Ward.

THE PARTS I'M NOT SURE ABOUT

Louise Plummer

YOU KNOW HOW you think you're best friends with someone, and then something happens and you realize maybe it was only you who thought you were best friends? Maybe your best friend doesn't think of you as her best friend? Get what I mean?

I've known Becky all my life. We went to the same nursery school up at the Unitarian Church on 13th East; we both went to Emerson School and had Miss Nordvall in the morning kindergarten, who used to count the number of squares of toilet paper you used after you went to the bathroom. If you used more than six, she'd make you sit in the corner. Becky and I played "O Holy Night" on violin and flute for the sacrament meeting before Christmas when we were twelve. And that same year, Becky wore a dress to school and her slip fell down in front of Mr. Peterson out on the playground. She picked it up and hid it behind her back. Mr. Peterson said, "You don't have to be embarrassed, girls; I have daughters." We laughed so hard, we nearly got sick. Becky can still do an imitation of him saying that in his high nasal voice.

Becky tried to kill herself the week before Christmas. I found it out thirdhand. Becky's mom, Sister Chase, told the bishop, and he told my mom, and my mom told me. I went upstairs and sat on my bed, looking out of the window at the iris bed now covered with a fine layer of snow, the iris bed where Becky and I had buried my Barbie and Ken dolls in a hat-box on my thirteenth birthday. Becky called it my rite of passage. I had a dozen of them. Sometimes I miss those dolls and want to dig them up, but I'm afraid there'd be worms in the box.

I try to think of clues in her recent behavior that would explain Becky cutting herself, but I come up with zip. The last time we were together, she and Alison and I went to a movie and then to Hires for a hamburger. Becky told us about the time when she was three and ran away from home. She filled a Luv's diaper box with her books and pulled them along the sidewalk. "I couldn't sleep without *Good Night, Moon.*" She had laughed. Then we had gone to my house and tossed M&M's at each other, catching them with our mouths. The night after that, she tried to kill herself. Shouldn't I have recognized something?

My mom thinks I should go visit Becky in the hospital, and she calls about visiting hours, but Becky can't see anyone for three days. I'm relieved. I don't know what to say to her. It's like Becky's crossed some line—like she's an adult with adult problems and I'm still a kid. It's like if I see her she'll be this stranger. I figure I can just write her a note, but when I try, all I can think of is "Hope you're feeling better," with lots of XOs after it. My head fills with questions I don't dare ask her: *Did you have a nervous breakdown? Why would you cut yourself? Why didn't you tell me you were unhappy? Haven't I been a good friend?*

I go to the What-Not-Shoppe over on 9th South to buy a get well card. Most of the cards are for old geezers, as if kids don't get sick. Others insult the receiver. I have a feeling Becky's not up to being insulted, even if it's funny. Finally I pick one that has Lucy pulling the football away from Charlie Brown. It says,

"Feel like you've been dumped on your head? Get well soon."

I write a lot of XOs after it and sign it, "Your friend, Trish." Then I feel dumb that I wrote "Your friend," as if she didn't already know. How many Trishes does she know? Your teacher, Trish? Your grocery clerk, Trish? Your insurance rep, Trish? But I can't cross it out, because that's even dumber. I put the card in its yellow envelope and lick it shut.

My mom is in the kitchen sprinkling powdered sugar over rosettes when I ask her for a stamp. "It's a card for Becky," I say, waving it at her.

"Nice, honey. The stamps are in my purse—in the side pocket."

I find them, lick one, and set it in place. "I'm going to mail this," I say.

"Great," she says. And I escape. When I mail it at the corner, I feel good. I feel *mature,* as my mom says. Becky will know I don't think any less of her and that I'm still her friend. The card says all that. Then too, it's now her turn to send me a letter or call me, or come by when she's out of the hospital—maybe by that time, I'll know what to say to her.

But on Monday, I come home from babysitting at the Wakefields and my mom tells me that tomorrow we can visit Becky at the hospital. She says I should buy her a present. Something nice, she says.

"Like what?" I say. I can't imagine what to buy a suicidal person. "You mean a Christmas present—I've already got that."

My mom turns away from the fruit baskets she's putting together and looks at me as if I've just turned into a three-year-old. "No, Trish—I mean a get well present." She cuts a long piece of red ribbon from a roll. "Are you all right?"

"Yeah, I guess." I open the refrigerator and pull out a lemon yogurt. *A get well present? Hi, hope you get well soon from that self-inflicted wound. Or worse—hope you're back on your rocker soon.*

"I don't want to visit the hospital." I speak softly into the yogurt carton, because I'm not sure if I want Mom to hear me.

She lays the red ribbon on top of one of the fruit baskets. "I know," she says.

"If it were to celebrate something, I'd know what to buy—"

"But this is more serious," Mom says. Her hands are on my shoulders, but I can only stare into my yogurt.

"Mom, Becky's always been the one who made me laugh. I don't know how to be with Becky when she's in this kind of trouble. I'm sure I'll say the wrong thing. I'm sure I'll make it worse." I start to cry like the big baby that I am.

Mom hugs me and rubs my back. "You'll think of something," she says. "Becky just needs to know that you're still her friend."

"I don't know if I still am." I've said the worst, and my mom doesn't drop over dead or even wince.

"Then you'll find out tomorrow evening, when we go visit her."

"I'll get her some roses," I say. "Becky's nuts about roses." And then, catching myself, "I mean, she loves them."

Mom smiles. "I think nuts may just about cover it."

Last summer, Becky stole roses from all over the neighborhood and dried them by hanging them in bunches from her ceiling. Her yard is filled with roses, but she said it was more fun to steal them from neighbors, where there was a possibility of being caught and humiliated. Once, when I had slept over at her house, I went out with her on her early morning rose hunt, but I wouldn't step off the sidewalk into anyone's yard. "It's immoral to steal," I said. I could tell my voice sounded prissy.

"Yeah, sure." She clipped a couple of roses out of Mrs. Keddington's front yard.

"Any of these people would gladly let you clip a few roses if you asked them, so what's the point?"

She looked up at me then, her eyes squinting from the sun beyond my shoulder. "The point is that I'm not living my life anymore by somebody else's rules." She sounded mad, but then catching herself, she lightened up and said, "Besides, this is more fun." She turned back to clipping roses. "You can stay on the straight and narrow sidewalk if you want."

How did Becky do that? How did she make me feel guilty for *not* stealing roses with her?

Mom and I wait for Becky in a room with two banquet-sized tables and folding chairs around them. There's a blackboard on one wall, and it has notes about "A & P" written on it. My legs are crossed and my foot twitches nervously back and forth, so that the roses on my lap flop about in the vase. I can't stop though. The security for the adolescent unit of the hospital unnerves me. This room has a window, but there's a metal mesh that runs through the glass. It's like Becky's in prison.

My mom must feel the same way, because she's drumming a finger on the tiny wrapped package she's holding. It's a second gift for Becky. I thought of it later in the day. Mom smiles at me and whispers, "It'll be okay," but I think she's just trying to set an example. I wonder if Becky will be wearing a hospital gown and slippers. I wonder if she had to be in a straitjacket.

Becky appears in the doorway, a nurse behind her. "Hi," she says. I see everything at once: the familiar slacks and high-top boots, her bony frame under an extra-large sweatshirt, the sleeves falling below her wrists, hiding bandages, I'm pretty sure. Maybe not. Maybe it's all just a rumor.

"Hi," I say back. I try to smile. I try to stand. I feel like I'm suspended in Jell-O.

But my mom is quick. She's crossed the room by the time I stand and has her arms around Becky. She holds her tightly and I can see Becky's eyes close against my mom's neck, as if she feels safe for the first time in a long time. She clutches her as if she doesn't want her to stop the hug too soon, but my mom isn't going anywhere. My mom is a good hugger. She doesn't pat Becky's back and treat her like some pet mouse.

It isn't until Becky whispers, "I cut myself you know," in Mom's shoulder that I realize she's crying.

Mom kisses her cheek. "I know," she says. "I'm so sorry you're unhappy." She kisses her again. They stand pressed together for a long time.

I feel too young to be here. I feel sheepish and on the outside of things. I feel jealous.

When they finally part, Becky wipes her face with the palms of her hands. She sees me, says "Hi" again, and smiles broadly.

"I brought you roses," I say holding the vase up. I hug her with my other arm.

She takes the vase of roses and buries her nose in them. "They're glorious," she says. "Oh my, yes." She cups them with her fingers. "Yellow's my favorite. I love them." She puts her arm through mine. "Thank you."

"I'm glad," I say.

I had forgotten about the nurse in the doorway, but now she comes forward and says,

"Let me put these in a plastic container for you."

I'm surprised by this gesture, since the roses are already in a nice glass vase, but Becky hands them over to her.

"I'll put them in your room, okay?" the nurse says.

Becky watches her leave. "They won't let us have glass in here," she whispers to Mom and me. "She'll take all the thorns off too. So I can't use them to cut myself." She tries to smile. "Can you imagine trying to kill yourself with rose thorns?"

I can't imagine trying to kill myself at all.

Mom and I probably look stunned, because she adds, "Don't worry, I'm not going to do it again."

Mom strokes her face with one hand and says, "Good." Then moving toward the door, she says, "I'm going for a little walk and let you two talk. I'll be back in a while." She blows Becky a kiss and disappears.

"Here, I got you another present," I say and lead her to the table where we both sit down.

Becky picks up the box and shakes it lightly. "Goody," she says. She picks at the ribbon, removes the lid, and squeals. "It's a charm bracelet!" She lifts the silver chain out of the box and holds it out with two hands. "Look a flute and violin—aren't they cute? And the letter *E*."

"For East High," I say.

"What are these lips for?"

"To remind you of the time that Alex Bradshaw kissed you on that hayride and then kissed me the next night at Lagoon."

She shrieks. "Ooh, Acne Alex! Ooh yuck!"

We pucker our lips at each other and say in unison, "You taste better than chocolate." The twerp had actually said that to both of us.

She shrieks again when she sees the miniature Barbie doll. "This is too good," she says and holds the charms in one hand close to her chest. I can see the white bandage wrapped around her wrist. "Remember when we buried all your Barbies and Kens?"

I can see that she's caught between laughing and crying, and I begin to wish my mother hadn't left. It is easier when Becky is laughing. "I remember," I say.

"Wouldn't it be nice to be ten years old again?" A kind of half sob, half laugh escapes her mouth.

I don't know what to say, how to look. "I'm sorry," I say finally. I've never seen anyone look so sad. *No one our age should be this sad*, I think.

"Well." She literally shakes off the sadness. "This is one Barbie doll that will never be buried."

There is a rose charm on the bracelet. "To remind you of your life of crime," I tell her. I am glad to see her smile again.

She has come to the last charm on the bracelet, and she looks at it closely. It's a heart with "My friend" engraved on it. She stares at it, runs her index finger over the engraving, her lips tightly pressed together. She is crying, I realize.

"We still are friends, aren't we?" I ask.

She can only shake her head up and down. We sit together without speaking, Becky clutching the bracelet in her fist, and me holding her fist in my hand. Once I rub my fingers along the bandage at her wrist.

"Visiting hours are over." The nurse stands in the doorway.

Becky stands up immediately. "I have to go. I can't afford to lose points." She hugs me quickly. "Thank you, thank you for being my

friend. Thank you for this." She holds up her fist with the bracelet.

I nod. "We'll come again," I say, and I mean it. "Love you."

"Love you too."

We both step out of the room. I watch her walk down the hall past the nurses' station, where a small Christmas tree stands with only paper garlands on it. Becky turns once and waves at me. I wave back and go to find my mom.

That night, I can't sleep. I keep thinking of my mom holding Becky in her arms and telling her she loves her. I think of her kissing Becky's face. Finally, I get out of bed and go downstairs. I walk through the dark kitchen and into the family room, which is lit with moonlight. Through the backyard, I can see the Wakefield's Christmas lights still blinking along the roofline. "Mom?"

She is standing in her robe, looking out over the snow-covered yard and turns when I call her name. "Can't you sleep either?" she says to me.

"I was thinking of Becky," I say, even though it's only half true.

"Me too," she says.

We stand next to each other, looking at the stream of moonlight cuffing across the snow and listening to a car alarm in the distance. I can smell my mother's hand lotion and perfume. She has worn the same scent all my life.

"Mom." There's an unexpected catch in my voice, but I continue: "If I did something like Becky did—" I can't even say the word *suicide*. "If I did that, would you hug me the way you hugged her tonight? Would you kiss my face and tell me you loved me?"

She turns then and looks into my face as if she's seeing me for the first time. Then she draws me in, and we are pressed together. "If I have taken you for granted, I am so sorry," she whispers and kisses my cheek. "You're everything I ever wanted in a daughter. Everything."

Seeing Becky tonight, I realized that the world is a dangerous place, that there is unhappiness even at Christmas, but for the time being I hold onto my mother and feel safe to be her child.

LOUISE PLUMMER lives in Salt Lake City, Utah, and teaches writing at Brigham Young University. She has published novels for the national market and a book of essays (*Thoughts of a Grasshopper: Essays and Oddities*) for Deseret Book Company. She and her husband, Tom, have four sons.

SNOWBALL LICKS MY HEAD

Dick Beeson

It's the Christmas season, 1950.

504 Cook, Government Hill
Anchorage, Alaska
(Just above the railroad yards.)

I am 8 years old. My name is Dick.
My brother David is 11.
My sister Jane is 15.
Georgia is my Mom.
Ray is my Dad.
Snowball is my dog.
(My sister, Iggygick, is not born yet.)

We're snowed in and
I'm teetering tiptoe on the back of a kitchen chair
    which is propped against the curved wall of our Quonset hut home.
I'm Good King Wen-sez-claus at the window,
    looking out on the snow, which lays round about, deep and crisp and even.
In a minute, I'm going to fall from the chair
    and crack my head and bleed all over and get a scar for life.

My dog, a black cocker spaniel, will sniff at the blood on the floor,
    then lick my curly head.
I think his name, Snowball, being opposite his color and all, is very clever.

My hair is curly because Mom has given me and David a Toni home permanent.
    It's an annual rhythm:
        Mom curls our hair in December,
        Dad shaves our heads in July
            (so we look more like boxers
                and less like Gorgeous George, the wrestler).

Mom and Jane are baking a chocolate cake.
    When it comes out of the oven
        they will lay Hershey bars all over the top
            to melt for frosting.
                It's our breakfast.

And we'll have music with our cake,
    Frankie Carl plays "The Nutcracker" on our record player.
        "Victrola!" Mom says.
            She knows magic words.

Like every Christmas before, Mom is helping Dad with his gift list.
Like every Christmas before, Dad will ignore her instructions.

"No knives or guns for David."

        Last year he blew his new Christmas gloves off
            with his aspirin bottle bomb packed with
            July's fireworks he'd cached somewhere.
        He'll be a dentist in a women's prison someday.

"And no swimming stuff for Jane."

        This is Alaska. Alas Dad's water-winged hope
            for Jane as Esther Williams.
        And Lake Spenard is mostly too cold.
            And, when so briefly warm,
                full of what we call "bloodsuckers."

"And no boxing gloves for Dicky."

        Dad and Uncle Harold (Mom's younger brother) love "the fights."
            Dad fought "Chiggerweight"
                all along Elm Creek in Nebraska.
            Harold was a middleweight
                in WWII army smokers.
        They think I have promise as a boxer.
            The truth is, I'll fight anyone for their praise.

"And what don't you want," asks Dad. He's excited.

        In the trunk of his Plymouth are his boxes
                just arrived from Sears catalog, stateside:
        In one, a hatchet for David
                and a squeaking plastic carrot for Snowball.
        In another, a snorkel and fins for Esther.
        In a third, hockey skates, a stick and puck (fighting on ice).
        In the last, the latest pressure cooker.
            All variations on a theme.

"No pots and pans, no kitchen gadgets.
　　Nothing practical. And no perfume."

　　Mom coughs. She suspects she's dying. She's right. She has TB.
　　　　She has begun to leave us, and she knows it.

　　And she knows that her gifts will be left behind,
　　　　tokens or symbols of her life.
　　　　　　Who was she?
　　　　　　　　What was she about?

　　And she knows we will need to remember her without perfume—
　　　　the smell of flowers taken in their bloom.

　　And she knows we will need to believe
　　　　that our love for her was more than just practical.

And so, my fall, the blood, the possibility of a scar,
　　are nothing to Mom.
She bandages the wound—small really,
　　with a "butterfly" she tells me.
　　　　It is sufficient. It is entirely practical.
Then, she wraps my head in a grand turban of gauze.
　　"Now you're one of the three kings, Dicky.
　　　　Which will you be—Gaspar, Melchior, or Balthazar?"

"I'm Good King Wen-sez-claus, like in the song.
　　And you're my mother.
　　　. . . You're my mother, The Snow Queen."

. . . .

It's the Christmas season, 1996.

611 East of Scera Park
600 South of the Public Library
(Just by the Church Farm.)

I am 54 years old.
My granddaughter Eliza is 2 plus.
My grandson Elliot is 1 minus.

I'm sitting in Grandma Reeve's rocker (she loved boxing).
　　Eliza is standing in my lap, stroking my bald head.
　　Elliot is staring up from my cradled arms.
　　　He tilts his head with a question, but he has no words.

"Chiggerweight," I answer,
    "a dog licked all my hair off.
        An Eskimo's black dog, named Snowball."

Eliza has found my forty-six-year-old scar.
    She's tracing it with her pudgy sausage fingers.
    "Papa, did the dog bite your head?"

"No, Eliza.
I fell in my home, full of gifts,
    and The Snow Queen bandaged my head
        with a butterfly, and a grand turban of gauze."

DICK BEESON is the director of the Orem Public Library—a great job for a reader and writer. He is married to Gaylene Gunn Beeson, a musician. They are the parents of six children

ALL IN PEACE AND QUIETNESS

Larry E. Morris

IT WAS A CLEAR, hot August afternoon, the temperature holding steady at 105 degrees. I pulled the rental car up in front of the old two-story house and stopped.

"This is where Duane and his wife lived," I said to my sixteen-year-old son, Scott, but I realized he was still listening to his music. I motioned to him, and he reluctantly took the headphones off.

"This is where Duane and his wife lived," I said again.

Scott fiddled with his CD player.

"We came over here every week for Scout meetings. Duane taught us to tie knots right out by that tree."

I pointed to my left. "That's Poitevan Park. In junior high we came here for P.E. when the weather was good. We practiced freshman football out there. Coach Tremain always said we looked like sixty miles of gravel road."

Scott put the headphones back on.

I got out of the car and walked across the street to the park. Scott and I had flown in from Connecticut earlier that day; this was his first trip to Idaho.

Every day, after practice, Coach Tremain had made us run several laps around the park. I could still smell the sweat and feel the weight of the helmet and pads, and I could still hear the grind of cleats as we crossed the street and headed back for the school, running all the way.

A month earlier, when I had picked up Scott for the weekend, my ex-wife had sent out a shoebox of items that belonged to me. In the bottom of the box was an unopened Christmas card, postmarked the previous December 15, the very week we had decided to get divorced. I must have moved out a day or two before the card arrived and hadn't seen it before.

Standing at the edge of Poitevan Park, breaking into a sweat from the hot sun, I pulled the card from my back pocket and examined the envelope. It had been mailed from Tendoy, Idaho, and was addressed to me in Duane's unmistakable handwriting, with an exaggerated swoop on the *T* and a long tail on the *y*.

I opened the envelope and read the card again.

Dear Terry,

How are you doing, pardner? Think of you and the other boys every Christmas, without fail. Course, you're not boys any longer. Imagine some of you have grandkids by now. Time goes by, doesn't it? For good or bad, it goes by.

Will never forget that winter camp we had just before Christmas so many years ago, thirty-five years, I believe. I live within a few miles of that spot. I work in Salmon, driving truck, of course, but I couldn't resist living in Tendoy, where I can walk out the door of the trailer and be standing on the Lewis and Clark trail.

Look me up if you happen to be in this part of the country. You've apparently raised your family in Connecticut and are probably settled there. But don't you sometimes long for the West?

Merry Christmas to you and your family.

Duane

I calculated the passage of time, using my fingers for both decades and years. Duane was right: it had been thirty-five years. My friends and I had been thirteen that winter, and Duane, our new Scoutmaster, had been maybe twenty-five. That would make Duane about sixty now.

A few days before Christmas, Duane had driven a carload of us from Idaho Falls to Tendoy, where Lewis and Clark had crossed the Continental Divide. I muttered something about the cold as we pitched the tent, but Duane wouldn't hear of it.

"Do you know what you've got?" he asked. "A chance to experience just a little of what Lewis and Clark experienced. But they didn't have nice sleeping bags and expensive boots. So don't complain."

After receiving the card, I made several unsuccessful attempts to reach Duane, finally deciding to go to Idaho and look for him. Scott agreed to come along after a good deal of pleading and the promise of a nice motel, with cable TV and a swimming pool.

I walked back to the car and drove the four blocks to the school. I got Scott to take his headphones off again.

"This was my junior high. We used to run out that door and down those steps on our way to Poitevan Park. We ate our lunches sitting right over there on that ledge. In the fall, I used to bring a transistor radio so we could listen to the World Series during lunch."

O. E. Bell Junior High was abandoned, no doubt condemned, with the windows boarded up and signs on the grounds warning trespassers to stay away.

I drove a block north and pointed out the building that had been the library. Then I showed Scott where the swimming pool had been, the pool area now filled in and covered with grass.

"Duane's favorite Scouting activity was

swimming. I got my Lifesaving merit badge here at the city pool. And Don Wilson Drug used to be right there, across the street. Sometimes in ninth grade we'd come down here and have lunch. Egg salad sandwiches."

Scott listened to his music; I drove west.

"There it is," I said a few minutes later, "the Snake River."

The river was high, the current strong—the way I remembered it. Scott was impressed enough to get out of the car.

I motioned to my right. "There used to be a hospital right there, where that church is. That's where I was born."

I turned back to the water. Duane had challenged me once to swim across the river, and we had done it together, starting at the dock near the bridge and reaching the east bank near the hospital. Duane had climbed up the bank, hoisted up his trunks, and then grabbed my hand as I slipped on the muddy bank. His grip was strong. "Now you can say you've swum across a real river," he had said, shivering.

Scott and I got a hamburger and drove north for Tendoy, passing within a few miles of Mud Lake, where Duane took the Scouts ice fishing, and then heading northwest, with Targhee National Forest to one side and Salmon National Forest to the other.

Scott listened to his music, using the CD player his mother and I had given him for Christmas eight months earlier, a Christmas that had turned into a nightmare. Never one to show emotion, Scott had cried when we told him about the divorce; his fourteen-year-old sister became angry and resentful. She had hardly spoken to me since and refused to visit me with Scott every other weekend. On Christmas Day, my wife had taken the kids to her mother's house; I had idled my time away in a Motel 6, alone.

No one had known how to celebrate Christmas like Duane. Thirty-five years ago, on the first day of December, he had gathered the Scouts at his home and announced what he called the "twenty-four days of Christmas." The next few weeks we had celebrated Christmas every single day—caroling at several rest homes, making music boxes for our mothers, collecting canned goods for the poor, sledding at the golf course, ice skating at Tautphaus Park, swimming at the indoor heated pool at Green Canyon, and making winter camp near Lemhi Pass. On the twenty-fourth day, Christmas Eve, Duane had stopped by my home with a present. "Merry Christmas, Terry," he said, handing me the small, awkwardly wrapped gift. I opened it that night—it was a Swiss Army pocketknife, which I still had.

Scott and I reached Tendoy in mid-afternoon. Like Lemhi, Tendoy was nothing more than a store with a gas pump. We went inside.

"Are you Mrs. Blake?" I asked the woman behind the counter.

"Yes."

"I called about a week ago; I'm looking for Duane Olsen."

"Yes, I remember," she said. "As I told you, he still has a post office box here, but I haven't seen him recently." She checked the box. "Your letter is still here; he hasn't received any other mail."

"Have you been able to find out where he lives?"

"I asked several people in the area. No one seems to know him. But I did hear there's someone living in a trailer over near the Lemhi Pass road."

She gave me directions, and Scott and I drove east, finding the trailer without difficulty. A woman answered the door, but she had never heard of Duane.

"How long are we going to keep looking?" asked Scott.

"Just a little while."

I left the main road and followed a dirt road up Lemhi Pass.

A few weeks after becoming Scoutmaster, Duane took the troop swimming at Lava Hot Springs. He worked with us on our Swimming merit badge and then challenged us to a cannonball contest.

"No problem," said my best friend, Chad, climbing out of the pool. He jumped off the side, grabbed his knees, and splashed into the water.

Duane laughed. "Not a *teeny, weeny* cannonball."

He got out of the pool, hoisted up his trunks, and walked to the high dive. He climbed up the ladder and strode and bounced off the board like a champion diver, even spreading his arms in an apparent swan dive. Then he tucked into a cannonball position and disappeared into the water, all two hundred and seventy pounds of him, a perfect arc of water shooting up from the surface.

Chad and I yelled with delight and then followed Duane back up the ladder.

Scott and I came to another trailer, parked haphazardly next to a stream; I got out and knocked on the door. After a minute I heard a shuffling inside.

"Come in," yelled a voice.

I opened the door. The trailer was musty, shrouded in darkness. I could barely make out a man lying on a couch.

"Excuse me," I said. "I'm looking for Duane Olsen."

"You found him."

"Duane," I said, peering into the darkness and still unable to see his features, "it's Terry Hayward."

"Terry, Terry. Please turn on the light—to your left on the wall."

I turned on the light. The voice sounded like Duane, but I couldn't recognize him. He looked to be at least seventy and was thin and gaunt.

"Come over here and shake my hand, son."

I stepped over and extended my hand; he shook it weakly.

He looked me over and smiled. "You're a bald old man," he said, laughing, but the laugh turned into a cough.

I rubbed my head. "I'm certainly bald. And I feel old."

"It's an amazing thing to go almost thirty-five years without seeing someone," he said. "Makes you realize how short life is."

"It sure is good to see you, Duane. How are you doing?"

"Sick. Had to stop working."

"The woman at the store said she hadn't seen you lately."

"No. My neighbor down the road checks on me occasionally and brings me a few groceries."

"My son is out in the car. Let me get him."

Scott entered the trailer suspiciously; I introduced him.

"Hello, Scott," said Duane. "You look like you're about eighteen."

"Almost seventeen," said Scott.

"Very glad to meet you. Has your dad told you about me?"

"Yeah."

"Don't believe a word he says."

Scott surprised me by laughing.

"Scott, did you see that stream outside?"

"Yeah."

Duane leaned over and took a book from the bookcase next to the couch. I recognized it immediately—Duane's paperback copy of DeVoto's *Journals of Lewis and Clark*.

"Have you ever read this book?" Duane asked Scott.

"No."

"You mean your dad has never mentioned it to you?"

"I don't think so."

"Well, this book tells about that stream outside. Will you do me a favor?"

"Yeah."

"Hike up the stream a ways. And I want you to remember Meriwether Lewis, who followed that very same stream in the opposite direction, almost two hundred years ago."

Scott surprised me again by looking interested.

"Okay," he said, walking out of the trailer.

"A good young man," said Duane.

I told him about the divorce, and how I had discovered his Christmas card.

"How long were you married?" he asked.

"Twenty years."

"I'm sorry, Terry."

"I'll survive."

"Surviving's not the point, is it?"

"I guess not, Duane."

"Gloria and I got divorced right after we left Idaho Falls."

"Did you ever have any children?" I asked.

"No, and two years ago I got word that Gloria had died. She had diabetes, you know."

"Yes, I remember that."

"Terry, you're the only Scout who stayed in

touch with me. That meant a lot to me. I really appreciated those Christmas cards."

"Well, I'm sorry you haven't heard from me in such a long time—it must be ten or twelve years since I sent you a card."

"I knew you hadn't forgotten me."

"You gave me the most memorable Christmas of my life."

"The twenty-four days of Christmas," said Duane, smiling. "I planned on doing that with a Scout troop every year for the rest of my life. I never did it again."

"Like you say, 'Time goes by.'"

Duane nodded.

A moment later Scott returned.

"Did you hike upstream?" asked Duane.

"Yeah."

"And did you remember Lewis?"

"Yeah."

"That's good, son. Would you please help me off this couch?"

Scott stepped over and held out his hand.

"Thanks," said Duane, leaning on Scott as he stood up. "I want to stand near that stream for a minute; I want to tell you about Meriwether Lewis."

Then Duane turned to me. "You stay here, Terry."

I laughed. "Yes, sir."

Through the small window in the kitchen, I watched Scott help Duane out to the stream, the same stream we had camped next to thirty-five Christmases ago. I got the copy of DeVoto and found the passage Duane had quoted to us that night in the tent:

> Tuesday 25th Decr 1804, cloudy.
> [Ordway]
> we fired the Swivels at day break & each man fired one round. our officers Gave the party a drink of Taffee. we had the best to eat that could be had, & continued firing dancing & frolicking dureing the whole day. the Savages did not Trouble us as we had requested them not to come as it was a Great medicine day with us. We enjoyed a merry christmas dureing the day & evening untill nine oClock—all in peace and quietness.

Through the window, I watched my son and the friend of my youth, Duane, gesturing to the stream with one hand and putting the other hand on Scott's shoulder.

LARRY E. MORRIS has published more than eighty articles in such magazines as the *Ensign, This People, Honolulu,* and *LAN Times.* He is the coauthor of *The Mormon Book of Lists* (with Jay A. Parry); his latest novel is called *Aftershocks.* He and his wife, Deborah, live with their four children in Salt Lake City.

CHRISTMAS LIGHT

*LaRene Gaunt**

I'VE ALWAYS LOVED CHRISTMAS. Ever since I was a little boy, I've gotten swept up in the whirl of bright lights and excitement around me. Ironically, we celebrate the birth of the Savior—the light of the world—just four days after the winter solstice, the darkest time of the year in the Northern Hemisphere. Yet amid this Christmas darkness, even the Earth itself tries to compensate by reflecting the available light off the snow, thus creating some of the brightest days of the year. Most people do the same thing at Christmastime by stringing colored lights, building roaring fires, singing songs, and wrapping presents in brightly colored paper. For some, however, this proves to be too much, and they fall into darkness and gloom. I never understood those people. Christmas has been such a magical time for me, I always wondered how someone could get the "Christmas Blues." That is, until this year.

This would be my second Christmas since returning home from my mission and it promised to be a great one. I was enjoying the independence of college life, studying photography and sharing an apartment with three returned missionaries. I had a good job, and although I didn't make lots of money, I paid my tithing, and had enough to get by. Besides that, in an unusual situation for me, I had become good friends with two wonderful young ladies—Jenny and Christine—and I was

---

* This is a fictionalized account of a true story, told to the author by a young man who prefers to remain anonymous.

in the early stages of dating both of them. I liked them both but for different reasons. Jenny, an Australian, was trying to get a work visa. She and I had become fast friends three months earlier when we realized that her younger brother and I had been missionary companions. Knowing she might have to leave if she couldn't get a visa, we had tried to keep our relationship simple. It was comfortable and filled with laughter and long talks.

Christine was the choir director in my singles ward, and she seemed to reciprocate my affections. She had a quiet grace about her that suggested a deepness of soul beyond her nineteen years. Knowing she was young, I had tried to give her space and allow our relationship to develop slowly. Music and activities at the singles ward filled our time together.

Yes, things were looking good!

Then, as the winter solstice approached, to my surprise the light began to drop out of my life also. The first hit was financial—one of my roommates left for two months leaving us to split the expenses three ways instead of four. As I looked over my budget, I realized that I would have to "skip" buying Christmas presents if I wanted to survive financially. I basically told my family and friends that I loved them but not to expect any gifts from me this year. My running joke was that I couldn't even afford to pay attention.

As the days passed and the Christmas frenzy intensified, I felt less and less a part of it. I could feel myself being pulled down. In an effort to save myself, I decided not to abandon Christmas entirely and made plans to give gifts to Jenny and Christine.

Then, just when my spirits brightened at the idea, came hit number two—Jenny told me that she had to return to Australia until she heard about her work visa. We were insepara-ble for a week. I took her to a concert by her favorite LDS musician as my Christmas gift to her. The next morning, we went to the temple, and then later that day I took her to the airport. Though I had tried to restrain my growing feelings for her, it was difficult to see her go.

I lost myself in my photography, spending long hours in the darkroom trying to create just the right print for Christine as her Christmas present. Finally, I had it—a shadowy photograph of a black swan silhouetted against a shimmering silver lake. I gave it to her Sunday evening after choir practice. She loved it. Unfortunately, so did Larry, a young hot-shot who had just returned from his mission. Christine had caught his eye his first week in the singles ward. He happened to be nearby when I gave Christine her gift, and as he came over to look at it, I saw Christine look at him. It's hard to describe how she looked at him, but suffice it to say, I should be so lucky as to have a young woman look at me that way. I tried to ignore it, thinking I was jumping to conclu-sions, but still, it kept bugging me. It was hit number three.

I talked to my best friend Steve about it. He said not to worry, but Steve was getting mar-ried in a week and I knew he had more impor-tant things on his mind than how Christine looked at Larry. Steve and I had been friends for more than a year. We had so much in com-mon that we often joked that we shared the same frontal lobe in our brains. When he met Heather and they fell in love, the three of us shared great times together. I often brought Jenny or Christine when we double dated. But I knew that after Steve and Heather got mar-ried and moved away things would be differ-

ent. My despair darkened as I realized that I was losing my best friend—hit number four.

The days dragged on, and dragged me down. Then hit number five—I fell into a cre-ative slump and lost my desire to do any pho-tography whatsoever. I tried to keep up my facade with Steve and Heather because I was going to photograph their wedding, and I didn't want them to see me in my ever-increasing gloom.

Things came to a head at Steve's wedding two days before Christmas. I was with Steve and Heather most of the day, constantly stick-ing a camera in their faces, and ironically, con-stantly on the lookout for the next batch of good light. That evening, near the end of their reception as I was taking some candid shots, Steve left his own reception line and came over and tapped me on the shoulder. "Christine just came through the line," he said simply, "she said she's been going out with Larry every night for the past week."

If someone had been videotaping me I could have gone back and tracked it frame by frame, until I stopped on the exact instant when I felt my heart burst. I'm not kidding. As soon as my brain registered what Steve had said, I felt an actual, tangible pain in my heart. It was similar to pains I'd felt before, but never this intense, nor this prolonged.

I knew it wasn't just Christine. It was every-thing—uncertainty about my whole life and future. I was tired of being single. It seemed like everyone else, including my best friend, was getting married. I wanted to meet the right girl and it just wasn't happening. In addition, I was tired of not having any money and struggled with my choice of photography as a career. I wanted to start over in another major but I knew I didn't have enough money to go to college full time—or to do anything else for that matter. On top of all this, I hated losing my best friend right when I needed him.

I left the reception, went home, and lay awake in the dark for a long time.

The next day was Christmas Eve. I wasn't due over at my parents' place until early afternoon, so I sulked around my apartment with the pain still lingering in my heart. If ever there was a pitiful picture of the "Christmas Blues" it was me sitting there on my couch unshowered, unshaven, and totally engrossed in a music video of Bing Crosby and David Bowie singing "The Little Drummer Boy," circa 1972.

As if that weren't enough, all the stress and gloom had given me a searing pain in my neck. I went to my parents' house, but by the time dinner rolled around, I'd had it with "Hark! the Herald Angels Sing" and blinking Christmas lights. I felt bad, but even worse than that, I didn't want to feel better. I told my mom that I was sorry, but that I needed to be by myself for now. Then, in an act I shall always be grateful for, she understood. She didn't protest, didn't try to talk me out of it; she just understood, and let me go.

I'd heard that sometimes you just have to lie down with your pain, so I drove back to my apartment in silence planning to sit on the couch in the dark. "There is no coming to consciousness without pain," said psychologist Carl Jung. I pulled into my parking spot, and as I got out of my truck, I stepped on something. I looked closer, and there, lying in the ice and dirt, was a copy of a standard, blue-cover missionary-issue Book of Mormon—just like one of the many I had given out while on my mission. It was even dog-eared on 3 Nephi 11.

It was too much of a coincidence to be real, but it was real. As much as I resisted the idea, I knew it was no accident I had stepped on that Book of Mormon. Maybe it was the Lord's way of getting my attention. Here I was drowning, and the Lord was tossing me a lifeline—right at my feet.

I picked it up, and went into my apartment. Against my original plan, I turned on the lights. I looked at the book again.

Opening up to the dog-eared page, I began reading 3 Nephi 11—the one chapter I'd read more than any other chapter in the Book of Mormon, having read it with every investigator I'd ever taught while on my mission. However, there was something different this time. I felt as though the images in my mind were clearer than ever before, and I could see the Savior appearing out of the darkness to the Nephites. I kept reading on into chapter twelve until I got to the verses that read:

"*Behold, do men light a candle and put it under a bushel? Nay but on a candlestick, and it giveth light to all that are in the house; therefore let your light so shine before this people, that they may see your good works, and glorify your father which is in heaven.*"

I read it, re-read it, and re-read it again and again, until I cried out, "I just don't feel like shining!" That was it. That was the catalyst that started the tears flowing for the first time in who knows how long. All the anxiety, frustration, anger, sadness, and heartache that I'd let well up inside finally came pouring out in a flood of tears and a paroxysm of emotion. I could not feel the pain in my neck, so great was the pain in my heart. I wept openly and unashamedly for hour-long minutes, clutching the Book of Mormon to my chest. I do not believe that I have ever experienced a darker time in my life. Then, in the midst of this maelstrom decay, I *felt* a light inside my soul, growing brighter, and calming me. In that instant, I *understood* many plain and specific things pertaining to my life, and things unlawful to repeat. I felt a voice speak to my soul and say, "I understand pain. I have descended below all things." Then I remembered that my relationship with the Savior had always been there; I had just moved away from it.

I also felt something else—peace. I realized that a measure of peace in life goes a long way in helping us deal with pain. I knew that my problems were not going to be solved instantly, but I finally felt hope. My troubles might not seem like much to anyone else, but my pain was real to me. Now I knew that the Lord was aware of me in the details of my life, and that if it was important to me it was important to him. I found myself smiling, something else I hadn't done in weeks.

Elder Neal A. Maxwell of the Quorum of the Twelve Apostles said, "If you can know that God loves you, even when you don't know the meaning of all things, *it will sustain you.*" I knew God loved me. I knew his light would always be there for me.

No sooner had this moment passed, than the phone rang. It was my mom. She realized that I'd left without eating and offered to bring me some food. I said no thanks, I was fine. I hung up the phone, then looked down at the Book of Mormon still in my hands. Was the phone call another "coincidence"? I don't think so. It was another testimony that the Lord was aware of me. I realized it was pretty dark back home, in no small part due to my refusal to "put my light on a candlestick." I knew what I had to do. I got on my knees, thanked the Lord, and raced home.

My winter solstice had passed. I had been rescued by the light of the Savior. It seemed to me that this life was as the winter of time, with but a little light to go around. To be one of the Lord's disciples, we must be as the pure driven snow, willing to reflect whatever available light he sends.

"He that ascended up on high, as also he that descended below all things, in that he comprehended all things, that he might be in all and through all things, the light of truth. Which truth shineth. This is the light of Christ" (D&C 88:6–7).

LaRene Gaunt was born and reared in San Diego, California, the daughter of Worth and Florence Porter and the oldest of five children. She graduated from Brigham Young University with a B.A. in Art in 1965. While working in the San Francisco Bay area, she met David Gaunt. They married in the Salt Lake Temple in 1968, and moved to a small town in east central Indiana. The parents of six children (three deceased), the Gaunts moved to Sandy, Utah, in 1979. LaRene has published five books, a board game, three card games, and numerous magazine articles. An accredited genealogist, she has a passion for family history. She is currently an associate editor for the *Ensign* magazine.

Dad's Season

Chris Crowe

Most people think the Christmas season begins right after Thanksgiving. Well, in a narrow sort of way, they're right, I guess, but people who link Christmas to Thanksgiving are probably—

1. Couch potatoes,
2. Old people,
3. Department store managers,
4. Culturally illiterate, or
5. Nerds.

Real people—including *girls*—know that Christmas season begins shortly after the start of basketball season. It's not the smell of pine trees, the glow of Christmas lights, or the sound of Christmas carols that signal Christmas's coming. The surest signs are the bammata-bammata-bammata sound of a dribbled basketball echoing in a gym and the pungent gym-smell of varnished hardwood, locker room disinfectant, and sweat.

Basketball is my life. I've got a picture of my dad, who coached at Valley High before he died, holding one-year-old me under one arm and a basketball under the other. In the background, a handful of players are trailing off to the locker room at the end of practice. Dad's tan face is flushed, a few beads of sweat trickle down his cheeks. He looks tired but happy.

I'm reaching across his body for the ball. My right hand is almost there, just about ready to poke it free and chase after it when it hits the floor and bounces away. My face is tight, framed in concentration, like I'm trying to solve a monster calculus problem.

"Carrie-Jo," says Mom. "That's how you always were, even as a baby—going for the ball, wanting to hold it. At three, you were starting to dribble, and when you were six or seven, you started shooting on the real baskets. The first time I saw you making bank shots from six or seven feet out, I knew you were destined to be a gym rat, a basketball fanatic just like your father."

Anyway, that's my favorite picture of me and Dad. I like how I'm on one side, basketball's on the other, and Dad's in the middle, holding us both and smiling.

He died at thirty-one, just two weeks before Christmas. He'd been out jogging that night—Dad was a total fitness freak—came home, showered, did the regular night things: read scriptures and said prayers with me, tucked me in, then went to bed himself. He never woke up.

I was five years old.

But this isn't about Dad; it's about me.

Me and basketball.

* * *

When you're a basketball player, a *real* basketball player, you learn to do without all the Christmas stuff. I'm not saying you forget about the holiday; I'm saying that Christmas falls smack in the middle of basketball season, and if you're not playing in a Christmas tournament, you're at school practicing. And if you're not at school practicing, you're playing pickup games in the stake center with your buds. There's no time for shopping, carolling, service projecting—no time for anything but basketball. Sure, you take off part of Christmas Day to open presents, eat, and do the family thing, but you still find time to shoot some hoops. Somewhere. Sometime. Anywhere. Anytime. I love being basketball-busy during the holidays. The best Christmas vacations are the ones where we have two-a-day practices on the days we're not in a tournament. I take Sunday off, but I try to fill the rest of my vacation time with basketball. It feels great to stay in shape, to use my body, to improve my game.

It also helps me forget that I'm spending another Christmas without Dad.

Mom, basketball widow that she is—and was—understands, sort of. She's used to doing the Christmas decorating, shopping, and cooking alone. She's used to spending half of Christmas Day alone, but it's hard for her. Believe me, *I* know.

This Christmas, though, she's going to have me with her.

* * *

December 7: a day that will live in infamy for me. We're playing Pineview High, the fourth game of my senior year. I already hold most of the school basketball records, including points scored, and a few college scouts are in the stands. Life and basketball are terrific and looking better all the time. Third quarter, I go up for a three-pointer. It snaps through the net, but I don't see it because a Pineview player shoves me just as I release the shot. I come down wrong on my leg and my world blows up. An explosion of pain rips through my knee. I feel like I've been shot or knifed or mortally wounded. I hurt so bad I can't see or even breathe for a few seconds.

When I catch my breath, I scream. Sweat and tears drench my face, and through it I see foggy images of teammates starting to huddle around me, not sure what to do.

* * *

ACL: anterior cruciate ligament. The orthopedic doctor who examined me that night said mine had shredded on impact, leaving me with a blown knee. "It looks pretty bad, Carrie-Jo," he said. "Lots of athletes come back from ACL injuries, but with all the damage I suspect we'll find when we get inside there, surgical repair is going to be difficult. Rehab and therapy will help, but . . . " he paused and looked away. Mom was standing at the head of the gurney, stroking my hair. She had been crying. The doctor looked at her and continued, "Some basketball players never come back from ACL surgery. The game just puts too much stress on knee ligaments."

That about killed me. I'd been holding back the tears, trying to be tough, but when he said that, I let out a loud, sorrowful sob. He looked at me again and rested a hand on my ankle. "I'm not saying it's 100 percent certain that your basketball days are over, but, well, it's going to be rough."

"Rough" hardly describes how I felt when I woke up from surgery; I felt like I'd been crammed into a washing machine and run through a week's worth of spin cycles. I was still half out of it when a therapist-nurse–serial killer came in and fitted my knee with a Velcro and metal leg brace and made me get out of bed. When I stood up, hot wires of pain shot up my leg and the room spun crazily. I wasn't sure if I'd vomit or faint first. I didn't care. I just wanted to die.

I'm not a wimp. I've played enough basketball to have learned to live—and play—with all sorts of pain: sprained fingers and ankles, bruises, bumps, and cuts. My knee hurt worse than anything I'd ever felt before, but I could have handled that. I wanted to die because the knee injury was the one thing I couldn't play with. And if I couldn't play basketball, I certainly didn't feel like living.

I came home from the hospital angry and depressed, prepared for my worst Christmas since Dad died.

"Look on the bright side, Carrie-Jo," said Mom as I settled into the couch in the family room. "At least now you'll be able to enjoy the Christmas season."

"I don't care about the Christmas season, Mom. I care about the basketball season. And mine is shot."

"But we'll have some time together, and you can get some good rest before you go back to school and start rehab on your knee. There's always next year."

"Next year? My career is over. What college is going to take a chance on a girl with a blown knee? My career ended on the floor of the Pineview game. And now what am I going to do?"

Mom paused and her face got all serious. "Have faith, Carrie-Jo. This isn't the end of everything."

"Yeah, right. My knee is blown. My career is ruined. Faith is really going to fix that." My throat tightened, but I was determined not to cry. "It's not fair. It's not right. What's left for me?"

"Your whole life is left for you. You're young, bright, healthy," she tapped my leg, "even with an injured leg. That will heal in time. You can still do whatever you want to do."

"I want to play basketball. I've got to."

"But, Carrie-Jo, you can't play basketball forever. Surely you knew that it would all end one day."

"But not now. Not right now. I'm not ready for this to end. I'm not done with it yet."

"I sincerely hope you're not, but you've got to face the possibility that you might be. If you never play again, it's not the end of the world. There's more to life than basketball."

"How can you say that? I've already lost enough in my life. To lose this, *this,* it's the last thing I can afford to lose." I was crying now, trying hard to talk without sobbing. Mom left me alone. She knew she wasn't going to be able to talk me out of feeling sorry for myself.

I sulked around the house for a week. Mom let me sleep as long as I wanted to, and I spent most of my waking time watching basketball on ESPN or doing some low-key rehab exercises. Some teammates visited one afternoon and invited me to come watch a few practices. Coach Zinke called almost every day to see how I was doing.

"Fine," I told him. "How's the team?"

"Not the same without you, of course. Looks like we're going to make it to the finals of the Christmas tournament. Sure wish you'd come cheer us on."

"Yeah, well, I'd like to, Coach, but my knee's still kind of sore, and besides, I'm not very good on crutches. But tell the girls I said good luck. I'm sure you guys'll do fine without me."

He was silent a moment. "Carrie-Jo, you're going to be okay. I know this must be hard for you and all, but really, you're a great girl. Things will turn out . . ."

Now my coach was sounding like Mom. "Look, Coach, I've really got to go now. Thanks a lot for calling, and good luck." I hung up the phone.

Mom did her best to make the house a happy place. For the first time in my life, I noticed how hard she worked to make everything Christmassy. She had Christmas CDs on the stereo, the Christmas tree glittered and glowed in the corner of the family room, the kitchen overflowed with Christmas goodies. Sometimes, I felt like I was trapped in Santa's Workshop. Through it all, Mom stayed upbeat, cheerful, a Cratchit to my Scrooge. As Christmas grew nearer, and as my boredom and unhappiness deepened, I got grouchier, uglier, meaner.

"This is stupid, Mom. I'm not a little kid anymore. We don't need to waste your time and our money on all this Christmas stuff. Haven't you got better things to do?"

She smiled. "I like Christmastime. I like the feeling, the traditions."

"It's dumb. Who cares about all this stuff, anyway? It's mostly a commercial rip-off. All this junk doesn't have anything to do with Christmas."

"I like it anyway, especially the memories."

"Memories? What are you talking about? Don't you remember Dad? Don't you remember what happened to him?"

"Of course I do. Christmas was his favorite time of the year, even though it was his busiest. He always said December combined two very important things in his life: basketball and a celebration of the birth of Christ. I don't think he'd want his death to ruin his favorite season, do you?"

"Are you crazy? It did ruin Christmas, and it's ruined every Christmas since then. How can you celebrate Christmas without a husband? How can I celebrate it without a father? I hate this time of year. If it weren't for basketball, I would have gone insane years ago. All this stuff brings back too many memories; it reminds me of how unfair it was that Heavenly Father let my dad die. And then this," I smacked my leg brace, "this is almost as bad. Christmas is supposed to be a time of giving, but for me it seems like it's a time for losing. I *hate* it!"

Mom came and sat by me. Without speaking, she placed one hand on the back of my neck and began squeezing it gently, a firm massage, one she'd done since I was a baby. I felt the warmth of her hand work its way into my neck. The tightness and tension eased, but I continued to frown.

"I never knew you felt that way, Carrie-Jo. I knew it was hard, I knew you hurt—we both hurt—but I didn't understand how you were dealing with it." She looked at the Christmas tree and sighed softly. "This time of year is my connection to Dad. Basketball, Christmas—it was all one for him, and now for me, the entire Christmas season reminds me of him. It's a memory I don't want to forget. I know I'll be with him forever, of course, that all three of us will be together one day, but while I'm waiting, I like to keep him fresh on my mind. All this," she gestured to the tree and decorations, "helps. It helps more than you can know." She let her arm slide down around my shoulders and hugged me. "I love him," she whispered. "I love you."

I thought of that picture of me and Dad, of how I was connected to him. I had always figured basketball was my connection to him, my last connection to him, and I didn't want to let it go, ever. As long as I played, I had a part of him with me, in me. Playing basketball was my way of holding on to Dad, just like Christmas was Mom's way. My knee still hurt. I was still mad at God for letting me get hurt. But with Mom sitting there massaging my neck, gentle Christmas carols playing in the background, the tree shimmering in the corner of the family room, something was changing. Maybe I needed to get to know more about Dad, more about his life outside the basketball court.

"Mom, tell me about how Dad celebrated Christmas."

CHRIS CROWE, father of four children, two of whom are basketball-playing girls he can rarely defeat in one-on-one, is a former high school teacher and coach who is now an Associate Professor of English at Brigham Young University. He has written many stories and articles for the *New Era* and most recently published *For the Strength of You: A How-To Handbook for LDS Teens.* He lives in Provo, Utah, and serves in the bishopric of the Edgemont Fifth Ward.

A BLUE CREEK CHRISTMAS

Richard Peterson

THE WINDOWS OF THE DINER on Main Street in Tremonton were steamed up when Walter Glenn and his young grandson stepped from the cold afternoon into the warm cafe. The tables were all empty, but six of the dozen stools lined up in front of the counter were occupied. A strand of gold braid looped around the pass-through window to the kitchen and a squatty Christmas tree by the front window were the only concessions to the holiday.

The men on the stools were all farmers, and they turned to look at the front door when it opened.

"Walter," one man said.

"How's it going, Walt?" another asked.

Walter eased onto one of the stools and patted the one next to him for Nelson to climb onto.

"Who's your helper?" one of the men asked.

"This is my grandson, Nelson," Walter said, reaching to pull off the boy's cap and ruffle his blond hair. "We're headed out to thin the jackrabbit population of Blue Creek."

"The boy must be one heck of a shot," one man said. "Cause *you* ain't likely to hit any."

Nelson grinned, pleased to be noticed by his grandfather's friends.

Ignoring the barb, Walter turned to the waitress, who had taken up a defensive position in front of him on the other side of the counter.

"And how are you on this fine day before

Christmas, Miss Luellen?" he asked, flashing a grin at her.

"I'm Doris. Luellen's my sister."

"That's right. I believe you mentioned that the last time I was in here," he said, winking.

"The last time you were in here, and a hundred times before that," she said, without smiling. "What'll you have?"

Turning to his grandson, Walter said, "How about it, Nelly? Want a piece of pie?"

The boy nodded enthusiastically, and Walter said, "Why don't you give us both a piece of pie?"

"Apple okay?"

"That'll be fine, but put a scoop of ice cream on my grandson's."

While they were eating, Walter visited with the men at the counter. He ate only a little of his pie but coached Nelson on slicking up his plate; when the boy was through eating, Walter paid the bill, leaving "Miss Luellen" a generous tip. The men at the counter had fewer farming duties this time of year and would spend a part of the day nursing coffee refills, trading jokes, and jawing about machinery, crop prices, and the weather. Frankly, they were grateful to be out of their wives' way on Christmas Eve day.

As the boy and his grandfather climbed off their stools to leave, one of the farmers said, "When you're out there shooting, Nelson, take care to stay out of your grandpa's way. He ain't likely to hit anything he's aiming at, but he's been known to shoot quite a few things by accident."

* * *

Walter Glenn was only a part-time farmer. For nearly forty years he had taught English and history at Box Elder High School in Brigham City, Utah. But he also operated a dry farm in Blue Creek Valley, west of Tremonton. Every summer while their children were young, he and his wife, Arba, had moved their family, a couple of beds, and a few household furnishings out to the farm. For three months, the Glenns lived there in virtual isolation.

After threshing time, when the crop had been sold, the Glenns would pack up and move back to town. It would take a week or two to break the children of their wild, range habits, but they would eventually settle once again into school and the social swirl of town. Walter had enjoyed his dual careers and was especially grateful for the summers he and his family had spent on the farm. The children had had their share of squabbles, but necessity had also made them best friends.

* * *

Leaving Tremonton, Walter drove his battered pickup west, through a pass in the range of low, rounded hills. It was about fifteen miles out to the farm, and he was anxious to see how the wheat he had planted in the fall was making out. It had been an open, dry winter, and the farms on either side of the road were bare of any snow. Much of the ground they passed had also been seeded in the fall, and Walter was glad to see a green haze on the fields.

He enjoyed being with his grandson. Seven-year-old Nelson was a handsome, blond-haired boy, small for his age but full of life. As they rode along, the boy jabbered about Christmas and asked an endless string of questions. Walter occasionally reached to ruffle his hair or playfully pinch a ticklish knee. More than any others, this grandson reminded Walter of his own youngest son, Franklin. Nelson looked a lot like his uncle had when Franklin was a boy that age.

After a few miles, they pulled off the black-top onto a rutted dirt road that snaked up into the hills. A half mile on, the farmhouse and barn came into view. The two buildings, their unpainted wooden exteriors weathered nearly white, were silhouetted against a darkening late afternoon sky. The pickup truck bucked and pitched on the bumpy road, bouncing Nelson on the seat and making him laugh.

Pulling into the barnyard, Walter braked to a stop and got stiffly out of the cab. Stretching to ease the pain in his lower back, he looked with satisfaction at his acreage, which fell away to the south all the way back down to the main road. The seed had germinated, and the sprout looked promising. It was a good beginning, and barring drought, hailstorms, rodent infestations, disease, or wildfire, there would be a harvest in late August. Dry farming was a risky venture—the outcome always in doubt until the grain was safely delivered to the elevator and your check was in the bank.

Nelson climbed out of the cab and stood beside his grandpa. A cold wind blew from the north, pressing at their backs.

"Can we hunt for jackrabbits now, Grandpa?" the boy asked.

Looking to the north at the darkening sky and feeling the wind, Walter said, "I think maybe we'd better get at it. Let's walk up the draw a ways and see if we can jump any."

Walter took the .22 from behind the seat of the pickup and the old man and the boy walked up the hill, away from the house and barn. They had not gone a hundred yards when a big jack sprang out of the sagebrush and sped with long, desperate bounds across the open farmland, too far away and moving too fast to provide a target. Walter pumped a shell into the chamber, but the two just watched the rabbit run.

Turning his attention back to the draw, Grandpa put his hand on Nelson's shoulder and made a sign for the boy to be quiet. About twenty yards ahead of them, a big jack sat poised on its haunches, its long ears up and its head still, watching the two humans.

Walter took the safety off and slid the small caliber rifle into his grandson's hands, bending to help the boy take his aim. The rabbit continued to stand very still as Nelson struggled to steady the barrel of the rifle.

In the open, with the wind blowing harder now and snowflakes beginning to fly about them, the .22 made only a snapping sound, but that was followed immediately by a cry from the rabbit, which took one leap, thrashed briefly, and then shuddered to stillness.

"Good shot!" Walter said, taking the rifle with one hand and clapping the boy on the back with the other. The storm was now suddenly on them, and big, heavy flakes blew horizontally into their faces. The old man and the boy leaned into the wind and walked to where the rabbit lay.

Standing over the bloodied animal, Walter and his grandson looked down at their prize. It was snowing heavily now, and the wind-driven flakes stung their faces and began sticking to their hats and woolen coats and coating the ground.

"He cried, Grandpa. Did you hear him cry?" the boy said, looking up at the old man through the beating snow.

"I know, Nelly, I know. C'mon, we'd better get going. It's starting to come down pretty hard." He turned Nelson, gently nudged him down the hill toward the farmhouse and barn, and turned to slowly follow.

By the time they reached the truck, the storm was in full swing and daylight was fading. The tires spun as Walter backed the truck around and then steered down the road toward the highway. The wipers couldn't keep up, and snow plastered the windshield, making it a guess where the road was. Walter was glad that this was not the first time he had ever driven the road and that he had a pretty good sense of where it was supposed to lead. However, when they reached the steep part, Walter braked a little too hard, and the truck slid off the road into the shallow ditch alongside. There wasn't time to panic—only to get mad.

"Dang!" Walter said sharply, gunning the engine and trying to steer back onto the road. The truck settled instead more deeply into the snow-slick wash.

After a moment, Walter turned off the ignition. Looking over at his grandson, he smiled thinly. "It looks like your old grandpa has gotten us stuck, Nelly."

"What are we going to do?" the boy asked.

"I'm not sure." But after a moment, he added, "We'd better walk back up to the house and get out of this storm. Don't worry, your mom will miss us and send someone out."

After slogging up the long hill in the gathering darkness and falling snow, the old man and the young boy were glad to get into the cold, dark farmhouse.

Stamping his boots on the bare wooden floor, Walter said, "Stand right here, Nelly, and I'll see if I can get us some light." The old man felt his way to the cupboards where he located a kerosene lantern and a box of wooden matches. The lantern gave off only a pale glow in the gloom of the bare house. Grandpa looked over at his shivering grandson. The snow-covered boy was trying not to cry.

"Hey, Nelly. C'mon, son. It's all right." He stepped to the boy's side and hugged him, rubbing his grandson's back vigorously. "We'll get a fire going, and I'll bet there's even something to eat in the cupboards. It'll be like camping out. What do you say?"

"I want to go home," the boy said.

"I know you do. So do I. But it looks like were stuck. Someone will be out early tomorrow morning. We'll get the truck pulled out and be home by noon."

Nelson started crying.

"We'll have fun."

There was still some kindling and several chunks of coal in the wood box, and Walter quickly got a fire started in the cast-iron cooking stove. He left the door to the firebox open and brought Nelson over to stand in front of the crackling flames while he searched the cupboards by lamplight for something to eat.

"Are you hungry, Nelson?" he asked.

"I want to go home," the boy said.

"Well, we can't go home," Walter said, somewhat sharply. Then he spoke more softly, "It'll be all right. We've got plenty of coal, and we won't starve. He opened a cupboard next to the sink. "Here's a can of . . . sardines and a jar of your grandma's stewed tomatoes," he said brightly.

The fire glowed in the open firebox of the range, which gradually warmed up, throwing a little heat into the area right in front of the stove. Walter dragged in a worn overstuffed chair from the other room and set it in front of the fire. Then he took the lantern and went upstairs to search for a blanket. He found a musty quilt in the closet of one of the empty upstairs bedrooms. He helped Nelson take off his boots and wet coat and wrapped him up in the blanket in the chair before organizing their meal. Nelson turned up his nose at the oily little fish and the stewed tomatoes, but he did take a sip of heated evaporated milk sweetened with some lumpy sugar.

After they had eaten, Walter poked the fire, stoked the stove with some more coal, and blew out the lantern. Nelson climbed onto his lap, and they drew the quilt around them, facing the glow from the open firebox in the stove and snuggling together. Outside, the wind had died, but snow continued to fall. Sitting in front of the stove, they were warm and comfortable, though Grandpa's hands and breath smelled of sardines.

They sat for a time in silence, staring into the fire.

"Grandpa, was that rabbit really crying?" the young boy asked.

Walter didn't know what to say. He shifted his weight in the chair and adjusted his grandson's position. He cleared his throat and stared into the fire.

After a while he said, "Hey! It's Christmas Eve, Nelson. Old Santa's probably out making his rounds right now. Did you tell him what you wanted?"

"I wrote him a letter. Will he come here?" the boy asked, sitting up on his grandfather's lap.

"I don't think so. I'll bet he'll leave your stuff at your house. It'll be there when you get home tomorrow. That will be fun, won't it?"

"Mom's gonna be mad," the boy said glumly.

"If she's mad, it won't be at you," Walter said, shaking his head and imagining what his wife and daughter would have to say when the two women finally got hold of him.

Patting his own chest, Walter invited Nelson to lie back down, then pulled the covers around the boy again.

"Go to sleep, son. We'll have all day to celebrate Christmas."

"When will Mom be here?" Nelson asked.

"Probably right after it gets light. Are you cold?"

"A little."

Walter pulled the quilt more tightly around them, and they sat together quietly, staring into the fire.

"Do you think she's worried?" Nelson asked.

"Sure. She's probably been praying for you all night and making plans to get someone to come and get us."

"My mom doesn't pray anymore," the boy said.

"How do you know?" Walter asked.

"We used to take turns, but now she makes me do it."

"She probably says her own prayers, don't you think?"

"I don't know. Do you pray, Grandpa?"

Walter didn't answer for a moment. "You know, Nelson, to be honest, I guess I'd have to say I haven't really prayed for a long time."

The two sat in silence for a while.

"We should pray now," Nelson said.

Walter tried to think how to respond. He was stumped—he didn't know what to say. Instead he just hugged the boy more tightly.

"Jesus loves us," Nelson said.

"How do you know?" Walter asked.

"My dad told me."

"He did? When did he tell you that?"

"He said it a lot. He said that Mom loved me and that he loved me and that Jesus loved me too. He said that's why we have Christmas."

"Why do we have Christmas?"

"Because Jesus loves us. That's why he came down from heaven."

Walter shook his head and smiled in the dark. "You're a pretty smart guy, Nelson."

Just before he fell asleep, Nelson reached up with his hand and touched his grandpa's grizzled face. Later, looking down at the sleeping boy's face, only dimly lit in the fire's glow, Walter felt a rush of affection for his grandson. After the divorce, Nelson's father had moved from Brigham City to Las Vegas. It hurt to think of the boy growing up without a dad.

Walter thought again of how much this grandson resembled his own youngest son. Franklin had been just Nelson's age—only seven years old—at the time of the accident, which had happened not a hundred yards from where they now sat. Walter wondered if there had been a day since then when he hadn't thought about it.

* * *

Walter and his brother Howard and their oldest boys had spent three days hauling wheat from the farm into Tremonton. It was a hot, August day in 1934, and in the late afternoon the two men stood visiting while the last truck was being loaded for the run to town.

The combination barn and granary stood just north of the house, across the hard-packed dirt yard. One half of the tall wooden building housed the work horses and machinery, with a hayloft overhead; the other half of the barn was a granary—a great wooden bin nearly two stories high. The building had been set against a hill, and the harvested grain was dumped into the tall bin through a chute cut into the roof. After years of use, the steel chute had been pol-ished by the flow of the grain, and the boys often made a game of sliding into the darkened bin onto the pile of grain below. There was room on the underside of the granary to back a truck under a spout cut into the floor of the bin. The grain flowed down from above in a steady stream that kept two of the older boys busy, shoveling the wheat away from the growing mound and into the corners of the high-walled truck bed.

* * *

After sleeping for only a couple of hours, cramped and uncomfortable, Walter struggled out from under Nelson and stood up. He settled the sleeping boy back into the chair and tucked the blanket around him, then walked to the window by the front door.

The snow had stopped falling, and the sky had mostly cleared. A small, round moon stood in the sky to the north, backlighting the darkened barn and granary. The building loomed huge, its size exaggerated by its black shadow being cast on the snow-covered yard between the barn and the house.

* * *

The flow of wheat stopped, and the two boys in the back of the truck looked up from their shoveling toward the spout above their heads. Dangling from the opening and clogging all but a trickle of grain was a boy's leg, his bare foot and ankle hanging limply out of a dusty trouser leg.

What had happened didn't immediately register. Then shouting for their father, the boys in the back of the truck tried to force the leg back up through the valve and into the bin above. Others ran up the hill to the chute.

Peering down into the gloom, they saw only the still mass of brown wheat, the great pile sloping away from the walls into a sinkhole in the center of the bin. Two of the boys slid down the chute into the granary, where they tried to dig down with their hands to where their little brother was buried. But the wheat settled back into the sinkhole as quickly as they threw it aside.

Crazy with fear and anger, Walter tore at the wooden planks on the side of the granary, trying to pry them away with his bare hands. After a minute, his brother brought a steel bar, and together the two men wrenched a hole in the wall, releasing a great flood of wheat onto the ground. But it was too late. Franklin had been playing with his dog in the top of the granary, and when the valve was opened, both the boy and the dog had been sucked down into the flow and smothered.

The funeral had been little comfort. Oh, Walter knew the dogma, and he *wanted* to believe it. The bishop had spoken, reminding the parents in a sad voice that there lay over the horizon a happier day. He promised them they would once again embrace their precious boy and that in the Resurrection the family would again be whole. Their son would be restored to them.

But the Resurrection wasn't *now!* Losing that precious boy was a blow Walter at first didn't think he could survive—didn't *want* to survive! His grief had turned into a monster that stood between him and his wife. For months, Arba was inconsolable; and struggling with his own loss, Walter lacked the energy to provide her any comfort. He was haunted too much by the vision of Franklin, floundering in the avalanche of grain, struggling in vain to keep his head out of the flow until finally,

exhausted, he was sucked down and silently covered over.

Walter had carried the limp little body from the granary to the house where his wife collapsed in tears and screams of disbelief and grief. The trip in the car from the farm to Brigham City—with Arba at first wailing uncontrollably, rocking the body on her lap, then falling into stony silence—had been almost unbearable. For years, he couldn't imagine how they had survived that long drive and the pain of delivering the body of their youngest son into the hands of the undertaker.

Walter's grief turned to bitterness. Sometimes he blamed himself for Franklin's death, and he often imagined his wife also blamed him. Unable for a long while to ever discuss it, the tragedy drove a wedge between them. The thought of going back into the chapel where the funeral had been held was also more than he could bear, and for several years Walter stayed away from church, though his wife and children continued to attend.

A bitter irony dominated his thinking—Franklin had suffocated in a bin of *wheat!* Wasn't the Lord supposed to have said that "all grain is ordained for the use of man, to be the staff of *life*"? That his son should have drowned in "the staff of life" became the linchpin in Walter's unspoken litany of excuses about why he could no longer attend church or even pray.

Turning away from the Lord, Walter sought comfort in other things: his teaching duties, his farmwork, and, for a number of years, periodic beer binges. It was a way of masking his pain and avoiding the guilt he felt for not going to church. However, the alcohol made him sick and left him with horrible hangovers and headaches. Getting drunk also made him maudlin, and, when he sobered up, left him depressed. He drank alone and in secret, but in a town like Brigham City, he knew he wasn't fooling anyone. Everyone was aware of his weakness, and he hated being thought of as the town drunk by his family, members of the ward, and by everyone at school. After a few years he gave up drinking, much to the relief of Arba and their now mostly grown children. Eventually he even went back to church. But deep down, he held a grudge against the Lord, wondering always how a "loving" God could permit an innocent child to die in such a hideous way.

* * *

Standing there in the darkness and cold of the farmhouse and looking out of the window at the granary across the way, Walter thought again of some lines from Ben Jonson. The English poet's son had been only seven years old when he died, and in his grief the father had written:

> Farewell, thou child of my right hand,
> and joy;
> My sin was too much hope of thee, loved
> boy:

Walter understood that. And he also understood Jonson's sad promise to himself:

> Rest in soft peace, and asked, say, "Here
> doth lie
> Ben Jonson his best piece of poetry;
> For whose sake henceforth all his vows be
> such
> As what he loves may never like too
> much."

Walter stepped from the window back to the stove. He poked the glowing pieces of coal and dropped a couple of new chunks into the fire. The fire flared up, briefly illuminating his sleeping grandson's face. The boy was breathing evenly, and Walter was glad he wasn't awake and fussing.

Remembering his grandson's innocent reprimand about not praying, Walter began to think about when he had abandoned his prayers. He couldn't remember when he had last poured out the feelings of his heart, or if he ever had. He began to think about his life. To pass the time, he decided to list the things he enjoyed. He had to admit, for all the risk and hard work that it involved, he liked dry farming. He had particularly enjoyed the old days when he had broken the ground behind a strong team of horses, watching their great haunches work and feeling their power. On the endless, solitary rounds made plowing, he had often spent the time reciting poetry and thinking about the books he loved to read. Thinking about that now reminded him of how much he enjoyed teaching school, and that reminded him of their comfortable old house in Brigham City and of his family. He had to admit, in many ways he had lived a rich and satisfying life.

Walter found himself speaking out loud, in a quiet voice. It wasn't exactly a prayer, but he felt a need to go on. He was grateful for a place to be out of the storm, and he expressed hope that someone would come to rescue Nelson and him. He spoke the name of his wife, then his children, then all his grandchildren, and he was surprised that their names came easily to him, without having to concentrate on them—something he found increasingly difficult as their number grew. Picturing his family, love welled up from within and overcame him—a feeling that intensified as he turned his thoughts to Franklin, remembering the joy he had taken in the little boy. He was surprised. It was the first time since the accident that he had been able to concentrate on Franklin's life rather than on his death. He remembered how grateful he was for the seven years that his son had lived, and he found himself weeping.

Walter's thoughts turned to his sins, and he was suddenly ashamed. He marveled at the bitterness he had nursed as the result of Franklin's death. He saw clearly Arba's face and her anguish, which he now realized was no longer caused by the death of her son but by the hardness of her husband's heart.

He pictured a nativity scene, different from the traditional ones. This was a real scene—a frightened young woman going through the pain of childbirth without any comfort from another woman, surrounded by dumb animals who were indifferent to her suffering and fear. He saw the newborn baby and somehow sensed the bond of love between the woman, her baby, and the man—a youth himself—who was embarrassed by his inability to provide the comforts his wife and baby so desperately needed.

The events that would lead from Bethlehem to Gethsemane to Golgotha to the garden tomb flooded Walter's mind. And, finally, he saw the resurrected Lord, standing in the air, his wounded hands outstretched, gazing sadly at those who milled about below, apparently unaware of his presence or of his yearnings for them.

How long he had prayed, if that was what he had been doing, Walter didn't know. He only knew the experience had been sweet; and keeping his eyes closed, he struggled to hold on to the feeling. When he finally opened his eyes,

the interior of the farmhouse was bathed in a dull gray light.

Whether he had been asleep or awake, he was unable to say, but he did know that he was filled with a feeling of sweet contentment. *Delicious* was the word that came to mind when he tried to verbalize what he had felt.

The sound of a diesel engine droned in the distance, and Walter stepped outside and around the corner of the house. A Caterpillar tractor was clanking and squeaking its way up the snow-covered road toward the farmhouse, pausing once to spew a puff of black smoke from its stack before continuing to lumber up the hill. Spotting Walter next to the house, the driver waved and came on. Walter waved back, then went in to wake Nelson.

Thinking of the way his wife and daughter were going to light into him, Walter smiled and shook his head. He could get through that.

Then they would have Christmas—maybe the best they'd ever had.

RICHARD PETERSON is an editor for Deseret Book Company. He and his wife, JoAnn, are the parents of five children and the grandparents of nine, including a grandson named Nelson.

THE LAMB

Virginia Havens

THE LAMB WAS YONATAN'S to raise from the moment of its birth. And nine-year-old Yonatan knew from that moment that its whole purpose for existence was to become a sacrifice at the great temple in Jerusalem.

But that moment was lost in the little boy's joy at having a lamb of his own to raise. Oh, since he was old enough Yonatan had always helped his father, Eli, and his now 12-year-old brother, Nathaniel, with the family's flock, but this time he was given the responsibility of raising a lamb himself.

Yonatan was typical of the little boys who lived in the Jerusalem area; however, his bright brown eyes and his dark curly hair were something of a contrast to his fairer brother. He loved animals, playing in the hills, and carving, but he only tolerated synagogue.

"It's perfect," his father said as they watched the lamb struggle to its feet. "There seems to be no blemishes, and it's the ewe's firstborn."

"Yes, Father," replied Yonatan. "He's a good one."

"I want you to take care of this lamb, son, so it will still be perfect when I take it to the temple to be sacrificed on the altar at Passover."

"Yes, Father. I'll take care of it as if it were my own." Yonatan reached down and lightly stroked the fuzz of the lamb as it wriggled in delight, its nose pushing again and again with all the force it could muster to nurse, its long tail whipping in ecstacy.

"He's my lamb," Yonatan whispered. "My lamb."

"Just to raise," Eli repeated, but Yonatan didn't hear.

"Father," he said, looking up. "I will name him *Mattan,* for to me he is indeed 'a gift.'"

"But you must remember, son, though his name may mean 'a gift,' he is just on loan to you until we take him to the temple next spring to sacrifice. The only gift involved in all this was saving of our people by the lambs' blood at the first Passover. Don't get too attached to it. You'll just feel bad when it must be killed."

Yonatan was as good as his word in caring for the lamb. He was careful that the mother ewe was herded to special grazing spots on the hillsides so she would make the best milk for Mattan. He took special care to see that his lamb didn't stray or get lost—except once.

On that day, Yonatan came home from his studies at synagogue to find the ewe bleating for a lamb that wasn't there. Mattan had apparently squeezed out through a small break in the fold trying to follow Yonatan to synagogue.

"Mother!" he screamed, running into the house. "My lamb! Where's Mattan?"

Eunice looked up from the bread she was making. "I don't know," she said. "I didn't know he was gone. But you'd better find him before he gets hurt—or worse."

Crying and praying at the same time, Yonatan ran to the hills where the little flock often grazed.

"Mattan! Mattan!" he called as he searched the gullies and caves of the area. Finally, he heard a bleat. "Mattan! Mattan!" Yonatan half ran, half rolled down the hillside to a thicket at the bottom where the sound came from. There, caught in the branches of a bush, was the stray lamb.

"Mattan! I found you!" Yonatan freed the

small animal. He carefully felt its legs, ran his hands over the soft wool. "You're okay. Not even a scratch," he marveled.

He buried his face in the lamb's wool and shuddered at what might have happened. Picking it up, he gently carried it home, talking to it all the way.

Mattan learned early to recognize Yonatan's voice and would run to meet him. The lamb would nuzzle the boy, looking for tidbits of bread or cheese sneaked from the table and hidden in his knapsack. Finally, Yonatan would pull out the tidbits, and Mattan would eat from his hand.

Together they ran and leapt as Yonatan watched the flock grazing in the hills, and the boy often sought out specially choice grasses to hand-feed his pet. Especially in fall and winter, when green, succulent feed was scarce, he watched for tender morsels. On other occasions, he would gently pull briars and burrs from the lamb's wool and brush it until it was clean and soft.

Winter turned to spring, and the hills where the flocks grazed began to take on various shades of green. Mattan was nearly grown, and his mother was soon to lamb again. In this season of new life and hope, Eli brought up the unthinkable subject that Yonatan had put out of his mind.

"It's soon Passover," Eli said one night at the evening meal. "Is the lamb still in perfect condition, Yonatan?"

Yonatan stopped eating in midbite. Suddenly he was not hungry. "Yes, Father," he replied quietly. "Mattan is perfect." Yonatan remembered his father had invited Uncle Timothy and his family to share Passover with them. At least ten or twelve were required for the Passover feast. But at the time of the invi-

tation, he'd thought only of his cousins coming—his will had simply closed out all thoughts of Mattan's sacrifice.

"Good," Eli responded. "I knew you would do a good job of raising our Passover lamb."

Yonatan's shoulders drooped. Mattan for Passover. It couldn't happen. It just couldn't. Not Mattan. There must be some other way.

"Father," he pleaded. "Does it have to be Mattan? I know he was raised for Passover, but why not Julius? Or Zuzim or Jaalam? They're males, and they're good."

"They are good, son," Eli agreed. "But Mattan is perfect. We have to give the best."

Yonatan started to protest again, but his father ignored the open mouth and patiently continued: "My son, this event means much more than merely taking the life of a pet. As you know, that lamb is a symbol. It represents the Atonement that the God of our fathers has prepared for us. In some way that I do not understand, He will take our sins on Himself when we truly repent. Somehow the blood of this perfect lamb represents the perfect Atonement of the Messiah."

"Yes," added his mother. "You have learned about our annual rite of sending a scapegoat into the wilderness, a goat who is supposed to take our sins with him. Both the goat and the lamb are symbols that represent this Atonement."

Yonatan knew all this. He had attended Passover for as long as he could remember, had learned the stories and heard the questions about unleavened bread and bitter herbs over and over, and had sung the Hillel since he could talk. But this was Mattan now. Maybe he could hide the lamb in a cave until it was too late for the sacrifice. He would sneak up at night and secretly feed it. But even as he thought of it, he knew it wouldn't work. Other schemes came to mind, but he rejected them just as quickly. Father would know. Then he had one more idea.

"Father, couldn't we go to Uncle Timothy's this year and they could give the lamb?"

"Yonatan, it's all been arranged already. Now don't behave this way." Eli's patience was beginning to wane.

"You knew from the beginning, little brother," Nathaniel spoke for the first time. "I had to give my lamb up, and now you have to, too."

"It hurts to give up Mattan," Eunice said, trying to comfort her son. "Maybe it's supposed to. Maybe the Messiah has to hurt, too, to atone."

"Some people don't believe in the Atonement," Yonatan protested, muttering under his breath.*

"Not many do. But *we do believe,* Yonatan; therefore, we will sacrifice our perfect lamb. Now, we will have no more discussion on this," Eli spoke sternly.

Yonatan fled from the room in tears.

Early the next morning he quietly crept out of the house. He went to his lamb and hugged him one last time, wetting its wool with his tears. Then he began to walk, anywhere—just to get away from the pain of his own sacrifice. In time, he found himself in the garden they called Gethsemane. There he sat down under the olive trees and wept again.

In time he quieted and felt the physical

---

* According to Elder Bruce R. McConkie, some few people did understand the connection between Passover and its sacrificial lambs and the Atonement of the Savior (see *The Mortal Messiah* [Salt Lake City: Deseret Book, 1979], 1:133–34).

need to shift, but when he did so, his sandal-clad foot caught a piece of olive wood and kicked it up. Yonatan picked it up, brushed off the dirt, and turned it over and over. Almost unconsciously he took his knife from his knapsack and began carving. When he had finished, in the palm of his small, grimy hand lay a lamb—head erect and ears straight out as though listening for its master's voice.

"Now I will always have you with me, Mattan," he said.

*   *   *

The stars seemed exceptionally bright, and the air was warm for an early April night. Yonatan shifted his position as he leaned against a large rock, and his eyes wandered across the valley to the little village of Bethlehem. He was one of the skilled and chosen ones in charge of the temple flock kept especially for the sacrifices; this night was his turn at keeping watch, along with several of his fellow shepherds.

He reached into his knapsack for a piece of pita bread and cheese that his wife, Sarah, had prepared for him. She always took such good care of him and their small son, Daniel. He smiled as he remembered a scene from earlier in the day: The toddler had run across the floor—he never walked—with a small item in his hand. Then he held it up, offering it to his father.

"Abba!" Daniel exclaimed with his usual enthusiasm. "Sheep!"

Yonatan took the proffered object. *Where did he find this?* he asked himself, for there in his hand was the carving of Mattan he had made many years ago.

"Thank you, little one," he said, dropping

the carving into his knapsack for a lack of a better place to put it at the moment, and of course to please the child. Then he swung his young son into the air. Daniel laughed with delight and gave him a fierce hug. Handing him to Sarah, Yonatan gave her a kiss, picked up his staff, and headed for the hillside where the sheep waited. . . . Yonatan shifted his position again. He felt restless. There was something in the air, a sort of feeling of anticipation. Perhaps it was the excitement of the Passover season that was now upon them. Or maybe it was just the large numbers of people in the area, coming at the command of that scoundrel Herod to be registered at the place of their birth. Much activity was centered in Jerusalem, only a few miles away, but there was a large influx of people here, too, settling themselves for the night at caravansaries, caves, wherever they could find a place to sleep. The livestock seemed to be settling down, too. Only an occasional sheep's bleat or donkey's bray carried across the air.

Yonatan looked over at David, Abel, and the other temple shepherds to see if they felt the same thing. They too were looking across the valley at Bethlehem, as if they were all players in a well-choreographed drama. He looked up again at the stars.

Suddenly a bright light appeared. What was happening? The light grew rapidly in size and brilliance until it completely surrounded the men. Yonatan fell to the ground in terror, unaware that the others had done the same because he was unable to take his eyes off the light.

Then he could see within the light—a man, an angel! If Yonatan could have closed his eyes, he would have squeezed them tight against the penetrating brightness; had he been able to

run, he would have sped like the quickest of roes—but Yonatan could do none of these. He was frozen in his fear of the unknown messenger. Then suddenly the angel spoke, and with his words all fear vanished.

"Fear not," the angel said, "for, behold, I bring you good tidings of great joy, which shall be to all people. For unto you is born this day in the city of David a Saviour, which is Christ the Lord. And this shall be a sign unto you; Ye shall find the babe wrapped in swaddling clothes, lying in a manger."

The angel finished his message, and immediately the whole sky was filled with a mighty chorus of the hosts of heaven with a message of praise to God, saying, "Glory to God in the highest, and on earth peace, good will toward men." It seemed the heavens would burst with the joyful news of the Messiah's coming. Yonatan could only lie there and look up at the marvelous spectacle, for his whole soul too was filled with joy, and his heart sang with the angel chorus.

Then, the message given, the rejoicing complete, they were gone.

When his strength returned, Yonatan sat up and looked at his fellow shepherds. They too were rising, wonder still on their faces.

"You saw it too," he almost whispered. It was more an acknowledgment than a question.

"Yes," was all Jarom could say.

"They said Messiah is born," Yonatan marveled. "He has come."

"And the angel told us where to find Him," added David. "Come, brethren, let us go!"

"What about the sheep?" asked Abel.

"God will care for them a little while," David reassured. "Come, let's go."

The shepherds found the place the angel had described. It was a stable normally used for costly animals, which had been turned out into the courtyard to provide additional lodgings for travelers during this busy night, a common practice of the time. The particular lodgings were on property reputed to have belonged to Boaz, Obed, Jesse, and David of old, and since property in the Holy Land was never sold, it was the place that the mother of the Messiah would be expected to go when coming to Bethlehem to register in Herod's census.*

The stable had been swept clean, with fresh straw scattered around. The shepherds realized that its occupants would likely have paid well for their accommodations, the innkeeper being able to ask for and receive much more than for the regular chambers in such circumstances. It was no sign of poverty to sleep in the stable at such a time. This young couple now here did not seem to be in dire financial straits, but appeared used to modest living. They were just too late to get a place in the inn.

The shepherds were not ignorant of the tradition that young David had been seated in a manger to be crowned king of the shepherds. The legend had been handed down for years.

There, lying on some clean straw, was a young woman, perhaps in her teens. She looked rather pale, but there was a serenity about her that touched the men. Sitting by her side was a young man who appeared to be her husband. He held her hand and gently stroked her hair. She sat up as the shepherds approached. Yonatan introduced himself and his companions, but he hardly looked at the couple—there before his eyes lay her newborn

---

* Richard C. Galbraith in "No Room at the Inn?— Oral Traditions from the Holy Land" (*This People*, holiday issue 1995), provided information concerning the stable, inn, and related details.

Son, the Messiah of all the world! Yonatan marveled that the Messiah should begin his reign in a manger, like David. The words of the angel echoed in his ears: "Lying in a manger . . . a Saviour who is Christ the Lord."

The Baby was wrapped in swaddling clothes, as the angel had said, the clothes in the colors of the tribes announcing to the shepherds His royal genealogy. He looked much as any newborn babe, curled somewhat in a ball. His eyes were closed in sleep, and the tiny mouth moved as though He dreamed of nursing. He stirred, waved His tiny arms, with miniature fists closed in the way of babies, and opened His eyes. Although the eyes were those of a newborn, still somehow, for an instant, they seemed to look at Yonatan and into his soul. It was as though He were a grown man and knew all things.

All things. Yonatan wondered at this. The Messiah. The Lamb of God. The One who would atone, would take upon Himself the sins of the world. The One that all those sacrificial lambs represented that kept Him in man's remembrance. Would He have to give His blood somehow, this tiny, innocent, perfect One?

As he thought of the Passover lambs now being readied for sacrifice, Yonatan thought of the pain that God the Father would feel to see His Son, His Lamb, sacrificed, even though it meant atonement for His people. Yonatan thought of his own little son. He could still see that happy face of earlier that day, the chubby hands reaching for him. How it would hurt to sacrifice his child! And Yonatan began to understand.

The Babe began to cry, and His mother took Him in her arms, kissed His cheek, and comforted Him. Then she again placed Him in

the manger bed. As she did so, Yonatan reached into his knapsack and felt around. Then he withdrew from it the small carving of a lamb, his teacher. Mattan. The gift. Yonatan laid it gently in the manger near the Babe, and His mother smiled.

VIRGINIA HAVENS grew up in Salmon, Idaho, the second of five children. She graduated from Brigham Young University in 1953 with a bachelor's degree in journalism. She has worked as a reporter for *The Daily Herald* in Provo, Utah; *The Deseret News* and BYU News Bureau; was promotion writer for KSL-TV; and served as information officer for the Utah State Retirement Office. She was a member of Utah Press Women and has received 1st, 2nd, and 3rd place awards for her Retirement Office annual reports and brochures. She also is a member of the League of Utah Writers, and has written two novels, *The Link and the Promise,* and *Roxey's Choice.* She has held numerous positions in the Church, including serving a mission in California. Presently, she is serving in the Salt Lake Temple.

THE PEOPLE IN THE BUILDING

Gary L. Davis

DEAR HEATHER!
Merry Christmas—ho ho ho!

Well, it was a long, tiring car trip, but we got here okay. It's different here in Iowa, sort of like culture shock after Twin Falls! No mountains anywhere. I'm sorry I didn't write sooner, but this has been the unmerriest Christmas of my life! I've been so depressed that the stationery would have been soggy. Fortunately I've been really busy unpacking and cleaning and stuff. Grandma Sawyer had me dig an old artificial tree out of the basement to decorate. It looks like something the Grinch brought. Grandma and Grandpa Sawyer have a big old farmhouse a few miles from Indianola. Gramps used to own a large farm, but he sold it all except the house and a couple of acres.

My grandma isn't doing so hot. Mom takes her into Des Moines a couple of times a week to the doctor. I've been helping a lot with the housework and cooking. Grandpa can't do much anymore because his eyesight is pretty bad. I don't think he ever did much housework anyway. It's good for Mom to be busy. She has less time to think about the divorce. I often wonder if having the gospel would've changed things for my parents. It's hard to say.

Which is a good time to say that I'm grateful for your friendship and influence in introducing me to the Church.

The high school is pretty small here, and so is the Church. I'm the only Mormon girl in our school. There's one LDS boy, but he's a freshman (much too young for a mature senior like me!). His name is Ara, which is sort of weird, but he's nice. His dad is the branch president.

I have almost a whole floor to myself in this house! That probably sounds great to someone like you with four sisters, but it's actually kind of lonely.

It's getting late, so I guess I'll close for now. Say hello to Sister Betty and all the kids at church. Oh! Thank you for the CTR ring. It was my favorite present. Mom got me some clothes, and Grandpa gave me some dorky looking boots. They're warm, but they don't make any fashion statements.

They're having cheerleader tryouts at school next week. I think I'll sign up. The old group of cheerleaders was sort of disbanded because two of the girls got kicked out of school for drugs and another dropped out to get married and have a baby. (But not in that order.)

Okay, I'm really quitting now.

Love,

Andrea

* * *

Dear Heather,

Hard to believe it's been two months since I left Twin Falls. I sure miss my friends in Idaho!

You asked in your letter about the cheerleader tryouts. I guess you could say there's good news and bad news. The good news is that I was one of the five girls selected out of the twenty or so that tried out. The bad news? I'm not on the cheerleading squad, not anymore at least. Some of the girls that didn't make it resented me, because I'm new I guess, and two of the girls who made the squad were mad at me because their friend was picked as first alternate. Naturally, without me she would have made the top five. I had hoped that everything would be okay once rehearsals got started. I thought we could all become friends. Dream on, Andrea! They were so awful to me that I decided it just wasn't worth it.

They made fun of my clothes, my hair, my braces, my dancing—everything! Then they found out I was a Mormon and it got twice as bad. Miss Wu, the coach, knew what was going on, but this is her first year teaching and she didn't know what to do. She offered to kick the two meanest girls off the squad, but that would've caused trouble for her and probably more for me, so I quit. I prayed and prayed that things would get better, but they didn't. Just like I prayed that my mom and dad could patch up their differences, but that didn't happen either.

I asked Brother Stillwell, my branch president, why the Lord didn't answer my prayers. He said that the Lord sometimes says no and that we all have our free agency to act how we want. He also told me that God has a different timetable than we do and that trials can help us grow and make our faith stronger. If that's what it takes, I don't think I want my faith any stronger for a while.

They called me to teach a Primary class at church. Some of the kids know more about the gospel than I do. That's a little scary.

Love to all,

Andrea

* * *

Heather,

Thank you for the letter and the pictures. It looks like you had fun skiing. Wish I could've

been there. So Scott asked you to the Winter Formal! My face is green.

How's my social life? Frankly, my dear, I have such a full calendar that I hardly know where to begin.

Let me start with this—I'm getting straight A's in school. Is that because (1) I'm brilliant? (2) I have lots of time to study? (3) None of the above? (4) All of the above? If you chose "2," you win an all-expense-paid trip to Blackfoot!

Want to hear about my date? That's "date" as in singular, past tense. It was memorable! His name is Kirk, probably the cutest boy in school. When he asked me out, I was elated. He's a football player, a track star, and he drives a Corvette. I'm not kidding. But my LDS friend told me Kirk was a jerk (hey, that rhymes—Kirk the Jerk); anyway, I thought Ara was just jealous.

It turned out that *jerk* was a compliment for this worm. He asked me out on a bet! Really! Seems he was bragging to some of his buddies that he could do what he wanted with any girl in the school, and someone bet him that he couldn't get far with the "Mormon chick."

So we went to a movie, which was okay, then he takes me to a party with no chaperones and a bunch of people I'd never seen before. They were drinking, smoking marijuana, and playing vulgar music videos. When I told Kirk that I wanted to go home, he laughed and said, "Loosen up and enjoy yourself."

I was really mad, but I was scared, too. Know what I did? You won't believe this. I went into the bathroom and locked the door. Then I climbed out of the window, ran three blocks to a mini mart, and called my mom. I hid behind the store until she showed up. When Mom got there, I jumped in the car and started bawling.

It was terrible. Later, we had a long talk. I needed that.

Do you know what I hate most about my situation? I hate being an outsider. I hate not being part of the "in" crowd. It's sort of like Lehi's dream in the Book of Mormon, where the people in the big building are mocking and laughing at those gathered by the Tree of Life. I think I understand those people who were ashamed and turned away. Nobody likes being ridiculed!

This whole experience has forced me to rely more on my Heavenly Father. I'm praying that I can be strong and not care about what others think as long as I'm doing what's right.

Hope I don't bore you with my problems—I'm grateful for your friendship.

Take care and look out for the "people in the building."

Love,

Andrea

* * *

Heather,

Sounds like the Winter Formal was eventful! Too bad you didn't get a picture of Scott and Mike changing the flat tire in the snow with their tuxedos on! I hope you and Bonnie didn't laugh (out loud).

I've got some good news for a change. My mother went to church with me last week. Everyone was really nice to her, and she said she enjoyed it. Cross your fingers—better yet, *pray!*

I probably should admit to you that it wasn't entirely my sterling influence that got Mom to church. Grandma Sawyer has been doing much better lately, so Mom got a job three days a week with the local bank, and the bank manager is a recent convert to the Church. He just transferred here from Sioux City. I heard that his wife died a couple of years ago. Anyway, I met him at church and told him about Mom, and he invited her out. He seems like a neat man. I told Mom that if she got baptized, she'd probably get a big promotion—*ha!*

Love,

Andrea

* * *

Heather,

Are you ready for headline news? I'm engaged! Just kidding, I'm only writing to a missionary (who isn't?). It's Ara's brother, Cris. He's in Japan. I've gotten two really sweet, spiritual, funny letters from him. He'll be home in a couple months. Actually, 57 days, 6 hours, and 14 minutes, but who's counting? I asked Ara if he was nice. He said I'd probably like him better than Corvette Kirk. Ara has a great future in comedy. Cris was a student at Iowa State before his mission He plans to return to college and major in business administration with a minor in Japanese. I'm thinking about court reporting school. What are you thinking about, besides Scott?

Love,

Andrea

P.S. Beware of boisterous babbling baboons in big buildings.

* * *

Heather,

Did I mention to you that I have a date for the Senior Prom? *The Senior Prom!* You must be saying, *That's well over a month away!* But of course, my dear. If one desires to spend an evening with the popular and glamorous Andrea Brown, then one must book weeks in advance. *And just who is the lucky fellow?* I'm sure you're asking. Oh, merely the eldest Stillwell chap. Just returned from abroad you know. Comes from good stock too. Father's a branch president; mother teaches piano; brother is a comedian. Hey, two out of three isn't bad.

Okay, okay, here's what happened. The first Sunday after Cris got home from Japan, the Stillwells invited Mom and Stan (her boss) and I over for dinner. I, of course, was witty, charming, and totally captivating. (Did I tell you I got the braces off my teeth? I got the braces off my teeth. Boy, do I have great-looking teeth. Nothing sticks in 'em anymore.) Anyway, after dinner Cris and I went for a drive and had a terrific talk. We've been seeing each other every day since. We're deeply in like. He's planning to return to Iowa State in the fall, and I'm going to begin a course in court reporting at a school in Des Moines. Are you still planning to go to Ricks? My mom is seeing a lot of Stan now. She also started the missionary discussions!

I'm not sure how this book turns out, but this is a great chapter!!!

Love,

Andrea

P.S. So take that, you bozos in the building!

* * *

Heather,

"Would you like fries with that burger? How 'bout some dessert? We've got fresh pies. What kind? Well, there's apple, berry, peach, pecan, and rhubarb. Rhubarb!? You must be kidding! That stuff is terrible!" Think I make a

good waitress? Yup, I'm the best. At least the best one at Boog's. It's a restaurant in Indianola that's owned by a man who used to be a football star at Iowa. It's a popular place and I get good tips. Cris is working for the state on some statistical project that's probably a waste of the taxpayers' money, according to Cris. We're still seeing lots of each other.

My mom set a date to get baptized! I've got a feeling she and Stan will be setting another date pretty soon too. If that happens, I'll have a little brother. Stan has a seven-year-old son who was staying in South Dakota with his aunt this summer.

Did Scott send in his mission papers yet? How do like working for your dad? Will you ever get a room of your own? Why *did* you cut your hair?

Life is good. The gospel is true.

Love,
Andy

* * *

Heather,

Another Christmas season! Time flies. It's hard to believe a year has passed since we said our tearful good-bye. This December I've given a lot of thought to the birth and life of our Savior. Mom found a box in the garage with a beautiful nativity set in it. The figures are all hand carved. I put it on our kitchen table. Sometimes late at night, I sit there at the table and talk to the baby Jesus. This is going to sound strange, but I think sometimes he answers me. Really, I get thoughts and insights that I never had before—thoughts about his sacrifice and Atonement, about how much our Heavenly Father loves us to allow his Son to suffer, and about how obedient and loving

Jesus was. Then I just feel so thankful that I want to cry.

Remember the CTR ring you gave me last year? Well, I got another ring this year. Pretty boring, huh? This one came from Cris, and it's a diamond!!! Could you make it down to Salt Lake City in March to be my maid of honor? His parents got married in the Salt Lake Temple, and Cris and I both want to go there too. Call you soon.

Love,
Andy

P.S. I bet those people in the building aren't laughing now.

GARY L. DAVIS was born in Provo, Utah, and raised in southern California. He returned to Provo following high school to attend Brigham Young University for two years before serving a mission for the Church in Minnesota and South Dakota. Gary describes his academic career as "singularly undistinguished." He got involved in comedy while at BYU, and continued to write and perform comedy upon his return to the Los Angeles area. He has had three novels and a number of short stories published; he has also written weekly columns for two newspapers. *Lori, I Love You . . .* and *Friends* are his most recent books.

Gary is married to the former Jean Dalton. They have four children and five grandchildren. Jean and Gary presently reside in Frazier Park, California, a remote hamlet in northern southern California or southern central California, depending on your point of view.

Gary is presently working on a new novel, *Borrowed Light,* inspired by his friendship with a blind woman he met at a booksellers' convention in Salt Lake City a few years ago.

Going Home for Christmas

Jennie L. Hansen

WIND HOWLED ACROSS the empty desert, carrying bits of stinging ice. They struck Julie's face, causing her to turn away from the huge stone outcropping she and David had stopped to see. Burying her face in her collar, she stifled her disappointment. She'd been looking forward to touching Independence Rock, perhaps even discovering the names of ancestors who had passed this way. But neither this small disappointment nor dire weather forecasts dampened her happiness for long. They were on their way home for Christmas. At long last they were going home.

She and David had arrived at Independence Rock to find the gates locked and signs advising visitors not to proceed along the walkways. Though the building was open, it appeared abandoned in the desolate landscape. David's shabby pickup truck and her small Escort were the only vehicles in the parking lot.

As the wind took on a high keening wail, she thought about her pioneer ancestors who were buried not far from here along the Sweetwater. Her mother would be disappointed that Julie had come this close and hadn't actually touched the huge stone.

"We'd better go." David urged her toward her car. "There's snow on the way, and I'd like to reach Green River before dark."

"All right," she conceded. It wasn't his fault the trail was closed, and she had to admit that she wasn't any more anxious than he was to get caught in a Wyoming snowstorm. Besides, she could hardly wait to get back home. "Just think! Tomorrow we'll be in Salt Lake City."

"Julie," David held her door for a moment. "I'm really sorry the past year has been so rough for you."

Placing one finger across his lips she silenced him. "Quit your jawin', cowboy. It's time to ride."

"Yes, ma'm." He grinned broadly as he slammed her door shut and quickly stepped around to the driver's side of his truck. As his faded jeans and worn sheepskin coat disappeared inside the other vehicle, she gave a little sigh. At moments like this, David seemed almost like the man she'd married two years ago.

This trip would be a lot more fun if we could ride together, she thought wistfully as she shifted gears. *Fun!* She laughed at her choice of words as she backed out of the parking space. It had been so long since she and David had had any fun, she didn't know if they remembered how.

They'd met and married while attending the community college in Salt Lake and were planning to transfer to a university when David's father had become ill and had insisted that his son come home to run the small ranch in South Dakota where David had grown up. Back then Julie's usual exuberance had led her to anticipate that ranch life would be a big adventure.

The big adventure had turned into drudgery as day after day she cooked and cleaned with meager supplies, did farm chores, and cared for a cranky old man who found fault with everything she did, while David rose before dawn and crept back into bed long after dark. When she complained that she never saw him, he reminded her there was no money to hire help and the ranch was in financial trouble. As David's father became more demanding and his care increasingly difficult in the months before his death, she longed to place him in a care facility and escape back to Salt Lake. Something, perhaps stubborness, had kept her there. But it was over now; David's father was gone and the ranch sold.

Julie scanned the vast empty landscape before her and uttered a little prayer of gratitude that tomorrow she'd be back in Salt Lake. The tree would already be up and the house would be filled with the aroma of pizza. Dad always ordered pizza on Christmas Eve. He said Mom had enough to do without cooking a big meal on Christmas Eve.

Up ahead she saw David's signal light come on, so she eased over to the side of the road to park behind him. Seconds later he tapped on her window.

"A corner of the tarp came loose. I'll just tighten it and we'll be on our way again," he shouted over the wail of the wind. From the protection of the car, Julie watched him struggle with the flapping canvas. Each time he pulled it into place and reached for the rope to tie it down, the wind caught it, whipping it out of his grip. Everything they owned was in the back of that truck or piled in the cargo space of her small car. It wasn't much—there hadn't been much left after David's father's bills had been settled.

A gust of wind rocked the small car, and Julie reached for a scarf to wrap around her face. If she didn't go help David, his fingers would be too stiff with cold to lace the rope through the tarp by the time he got the two together.

A sensation much like the time she'd had the wind knocked out of her when she fell

from a swing struck her as she left the shelter of her car. David glanced up but didn't waste energy speaking. He pointed to the rope, and in minutes they had the load secured and were climbing back into their respective vehicles.

With a sigh of relief she closed the door against the howling wind. Her teeth chattered and her fingers felt numb in spite of her gloves. She pulled them off with her teeth and blew on her fingers before reaching for the ignition. She turned the key and . . . nothing. Glancing down she made certain the car was in park and twisted the key again. Once more the engine failed to start.

Maybe David could fix it; he was good with engines. Her fingers clutched the door handle, and she looked up to see his truck just pulling back onto the highway.

"David!" She screamed as she flung open her door and raced toward the other vehicle. "David, wait!"

The truck rolled smoothly on, picking up speed as it went. Julie watched in horror as it topped a small hill, then dipped out of sight. Standing alone on the windswept plain, Julie felt more alone than she'd ever been before in her life. Even more alone than she'd been all those months in her father-in-law's bleak ranch house. No matter which way she turned, there were no houses, no cars, no trees, no sign that anyone other than herself existed anywhere.

Panic drove her back to her car. Frantically she twisted the ignition key and begged the engine to respond. In frustration she pounded her fists against the steering wheel and gulped back sobs. Okay, she was an adult, she reminded herself. She wouldn't give way to hysteria. After all, she was far better off than her ancestors had been. She had food—a cooler full of soft drinks, sugar cookies, apples, and carrots. The Relief Society president had brought over a fruitcake, and the realtor had handed David a two-pound box of chocolates just before they left South Dakota. She wouldn't starve.

She wouldn't freeze either. There was a big difference between a handcart and a Ford Escort loaded with clothing and bedding, including the four quilts her grandmother and aunts had given them at their wedding. And it wasn't snowing—yet.

The car rocked as a diesel truck flew past. Julie's eyes turned to the window. She was being foolish. She could always flag down a truck. Besides David would soon notice that she wasn't behind him and hurry back for her. Tomorrow night she and David, along with her whole family, would laugh together at her foolish fantasies as they sat around the fireplace sipping hot chocolate and eating pizza as they reminisced about Christmases past. Then Dad would reach for the big family Bible to read of the first Christmas.

A tap sounded at her window and she looked up to see David. He slid in beside her and, after a couple of futile attempts to start the car, stepped back outside to bury his head under the hood. Time dragged as he made repeated trips to his truck for tools. When she attempted to join him, he ordered her back inside the car out of the icy wind. Several times he asked her to try to start the car, but each attempt failed.

Giving up at last, David joined her in the car. "I'm going to have to tow you into Rawlins." He cupped his hand in front of his face and blew on his fist. "I don't have a tow bar, only a rope, so you'll have to keep your eyes on my brake lights. If my lights come on,

hit yours or you'll run into me. Otherwise keep your foot away from the brake."

"David, that's seventy miles."

"I know, honey." He touched an icy knuckle to her chin before plunging back out into the wind. She wished he'd wear gloves, but he insisted gloves hampered his ability to work. He only wore them when he bucked hay. She couldn't imagine how his cold fingers could possibly tie knots to join their two vehicles. A picture of ragged men, women, and children huddling beneath handcarts along this desolate stretch in a raging blizzard flashed before her eyes. At least as David crawled under her car with the rope he'd be on dry ground.

Without a running engine, Julie soon realized that she had no heat, no radio, and no lights. At first she didn't miss the heat. Nervous tension—as she struggled to concentrate on David's tail-lights and swallow her fear as he towed her up hills, then outran her on the down side—kept her warm enough. Only when she noticed her breath forming clouds before her face did she remember the heater had quit in David's truck last winter and he'd never found the money to replace it. He'd been without heat since they left South Dakota!

The radio would have only been a distraction, but roiling clouds brought on dusk early, and with it came concern that without tail-lights one of the big diesels that roamed this road might run them over from the rear.

By the time the lights of Rawlins came into view, Julie's focus had narrowed to two points; she was so cold her teeth were chattering and she desperately needed to find a rest room. David gradually slowed their speed, and her peripheral vision caught a No Vacancy sign in front of the first motel they passed. A similar sign lit the next one. A giggle erupted out of nowhere. It was Christmas, and once more there seemed to be no room at the inn.

Seconds later David pulled into a wide graveled area and shut off his engine. Julie watched as he bolted from the truck and ran toward a brightly lit shack. It took a moment for the flashing neon signs to register in her mind. The place was a bar—and where people drank, there had to be rest rooms. Obviously David faced the same problem she did. She struggled to release her grip on the steering wheel. Either the harrowing ride or the cold had nearly immobilized her hands in a white-knuckle grip. She jerked herself loose and sprinted after her husband.

Minutes later Julie found David waiting for her at the door.

"Sorry," he mumbled.

"Don't be," she laughed. "I couldn't have made it past one more No Vacancy sign. Besides, I've never been in a bar before. Interesting place."

David coughed. "Yeah, real interesting. The smoke in here is worse than the cold out there." He opened the door and ushered her through. The flurries of ice carried by the wind immediately assailed them, and they hunched inside their coats.

"Look," David pointed to a faint neon sign. "There's a motel and I don't see any No Vacancy sign. I'll pull your car over there and go inside. You wait in the bar."

Clean was about all that could be said for the room they were assigned. A double bed with a worn bedspread took up most of the cramped space, and a tiny bathroom opened off the opposite corner. Cracked linoleum covered the floor.

"Strangest desk clerk I ever met," David shook his head as he carried in their bags. "He

acted like he didn't know what I was talking about when I told him we'd only be here one night."

"It will be only one night, won't it?" Julie asked anxiously. "I told Dad we'd be there around noon."

"We won't make it by noon, but if I can get your car running we should reach Salt Lake by early evening. Here." He tossed her a couple of packets of hot chocolate mix.

Julie removed her shoes and climbed onto the bed to sit cross-legged with a warm cup in her hands. A steady stream of heat blasting from base heaters created wonderful warmth, and she wished David hadn't gulped down his chocolate so quickly and gone back outside. At least the L-shaped building would provide him some protection from the wind.

The roar of an engine caught her attention, and she leaped from the bed to peer out the window. David had done it! He'd fixed her car. They'd make it home tomorrow!

While she prepared for bed, David took the car for a short test run. When he returned, he lost no time scrambling out of his clothes and into bed.

"It's not really fixed," he warned her. "But I think it will run until we get to Salt Lake." His feet felt like blocks of ice, and his body shook as he snuggled deeper into the quilts Julie had piled on the bed. He drifted to sleep, but she lay awake for some time. Through the thin walls she heard a shower come on, a high-pitched giggle, and a man's deep rumble of laughter. Car doors slammed at frequent intervals, and she noted that for a shabby run-down motel in a small town, it seemed to attract a lot of business.

She woke with a start when David sat

straight up in bed. "We're getting out of here," he announced.

"What? Now?" She glanced sleepily at the illuminated dial of her watch. "It's only a little after four." David wasn't the only crazy person; the people next door were showering again.

"I don't care. We're leaving." David reached for his pants. "No wonder the desk clerk and I didn't communicate. He probably doesn't get many customers who book a room for the whole night!"

It was snowing lightly as they left Rawlins, but as they approached Rock Springs the storm's tempo increased. The windshield wipers flapped at a rapid pace, and Julie leaned forward to peer through the driving snow. A shrill sound came once, then again, and she watched in horror as the wiper blade disintegrated in peeling strips of rubber. She flashed her lights to warn David that she had to pull over. When she rolled to a stop on the shoulder of the road, the engine died.

David was beside her in seconds. He could replace her wiper blade, but he couldn't restart her car.

"We've got to get off this shoulder before someone hits us," he shouted into her ear over the din of the storm. "The flashing light up there by the tunnel means that the highway patrol is closing this road. I'll have to tow you into Green River."

While he backed his pickup into place, a truck pulling a second trailer roared by burying her car in an avalanche of slush. This time when she felt the tug as the rope tightened and the car began to move, there were no tail-lights to follow. Only an occasional flicker of red made its way through the thick layer of mud and snow. In seconds even that small amount of visibility disappeared. She knew by the change of sound when they passed through the tunnel and was vaguely aware they had left the freeway before plunging into a kaleidoscope of terror as David took the spiraling exit at a flying speed. Visions of slamming into the back of the truck or skidding out of control brought a scream to her lips. When David slowed and gradually rolled to a stop, she applied the brakes with all her might and prayed she was doing the right thing.

"You all right?" He jerked her door open and helped her out.

"I—I'm fine," she stammered and promptly collapsed against his side. His arm came around her, and they stood locked in an embrace as the storm swirled around them.

"There's a Motel 6 behind us a hundred yards or so. We'd better see if we can get a room." David reached for her hand, and together they trudged through knee-deep snow. Julie kept her head down; she didn't want the motel clerk or David to see the tears sliding down her cheeks. Even if David repaired her car, they wouldn't be home in time for Christmas.

David insisted she stay in their room while he brought in their luggage from her car. She moved to the window and stood watching the snow. For a whole year she'd dreamed of being home for Christmas this year. Last Christmas had been devoid of any celebration. David had spent the entire day struggling to get feed to stock trapped by drifting snow while she'd been stuck with her father-in-law's belittling comments as she did her best to turn a tough piece of venison into a Christmas dinner that the old man had turned his nose up at and her husband was too tired to eat.

"Julie." In her intense solitude she hadn't heard David return. She turned to face him,

and he hurried to her side. With one big cold-reddened hand he brushed the tears from her cheeks.

"I'm so sorry." There was a catch in his voice. "I never should have hauled you off to South Dakota with me. I hated seeing you work so hard and give up school. I spent last Christmas making you a lot of promises while I dug through drifts and urged a bunch of stubborn cows closer to shelter. I know how much you miss your family. Many times I thought you were going to give up on me, and I wouldn't have blamed you if you had, but you stayed. I thought maybe I could make it up to you by getting you back to Utah for Christmas—I've failed at that too."

David stood before her in run-down boots and faded jeans, soaked through from the snow and slush, with his face and hands red and chapped, and his coat smeared with grease—it was as though she really saw her husband for the first time in months.

"You tried," she whispered.

"I let you down," he derided his own efforts. "I should have noticed the timing belt on your car needed to be replaced before we started. I not only endangered your life, but I took you to a bar and rented a room in a red-light motel. On top of everything else, you'll miss Christmas with your family again."

"It's all right." And suddenly it was all right. "You're my family and we're together. That's more than we had last year."

He cupped her face with his big hands and whispered hoarsely, "You deserve better than this." And deep in her soul she recognized how great had been his effort.

Like an echo from the past his words repeated in her heart, and she wondered how many of those snow-shrouded ghosts from her pioneer past had spoken those same words. Had they looked down at the mounds of snow covering their loved ones and blamed themselves? Had they cried, *"You deserve better than this!"*

"I'd better go work on the car." David dropped his hands and moved toward the door.

"No," she insisted as she caught his sleeve. "The car will wait. You need a warm shower, something hot to eat, and a good long sleep."

"Julie, I hadn't counted on a motel room for two nights. We can't go out to eat or we'll be short on gas money."

"All right, we'll make the hot meal soup. We still have some dried soup packets left. Hit the shower, cowboy."

"Yes, ma'am." A tired smile reached his eyes, then faded. "While I'm in there, you'd better call your parents."

When he emerged from the bathroom, Julie sat on the bed with the telephone in her lap. He sat down beside her and placed a hand on her shoulder. "You okay?" he whispered.

"Yes," she blinked back a tear and smiled radiantly at him. "Daddy read me the Christmas story, and I heard a different story this time. I could see Joseph shouldering the responsibility for his pregnant young wife on what must have been a nightmare journey. He tried so hard to find her lodging. He did his best, and she still had to give birth alone in a smelly barn. He must have been quite a man. Something like you." She turned and coiled her arms around his neck.

"Me?" he gulped in disbelief.

"You. Kind, hardworking, faithful, and he loved his wife."

"I do love you, Julie."

"And I love you," she whispered back.

A knock sounded on the door. They looked at each other blankly, then David rose to his feet and thrust open the door.

"Pizza delivery," grinned a young man from under a liberal sprinkling of snow.

"We didn't order pizza." David began to close the door as the tempting aroma filtered into the room making Julie's mouth water.

"Nope, you didn't," conceded the grinning kid. "Some guy in Salt Lake called, said he promised his daughter pizza for Christmas Eve and to get it to her quick. So here it is."

Julie began to laugh. Pizza didn't quite compare to the teams Brigham Young had sent out to rescue the handcart company, but she'd take it. This was going to be a merry Christmas after all.

JENNIE L. HANSEN, author of five LDS novels—*Run Away Home* (1993), *When Tomorrow Comes* (1994), *Macady* (1995), *Some Sweet Day* (1997), and *Journey Home* (1997)—was born and raised in Idaho and currently lives in Salt Lake County. She graduated from Ricks College in Rexburg, Idaho, and Westminster College in Salt Lake City, Utah. She has been a reporter, an editor, and a messenger for the Utah House of Representatives. She currently is a technical services specialist for the Salt Lake City Library System. She served two terms on the Salt Palace Advisory Board, represented Utah at the White House Conference on Libraries and Information Services, and has received numerous journalism awards. Her Church service has included teaching in all auxiliaries and serving in both ward and stake Primary presidencies. She has also served as stake public affairs coordinator, stake literacy specialist, and is currently a counselor in her ward Relief Society. Jennie is married to Boyd K Hansen; their family consists of four daughters and their husbands, a son and his wife, and three grandsons.

THE MISTAKEN GIFT

Laurel Mouritsen

THE GLOW FROM the Christmas lights strung around the storefront window was muted by the onrush of falling snow. As a result, the twinkling red, green, and white lights provided a somewhat haunting background to my reflection in the glass—striding with briefcase in hand, thin coat buttoned up around my chin, and face scowling. Admittedly, the scowl was out of place for this merry season, but I was filled with none of the cheer and goodwill that characterized the holiday's approach.

Even the ornamented and tinsel-draped tree in the large window of J. R. Smithie's didn't dispel the air of gloom. Christmas music from someone's radio glided on the frosty air, and the strings and brass of "O Little Town of Bethlehem" played a discordant rhythm to the sound of my steps on the slick and icy pavement. Dusk was gathering, but it was still light enough for me to see people's expressions as they passed by on the sidewalk. Many were somber, even discouraged. Others appeared harried and distracted. Few, I thought, reflected the spirit of the Christmas season.

And no wonder. We were in the midst of the greatest economic depression in our country's history. I was fortunate to have a job and treasured the few dollars it paid each month. That was more than many people had. Some men had been out of work for months. A few were even reduced to begging. *Take for example that thin, ragged man standing on the street corner just up ahead,* I thought. He was truly pathetic, standing coatless and hatless in the chilly December air. I could see his lips quivering from the cold. A jagged hole in one sleeve of his red-and-brown checkered flannel shirt revealed a bony elbow. His trousers hung two sizes too large on his lean hips. He had no gloves to warm his rough and reddened hands.

"Brother, can you spare a dime? I've a wife and children, without means to feed or clothe them."

I shook my head as I strode quickly past, mumbling, "No, I'm sorry," under my breath. After all, how could I help—I had my own welfare to worry about. Since my father's death early last spring I had become the primary wage earner in my family; I had a responsibility to manage my meager earnings wisely.

I scurried on down the main street of town, past several more lighted windows and wreathed doors. To my left stood a vacant building—taller than most of the other buildings, but unkept and dilapidated. Yet someone had affixed a large illuminated star atop the roof of the building. The snowfall had nearly stopped, and the star's shining yellow light created a soft glow on the muffled landscape below. I wondered why the owner of the building would want to pay for the cost of lighting that big star when money was such a scarcity. *A foolish waste,* I thought.

By the time I reached the screened back porch of my mother's home, my feet were wet from the slush that had leaked through the nickel-sized holes in the soles of my shoes. I determined to use the few cents I had managed to save out of my paychecks to get my shoes resoled, even though the money should more rightly go toward food and fuel. As I entered the house, I glanced at the decorated Christmas tree standing in the living room. We

had gone on an excursion into the mountains to cut down the tree and bring it home. Its fragrance of fresh pine and homey appeal of handmade paper stars and strings of popcorn and cranberries barely penetrated my consciousness as I tramped down the hallway.

"Supper is ready, Winston." My mother's voice floated from the kitchen of our modest frame house. "Take off your coat and come and eat."

The enticing smell of stewed meat and vegetables tickled my nose. I shucked off my coat and hurried into the kitchen. Mother was standing over the black enamel stove, stirring a small amount of stew bubbling in the pot.

"Umm, it smells good. I'm starving."

A smile crossed her cheeks. "The girls have eaten already. I saved a bowl for you," Mother reported.

The girls consisted of my three younger sisters. The oldest one, Vivian, had a job as a switchboard operator in a downtown hotel. The other two were still in school.

"How was your day, son?" Mother asked as she set a bowl of steaming stew before me on the table. I couldn't help but notice her chapped hands, worn raw from the harsh lye soap she used to launder clothing.

I picked up my spoon and dipped it into the depths of the chipped earthenware bowl. "Busy. A steady stream of clients came into the office. It's amazing to see so many people willing to spend large sums of money on litigation. It seems in times like these, people would work out their problems without resorting to the expense of legal counsel."

Mother sat down opposite me at the table, her hands folded in her lap.

I sucked the stew from my spoon. "Lucky for me that they don't, or I wouldn't have been able to land this job as an apprentice book-keeper at the firm."

"It's a pity those people have to hire a lawyer." Mother shook her head sadly.

I frowned. Mother's sympathies invariably rested with the unfortunate. Or the needy. Or the ill. If goodwill could be carried to a fault, then that was Mother's burden in life.

"My appointment with the dean of the business college is tomorrow evening, Mother. I'll leave work a little early, come home to change, then take the streetcar up to the university for the meeting."

Mother nodded.

"I hope to make a good impression. This interview carries a lot of weight. I need to wash and press my white shirt for the appointment tomorrow."

"I've already done it for you, son. It's hanging in the closet."

I smiled my appreciation and swallowed another spoonful of stew. Trust Mother to take care of everything for me. She had probably laundered my best white shirt in the washtub with the neighbors' clothing. Theoretically, she did their laundry to earn a few dollars, but most of the time they neglected to pay her; and more often than not she refused to take their money.

"That's my only good shirt, you know, Mother. Don't inadvertently get it mixed up with someone else's laundry. I can't afford another one. And I need it ready for tomorrow."

"I know, Winston. Like I said, it's clean, pressed, and in your closet."

"Thanks, Mother." I scraped the bottom of my bowl to get at the last snippets of meat. "How about another spoonful or two of stew, Mother? It tasted awfully good."

"I'm sorry, it's all gone. I gave a bowlful to a nice young man who stopped by. He hadn't had a meal all day."

"Mother! I keep telling you it's dangerous to open your door to strangers. This guy was probably some hobo who just stepped off the train. He could have robbed you, or worse." I scowled and made sure Mother heard my sigh of disapproval.

Mother's ready smile sprang into place. "Oh, no, Winston. He really was a kind fellow. And I only invited him onto the screened porch; I didn't actually let him in the house."

I rolled my eyes to the ceiling. Our home was located two miles from the railroad tracks, and the hobos who rode the trains from city to city looking for work were a common sight on our side of town. They often went from one door to another looking for a handout, a place to sleep, or an opportunity to do odd jobs for pay. Mother never refused any of them. If one appeared at the door, she'd usher him inside the screened back porch and fix him something to eat—a sandwich, a biscuit with cheese, or a bowl of hot stew. *My* portion of hot stew, to be more exact. Occasionally, she set him to work doing some task around the yard, then she'd give him a quarter or two. That one irritated me the most—giving her hard-earned money (and sometimes mine) to someone she didn't even know. Once she gave away Vivian's new pair of winter gloves to a transient who happened by. I shook my head in dismay at the thought of it.

"I can find you something else to eat, Winston," Mother offered.

"No, thanks. I'm not hungry anymore." I pushed my chair away from the table and stood up. "I'm going to read for a while and then go to bed. 'Night, Mother." I kissed her cheek. It smelled of the same harsh soap she used to wash clothing.

I slept poorly that night. I guess I was nervous about my interview with the dean of the business college. My future education depended on getting a scholarship, and it was to be awarded at the dean's discretion. The following day lasted nearly an eternity. Though I tried to focus on my work, my eyes were incessantly drawn to the big clock hanging on the law office wall. At last the allotted hours were used up, and I put on my coat and left the building.

The sky was steel gray and once again threatening snow. I hurried down the sidewalk, hoping to reach home before the weather turned foul. I paid scant attention to the silver tinsel strung between the lampposts or the bright Christmas lights that gleamed from nearly every store and office window. Even the large yellow star perched on the roof of the vacant building, creating a halo of light, failed to sway my thoughts from the crucial meeting I had scheduled with the dean.

I hastened along, nearing the corner where I had spotted the ragged beggar the day before. I decided this time to avoid eye contact with him, but when I reached the corner I discovered he was not there. Though the sidewalk was alive with passersby, the beggar was nowhere in sight. *Good,* I thought. *He's probably begging on some other street corner tonight. Now I won't have to be troubled with him.*

When I arrived home I went straight to my room to wash and change clothes. As I rehearsed in my mind answers I would give to possible questions the dean might ask, I pulled on a pair of clean trousers and reached in the closet for my only good white shirt. My fingers snatched at empty air. My white shirt was not hanging where it should have been. Hurriedly I sorted through the few threadbare shirts I had in the closet, expecting my good one to be sandwiched somewhere between them. But it wasn't. My best white shirt was gone. *Perhaps Mother forgot to hang it in the closet after she pressed it yesterday.*

"Mother!" I zipped out of the room, consternation flooding through me. "Mother," I shouted again.

"I'm in the living room, Winston," I heard her reply.

I dashed into the living room. The Christmas tree lights were glowing a cheery red and green, and Mother stood next to the tree threading a string of popcorn through the branches.

"My shirt," I half-bellowed. "Where's my white shirt, Mother?"

She finished wrapping a portion of the popcorn string around a scrawny branch and then turned to look at me. Her eyes were soft and shining, and had I taken the time I would have noticed our Christmas tree lights reflected in them. "I gave it to that poor man who came to the house today. He had no coat, and his shirt was worn clear through at the elbows."

"You what?" I shouted incredulously. "You gave away my best white shirt?"

"Yes, son. You have other shirts. That man had only the tattered shirt he wore on his back."

"But—but—" I stammered.

"I'm sure you would have done the same if you had seen him. That poor man. No coat. No hat. And his hands were as red as a lobster from standing in the cold without any gloves."

An image fluttered into my mind. "He wasn't wearing a red-and-brown checkered flannel shirt, was he? And brown baggy trousers?"

"Yes. That's the man. How did you know?"

I groaned and slumped into a chair. "Oh no, Mother. That man was a vagrant I saw begging on the street corner yesterday."

Mother shook her head adamantly. "He was no vagrant, Winston. He said he had a home, a little makeshift shelter of tin down by the railroad tracks. He has no heat or electricity in his place, Winston. He needed the shirt. It will help to keep him warm."

I moaned. "You know I was planning to wear that shirt to my interview tonight," I said dismally.

"You can wear another, son."

I lapsed into a miserable silence.

"Would you help me string this popcorn through the branches, Winston?"

I rose dejectedly from the chair, taking the popcorn string Mother handed me. She had threaded a cranberry between each puffed kernel of corn, so that the string was a gaily colored red and white. "If you had to give that man one of my shirts, why did it have to be that one?"

"Because it was the finest one you had, Winston," she answered simply.

I stared at her. I could hardly believe what I was hearing. She had deliberately chosen my best shirt to give to that ragged, tawdry beggar. Suddenly I was consumed with anger—not toward Mother, who had only responded out of the goodness of her heart, but toward that wretched vagrant who was now wearing my best white shirt, the very shirt I needed to wear in just a few minutes to the most important interview of my young life. Rage got the best of me, and I flung the popcorn string to the floor.

"Where did you say that beggar's house was located?" I growled.

"He said it was down by the tracks. Why?" she asked wide-eyed.

"I have to go out for a while. I'll be back," I replied. I grabbed my coat, forgetting to take my hat and gloves, and stormed out of the house. I heard Mother call my name, but I didn't turn or pause to answer.

The snow had started to fall—big fluffy flakes that caught on my eyelashes and slid off the bridge of my nose. I ignored the wet splattering on my face and trudged forward with a grim dedication to my purpose: I was going to find that beggar and get my white shirt back.

I tramped the two miles to the train tracks in record time, my jaw set in an intractable line. As soon as I had the tracks in sight, I stared up and down the line. A few hundred feet away, tucked back in among some brush, I glimpsed the corrugated tin roof of a small shelter. As I approached, I could see that it was more a hut than a building, surely no bigger than my mother's living room, and our living room was by no means spacious.

I hesitated. Now that I was here, I wasn't sure exactly how to proceed, how to phrase my demand. I steeled myself with a deep breath. The intake of cold air hurt my lungs. I shivered, then stuffed my hands into the pockets of my coat and walked the remaining distance to the tin shelter. I didn't know for certain if this was the abode of the man I sought, but I had only one way of finding out. I knocked on the metal door.

Seconds later a middle-aged man wearing a familiar red-and-brown checkered flannel shirt opened the door. As he stood there expectantly, I noticed how withered he looked. He was as thin as the rails that ran past his house.

"Pardon my intrusion," I said haltingly. "I'm afraid I have a rather unusual request, but it deals with a matter of some importance."

"Come inside, brother. The wind's cold tonight," the man replied. He swung wide the door of the little tin hovel and beckoned me to enter.

My eyes took in the sum total of the house in a single glance. One tiny room held his possessions—a shabby mattress set on a crooked wooden floor, broken apple crates for table and chairs, a few tin cans of food stored in a cardboard box.

"Now what can I do for you, brother?"

The question seemed absurdly out of place. Standing before me was this destitute man, dwelling in a tin shack, asking what he could do for *me*. I felt my cheeks flush with shame.

"This afternoon, I believe you may have stopped by my mother's home," I began, fidgeting uncomfortably with the words I was in the midst of spouting. "She apparently gave you, by mistake, a white shirt. I'm afraid it was my best white shirt." I paused, feeling foolish and incredibly selfish.

"Ah, yes. The white shirt. Your mother is a very kind lady."

"Yes, she is," I stammered on. "But you see, the white shirt was a mistake . . . that is to say, *giving away* the white shirt was a mistake. I need to wear it to . . . " My voice faltered, and then died a miserable death in my throat. My shoulders drooped. I hoped he would retrieve the shirt for me without discussion and spare me further embarrassment.

Instead, he took a seat on one of the wooden crates and motioned for me to do the same. "That white shirt was the nicest shirt I ever owned," he mused.

"Owned? Are you saying that in the past tense?" I whispered hoarsely.

"That shirt was too fine for me to keep. A young friend of mine needed it far worse than I did."

"A friend?" I gasped.

"Yes. He's gettin' married in four days. On Christmas Day. That white shirt was a gift sent straight from heaven. Yes, indeed. Your mother was an angel to hand me that nice white shirt."

I swallowed noisily. "Are you saying your friend has my white shirt? Does he live close by?"

The man nodded. "He has a little place on the edge of town. Reminds me of the cottage I used to own back East. That's where my wife and young 'uns are, back East, livin' with relatives until I can get myself some employment."

"Yes, go on," I encouraged, hoping he would tell me exactly where his friend's house was located.

"I came out here lookin' for work. I hope to be findin' a job real soon. If not, I'll be movin' on until I do locate myself a position. My wife and me aren't tramps, you know. We're hard-workin' folks. We're just down on our luck 'cause of the hard times and all."

I stared at him without speaking. I could see the gleam of pride that flickered in his eye as he spoke about his family and his anticipation of obtaining employment. My gaze traveled to the four corners of the man's tin dwelling. Although there was next to nothing in the way of furnishings, the man's home was clean and neat. Mother had seen through to the heart of the situation. This man was no vagrant or beggar. He was simply a casualty of the Great Depression.

My feelings were sympathetic, but my mind was still bent on reclaiming my white shirt.

"You say your friend lives on the edge of town. Which direction would that be?"

"South, brother. Due south. Just follow the train tracks south and you'll come upon a little frame house painted apple green. That'll be my friend's place. His and his bride-to-be."

I thanked him and prepared to leave. I wished I had something to give him to make his Christmas season brighter, but I'd brought nothing with me in my mad dash to leave the house in pursuit of my white shirt.

The man rose from the rickety crate he'd been sitting upon. "Here, brother," he said, walking to the cardboard box that served as his cupboard and reaching inside it. "Take this candle with you. It will be dark outside soon, and you'll need the light to find your way." He put a match to a short, stubby candle and handed it to me. Its flame burned blue in the dimness of the tin shanty.

I thanked him again and started for the door.

"Merry Christmas, brother," the man said in farewell.

As soon as I stepped outside, the wind licked at the weak blue flame of the candle; it sputtered under the press of falling snow. I cupped my hand around the flame to protect it. As I walked away from the tin hovel, following the train tracks southward, my thoughts lingered with the unfortunate man I had just met. Unfortunate, did I say? Perhaps not. This man possessed a concern and charity for others that obviously transcended his own desperate poverty. He carried in his heart the true spirit of Christmas.

I hadn't traveled but a few yards when a stiff gust of wind buffeted me, abruptly extinguishing the tiny flame burning from my candle. I muttered under my breath and stuffed the now useless candle into my coat pocket. Dusk was quickly settling upon the snowy ground, and soon I would be walking in darkness. I quickened my pace, anxious to reach the apple green house the man had described to me. My conscience scolded me for pursuing the quest for my white shirt, but I squelched its censure. I *needed* that white shirt. The hour was drawing nigh for my appointment with the dean. I'd really have to hurry in order to find my shirt and get to my meeting on time. The slushy snow underfoot seeped through the holes in my shoes. I shuddered with the cold. Grimacing, I glanced skyward. The snow fell like streaks of white light, pelting my upturned face. I turned away, pitting my concentration on reaching the green cottage where my best white shirt awaited me.

Ah, that must be the house. It was nestled among a clump of similar small cottages, but it was the only green one. Boldly I climbed the front step and knocked on the door. A moment later a young man who appeared to be near my own age answered.

"Yes?" he said. "Can I help you?"

"I hope so," I replied. "May I come inside for a moment?"

"Of course." He moved aside to allow me to enter—it was then I noticed the heavy metal braces on the young man's legs and the metal crutches propped under his arms. "Have a seat," the young man offered.

I took a place on a worn couch, its fabric shredded in spots from too much wear. My eyes assimilated the spartan surroundings in a quick glance. The tiny living room was joined by a smidgen of a kitchen to the left and a closet of a bedroom to the right. The young man hobbled away from the door and lurched into a chair. He placed his crutches on the floor beside him.

I cleared my throat. "Excuse my intrusion," I began lamely. "Would you be the fellow to whom was given today a white shirt?"

The young man's brows rose in surprise. "Yes. How did you know that?"

"I just finished speaking with the fellow who gave you that shirt." I blinked and loosened the collar of my shirt with my finger. I was feeling awkward and uncomfortable. I tried not to stare at the young man's legs, which draped lifelessly from the chair.

"Oh, yes. I'd only met that gentleman yesterday when I was walking past his home. I happened to mention to him that I was getting married shortly, and this afternoon he showed up here at my place with that nice white shirt."

After the first few words, the rest of the young man's explanation passed over my ears. *He was* walking *past the other man's home? How could he walk anywhere with those useless legs?* I wondered silently.

"Whether it was coincidence or an answer to prayer, I don't know. But that nice white shirt was exactly what I needed. When I was struck with polio," he glanced down at his listless legs, "both of my parents had to get work in order to pay for the extra medical costs. But now, with the economy the way it is, my father has been laid off and my mother's work has been cut back to only a few hours a week. So we can't afford new clothes for the wedding."

I nodded my head, watching the muscles in the other man's face work with the emotion of his words.

"I wasn't well acquainted with the fellow who made a gift of that shirt to me, but he looked like he needed the shirt more desperately than I did."

I skulked down into the depths of the couch cushion. *How can I ask for the return of my shirt now?*

"But now I've rattled on when you're obviously here on some errand. What can I help you with?"

I changed position on the couch and wiped a bead of perspiration from my forehead. In spite of my empathy for the young man's plight, that shirt was important to my future as well. I couldn't afford a new shirt, either. "Well, you see," I began. "The man who gave you the shirt acquired it himself quite by accident."

"Accident?"

"Yes. The shirt actually belonged to me and—"

"Oh, I understand," the young man interrupted. A smile appeared on his face. "You wanted the shirt to be a Christmas gift, didn't you?"

"Well, not exactly." I squirmed in my seat.

"What a kind gesture! He told me how much he appreciated receiving the shirt." A frown suddenly appeared upon the young man's brow. "Are you upset with him for offering me the shirt? I didn't know it was a special gift. If I had of known, I never would have passed it along to that little girl."

I stared at him. "Little girl, did you say?"

"Yes. That sweet little girl with the yellow ringlets and bright blue eyes who lives down the road. She and her mother came visiting not more than an hour ago and the little girl told me she wanted to be one of the angels in her school Christmas play. But she didn't have an angel costume, so she probably wouldn't get to play the part."

"The angel part?" I asked in confusion. Trying to follow in the wake of my white shirt was becoming more perplexing by the moment.

"Yes. The white shirt was so big for her that it reached to her ankles, making a perfect angel costume. So I gave it to her."

I closed my eyes and leaned back against the couch in despair.

"You should have seen it—her face lit up like a Christmas tree."

"I'm sure it did," I muttered. My crisp white shirt. A costume for some child's school play. I doubted I would ever get it back now. "Can you tell me where that little girl lives?" I asked wearily. I glanced at my wristwatch. One hour left before my appointment with the dean.

"Yes. She lives with her widowed mother just a few blocks from here." He shifted position on the couch, adjusting his legs by lifting them with his hands into place. "It's a small yellow house surrounded by a picket fence. There's just the little girl and her mother. They don't have much, but they bring a beam of sunshine whenever they come to visit me."

I stood up, ready to go in search once again for my errant white shirt.

"Wait. Before you leave, I'd like to give you a little something. Sort of a Christmas gift." The young man grasped his crutches from the floor and then struggled out of his chair. I resisted the impulse to reach out and help him to his feet, but in a moment he was up and lunging to a bureau that stood beside the wall. He pulled out the top bureau drawer and removed an object from it.

"Here," he said, returning to my side in lurching steps. "I'd like you to have this. To brighten your Christmas." He pressed into my hand a miniature manger scene carved in glass. "If you put a light behind it, the rays will dif-fuse through the glass and make a pretty shine."

I peered at the trinket. Joseph, Mary, and the baby Jesus lying in the manger—all molded out of a single piece of clear glass. The entire piece fit within the palm of my hand. "Thank you," I said. I wished I had something to give him in return. I headed for the door, thrusting the glass manger scene into my coat pocket.

"Merry Christmas," the young man called. I waved a hand in return and then shut the door behind me so he wouldn't have to hobble over to do it himself.

I stood uncertainly on the front step for a moment, wondering if I should continue to track my white shirt or turn around and head for my meeting. But I had no suitable shirt to wear to the meeting. How could I appear for the interview wearing a faded and worn old shirt when it was so important that I make a good impression? If I hurried very quickly and accomplished my task without delay, I could still make the meeting on time. I pulled the collar of my coat up around my ears and set off in search of the yellow house with the picket fence around it. The snow was still falling, piling up along the fence posts in little mounds. There were no streetlights in this section of town, and the houses were scattered farther apart. I walked the dark block with rapid steps.

A few moments later I spotted the yellow house, encircled by a white picket fence just as the young man had described. It was a tiny structure, situated in a minuscule yard. I let myself through the gate and marched up to the front door. My shoes were sodden and my feet numb from the wet and cold.

My knock at the door was answered by a small girl with long yellow ringlets, pink cheeks, and the prettiest blue eyes I'd ever seen.

"Hello," she said simply on seeing me on the doorstep.

I bent down until I was her size. Her pretty eyes gazed at me unflinchingly. "Hello, there. Would your mother be at home?"

In reply to my query, the little girl turned and shouted, "Mama! A snowman is at the door."

I smiled at her perception of me. I must have looked, in fact, like a snowman with the snow crusting on my coat and bare head. My eyebrows were caked with snow, and my nose was surely as red as a carrot.

I caught sight of the little girl's mother coming from a back room and into the hallway. She paused an instant when she saw me, then she hurried to the child and put a protective arm around her. "Can I help you?" she asked warily.

She didn't invite me inside, so I stood on the doorstep shuffling my feet. "I hope so. The crippled young man living down the block—" I pointed with my finger—"he told me you and your daughter had come to visit him, and he gave your daughter a white shirt."

"Yes," the woman answered slowly, still keeping her daughter tucked close. I noticed the woman's attractive face and shoulder-length honey-colored hair. Her eyes were the same shade of blue as her daughter's, but framed by longer, curling lashes. I shifted my weight, feeling the sogginess of my socks inside my soaking wet shoes.

"Well, it so happens that the white shirt belongs to me. Through a rather long and jumbled turn of events, the shirt ended up in your daughter's hands. I wondered if it could be returned to me." There. I'd said it. I'd actually asked for the return of my shirt. I let out an audible sigh, relieved that I was finally about to see my nice, new white shirt again.

The woman's pretty face creased into a frown. "My daughter was planning to use that shirt as a costume for her school Christmas play," she began.

I interrupted her in midsentence. "Yes. I know. But it really is imperative that I have the shirt back. I have an important meeting I must attend and . . . " I paused as an awful thought struck me. "You do still have the shirt, don't you?"

The child twisted out of her mother's grasp. She took a step toward me, peered up into my face, and said, "I'll show you where the shirt is. Can I, Mama?" she added, looking over her shoulder at her mother.

Her mother's frown deepened as she considered her daughter's request, then she nodded slightly. The little girl slipped a warm, soft hand into mine. The unexpected contact caught me by surprise. I glanced into the child's face and saw a smile settle across her cheeks. She tugged at my hand. "Follow me," she said.

The child's mother stepped aside from the doorway, allowing me to enter the cramped house. She followed behind us as the child led me toward an open door that I assumed to be a bedroom located at the end of a short hallway. I felt her mother's eyes stabbing into my back, ready to rescue her child at the hint of one false move from me.

The child walked me through the open door into a small room. The room was filled by a narrow bed, square bedside table, and a chair. My eyes widened as they settled on two figures resting on the bed—a young woman with straight black hair and an olive complexion cuddled a tiny infant in her arms as she lay in the bed. The woman's face radiated joy. Or perhaps the glow came from the reflection of cheery colored lights strung around a small Christmas tree standing on the table beside the bed.

The little girl led me a step closer to the woman's bedside. "This man wants to see your baby," she said to the dark-eyed woman.

My eyes drifted to the infant. Although I knew next to nothing about babies, I could see this baby was newly born, perhaps only hours old. And with a shock, I realized the infant was swaddled in my nice white shirt.

"Isn't he beautiful?" the little girl murmured. She bent down and stroked the baby's tiny head. The head was covered with soft black fuzz. "His name is Immanuel. He was born last night."

I peered more closely at the baby. He had the same dark complexion as his mother, and his fine hair and eyes were as black as hers. The two were obviously of Hispanic descent. I murmured an appropriate compliment concerning the child, and his mother smiled. I didn't know if she understood my English or not.

"Maria's husband is in another city looking for work, and she had no place to stay. So we invited her here with us. The child was born a few weeks earlier than anticipated; that is why her husband is not yet here," the little girl's mother explained. Her face softened into a smile as she gazed at the infant. "She named the child Immanuel, in honor of the Savior's birth."

I stared at the infant. His tiny lips pursed into a bow, and his scant brows wriggled with expression. My white shirt was wrapped tightly around his little body. I bent down and ran a

finger across the baby's cheek. It was as soft as down. His round black eyes fixed on mine.

As I gazed into the depths of those small dark eyes, I was acutely reminded of Him whose birth the world was about to celebrate. The babe who was born at Bethlehem nearly two thousand years ago was not unlike this infant before me. As Mary lovingly cradled her newborn son, what thoughts filled her heart? Did she fully comprehend the greatness and goodness and glory of that tiny baby?

I felt suddenly overwhelmed with shame. During this whole Christmas season I'd been thinking only of myself—my needs, my goals, my desires. My heart had been turned only inward. I had failed to appreciate the miracle of the birth of my Savior and Redeemer. Without realizing my eyes were moist, I felt a tear roll down my cheek, and fall onto the folds of the white cloth swaddling Maria's baby.

I looked up to find the eyes of the little girl's mother fastened on me. Her face was a soft smile. "As you can see, your shirt has been put to good purpose," she said quietly.

I could only nod. A lump in my throat prevented me from speaking. The next moment I was conscious of a small paper object being pressed into my hand. The little girl with golden curls stared up at me. "I made this paper star. It's for you," she stated. I studied the tiny star resting in my hand. The folds forming the points of the star were uneven, and the glue holding the gold glitter to the paper was lumpy and streaked, but to me that star was one of the most beautiful treasures I'd ever been given.

"Thank you," I choked with emotion.

"I just love stars, don't you?" the child said to me. "I especially like great big ones. I'll bet it was a great big star that shone on the night Jesus was born," she added.

"Come along now, Annie. Let this baby sleep." The little girl, Annie, took hold of her mother's hand and followed her out of the room. I quietly followed. When the three of us were back out in the living room, Annie's mother said to me. "I started to explain to you how Annie was planning to use that nice white shirt as an angel costume for her school play, but we found a much better use for it." She hooked up one blonde brow and nodded toward the room we had just left.

"It's the best use possible," I agreed, grinning at her. "That shirt is serving a far better purpose than the one I had in mind for it."

Annie's mother flashed me a broad smile. Her smile was riveting. I glanced down at the star in my hand. "Thank you for this lovely gift, Annie," I said to the child standing at her mother's side. "It has reminded me of the true meaning of Christmas—a meaning, it seems, I had nearly forgotten."

I looked at Annie's mother. She was watching me with a studied expression. "You know, I haven't even introduced myself yet. My name is Winston Langley. I live with my mother and three sisters a few miles from here." I held out my hand to Annie's mother. She took it—her touch was as light as a feather. I was enchanted by her softness and sweetness, and her lovely blue eyes.

"Margaret Wyatt," she said in return.

"I'm pleased to make your acquaintance, Mrs. Wyatt."

"It's Margaret, please. My husband passed away two years ago." I saw a curtain of sadness fall across her eyes. But then she brightened again. "Annie is a very good companion to me. She and I enjoy our time together." Annie affirmed her mother's words with a vigorous nod of her head.

"I can see that. I'll bet the two of you are looking forward to Christmas," I replied.

"Maria's husband should be here by then. Annie and I will be spending Christmas Eve quietly here at home. Just the two of us. You wouldn't like to perhaps join us for dinner . . ." Her voice trailed off into silence, as if she were embarrassed for extending the invitation.

"I'd love to have dinner with you and Annie," I answered quickly. I astonished myself with how promptly my reply came.

"You would? Your mother and sisters wouldn't be disappointed if you didn't join them for a Christmas Eve supper?" She looked as surprised by my answer as I had felt in giving it.

"We always celebrate Christmas Eve late in the evening. Mother won't be expecting me until then."

"All right. How does five o'clock sound to you?"

"Five o'clock is perfect." The evening was growing late and I knew I should be going, but I almost hated to leave the cozy home of Margaret Wyatt and her daughter. I shifted the paper star Annie had given me into my left hand and extended my right to Margaret. "I guess I need to be on my way. I have an appointment for which I'm overdue. Thank you for inviting a cold and wet snowman like myself into your home."

I heard Annie giggle.

"I'm sorry you came all this way for your shirt and have to leave without it," Margaret said.

"That's the miracle of Christmas, isn't it? Discovering that peace, hope, and charity still exist in the world today."

Margaret and Annie walked with me to the door; Annie stood on the porch waving until I was out of sight. I put the paper star Annie had given me into my coat pocket along with the candle and manger scene. The snow had stopped falling, and winds high above the surface of the earth were quickly clearing away the clouds.

I strode quickly toward home. The slushy snow squished into the holes in my shoes, but I barely noticed it. I began whistling the melody to "O Little Town of Bethlehem." Soon I had retraced my steps past the small home of the crippled young man. I remembered that he had no new clothing to wear on his wedding day. A few steps more brought me near the door of the impoverished gentleman who lived in a tin shelter because he had no job. I walked on, my mind filled with reverent thoughts of the Savior and the blessings he had extended to me.

From up ahead a luminous yellow light issuing from the top of a building unexpectedly sprang into view. I paused on the sidewalk, staring up at it. Suddenly, an idea formed in my head. I knew what I could do to make my new friends' Christmas a little brighter. I chuckled with glee.

The sky was now clear and brilliant with stars. I stared at the heavens. It looked like a ceiling hung with Christmas lights. One particular star seemed brighter than the rest. Perhaps that was the same star that shone so gloriously over the stable where the baby Jesus was born.

By the time I reached my own door, the appointed hour for my interview with the dean of the business college was well past. Mother was waiting for me in the living room. A look of consternation flooded her face. "Winston, your appointment!" she exclaimed as I entered the room.

"It's all right, Mother. I'll go in tomorrow and apologize to him for missing it." I grinned, and kissed Mother's cheek. "Merry Christmas, Mother," I sang. Her jaw fell open in amazement. I left her standing in the living room, staring after me as I went to my room.

Inside my bedroom, I took off my wet coat and hung it on a peg fastened to the door. Then I reached into its pockets and withdrew the candle, the manger scene, and the paper star. I carefully placed each item on the windowsill, then stood back to study them. I looked at the scene for a long time, thinking about the people I had met that evening and the Christlike examples they had been to me. The plan growing in my head took on more clarity. I had a lot to do before Christmas Eve—calls to make, arrangements to set in place. I smiled to myself. This Christmas was suddenly shaping up to be one of the best I had ever had.

The following morning I arose early and went into work a few minutes before the usual hour. During lunchtime, I made another appointment with the dean. I couldn't get in to see him until after Christmas now, which wouldn't leave much time for him to consider my candidacy for the scholarship. But I had a feeling that everything would work out all right. After finishing for the day, I made a stop at the department store. That evening I did a little research to determine who owned a certain abandoned building on Main Street. I could hardly wait until Christmas Eve.

The day before Christmas arrived amid clear sunny skies and mild temperatures. I had a difficult time keeping to my desk as the hours ticked by at the law office. I was so grateful when the company director finally gave the signal for dismissal. As each of the employees filed out of the office, he wished us a merry Christmas and presented us with a wrapped gift. When I untied the big red bow and removed the wrapping paper, I discovered a round tin from which emanated the most delicious smell.

I carried the tin under my arm as I strolled along the street past the storefronts, admiring the glittering Christmas lights adorning the windows. A beautifully ornamented Christmas tree stood against the glass of one large-paned storefront window. I stopped to enjoy the gleaming tinsel threaded through the branches of the tree and the charming handcrafted decorations—wooden clothespin dolls with yarn hair and painted faces, bows and wreaths made of fabric, colorful glass ornaments. Why hadn't I noticed the beauty of this particular Christmas tree during any one of the dozen times I had passed it on my way to and from the law firm?

I moved on down the sidewalk. People hurried by, anxious to get home to their families and their Christmas Eve festivities. Again, many faces were somber, their eyes downcast and their brows a deep furrow in their foreheads. "Merry Christmas," I said on impulse to one passerby.

The recipient was an older, gray-haired woman. She looked up at me, startled, then her face broke into a smile. "And merry Christmas to you!"

"Have a good holiday," I declared to another. His preoccupied and worried expression lifted as he returned my salutation. The same thing happened every time I called out a greeting. It took only a kind word, a smile, or a touch of the hand to turn a frown into a smile. The change I saw taking place on people's countenances with just a word of cheer was

extraordinary. There was indeed something miraculous about this season of the year. Even though many were suffering from financial reversals or other serious problems, goodwill, peace, and joy were available in people's lives—brought to remembrance by the birth of a babe in Bethlehem.

I carried home the Christmas tin and placed it with the other items I'd prepared to take with me that evening. Then I changed into the *second-best* shirt I owned, the one with the fraying collar and cuffs and pinhead-sized hole in one elbow. I collected the objects I'd readied, kissed Mother and promised her I'd be back in time for the family Christmas Eve celebration, and set off in the direction of Margaret Wyatt's house.

The late afternoon sun was a brilliant ball in the cloudless sky. The snow underfoot dazzled like diamonds. I covered the two miles to the railroad tracks with a Christmas song beating time in my head. I carefully and quietly crept up to the door of a makeshift shelter constructed of tin, then reached into my coat pocket, and withdrew a short note. I glanced at the few lines I had penned.

Dear sir,

The law firm of Edwards, Jackson, and Fife is in need of a night janitor. Employment is between the hours of five and nine in the evenings. The pay is quite adequate. Your name was given to the company president, Mr. Bertrand Edwards, who is awaiting your call or visit. Hoping this bit of Christmas cheer makes your season brighter. A friend.

Chuckling to myself, I soundlessly taped the message to the door of the tin shack. The service was made sweeter by knowing the effort I had gone to in convincing the company president that he needed a night janitor and that I knew just the man for the job.

I tiptoed silently away from the tin shelter and then picked up my pace as I headed for the apple green house located at the edge of town. It took only a few minutes to get there. This time I removed a small wrapped box from the pocket of my coat, to which was attached this note:

Dear friend,

This small gift comes with a wish for joy and happiness on your wedding day. May this Christmas season be your merriest. An acquaintance.

I stole to the door with the wrapped gift and note and laid it on the front doorstep. In my mind's eye I saw the crippled young man opening my gift—what surprise and delight would be his in finding inside a new handsome tie to wear on his wedding day. I grinned with elation at the image, an image that made a few more months of saving to resole my shoes well worth it.

I chuckled aloud as I scrambled away from the porch and trotted down the block to Margaret's home. When I let myself through the gate of the picket fence, I saw Annie's face at the window looking out at me. She waved, then a second later the front door flew open and Annie stood dancing on the porch.

"Merry Christmas," I whooped. I dashed up the front step and squatted down to Annie's height. "There's the prettiest little angel I ever saw," I said, grinning at her. She put her two small hands around my neck and gave me an unabashed squeeze.

"Here you two are."

When I looked up, Margaret was standing in the doorway, a smile playing on her pretty features. I straightened and put out my hand in welcome. She placed her fingers in mine, and her touch sent sparks flying through me. She ushered Annie and me inside and offered to take my coat. I hurriedly pulled the last gift from my large coat pocket and then handed the coat to her to hang up.

When she returned to the living room, I held out the gift I'd brought for her. "Merry Christmas, Margaret. This is for you. Like my white shirt, I'm afraid this gift comes secondhand. But I thought we could all enjoy it together." I grinned like a nervous schoolboy.

She laughed, and the sound reminded me of the pealing of Christmas bells. She unloosened the lid of the tin, removed it, and then smiled with pleasure. "A Christmas fruitcake! Umm, it smells so wonderful. Look, Annie, smell all the fruit and nuts and spices."

Annie stood on tiptoe and sniffed, her nose only inches from the fruitcake. "Ooh," she squealed in delight.

I laughed at the sight of the two of them. "I guess it's safe to assume that you both like fruitcake."

"Thank you, Winston. What a lovely gift. It will be the perfect dessert for our Christmas meal."

The way she spoke my name turned me into a quivering mass of jelly. I was glad she invited me the next moment to sit down at the table. I think my knees would have buckled under me had I stood much longer.

I enjoyed a wonderful evening with Margaret and her daughter. The meal Margaret prepared was superb. I ate until my stomach ached, and then I still wanted more. I discovered that she possessed a quick wit and ready laugh; she was also charming, intelligent, and good-humored. And Annie was delightful.

After we'd each eaten a huge piece of fruit-cake, I turned to Annie and said with a mischievous gleam in my eye. "Why, Annie, I almost forgot about the Christmas gift I have for you."

Annie's eyes grew as large as the saucers on the table.

"Your gift is very special, however. I couldn't bring it with me. I'll have to take you to it. Have you a warm coat and boots?"

Annie nodded until her yellow ringlets bounced as if tied to a spring. Margaret sent me a questioning look.

"I'd like you and Annie to come with me for a few minutes. There's something I'd like to show Annie. Would that be all right?" I said to her.

"Trying to anticipate your next move is completely impossible, I've learned," she replied with a laugh. "I'll go get our coats." I smiled back at her. Her every word filled me with delight.

The three of us left Margaret's house and strolled leisurely toward the center of town. The evening was perfect for a walk. A three-quarter moon lit our path, and the temperature was cozy. It took us about twenty minutes to come within sight of the abandoned building on Main Street. From the direction we approached, the roof was hidden until we were nearly upon the building, and then the radiant star mounted on the roof burst into view.

Annie drew in a quick gasp. We paused on the sidewalk, and I bent down and put an arm around Annie's shoulder. "There's your gift, Annie. The biggest, brightest star I could find," I said softly.

Annie stood mesmerized. The star's light shone on her face, giving it an angelic glow. When I noticed a tear slip down Margaret's

cheek, I took her hand and gently squeezed it. "Let's go inside," I suggested.

We walked the few remaining steps to the building, with Annie's head craned up at the star, and I let them inside the door. Everything was undisturbed, exactly as I had left it. The electric light from the star outside on the building filtered through the windows, steeping the room in a golden glow. I was grateful to the owner of the building for allowing me to use it for the evening, and for his abundance of Christmas spirit. His star had delighted the heart of at least one little girl.

Annie's eyes immediately fell on the little scene arranged on a bit of hay in one corner of the room. She moved reverently toward it, her eyes fixed on the miniature glass manger with the candle behind it, and the paper star she had fashioned herself resting on top.

I let go of Margaret's hand and went to the manger setting, where I lit the candle with a match. The wick caught fire immediately and created a muted glow upon the glass, bathing the manger scene in rippling colors of light. Annie was speechless. She sat down on the hay I had spread around the scene, staring wordlessly at the little glass figures in the manger. Margaret and I dropped down onto the hay beside her. None of us spoke for several minutes, each caught up in his or her own thoughts about the birth of the baby Jesus on that starlit night long ago.

I was the first to break the silence. "This is for you, Annie," I said, pulling a wrapped package from underneath a spot in the hay. The package was done up in gold glistening paper and tied with green and red ribbons.

Annie's eyes sparkled. "Thank you ever so much," she whispered as she took the gift from my hand. Her mother and I watched her open the package. She withdrew from the box a crownlike circlet covered with dozens of tiny star-shaped, glittering bits of foil paper.

"It's an angel's halo," I explained. "My sister, Vivian, and I made it for you. Well, it was mostly Vivian who made it," I confessed with a grin. "Since you didn't get to wear the white shirt as a costume for your school play, I thought you might like to have this halo. It can always remind you of the angels that were present at Jesus' birth."

Annie placed the halo on her head. "You do look like an angel," her mother proclaimed. "It's a very beautiful gift, Annie."

Annie threw her arms around my neck and gave me a tight hug. "Thank you for the present. I love it!"

"You're welcome, Annie. Merry Christmas."

I sat back on my heels watching Annie and her mother exclaim over the halo, and the tiny manger scene, and the big, beautiful lighted star mounted outside on the roof of the building. Tears swelled in my eyes. The chain of events following one mistaken gift of a white shirt wrought a joyous change in me—Christmas had worked its miracle upon my heart.

LAUREL MOURITSEN holds a degree in history with a minor in English literature from Brigham Young University. She has taught creative writing for adult and community education programs, and has also taught classes in genealogy and family history. Laurel has written short stories, poetry, scholarly papers, and family histories. Three of her novels have been published. In addition to her interest in reading and writing, Laurel enjoys skiing, horseback riding, and traveling with her family. She and her husband, Robert, reside with their four children in Sandy, Utah.

DRUMSTICKS AND GERMANY

Tom Hughes

SITTING HERE TONIGHT, late on Christmas Eve, staring at the tree, I am thinking of three other Christmases. They span my lifetime, and lead my thoughts back to this Christmas, just a few minutes away. They are thoughts of what I share with my son, of what connects us to each other. They are thoughts of how lives become tied together, whether by design or by chance.

When I was four, I think, maybe five, we drove to my grandparents' home in Albuquerque. We were used to Missouri's severe and dramatic winters, with the cold that drove us indoors and the snow that pulled us back out. One winter our little town sat through a night's ice storm that left all the trees and lampposts covered in a sheet of ice. In the next morning's sun, our neighborhood looked like a crystal chandelier lying on its back. It was spectacular. Albuquerque would be different, they told us. Certainly not warm, but not at all like home.

As it turned out, New Mexico was having an unusually warm, dry winter that year. To our excitement, though, a dusting of snow fell on Christmas Day. Not enough to make even a single decent snowball, but enough to make everyone talk about a white Christmas. The snow is not why I remember that Christmas, though. I remember it for drums.

Christmas Day arrived with a little snow and a houseful of cousins rushing into the living room. In the center of that room stood just what I had asked for: a drum set, miniature but complete with a bass drum, two tom-toms, a snare drum, and two cymbals. I didn't have the first idea of what to do with all these wonderful noisemakers except to make noise, and I did plenty of that. I also had to let my brother and sister and cousins take turns making noise. With the other children I was very popular. Mom and Dad told me years later that I had not been especially popular with the adults.

The second Christmas that I think of tonight is my second Christmas in Germany. My first mission-Christmas had been difficult and lonely but also exciting and full of newness. My second was almost crippling.

I had known for a few months that Tracy was seeing someone. I knew that her family was not happy about it, and that mine was also concerned. At first she had assured me that they were just friends. Gradually, she stopped assuring me. So when I got a letter from her the day before Christmas Eve explaining all her reasons for marrying this friend, it was not a complete surprise. Of course, seeing the gun before it's fired doesn't mean you won't feel the bullet.

Ironically, maybe it was a good thing that the news came at Christmas. We had already been invited to spend the holidays with various members of the branch, so our time was filled with little children and good food. On the other hand, I hurt. I was missing her far more deeply than I had before—knowing that I would not be going home to her, trying not to think about her, trying to remember her exactly as she had been the last time I saw her, when she promised me she'd wait. Or the last time we spoke, the Christmas before.

Getting up was harder than usual on Christmas Day. I spoke to my family on the telephone. It was late Christmas Eve for them, of course, and there was that strange international call voice delay that makes those conversations so confusing at first, until you get used to waiting for answers. It was the first time I had spoken to them in a year. I thanked them for the gifts they had sent, which I had opened just a few moments earlier. They knew about Tracy, of course. What an eerie feeling I had during that call—exciting and painful, like pushing on a bruise—all of us trying to say the right things, to be buoyant and cheerful, supportive and positive. All of us knowing I was in pain. "Keep your mind on the work." "We're so proud of you." "What are your plans for today?" "I'll be fine." "I love you." "I love you." "Bye-bye."

Unlike the year before, I did not call Tracy. You can't call your girlfriend if she's engaged to someone else.

We were invited to the home of a member in tiny Buxtehude. It's a beautiful little town (I see it in the present tense, even though it's a long time away now) with a charming *Fußgängerzone* for pedestrian shoppers, lined with gorgeous old *fachwerk* homes converted into shops. The pre-Christmas season in Buxtehude had been so joyful, so tourist-poster German, it was hard to believe. Proselyting had been less productive than normal, but the town was so captivating that it hadn't seemed so bad. But on Christmas Day, the *Fußgängerzone* was empty. I mean truly empty. I have a picture of myself sitting on the short wall surrounding a fountain. I'm imitating the statue of some religious figure at the center of the fountain, something I would never have dared to do had a single person been there to see it.

We were invited to arrive at the member's home at 4:00, but finding things dead in the town where we lived, we decided to go ahead and take the train to Buxtehude around 1:00. We had thought there might be something going on there, someone to talk to. We were wrong.

I don't know what other missionaries are like, but I could never see my way clear to go tracting on Christmas. Our mission president encouraged it, I've heard General Authorities recommend it, but I never did it. I could only imagine Jehovah's Witnesses knocking on my door on Christmas. It just didn't seem right to me. So we wandered around Buxtehude for a few hours.

Truth to tell, I don't remember a lot about how we spent that day with the family in Buxtehude. We were there a long time, though. Long enough that we knew we didn't want to miss that last train back home at 9:20. We got to the train station about 9:15. By then, it was cold. At 9:45 or so, I went to check the train schedule posted by the track. We had taken that train many times, so I was sure the train would pull in soon. But I had nothing better to do, so I went to look. Sure enough, there was a train scheduled for 9:20 every Thursday night. There it was: "9:20*."

They're not usually this late, I thought, as I sort of absently looked at the bottom of the schedule to see what the "*" referred to. "*Ausser 25.12 und 1.1,*" it read. "Except for 12/25 and 1/1"—Christmas Day and New Year's Day.

It took another twenty minutes to find a cab. It took fifteen or twenty minutes to drive home. I sat in the back seat, looking out as a soft drizzle of wet snow began to stick to the window. I thought of the year before. When everyone else sent practical, cold-weather gifts, Tracy sent a picture of us walking together on a beach. The warmth of that beach felt far away as I leaned my head against the window; as I realized more than ever that Tracy was gone, really gone, an emptiness began to fill me.

It had started out as an awful day. Then came the partial solace of the phone call, but accompanied by the ache of not placing the other call. The day had become pleasant, even fun at times, certainly distracting, while we were with the family, but it ended as close to unbearable as I've ever known. Sitting here tonight, I wish nothing more than that I had no cause to think of it this year. I had hoped that this night would never come.

The third Christmas I remember was fourteen years ago, the Christmas when Lisa and I gave Scott a drum set. It was the first time I gave my son a gift I remember receiving, the first time I felt that we were having a truly shared experience.

We were home for the holidays, staying with my parents. Scott was six, and I couldn't resist. My parents tried to talk me out of it, but I was not interested in their warnings. I dragged them all into the music store with me. When I found the set I wanted, I waved over a salesman. I was laughing, my parents were chuckling and shaking their heads at me—the chuckle and shake of those who have been there before. Lisa was also chuckling and shaking her head at me—the chuckle and shake of someone trying to say, "Okay, but you're going to be the one who makes him keep the drumsticks off the furniture and his little sisters."

Since my parents live in Utah, we were kind of surprised that there was only a dusting of snow for Christmas that year. I've talked to Scott about that Christmas, and he doesn't remember much of it, except that he was very surprised to learn that a snare drum has little metal wires running across the bottom. I tried to show him a couple of the things I could remember from my junior high band days, but he was much more interested in seeing just how hard he could hit the cymbals. I giggled through the whole morning.

Dad and I sat and watched Scott banging away: the oldest son of an oldest son, smacking away at a set of cheap drums with a six-year-old's joyful abandon. I was touched, though not surprised, when my mom came over and kissed me, her eyes wet. "His daddy looked just like that," she said. Lisa came over and sat on the other side of me and held my hand.

I was so proud of our little boy. Hands that had first squeezed my fingers, then held a bottle, then tricycle handles, now controlled those sticks. I thanked God for a healthy little boy, and for his two healthy little sisters who, at four-and-a-half (-and-a-half, don't forget) and three were wise enough to give their brother and his drums a wide berth. I thanked him for parents whose love for me only became understandable as my own kids arrived and grew. I thanked him for a wife who had given me these children and been such a wonderful mother to them. I felt the kind of gratitude and love that you feel when you sit in a room with your parents and your wife and your children and it's Christmas.

It was no surprise when, later in the heavily drum-punctuated day, Scott rushed into my arms, his eyes wet, his round fist holding a broken drumstick. I promised him we'd buy him a new one tomorrow and told him to go get one of his new books to read to me. I looked at Lisa and my parents, chuckled, and shook my head—the chuckle and shake of someone who wonders just a little bit, "What was I thinking?"

I remember those three Christmases.

And now I'm sitting in an armchair in our living room and looking at the tree. Scott's sis-ters, seventeen (seventeen is fine by itself) and sixteen are downstairs watching something with Lisa. *It's a Wonderful Life* or *The Christmas Story* or something. Santa will be here soon. One of the nice things about having older kids is that Santa brings fewer some-assembly-required gifts, which means Santa can usually get to bed a little earlier. Mrs. Santa would normally have gone to bed about an hour ago. It's just a few minutes shy of Christmas morning here, but for Scott the day is underway. By now he's probably opened his very practical, cold-weather gifts. There won't be any impractical, affectionate gift from Rachel this year. He'll call us soon, then the girls will go to bed, then Santa will come, and then he and Mrs. Claus will go to bed.

"That's him," shouts Carrie, and we each rush for a telephone.

"Hello?" answers Lisa. There's a moment of empty air.

"Hello?" comes back Scott's voice.

"Hello, son," says his mother. "How are you?"

The pause. His voice catches. Another pause, and I am with him. I know him, and I know this moment. Maybe he is close enough to his companion that he can cry openly, but he is trying not to make it hard for us.

He tells us of his work, his investigators, his companion. He thanks us for the gifts. It's a terrible and thrilling conversation, hearing a young man so far away, so much a part of our lives, so much a part of me, and in so much pain. We haven't spoken to him in a year. The strength we have seen growing in him through his letters is muted today as we all try to find the right things to say, to tell each other how much we are missed and loved and prayed for, without pushing too hard on the bruises.

Fifteen minutes. He needs to let his companion use the phone. "I love you." "I love you." "Check the train schedule." He laughs lightly—he knows the story.

"*Fröhliche Weinachten,*" I say to him—Merry Christmas, words I haven't spoken in years.

"*Frohes Fest,*" he answers back, and we laugh lightly together.

"I know it hurts, son." No response. "I know. *Ich liebe dich.*"

"*Ich liebe dich auch.*"

"Bye-bye." "Bye-bye." "We love you." "We pray for you." "Bye-bye."

Lisa and the girls and I kneel down before going to bed. Lisa expresses the gratitude and love we share because we feel as if we are all together and it is Christmas. She tells Him of the pain we all feel because one of us is aching. She thanks Him for His son, and asks that our son will be comforted.

The girls go to bed. I kiss Lisa and tell her I'll come to bed in a while, then go back to my chair by the tree. Now that the call has come, now that I've spoken to him, I feel not really better, but somewhat relieved. I still hurt for him, and I know he is suffering. As much as at any time in his life, I want to put my arms around my son as I've done before, to hold him while he cries, to cry with him, for him, for both of us. I want to promise him that we'll fix it tomorrow, even though we won't.

We have always had many things in common, Scott and I. Now we have one more. I gave him the drums so that we could share something, so that a part of my childhood would be a part of his, so that I could see more of myself in him, so that he could share some of the joy I have known in life. I wish him many more of those joys: that he will find someone to love as much as I love his mother; that he will have his own children, his own son, to love as I love mine. I would like to share those things with him in Christmases to come. I believe I will.

Tom Hughes lives in New York City with his wife, Kristen, and their son, Steven. Tom is an actor and writer. He was an English major at Harvard, then returned for drama school at the American Repertory Theatre's Institute for Advanced Theatre Training at Harvard. He served in the Germany Hamburg Mission and is the elders quorum president in their branch. Kristen was a Theatre Arts major at BYU and served in the Florida Jacksonville Mission. She now teaches preschool and serves in the Primary presidency.

THE LITTLE CHRISTMAS TREE

Chris Hicks

IN DECEMBER 1968, a few days before the 25th, Christmas arrived in the northern sector of Vietnam.

It came in a box, wrapped in brown paper and bound with slightly frayed string. I assumed it was just another package someone had sent from "the world," as we referred to our homes back in the United States. But it turned out to be much more. The box contained Christmas, or at least the spirit of Christmas. And it manifested itself in an unexpected way to a small group of teenage soldiers laboring for Uncle Sam in an area called Phu Bai, about sixty miles south of the enemy border, near a beachhead we had dubbed "Phu Bai by the Sea."

Like everyone else in this army corps headquarters compound, we lived in "hootches"— eight of us squeezed into a sort of open bunkhouse on stilts that had been slapped together with wooden slats and capped with a slanted tin roof. It kept out the pounding rain and held back the roaring winds, but each day a new layer of dirt appeared on the floors, our bedding, and anything that had been left out in the open. The running joke was that this seemed to be the only place on earth where you could slosh through mud and choke on dust at the same time. But at least we weren't in "the bush," dodging bullets from hidden Viet Cong soldiers who knew the jungle better than we did. Instead, we were clerical workers, processing an endless stream of paperwork for colonels and generals who lived nearby in air-conditioned mobile homes.

It was easy to lose track of time as days turned into weeks and weeks into months. We all had jobs to do, tasks to perform, interrupted by guard duty, the occasional firefight on the perimeter, or artillery shells suddenly exploding around us, lobbed from afar by unseen rocket launchers. We worked odd shifts, ate in the mess hall, and slept when we could. Sometimes a movie was shown on a makeshift screen outdoors, most often John Wayne's *The Green Berets*. After a showing or two, we began to shout dialogue back at the flickering image of Wayne, who played the character of a special forces colonel in Vietnam as if he were still on horseback, leading a cavalry charge against an Indian raid in Monument Valley during the 1800s. A favorite moment was when Wayne would snarl, "Due process is a bullet," and we'd all say it with him.

For the most part, the only holidays we recognized were Care Package days, which could actually occur at anytime—whenever mail call delivered a box from friends or relatives to someone in our hootch. Real holidays, however—Lincoln's Birthday, Labor Day, Thanksgiving, and all the other annual pit stops for working stiffs—went largely unrecognized.

Christmas was different. We learned to recognize signals that Christmas was on the way, though they were not the traditional ones by any means. None of them came from the weather, for example. Not that I needed snow-capped pines to work up my holiday spirit. Having been raised in southern California, I was used to warm winters. But even my friends from the deep South complained that they weren't prepared for the kind of sweltering heat and heavy humidity we experienced in

Vietnam, which could aggravate the simplest task, such as writing a letter. By the time "Dear Mom" was written at the top of the page, the writer's wrist was soaking the bottom of the page. As December rolled in, though I had been in Southeast Asia for six months, I was still having trouble adjusting to the idea of a "sweaty" Christmas. (Bing Crosby never sang about *that!*) On the other hand, it wasn't always hot. The enemy was the only thing more unpredictable than the weather. During the week before Christmas, for example, it was quite cold one day, then it was 110 degrees in the shade the next, followed by torrential rains that flooded the mess hall, collapsed several sandbag bunkers, and knocked down a couple of those four-legged boxes we called home. Unpredictable, yes. But Christmassy it was not.

Our first hint that Christmas was actually going to happen this year arrived with packages that had Santa stickers or drawings of holly and snowflakes on the outside. Inside, smaller boxes were gift-wrapped with holiday paper. As a result, a certain unspoken excitement began to build over the couple of weeks preceding Christmas, and mail call was met with more enthusiasm than usual. We looked forward to anything that might in some small way remind us of the Christmas celebrations going on back home.

For most of the camp, the holiday really seemed close when the official army announcement came that the annual Christmas truce was in place, a 24-hour break from the war. We didn't have to worry about being shelled for a full day—no rockets landing in the compound, blowing things to smithereens and sending us scrambling for the shelter of those sandbag bunkers we had built around the hootches. We might actually get a peaceful night's sleep—

that is, if the truce was honored by the Viet Cong, which, according to veterans of several tours of duty, was more like an every-other-year occurrence.

And Christmas seemed even closer after the announcement that a special meal would be served on Christmas Day, as the mess hall prepared a genuine turkey and potato dinner to replace our steady diet of liver and rice.

But for the eight guys in our hootch, Christmas came a few days earlier. At first it appeared to be just another package. And though the arrival of a box instead of a letter always caused a bit of heightened excitement, I expected this one to be no different than many others that came on a fairly regular basis, although it seemed a bit larger than most.

As we retired to the hootch to open our mail, several of the guys gathered around my bunk to see if there might be some goodies they could mooch, joking about what "practical" Christmas gifts might be inside.

"Maybe it's an outboard motor," said Willie, grinning that perpetual grin of his.

"Could be a complete collection of Mantovani records," Kyle suggested with a laugh.

"A case of Turtle Wax?" said Charlie.

After a lull, the most realistic guess came from Robert, who didn't speak very often but was usually on the mark when he did: "More like two thousand cookie crumbs that used to be two dozen cookies."

The jokes subsided as the cardboard flaps were opened. Outside the compound, the war was still raging, but in the confines of our hootch, something very different was going on—something unexpected and quite surprising. Inside the box was . . . a tree. A genuine miniature plastic Christmas tree.

When I was a youth, I often said many unkind things about people who bought artificial trees instead of the real thing. Even when my father's allergies could no longer tolerate the aroma of pine and we brought a plastic tree into our own home for the sake of his comfort, in my own selfish, adolescent way, I would mutter snide comments and sing, "I'm Dreaming of a Fake Christmas." But at this moment my disdain for plastic pine evaporated forever. There was a thrilling exuberance in the air as we stared at the most beautiful bunch of do-it-yourself branches, twigs, and pine needles imaginable.

We all pitched in, putting Twig B into Branch A, and then tried to balance the minitree on its ministand as we added the small cloth balls of various colors and some gold tinsel garland that had been included for good measure. There were no lights, but that didn't matter—there was no place to plug them in anyway; a few of the branches were bent from packing, or maybe from being bounced around during the long journey; the tree stood slightly crooked when we placed it on the shelf I had built into the wall near my bunk; the green coloring was a bit pale; and the tree was unquestionably scrawny.

As we stood back to drink in our work, the laughter died down and the room became quiet. No one seemed to care that this wasn't exactly the tree in Rockefeller Center. We were like children again, going through the annual Christmas decorating ritual. And now that it was done, we stood silently for a moment, just staring at that wonderfully pathetic little image.

After a few moments, Willie, a large, muscular, imposing fellow, who nonetheless seemed to have a permanent smile fixed on his face, looked uncharacteristically serious as he broke the silence by going to the door and heading outside to his work duty. He glanced back for a moment and softly whispered under his breath, "Merry Christmas." There was another pause, and Kyle and Charlie turned to leave. "Merry Christmas," they said in one voice. The salutation was repeated through gentle, slightly sheepish smiles several times as we dispersed and headed for our respective assignments.

Over the next couple of days, acknowledging that tree became something of a ritual in the camp—in fact, it became a sort of shrine. People came from all over the compound to see it, including a group of gung-ho marines who happened to be passing through. The tree seemed to alter the atmosphere of the whole camp.

All these years later, when someone says "Vietnam," we tend to think of the war more often than the country. And compared to wars that had gone before, this one was unique. The tour of duty was set in a specific time frame—one year—during which a bonus was paid, an extra $65 a month in combat pay. When the year was up, the soldier returned to the states to finish out his term of service (two years for draftees, three years for volunteers).

Similarly, it seems rather odd to recall that we would leave the quiet comfort of that little tree and its religious symbolism—and, by extension, its message of peace on earth, goodwill toward men—to go out each day and "work" in the war.

Selective memory being what it is, I'm sure the wartime experiences of my former combat buddies have changed over the years as they've related anecdotes to their children and grandchildren. And as the story of that Christmas is told, I'm sure the tree has taken on very different characteristics. Perhaps it is a tall evergreen, with full branches and a shining star on top, tinsel on every branch, bright lights shining, and dozens of wrapped presents at its base.

Come to think of it, the tree really wasn't all that scrawny.

And it did have something of a glow. . . .

CHRIS HICKS is the entertainment editor for the *Deseret News,* Salt Lake City's afternoon newspaper, where he has been the movie critic for twenty years. Chris also reviews movies for KUTV, channel 2, the CBS affiliate in Salt Lake City. He was previously the movie critic for KSL television and radio for thirteen years. His book of video recommendations, *How to Pick a Family Flick,* was published by Deseret Book in 1993. Chris is currently preparing a new book for publication, *Cinema Saints: How Mormons Are Portrayed in the Movies.*

Born and raised in southern California, Chris joined the army at eighteen, believing a recruiter who told him that if he joined instead of being drafted he would not go to Vietnam. After being sent to Vietnam for a year, he spent eighteen months in Europe. Upon finishing his service obligation, Chris returned to California and a year later relocated to Ogden, Utah, where he lived for seven years, attending Weber State College and beginning a journalism career at the *Ogden Standard-Examiner.* In January of 1978 he was hired by the *Deseret News.*

Chris is married to Joyce Dearing Hicks and is the father of seven children, stepfather of six children, and grandfather of fifteen children—at last count.

A version of this story was published in the *Deseret News* in December of 1978.

THE BREAD OF THE ANGELS

Jerry Johnston

FIVE YEARS HAVE PASSED since the Night of the Widows, but my Brigham City friends and I still tell the story. We haul it out each Christmas—along with *A Christmas Carol* and *The Gift of the Magi.*

Since I have the best memory, they like me to tell it. And I always begin with the afternoon I pulled up in front of Danny's house, put the car in neutral, and watched as Danny plowed a swath through the heart of his front lawn with a snowblower.

The bare, little path veered through the drifts and into his orchard like The Road Not Taken.

I watched for a good two minutes. Danny glanced my way and nodded. I nodded back. I figured he was getting ready for a game of Fox and Geese; that he'd finally realized he was just a kid at heart. I stepped out of the car.

"Deer!" Danny yelled above the roar.

I cupped my hand to my ear.

"Deer!" he yelled again, spreading his fingers above his ears like a set of antlers. The move was supposed to convince me this was no laughing matter. Finally he killed the engine and walked over.

Danny was a chunk; an aging baseball catcher who'd kept his athlete's appetite but had stopped working out. He had a catcher's bad knees, pudgy face, and twisted fingers, but he'd come to look more like Yogi Bear than Yogi Berra.

"The deer come down at night and browse

my shrubs," he said. "I'm trying to steer them down through the lot with a trail."

"I see," I said. "So they'll go browse on Sister Hunsaker's shrubs."

Danny looked down the straight and narrow way he'd carved.

"I never thought of that," he said.

"Right," I said.

Years before, when my wife, Karla, and I left the city and moved back to our old hometown, we brought no illusions of small town bliss. We knew better. Brigham City had problems. The old people didn't care for change. The young people didn't care for old people. Like a big city, the town had its loose women, drunks, and crooked salesmen. Sometimes it had more than one of each. Still, there were enough "Dear Hearts and Gentle People" in town to bring us back. Besides, in Brigham City guys like Danny were liable to run snowblowers through the center of their lawns.

"Anyhow," Danny was saying, "forget the deer. You and Karla still up for caroling tonight?"

Going caroling was Danny's idea. He thought it would calm his holiday jitters. Get him in the right frame of mind.

"Far as I know, we'll be here," I said.

"What time?"

"I guess at 7:30," I said. "Like you told us. Vern and Dot said they'd be late."

"No surprise there," Danny said. "But they'll miss Yumi's chirashi sushi."

Danny's wife was Japanese. He'd met her while he was playing exhibition ball in Hawaii.

"Well," I said, "if they miss Yumi's sushi, that means more sushi for me."

It was the oddest sentence I'd ever said.

* * *

According to E. B. White, a small town consists of four stores and an excellent view of the mountains. He knew better, of course. A small town is more than a view. It's a point of view.

And at the time of our caroling expedition, Brigham's point of view had kept me working on the local newspaper for more than ten years. I didn't live in the provinces in spite of the provincialism, I lived there because of it. When some rugged individualist decided to raise ostriches or the mayor took up the zither, I had a story. I once pegged a column on a local Christmas tree salesman who left a box of money out so customers could make their own change.

"If somebody steals it," he told me, "my life would be simpler."

Such thinking wasn't Zen Buddhism. It was Village Mormonism. And I enjoyed it—even when it led people to see the Book of Job as a self-help manual or to rally the Boy Scouts to shovel the walks of able-bodied men.

It was sweet thinking. Warm thinking. And it was about to send six aging college chums out to sing carols for their well-to-do neighbors as an act of goodwill.

Vern and Dot liked Village Mormonism, too. They'd seen the world's grime and treasures, but every road had led them back to Brigham. And in Brigham they lived like gentry—the way Karla and I lived. We were part of the town, yet apart from it. We kept ourselves aloof, and—sadly—a little numb.

When Karla and I showed up at Danny's that night, Vern and Dot were already waiting for us. Vern was on his second plate of sushi.

"Welcome!" he said, his lanky limbs jutting from Danny's recliner. "Bet you thought we'd be late, didn't you. The hostess will serve you a surprise dish in a moment."

"I know what we're eating," I said. "I want to know what we'll be singing."

"The same thing we're eating," Vern said, "Panis Angelicus—the Bread of the Angels. Dig in."

Dot frowned at Vern from across the room, like a woman peering over bifocals. She'd taken up roost at the piano and had been thumbing through the hymns. Unlike her husband, who could spend hours in church counting the ceiling tiles, Dot got physically ill when not in motion. She was a dervish—a track coach at the high school, a pianist, a singer, and many other things.

Yumi appeared with two fresh plates of sushi. Danny walked in after her, saw his favorite spot had been stolen by Vern, and leaned up against the piano.

"Let's sing something from the *Messiah*," Vern said. "Think we can get a handle on it?"

Dot feigned another scowl, but even she knew that Vern's cheeky asides helped propel our little group along.

"Vern," I said. "You ever wonder who wrote the song the angels sang for the shepherds? Handel, maybe? Or Mozart?"

I was hoping to provoke a zinger.

"Mozart?" Vern said. "No way. We're talking 2,000 years ago. Those shepherds wouldn't even recognize Mozart as music. The angels probably chanted, like the Jews at the time."

Karla shivered. "Don't say *chanted*," she said. "I've heard enough chanting. I want to think of them singing, the way they do in 'Angels We Have Heard on High.'" She paused. "Why don't we sing that one tonight?" she said.

Danny gave a quick thumbs down. "No thanks," he said. "A couple of 'glorias' and 'Deos' go a long way with me."

Yumi had been sitting on the floor listening to all this. Our broad western gestures and loud voices often made her self-conscious. But now she spoke up.

"In Hawaii, 'Angels on High' was my father's favorite Christmas song," she said. Then she looked down into her hands.

Silence fell on us as an angel passed. We all looked at Danny. Danny shrugged.

"Well," Dot said. "Any better ideas?"

There were none.

Dot flipped the hymnbook to the song.

It took us ten minutes to knock together a working version. Vern was the only tenor, but he had a robust voice. And though Danny and I bogged down on the bass runs, it was good enough for Christmas caroling. We decided to do "We Wish You a Merry Christmas" in unison as an encore, then fade into the night. Karla wished we'd thought to wear Dickens outfits.

"Remember," Vern said, "we do eight families and out. I've got miles to go and promises to keep."

We were just wrapping ourselves up to leave when Danny stepped from the bedroom wearing his outfit—a large Russian hat that covered his head in fur.

We all stared.

"It looks like road kill," Vern said.

"It may be road kill," Danny said. "My brother got it in Canada."

We couldn't take our eyes off it.

"Stop gawking," Danny said. "It's just a hat. Are we taking hymnbooks tonight or winging it?"

"Dan," Vern said, slinging an arm around his shoulder. "How will you ever sing with the angels if you refuse to learn the words?"

Our plan was simple. We'd ride in Vern and Dot's minivan, sing at a few homes, then call it a night. At Vern's prodding we chose stake president Dixon as our first victim.

But President Dixon and his wife weren't to be found. The only soul at home was Roy, their teenager. Roy finally opened the door just as we went winding through the last of the "glorias."

He leaned on the door frame, looking lean and bored. When we finished, he stared at us like a man sizing up a lynch mob. His eyes stopped on Danny.

"Nice hat," he said.

"Thanks," Danny said.

Then Roy closed the door and went away. We didn't even bother to sing "We Wish You a Merry Christmas"; we just crunched our way back through the snow to the van.

"Gee," Vern said, "only seven more families to go."

The lights were out at Bishop Hopkins' home. Ditto for the Tingey family.

"So where to now?" Vern asked, easing the van along the snowpack.

"How about Sister Rose?" Dot said. "Since Lloyd died she doesn't have a lot of friends."

"When someone leaves you a million bucks you always have friends," Vern said. But off he sped in the direction of the Rose home. Danny, who'd been a counselor in the bishopric, pointed out a shortcut. He knew the ward by heart.

We took our places around the porch, rang the bell, and muscled up a hearty version of our carol, hoping for the best. When we got to "mountains in reply," Sister Rose stepped to the door, beaming like Our Father's mercy.

"Do the second verse!" Dot called.

But no one had a clue about the second verse. Someone sang the word *shepherds,* someone else added *we have heard on high,* and then like people scrambling onto a trolley car

we swung into the first verse again and held on for dear life.

Sister Rose applauded. "You just made my night!" she called. "No, you made my week. Thank you!" We bounced into "We Wish You a Merry Christmas," waved, and strode away to the humming van.

"Better!" Danny said. "Much better!"

"Shepherds we have heard on high?" Vern said. "What was that all about? It sounds like the name of a Billy Graham Crusade!"

Back in the van, Yumi sat closer to Danny, and Karla held my hand.

"How about another widow?" Dot said.

"Or a widower," I said.

"Sorry," Danny said. "All we've got is widows. The old boys remarry too fast."

Yumi laughed again and Danny boldly pointed Vern toward the home of Sister Fonnsbeck.

Opal Fonnsbeck may have won a beauty contest in her day, but it was certain she'd never been voted "Miss Congeniality." Our group avoided her. She had a sly way of showcasing her piety while scolding lesser souls. She once blamed a spate of my family's bad luck on our arrogance. To pay her back I often sang "How Great Thou Art" in her wobbly vibrato.

We stepped sheepishly to her door. My wife patted my shoulder. "Don't even think about doing the voice," she said.

"I won't," I said.

Sister Fonnsbeck stepped to the door before we could ring the bell. When we broke into full harmony on the chorus of our carol, she quickly put her hands over her mouth as tears began to slide down her cheeks. We all felt the rush of emotion but kept going. Except, that is, for Vern. The tenor part totally disappeared. I glanced over at him. He had a twisted expression on his face. He'd melted down. He couldn't sing.

On the last "Deo," Sister Fonnsbeck clapped.

"That's just wonderful!" she said. "You're such wonderful people! I'd come and go with you, but I haven't been well." Then she squinted out into the dark.

"Is that Sister Tingey in the back?" she asked. She'd caught a glimpse of Danny's hat.

"No," Danny said solemnly. "It's Danny Bird."

"Oh," she said.

"It's a hat, Opal," Danny said. "Now go back behind the door where it's warm. You'll catch your death out here. We'll sing extra loud."

We sang our farewell and waved. On the way to the van I caught up with Vern. I'd never seen him emotionally high-centered like that. I didn't know what to say.

"You okay, old-timer?" I said.

"I don't know," he said.

"Here," Danny said, tugging the big fur hat over Vern's eyes. "Wear it low so you can't see them cry. The song's no good without a tenor."

Whether Danny was kidding or not, the silly fur hat was now history for the night.

On we went, making the rounds of the widows. We sang for Sister Fisher, for Sister Kopinitz, and Sister Loma. All of them were home. Two of them cried. All offered us treats. We even serenaded Sister Knudson's dark house, on the chance she was there and couldn't get to the door. When she didn't appear we sang to an old woman we'd never met who'd come out to feed her dog. In the van we even sang to ourselves.

"This ward has more widows than a bad line of type," I said. It was a newspaper joke, but only Karla seemed to get it. She flashed me a sweet, indulgent smile. Smart-aleck remarks had fallen from grace. The mood had changed. The cold night was melting away.

"It's getting late," Danny finally said. "Let's do Sister Hunsaker, then call it quits."

Vern—who was singing again, but not talking—steered the van toward the white cottage on the ward's one dirt road. Sister Hunsaker was the widow who lived through the lot from Danny's deer trail.

Ivamae Hunsaker taught the Spiritual Living lessons in Relief Society. And women like her made that church auxiliary the one I longed to join but never could. It seemed to me the lesson manuals for men stressed knowledge while the manuals for women stressed service. I needed the women's manuals far more than they did.

Besides, I loved to listen to Ivamae. When she entered a room, her first impulse was to smile and go from there. There was no guile in her. And though, at age seventy-five, she'd come to look like a Mrs. Butterworth syrup bottle, her half-frame reading glasses showed she had more in her head than maple syrup. I admired her for being both firm and flexible in the faith—like the bendable birches in a Robert Frost poem. Dot once said that Ivamae was her idol. I'd never said as much, but she was mine too.

In fact, it struck us all as odd that we'd forgotten about her. So we gave her our best performance to make up for it. When we finished, she gave us one of her famous smiles in return.

"I've been baking all day," she said. "I've been expecting you!"

Danny gave a puzzled look.

"Who told you we'd be by?" he asked.

"I don't know," she said. "Who told you to come? Now come in, come in. It's colder out here than death on a spider!"

We brushed the snow from our coats and stepped into the living room. It was like a step back in time. Sister Hunsaker beckoned us through to the kitchen. The smell of fresh bread filled the house like the definition of "home" itself. Her kitchen was warm and snug, done up in fine Yankee crispness like a New Hampshire farmhouse.

Karla, who had a bad habit of exploring other people's homes, was quickly drawn to a large photograph on the wall.

"Is this your granddaughter, Ivamae?" she asked.

"Yes, that's Chelsea," Sister Hunsaker said, stuffing several loaves of bread into plastic bags. "Her Primary Christmas pageant was last night. And everything went wrong. The halos broke, the shepherds bumped heads. It was just like the real thing."

Danny looked up. "Like the real thing?" he said.

"Oh, you know," she said. "The Christmas story was a comedy of errors. Joseph shows up with his pregnant wife and has no place to go. Then the wise men come along with their gold and perfume—worldly things that brought the Savior nothing but grief. But in the end it all worked out, just like Chelsea's pageant. Mistakes just make the story sweeter, don't you think?"

We all agreed. By now, Sister Hunsaker had lined up three loaves of bread on the cabinet and was reaching into the cupboard for jars.

"Here's a loaf of bread for each couple," she said, "and a jar of chili sauce. Not salsa, mind you—Mormon chili sauce, made with brown sugar, tomatoes, apples, onions, and nutmeg."

She quickly passed out the loaves and sauce. Dot, who usually bubbled at such generosity, sat in a kitchen chair, serene as a Madonna. She seemed tranquil enough to count the ceiling tiles.

We all said "Thank you" and "This is way too much." Then Vern, who had finally ridden out his emotional white water, spoke up.

"Ivamae," he said. "What kind of song do you think the angels sang for the shepherds?"

"Pardon me?" she said.

"On the first Christmas, what type of music did the shepherds hear the angels singing?"

"Oh, I don't know," Ivamae said, working at the oven. "I'm not even sure they heard a song at all. I wouldn't be surprised if the singing was all in their hearts."

"You mean the literal music wasn't as important as the spiritual music."

"I guess what I'm saying," she said carefully, "is that the literal music doesn't matter to me."

She looked around as we digested the thought. It was pretty enterprising thinking for the old hometown.

"I'm an old lady," she said, "and it's taken God seventy-five years to teach me that the place where Jesus was born, the time of year and such, don't matter a fig. All that matters is that he's born in the lowly stable of the human heart. Compared to that miracle, what happens in the world tends to pale."

She paused to collect a thought.

"I guess I see tradition and history as a protective crust around God's spiritual bread," she said. "Now I have the bread, I think life's too short to chomp on the crust."

By now Karla had worked her way to the back porch to check out Ivamae's curtains. Suddenly she waved us to join her.

We moved toward the window like a tiny flock. Outside, three small deer had picked their way through the snow to browse on Ivamae's shrubs. We watched in silence.

"I've been going to make a trail for them," Ivamae whispered. "Make it easier for them to get at my bushes."

Danny gave me a guilty glance, but I pretended not to notice.

Yumi smiled, however, and nuzzled Danny's neck like a deer—a bold move for her. I looked over at Dot the Dervish. She seemed to be the most peaceful woman on earth.

"Look!" Sister Hunsaker said. "The middle deer's pregnant."

Karla looked at the deer, then looked at me. "Is that possible?" she said.

"Apparently so," I said. "It's pretty obvious."

"But what will happen to the baby?" Karla said.

I shrugged. Vern took a breath and softly blew it out. "I guess that's the question of the season, isn't it," he said. "What will happen to the babies?"

Ivamae shook her head. "Who can say?" she said. She paused, then went on: "But I do like the thought I found in a magazine recently. It said a new baby was God's opinion that the world should go on."

The thought hung in the air as we watched the three deer nibble, grow suspicious, and prance off into the dark. Then I felt it—the feeling everyone else was feeling—a feeling we were all bathing in the same sacred river. Sometime during the evening we'd flowed together at the edges—like raindrops joining in the sea. We were one, like the Good Book says. It felt like salvation.

I've wondered several times since then about our outing. Were such miracles small-town miracles? Could a wild, crazy city produce such grace?

Probably so.

Still, our little village—with its silences and "excellent view of the mountains"—did put a frame on such moments that seemed to set them off, made them appear more precious. Today, five years after our Night of the Widows, the wondering awe of that night still lingers. Each year since then my friends and I have tried to recreate the sweetness. Each year we've failed. Lightning has yet to strike twice. But we do have the story to share each Christmas. And Ivamae was right, inner music is what matters. What's more, memory can cue that inner music. And, as I said, I have a good memory.

As we watched the deer that night, for instance, I recalled a snippet of verse that I hadn't thought of since my college days—a few lines by James Dickey.

The poet goes to the pasture with a flashlight to check on the cattle. Once there, he finds a surprise—a mule deer. The beam from the flashlight strikes sparks in the deer's eyes that never ignite in the eyes of the cattle. But the deer doesn't bolt. It knows with one leap it can clear the fence to freedom.

The deer was with the herd, but not of the herd. It was a vision from another place, a wondrous little stranger come to live awhile among the cattle. It belonged, but it didn't belong.

It was, the poet says in the final line, like one of their own, who would rise.

JERRY JOHNSTON was born and raised in Brigham City, Utah, received degrees in Spanish from Utah State University (1974) and the University of New Mexico (1976), and has worked for the past twenty years as a writer for the *Deseret News*. He has published two books and won several writing awards. He is the father of one son, named Ian.

THE MATCHUP

A CHRISTMAS FOR THE NEW YEAR

Emma Lou Thayne

Loie AND FRITZ we named them. Mostly because he had bushy gray eyebrows like my cousin's husband, and she . . . well, Loie just went with Fritz. Had since days in the canyon and fifty years of family reunions where Loie and Fritz had entertained us younger kids with jokes and games. And the names had to be German sounding. For Schnauzer puppies.

Loie was all I had intended to buy. The thoughtful young vet had helped my alone cousin, my age—late sixties—to say good-bye to her pal Rosebud, a dying Russian wolf-hound, age fourteen (ninety, they say for a dog). When I asked, he advised me that three months was probably grieving time enough. A puppy different from that pet might just make Christmas. A Schnauzer, he said. Companion-able, loyal, gentle but sturdy, fourteen inches full grown, no shedding, good indoors or out. What did I know? Except that I wanted to find one. And he'd help me.

Four days later I was holding a smooth, fringed wriggler with no tail, and ears that perked up and fell over. The size of a new baby, she was licking my chin and then snuggling into my neck. I was a goner. The mama had noted my arrival with a quick bark and then lifted her Vandyke beard for a rub. The puppy would grow to be like this. Perfect. Christmas would be perfect. New life to comfort old grief.

And why not one, too, for our third daughter's family of seven? She'd been hunting for almost a year since Mishie, their white American

Eskimo, had also died—the puppy who had grown with their family, a gift from a groom to his bride on their first Christmas fifteen years before. "Yes!" she answered when I described the surprise I had in mind. So, two puppies were bought, to be picked up on Christmas Eve. And two portable kennels. And puppy food. And rawhide to chew instead of furniture. My husband, Mel, hadn't yet seen them, but I knew he'd like them—especially just in passing.

After dinner, two grandsons and I went for them. They were darling—bathed, groomed, as sweet as our intentions. And shaking, scared—of the cold, of leaving their home. Of strangers probably. But in two minutes they fit into our laps like part of our arms. Then suddenly we were at my cousin's—excitement and into the house, with a baby yip or two. But my cousin turned away: "I never want to see another dog." Tears. Too soon. Other comfort for now—a hug, a shared sadness.

We still could look forward to Christmas morning for the other puppy surprise. But late on Christmas Eve, when our daughter and her husband came to our basement to retrieve their stash of hidden gifts for five children (for Santa to assemble at home), that son-in-law was more than surprised. She had not told him about a new pet. Dog lover, he picked up one puppy and stroked it, she the other. Hesitation. Ecstasy. Then, still reluctant. "Nope," he said. "With nine live bodies at home already (two cats) and two of them little boys under three, it might be smart to wait a while for a puppy."

So. Merry Christmas, Mel. Loie and Fritz were ours. Loie, Fritz, and their newspapers strewn and their exploring unpredictable. Their deposits anywhere they wriggled behind, under, or into. Work. Odor. Bending, Straightening. Garbage cans filled. But also frolicking in the snow off the patio and coming to our arms for a beach towel rub. Attachment.

Dangerous.

We had passed our pet days—the resuscitation of kittens, the grieving for chicks, the arranging for animal sitters when our household of eight went on a trip. Turtles, hamsters, young dogs that dug to China in the geraniums. Grown dogs that played better than they trained (two were killed while on an adventure into the street). Now, like our brood, we were into another phase and off to where retirement or whim or need for solitude beckoned. This was not a time for loving too much these newcomers scrambling to be picked up, to lie in our arms cocking their heads at the television.

But no returning them to the pet store. Part of the bargain. We spent the next week making calls to neighbors, relatives, friends. Asking the milkman, the checker at the store, a passing jogger. By then knowing they had to stay together, not to be sold off alone—they were simply too amiable. Too good in the night, too . . .

Our ad read "Schnauzer puppies 8 1/2 wks old, 1 female, 1 male, papered, wormed, groomed, shots, sweet natured, need loving home . . . "

Calls. Some visits. No one we clicked with. Two days into the ad, New Year's Day, a youngish man on the phone: "I'm from Roosevelt [in eastern Utah, maybe three hours away] and I've gotta find a way to cheer up my family. Our little Schnauzer died on Christmas, and nobody's stopped crying." He'd be over to see the puppies the next day. I liked him. Please, no buyer show up before he did.

In the night the storm began. The puppies slept warm next to each other in the portable kennel by the furnace. The snow stacked up, broke records, continued to fall. Eighteen inches. Two feet. Not even snowplows yet. No way would anyone drive from Roosevelt for anything—even healing.

Then, about noon, into our twice-cleared driveway still a foot deep in snow, turned a big rig with four churning wheels, a Suburban, transport for major loads on any roads, iced and snow-covered. Out of it streamed what we'd find were two parents, an uncle, and not two or three but eight children. Urged, they flooded into our kitchen, filled the quiet with unboisterous telling of their little dog's being found silent and still under a fold-down bed, of how she was named Nestlés. (Their last name was Quick.) They told of her tricks and glowed in the telling.

I'd been watching Loie and Fritz bouncing in the snow in the backyard, almost disappearing, sliding to my feet for a climb and pat and then flopping over each other, racing back to the snow. The Quicks came out on the patio, picked up, quieted, romped with, passed along the pups. The six-foot sophomore basketball player gentled one into the arms of his two-year-old sister, who giggled as Loie squirmed toward her ear. Unafraid. All of the in-between kids took turns with the pups, in affections, not argument, some voting for Fritz, the dad saying he'd wanted a female. "They need to stay together," I blurted. "We've decided." (Actually, the Schnauzers decided; we just agreed.)

Without a blink Mel nodded and patted Loie's head, "Yep."

"Yes, Dad, yes. Please." Two were few enough to go around.

"Two for one," I said as if rehearsed. And a kennel. And puppy food. And rawhide. I liked them together, the whole bunch. Mel nodded again, relieved I was sure, though he'd been more than a sport in not blaming me for having two puppies by default.

We served salt water taffy, took pictures with all in front of the fireplace, exchanged histories and addresses, them promising to let us know how Loie and Fritz were doing, send pictures. Everyone was grinning a big grin. I swear even the puppies.

The Suburban had another two inches of snow on its top. The windows steamed immediately, took rubbings from within to round out a view; Loie and Fritz framed immediately, their paws activated like toys by invisible operators waving good-bye.

Good-bye, little friends. Good-bye, our eras of parenting puppies and babies and Christmases with five stockings for Santa and live actors for the manger scene on Christmas Eve. Good-bye and go well, new family to picture with a little Schnauzer probably sneaked into at least two beds and romping into the morning.

And thank You for the merriest Christmas since the last one.

(Oh, and they decided to keep the names Loie and Fritz. Like the whole thing, no doubt meant to be.)

EMMA LOU THAYNE of Salt Lake City, teacher, lecturer, has published thirteen books of fiction, nonfiction, and poetry and is listed in *A Directory of American Poets and Contemporary Authors.* She appears regularly as a columnist and contributor in women's, LDS, peace, outdoors, and travel publications. Her artistic and community involvement have been complementary to a life in home and mountain cabin with her husband of forty-eight years and the growing up and away of their five daughters and nineteen grandchildren. This story was originally published in the *Deseret News,* January 1994.

THE OTHER SHEPHERD

Jaroldeen Asplund Edwards

MY FATHER WAS A masterful storyteller. Every Christmas Eve he would tell us this story. In magical words he would transport us back in time to the windswept fields of another land, another place—and the lives of other children.

This is the story my father created and told to us all those long years ago . . .

* * *

The boy was only eleven years old, but tall and strong for his age. He was eager to be a man, but his mother doted on him and would have kept him by her side if she could.

His father, the chief shepherd of the tribe, knew that the boy was quickly approaching the age when every lad in Israel must begin to take his rightful place and to accept the responsibilities of wresting a living from the harsh and unyielding land. He had made his son an apprentice shepherd, and for almost a year the sturdy boy had spent each night in the fields with his father and the other senior shepherds.

The boy had learned to call each sheep and lamb by its own name. He had learned how to circle the flock and bed it down for the night. He had learned the soft whistles and calls that guided the sheepdogs in their tending, and he had been taught how to stay awake and alert to the sounds of the surrounding hills and the night winds.

With patience his father and the other

shepherds had taught him how to read the movement of the flock, the alertness of the dogs, and the cries from the darkness. He had been trained to recognize the signs of wolves and other predators and had been rehearsed again and again in the code of the shepherd:

"The sheep must never be left unguarded. They are helpless in the face of their enemies. They are without resource to fight back. An untended flock is ripe for slaughter by wolves, thieves, bears, lions, or wild dogs.

"A shepherd's first, last, and essential occupation is to protect the sheep. A shepherd would give his own life before he would allow his flock to be destroyed."

"You see, son," his father told him, "the sheep are our lives. If we lose them we lose everything—food, clothing, barter, wealth, purpose—all of these things are given to us freely by the sheep. In return, we give the flock our unfaltering care."

"I see," the boy said, with his eyes shining. For indeed, he did love the sheep—especially the tender little lambs. He had even trained two of them to follow him wherever he walked. They were almost like playmates, butting their heads gently against his legs and bounding back and forth in front of him as though asking him to play.

He would look at them sternly and try to make his voice deep and serious like his father's. "Go away, now, little lambs. It is time for you to sleep, and I must guard the entire flock." His voice took on a slight edge of importance. "I will play tomorrow, but tonight I have work to do."

The chief shepherd watched his son as he calmed the lambs and took them to their place in the sleeping flock. He was secretly very pleased with the boy's progress. The young boy seemed to have a natural feeling for the animals and instantly understood the importance of his father's lessons.

The father's eyes were wise and kind, narrowed to a constant squint by years of standing in the sun watching over a grazing flock. His eyes missed very little, and, while he stood as still as a statue in the midnight blue of the night, still his eyes constantly moved, noting even the slightest disturbance among his sleeping charges.

Looking at his father standing swathed in his striped Levitical robe, with the shepherd's crook balancing him as he stood on one leg, the boy knew that everyone and everything within his father's view was safely, valiantly tended. *Someday,* the boy thought to himself, *I will be a shepherd just like my father. I will care for the sheep, protect them, and the whole tribe will know their wealth is safe because I am watching over the flocks.*

* * *

This particular night, however, was different. Everything had gone wrong in the house that day. The water would not boil, the children had quarreled, and the bread had burned. The boy's mother felt strangely uneasy, and she stopped the father as he stood wearily and beckoned to the boy.

"Come, lad, it's time to join the night watch."

"Nay," the mother said. "It has been a tiring day, and I wish our son to remain at home. Just this once. You do not need to make a man of him in such a hurry."

The father smiled. "Well, little mother," he said chidingly, "haven't you noticed? He already is a man in all but name. I do not know a better shepherd on the plains than your son. We would be lost without him. He does a grown man's work."

The boy felt his heart swell with joy to hear his father praise him.

"Please, Mother," he exclaimed, "I am not tired at all. Please let me go, for they will laugh at me if they think I stayed home like a little baby."

The mother sighed. She could not even explain her feelings to herself. As she walked over to kiss them good-bye, she held her son for a moment longer in her arms, and then whispered in his ear. "You are as fine a son as any mother in Israel could ever wish. Go with peace."

The father and son trudged down the winding road from the crest of the hill where the village slumbered in the gathering dark, toward the sprawling, ridge-ringed fields where the flocks were being gathered for the coming night.

The evening hours passed slowly. The men by the fireside mumbled to one another, their cloaks pulled around their hunched shoulders. The dogs skirted the flock and nipped an occasional wandering animal back into its place. The moon had set, and the night seemed darker than any the boy could ever remember.

There was an odd restlessness in the air, even though there was not a breath of wind. The cold seemed to seep into the boy's bones, and he leaned against a stone, munching on unleavened bread and wishing that he had given in to his mother's wishes, and, just this once, stayed at home in his warm little bed.

His father's watch was over, and he came down from the rise to sit beside his son.

"This fire seems to give no heat at all," the father shivered, moving a little closer to the small flames. "I don't remember it ever being this cold at this time of the year."

The boy nodded. "Dark, too," he said in an uncertain voice.

The father smiled briefly, his teeth white in his sunbrowned face. "Sleep, lad. It will be morning before you know."

With a single, swift movement, the boy lay down and pulled the woollen cloak that his mother had woven for him over his head. In an instant he felt the comforting wing of sleep begin to enfold him.

Suddenly his father sprang to his feet. Bewildered and half asleep the boy raised his head and, to his astonishment, saw the sky above the black hills begin to shine with light.

"Is it morning already?" he asked wonderingly.

"No, my son," replied his father. "I know not what it is."

All the shepherds had roused and were standing with their faces turned toward the ever-increasing light. Wonder, terror, curiosity, and awe seemed to transfix them, and they could not turn away even though their frames trembled with the desire to run.

The boy moved to stand next to his father, as though the power of his father's strong, certain body would shield him. For one moment he knew how it must feel to be a sheep—helpless, powerless, and defenseless.

In the midst of the growing light suddenly appeared a being—more brilliant, beautiful, and glorious than any person the boy had ever seen. The night was filled with the sound of wind—but the air did not move. The shepherds heard a sound like the rushing of a thousand wings, and then a voice spoke out of that terrible and glorious arc of light.

"Fear not!" The voice was so magnificent—so filled with power, love, and joy that the boy astonishingly felt the fear vanish, only to be replaced by a splendid glory and happines that swelled his heart as though it would burst.

He listened with all of his soul.

"I bring you good tidings of great joy, which shall be unto all people. For unto you is born this day in the city of David a Saviour, which is Christ the Lord. And this shall be a sign unto you; Ye shall find the babe wrapped in swaddling clothes, lying in a manger."

Before the boy could even begin to comprehend what the words meant, the air was filled with a great choir of heavenly beings, and the night was made immense by the sound of music such as he had never heard before. The music seemed to play inside of him, as though he were an instrument too, as though he were part of the song.

The light grew brighter and brighter until the boy thought they would all be consumed and the earth would simply turn into light and beauty and disappear. The child wanted that moment to last forever. He had never felt happier in his life.

However, the light soon thereafter began to fade. The singing grew softer and softer until it was but a memory. Darkness returned, seeming ten times as dark and cold, and the little campfire seemed less than the spark of a flint in contrast to the radiance that had vanished.

The shepherds were beside themselves with excitement. "What have we seen?" they asked. "What should we do?" "Whom should we tell?" "Where should we go?"

The boy's father spoke slowly, but with the surety of a prophet. "It is clear. We are meant to go to Bethlehem and see this thing that the Lord hath made known to us. And we must go with haste. Now. Or be judged unworthy servants."

In instant agreement, all of the older shepherds gathered up their belongings and immediately began to hurry toward the road to Bethlehem. The boy struggled to keep up to his father's long, purposeful strides. His heart was beating with excitement, and he scarcely knew what to think, so much had happened.

"Halt!" his father cried, raising his hand with the shepherd's crook. "What are we doing? We cannot leave our flock untended. Especially on such a cold and dark night. If the fire dies, they will wander away and be devoured and lost in the hills. Someone must stay."

A great discussion ensued. No one wanted to stay behind. "The Lord has given us this commission," one said. "Surely He will guard our sheep for us while we are gone. It is a short journey. We will return long before morning."

Another shepherd raised his gray head. "We are all old men. This is the Messiah—and he is but a newborn babe. Few of us will live to see him grown. If we do not see him now, perhaps we never will."

The boy's father listened, and gradually the men came up with the idea that the boy should stay.

"He is yet young." "He will have ample time to know the grown Messiah." "He is well versed in caring for the flock—especially when it is bedded down." "It will only be for a short time, and then one of us shall hurry back to relieve him." "He is at an age where the experience will do him good. He is ready for responsibility." Such were the arguments and reasoning that the shepherds gave for their decision.

The boy stood, looking from face to face. Part of him was flattered and pleased that the older shepherds had confidence in him. Another part of him wanted to go to his father and beg not to be left alone with such an awesome responsibility, even if it was but for a few hours. Still, the boy was too proud to disappoint or embarrass his father, and so he said nothing.

"Do you think you could do it, son?" the father asked doubtfully. His voice was full of concern and love, and his heart was torn between the desire to be obedient to the command of the angel and the wish to do what was right for his son.

"Of course I can, Father. You have been training me for this for over a year. I know what to do, and I will stay and watch the flock if that is your decision." The boy's voice was firm, but inwardly he could feel his heart trembling.

"Haste!" the shepherds cried to one another. "We are commanded to make haste!" The men pushed into a bunch and began rushing toward the village road, using their crooks as canes as they stumbled over the field in the darkness.

"We shall be back before moonrise," one of the shepherds called to the boy.

The boy's father was caught up in the foreward thrust of the men. He glanced back with concern and saw his strong, sturdy son walking toward the sleeping flock. The boy threw a log on the campfire, and the flames shot up with a satisfying, crackle of light and warmth. The father felt reassured that his boy would be all right.

＊　＊　＊

After the sound of the shepherds' voices had faded in the darkness, the boy made his way to the rock where the shepherds kept watch. Away from the fire the night was darker still. The dogs prowled restlessly, as though, once wakened, they could not return to rest.

The sheep were nervous too. He could see their forms shifting and could hear soft bleating. The edges of the neat circle of the flock were looking ragged, and his instincts questioned whether the center would hold.

The boy knew that if one of the older shepherds had been there, he would have gotten down from the rock and walked the circumference of the flock, urging the errant sheep back into formation. However, the darkness at the outer edges of the sleeping sheep seemed mysterious and full of shadows.

He found himself staring at a movement at his feet, and he jumped down from the rock, landing on an unseen branch and twisting his ankle. Pain shot through his leg, and he gasped with fear as he felt something soft and wet on his ankle. It was the nose of one of his little lambs, who had wandered away from her sleeping mother.

One of the sheepdogs came to round up the lamb. The dog bared its teeth and growled at the boy as though he were a thief.

"Shadrack," the boy whispered, "It's me. Shadrack!" He whistled softly as the men had trained him to do, but the dog continued to growl at him so he backed away as the dog nipped at the lamb's heels and headed it back toward the flock.

The boy's ankle hurt too much for him to get back up onto the rock. He moved over by the campfire and saw that it was beginning to die down. When he checked the supply of firewood, he saw that the men had not replenished it before they left. Soon there would be no flame left unless he found his way into the deep shadows of the wooded canyon and brought back some fallen branches.

Glancing into the darkness, he saw nothing but menacing shapes and barren hills. As the fire grew lower, the flock was beginning to mill in confusion. The boy was shivering in the cold, and the darkness grew more ominous with every moment.

What would the older shepherds say when they returned and found he had lost control of the flock? Perhaps even now some of the lambs were wandering into the hills.

The fire would soon be gone, and the dogs would have no clear direction in which to herd the sheep. Already the boy could not see well enough to know what commands to give—even if the dogs would obey him, which he had begun to doubt.

Would the wolves that circled the fields already have figured out that the sheep were untended? Would he, a helpless boy, be able to fend off ravenous wolves? Or would he seem just another morsel for their dinner?

But overriding all these fears was the stunning memory of the dazzling light, the music, and the heavenly beings. As glorious as that moment had been, the boy could not help fearing that the experience might come again, and he would be alone—perhaps this time to be condemned for his inadequacies.

From the hills, just as the last flame in the campfire flickered out, he heard the lone cry of a wolf. At that terrifying sound, the lad's heart turned to ice. In unreasoning terror and panic, he began to run.

Without thought, without knowledge of what he was doing, without any conscious will, he ran, limping on his swollen ankle, stumbling on stones and bushes, falling headlong, and rising to run some more. He would find his father. He would find the shepherds. He would tell them he had failed. He would tell them they must come at once. He would explain that he had to leave the flock to save the flock. But he knew they would not believe him.

He ran and ran through the ink-dark night until, at last, with harsh breaths ragged in his throat, exhausted by fear and confusion, he fell headlong on the rocky ground and cried himself to sleep.

* * *

Morning came, and the boy woke shivering with cold. His ankle was swollen and painful, but his heart was more painful by far.

"What shall I do?" he asked himself. "I have committed the greatest sin. I have left the flock untended. I was made a steward and I have failed. Failed in every way."

He thought about the faces of the shepherds. He thought about his father's face. What did they think when they returned to the empty field? Could they ever forgive him? Could his father ever forgive him? Could he ever forgive himself? He had broken the code, betrayed the sacred trust that had been given him. He had committed the unpardonable act—he had left the flock untended at the mercy of wolves.

That was the awful truth. He had had no mercy on the sheep in his care. Now the world would have no mercy for him. He was enough of a man to understand what he had done.

He stood up in hopeless despair, not knowing what to do or where to go, and then a scrap of the glorious message of the night before came into his mind.

"Fear not," the angel had said. "Peace, and goodwill to men."

"And perhaps," thought the shepherd boy, hope springing in his heart, "goodwill to boys as well! Even though I know the shepherds cannot forgive me, there is One who can forgive me! I will go and find him. He will forgive me, and then I will know what I am to do."

The shepherd boy hurried into the small city of Bethlehem. It was market day, and with all the taxpayers in town the streets were bustling and crowded.

"Please, sir," the boy asked a captain of the guard, "could you tell me where the Messiah was born so that I may go and speak to him."

The soldier gave a rough laugh and pushed the shepherd boy aside. "None of your tricks, now. I'll not have you playing jokes on authority. Run along or I'll clap you in irons."

The boy asked his question of people on the street, of men entering the synagogue, of women in the market—but everywhere he was met with impatience, anger, or scorn.

Finally it dawned on him that others had not seen the great vision that he and the shepherds had witnessed, so he left his questioning and began searching for a manger with a child in it. By late afternoon, exhausted, in pain, and aching with hunger, he stumbled down the main street of Bethlehem where all the stalls for merchants were arrayed.

His hunger became sharper as he passed booths with roasted meat on skewers, dates, oranges, grape leaves steamed with lamb, figs, and nuts. As he came to the end of the street a merchant brought from his bakeshop a wooden paddle with fresh hot bread.

When the baker ducked back into his hut to lift the second batch out of the oven, the boy, almost by reflex, seized the moment to snatch a loaf from the table. Expecting at any moment to hear cries of "Stop, thief!" he sped around the corner, running zigzag through the alleys—the pain of hunger and fear erasing momentarily the physical pain of his weakened ankle—until he was certain that no band of angry merchants or soldiers followed him. Overwhelmed at his escape, he squeezed through a hole in a wall and, finding himself in an abandoned garden, he leaned against the peeling plaster, hidden by a pomegranate tree that had grown wild, and ate the loaf of bread, tearing at it with his hands and teeth as though he himself were a hungry wolf.

When the terrible force of his hunger subsided, he felt the agony of guilt wash over him. Now he was not only a betrayer of trust but also a thief. How could such terrible things have befallen him in so short a time? For such a sinner there was surely no hope of mercy or forgiveness from the laws of man. But still . . . if he could only find the babe, the Savior, the one who was promised. There he could find forgiveness and mercy. *Once forgiven,* the shepherd boy promised himself, *I will never sin again.*

* * *

Thus began a life of tumult for the boy. He grew into a young man, and then into a grown man. His face grew strong, heavily bearded, and harsh. His body was powerful and swift, and his mind was cunning and fearless. Much of his life was lived in hiding. His friends were friends of the moment; his employers were men of dark means and darker deeds; and he, who had feared the dark so much that he had betrayed himself, now lived in the darkness.

As he grew into manhood—and even those who had known and loved him as a boy would not have recognized him—deep in his heart remained the hope of the young shepherd boy he had been.

"Even though I have sinned and sinned again," he promised himself, "when I find the child who was born that night, he will understand and forgive, and *then* I will begin again, without sin, and I will be the man I was meant to be."

He looked for the promised Messiah whenever he thought of him—less and less as the years went by—but in his mind he kept careful track of how old the child would be. Over thirty years passed.

Often when he heard of a great preacher or a special high priest, he would make his way to the town or community where the man was said to be, and, covering himself with a cloak, he would try to get close enough to observe the object of his search. Always, though, he turned away, knowing his search was not ended.

Once he heard of a man who had healed a man who could not walk. He hurried to Jerusalem, only to discover that the man had been healed on the Sabbath. "That cannot be the one for whom I seek. Surely he would not break a commandment!"

So the shepherd boy grown to a man continued his occasional and halfhearted search for forgiveness, in the meantime keeping himself alive by thievery, treachery, worldliness, and political insurrection.

As the years passed the fugitive's name was whispered in fear by honest citizens, it was circulated in infamy, and the keepers of the law searched for him in vain, eager to arrest him and put him to death.

At last, through the treachery of a man he had called friend, he was trapped, arrested, and condemned to die for his many crimes.

Sitting in the silent cell, with its stone-cold walls, he put his head in his hands and looked back over a lost life. Remorse overcame him. "Ah," he said to himself, "if the angel had never come, I would have been a happy, ordinary shepherd today. It is not my fault that mine has been a life of sin. After all, I have searched in vain all of these years to find forgiveness."

He heard the clank of metal, and a key scraped against the lock of his cell. The heavy barred door opened.

"You are free to go," the jailor growled, "although how they could let such a one as you back into the world is beyond me."

"Free!" the prisoner exclaimed. "Free? It must be a trick!"

"No!" the jailor snapped, "It is no trick. Another poor soul is to take your place. You are free to go. Go fast, before I lose my patience!"

Still completely disbelieving, the prisoner stumbled out of the cell and staggered down the corridor, at every moment expecting to be called back. But no voice called, and in a few minutes he was out on the steps of the building and racing toward the crowded streets, planning to lose himself in the crowd before anyone found out that a mistake had been made. Surely it was a mistake! How could they possibly have let him go free!

For whatever reason, he was on his way. He'd go back to his friends. Maybe they could plan some kind of a quick theft that would give him a little money to live on—and then—oh, then, if he could find the time, and stay away from the law—well, maybe then he might start looking again for he who could bring him forgiveness.

"By now," thought the thief, "he must be at least thirty-three years old. Odd that I've never heard of him. Maybe I just dreamed the whole thing. Who knows? Well, can't think of that now. All that matters is that I find a way to get some money."

The street was so crowded that the thief could not press his way through. The people were shouting and staring at something. Probably some parade or visiting royalty. Anyway, the man was used to the back streets and alleyways. He easily found his path to a quiet street and began running toward Jerusalem's city wall, away from the tumult on the other road. Beyond the gate lay freedom— or so he supposed.

All I need is a start, Barabbas, the freed prisoner, the man who had been a shepherd boy, told himself as he turned his back on the street where the crowds lined the way to watch a mighty man, with tender eyes and noble face, carry his own cross to Golgotha.

*   *   *

Foolish, foolish Barabbas! Had he but turned his eyes, had he but taken a few steps, he would have found the Savior and all the mercy and hope that he had searched for these many years. Had Barabbas but known that the one who had set him free, the one who would die for him on the cross, the one who alone could forgive his sins was as close to him as the reach of his hands.

But Barabbas turned his back on the place where the Savior stood and hurried on his way toward the world.

*   *   *

When my father finished telling us this story we would all sit transfixed with poignant sadness.

How I wanted, just once in the telling, for the shepherd boy to be brave! How I wanted

him to stop sinning and change his life. How I wanted him to turn and see the Savior, go to him, ask him for forgiveness.

After Daddy finished telling the story, I was always convinced that the story continued and that one day Barabbas did find the gospel, repented, and became a righteous shepherd once more.

JAROLDEEN ASPLUND EDWARDS was born in Alberta, Canada, and is married to Weston Eyring Edwards. She is a graduate of Brigham Young University, the mother of twelve children, a nationally published novelist and essayist, and she loves Christmas—brimful and overflowing.

THE THANKSGIVING CHRISTMAS TRIP

Elinor G. Hyde

JEREMY AWOKE EARLY. He wondered if it were too early to get up and start the milking. Today, as soon as chores were done, the Jepperson family was leaving in a pretty, rented, silver-gray minivan, almost all packed and ready for their trip to the States—rented because their car wasn't reliable enough for that distance, rented with money saved from forgoing birthday gifts all year.

Although he'd been over the Canadian border to Great Falls, this was different. This time they were traveling all the way to Salt Lake City to celebrate the American Thanksgiving with Aunt Carole and Uncle Jeff.

That was exciting, but even more important, Jeremy was looking forward to seeing all the sights he'd heard so much about in Salt Lake City yet so far seen only in pictures—the famous Tabernacle, the statue of Brigham Young, Temple Square, the mountains where the pioneer wagons entered the valley, and, well, just everything.

Perhaps because he was named for the great-grandfather who had lived in Salt Lake as a boy before his family immigrated to Alberta, Canada, or maybe because it all was a central part of their religion, but Jeremy never tired of hearing of Salt Lake and pioneer stories.

He was particularly anxious to see the Christmas lights on Temple Square.

Aunt Carole sent a video of the lights last year; to ten-year-old Jeremy's eyes, it seemed that all the stars had dropped from heaven to celebrate the birth of Jesus. Stars weren't red and blue or green, of course, as the lights were in that video, but that made it all the more exciting to think about.

It almost seemed too good to be true, especially with all the rain this year. The first crop of hay turned moldy because of that rain, good only for bedding the smaller animals instead of being made into pellets that brought good money on the international market.

The other crops weren't top quality, either, but with the whole family helping, they'd managed to get the farmwork done without hiring an extra man this year so they could save for this trip.

Even Mom drove a truck during harvest, with twelve-year-old Amy doing more than her share by preparing meals and doing most of the laundry and housework. The whole season was touch and go, but somehow they finished harvesting only hours ahead of the first hard frost.

Jeremy shuddered as he recalled those frantic hours. They'd all worked until ready to drop. Despite the intense pressure and the constant race against time and weather, however, they'd made it. He liked the challenge, but longed to be able to do a man's share to help ease the load his father carried. He knew his father already appreciated all he did.

The Jeppersons seldom celebrated the Canadian Thanksgiving on the second Monday of October because it came in the middle of harvest; this year they had chosen to wait until the American one the end of November, again saving money by not having two celebrations, one for now and one later in Utah.

Looking forward to the Salt Lake trip was enough.

Jeremy chuckled as he imagined the look on Aunt Carole's face when he brought in those giant pumpkins that had grown so big despite all the rain. They'd been good for trip money, as well. Along with his 4-H prize money for his rabbits and what he'd earned selling pumpkins, he had nearly $35 to spend. Maybe he'd save some towards a new hockey stick or maybe more pumpkin seeds for next year or—

The pumpkins. He had forgotten to return to close the doors to the root cellar when he went to get them last night. All their winter produce would be frozen!

He dressed swiftly and dashed to the outdoor underground root cellar, zipping his heavy parka as he ran, praying for a miracle that was not to be.

The big cellar doors were as wide open as he'd left them last night when he trundled out the wagon loaded with produce for their trip. It meant disaster, not only in the loss of their winter food supply, but in money that it would take to replace the ruined vegetables—money they could not afford and still take their trip in a year when every penny had to be spent with such care.

Why hadn't he made two trips instead of trying to balance it all on one wagon load? Why hadn't someone noticed the doors open? Why hadn't he felt a warning to return and close them? It wasn't fair. All summer in his prayers he'd asked that nothing spoil their trip to Salt Lake. So much for prayers. For sure his weren't answered.

Jeremy's first impulse was to quickly close the cellar doors, go straight to the barn, and get the milking machines ready, pretending he knew nothing about the situation.

No, he knew he must face the truth. He returned slowly to the house, his stomach a leadlike lump.

As he shamefacedly shared his terrible mistake, Mother quickly turned away so he wouldn't see her shocked tears. If that wasn't bad enough, his father's quiet words of rebuke stung even more.

"Son, I thought I could count on you to be responsible."

On the farm being responsible was everything.

Jeremy gulped, as his father continued, "I guess you know this means no trip."

To make matters worse, Mark Chaffey, the young man who was going to do their chores, arrived just then for last-minute instructions. Mark needed the money he'd have earned to help pay for his university classes. It was bad enough letting his family down, but now he had also hurt Mark, who was always teasing and fun, like a big brother.

Jeremy escaped to the bathroom so he wouldn't have to face him, too.

When he heard Mark's pickup driving away, he knew the trip was really off. He could no longer hold back his tears.

The other children cried just as bitterly when they were told. The trip was as important to each of them as it was to Jeremy.

"You've ruined everything," Amy yelled, running to her room, and eight-year-old Sam stuck out his tongue and shook his fist as he slammed the door and stomped off to do his chores.

It wasn't fair. Why had it rained so much all year, and where were all the blessings Dad was always talking about when they paid tithing and tried to keep the commandments while most of their neighbors seemed to have more without bothering with such things?

As he thought on all it meant to be a Latter-day Saint, he knew he had to make it right with Mark Chaffey. He took the cordless telephone to his room and quickly dialed the number for their nearby neighbors. Thank goodness, it was Mark who answered.

"Mark? This is Jeremy."

Before he could say more, the young man interrupted him.

"Hey, pal. I'm sorry about your trip. I know how much it meant to all of you. Isn't there some way you can still go?"

"'Fraid not. But—but I want to pay you some of what you'd have earned taking care of things for us," Jeremy stammered, speaking as fast as he could before his voice broke with the tears he felt just beneath the surface. "I know you've counted on it for your university tuition and stuff, and I've got $35 prize money from my 4-H rabbits and from selling my pumpkins, and I'll make up the rest when I sell my 4-H calf next fall. And Mark . . . thanks. Thanks for understanding."

He hung up and then went out to do his chores. They didn't begin to take nearly long enough. He wished he could stay outside in the cold forever, long enough at least for the ache inside to go away, for it all to be a bad dream.

The depths of the torturous evening was having to kneel with his family in prayer. Jeremy would have skipped it, but he didn't dare. He'd caused enough trouble. He bit his lip as his father prayed: "Heavenly Father, we are grateful . . . for our blessings . . . and more so, in the midst of adversity. Please help us to forgive one another our shortcomings. Help us to accept that which comes to us, to help others in their needs . . . "

Likely the prayer would have lasted longer except for an insistent knocking at the front door. Mark Chaffey, his father, and several other neighbors stood like a small army in the quickly opened door.

Mr. Chaffey spoke for them, his words cutting warmly through the chilly winter air.

"You aren't gonna change your plans, you hear? Mark told us of your misfortune, and me and Mark and the rest of us are gonna clear out that root cellar, and then fill it up again with good stuff, and you're going to leave just as you planned."

He waved his hand to shush the protest Mr. Jepperson attempted.

"You're all the time showing us what that religion of yours means to you, and helping us. Now it's time to see if you really can live it, eh? The Good Book says it is more blessed to give than to receive, and this time it's our turn to give, which means you have to receive."

"That goes for you, too, young man," he said, gesturing towards Jeremy. "Don't you worry none about Mark getting off to the university. He's got a savings account we started for him as a kid that he don't know about. That was to be part of his Christmas, anyhow. He told us how you wanted to pay him out of your 4-H prize money."

Turning again to Mr. Jepperson, he said, "Now that's character, Jepperson, raising a boy like that, willing to pay my boy for chores he wasn't even going to do. Apples don't fall far from the tree, as they say.

"I'll let Mark speak for himself in a minute, but he wants to just take care of the chores in appreciation for all you've done to help us over the years, getting him involved in Scouts and coaching his hockey team and on and on. There's not a one of us here who hasn't been on your giving end, like when I had my accident a few years ago. Who got the neighbors together to get in my crops? We all've been wanting to do something to get even—and now we can."

The other farmers nodded in agreement.

"We'll give you one hour to be out of here, and if not, we'll think of something more to make you beholden to us. We know how you'll hate that."

Jeremy held his breath. His father looked hard at his mother, and then held up his hands in mock surrender.

"Okay, but just you wait. For this you'll all have to come and hear all about our trip—see our videos of Salt Lake and the Christmas lights and our family and everything, and maybe even listen to the missionaries to boot."

Mr. Chaffey grinned slyly, then shrugged.

"Whatever you say, Matthew. Whatever you say, *providing you're out of here in that hour.*"

The first load of frozen produce from the root cellar was already dumped near the pig pen as the Jeppersons drove off down the southern Alberta graveled road. At least it wouldn't be a total loss—what the pigs didn't eat would do for compost.

The American Thanksgiving with their relatives was all Jeremy dreamed of and more. Being with his Utah cousins was worth every minute of the 800-mile drive across Montana and Idaho, but the lights and choirs on Temple Square made it all just, well, nearly like heaven.

It was the lifelike manger scene, however, that touched him most. He could almost imagine their own neighbors there, humble men paying homage to the Christ child—men who made miracles of their own with pitchforks and pickup trucks.

He could hardly wait to get home. Wouldn't

showing the videos be fun! Jeremy knew each of his family savored their experiences as much as he did. Maybe Mark and his dad would even enjoy the Tabernacle Choir CDs the whole family had all pitched in to buy. And maybe, just maybe, Mr. Chaffey meant it about listening to the missionaries. Now that would really be a Christmas to remember!

ELINOR GODFREY HYDE is the wife of Alan A. Hyde, mother of six and grandmother to seventeen. She was born in Cache County, Utah, and grew up on a small farm in Blackfoot, Idaho. She attended Brigham Young University, leaving with her MRS. degree in 1955. She's published many essays and articles in the *Deseret News, Church News, Ensign, Mormon Women Speak* (Olympus, 1982), and various other publications; poetry in *Utah Sings,* volumes 6 and 7; a novel, *Canadian Windsong* (Randall, 1987); and many historical writings, including *Twenty Five Years of Company for Dinner,* a history of the Chuck-A-Rama restaurants in Utah. She was employed part-time for seventeen years as sales/public relations representative for Fernwood Candy Company and taught Blazer Scouts for twenty years. She is a member of the National League of American Pen Women, Utah State Poetry Society, and League of Utah Writers, where she is on the Speakers Bureau. She likes to travel, read, and make bread and quilts. Elinor currently serves part time, with her husband, as a missionary in the Salt Lake Family History Library. The Hydes live in the Mt. Olympus North 5th Ward, Salt Lake City.

SILENT NIGHT

Carroll Hofeling Morris

IT IS LATE AFTERNOON on Christmas Eve day in St. Cloud, Minnesota. Paul Avery sings "Oh, Come, All Ye Faithful" with robust enthusiasm as he combs his hair. He has an unfortunate tendency to go flat. His wife, Maggie—she of perfect pitch and much sought-after vocal skills—grimaces as she clears the dishes from their early supper. It isn't just his intonation that irritates her; it is his uncomplicated joy in the season. She would like to trade her heart for his: let him feel what it's like to have a black hole beneath his rib cage, to go through the motions of celebration, hoping they will somehow turn into real feelings.

She has gone through every motion required by the season. She has done the Christmas shopping for Paul and their grown children and mailed packages to the boys and their families. (The presents for daughter JanaBeth and her husband she put under the tree; they'll be driving up from Minneapolis Christmas Day.) She addressed and mailed the Christmas cards, helped plan the ward Christmas party, sang in the ward choir, and performed several times with a chamber choir.

And she baked cookies, dozens and dozens of cookies: nut-coated thumbprints with glistening jelly centers, sugar cookies elaborately decorated with frosting and sprinkles, buttery spritz stars and wreaths, and chestnut fingers with one end dipped in milk chocolate. When she finally stopped baking, she had cookies enough to fill twenty foil-lined tins. She and Paul have spent the best part of this afternoon delivering them—some to friends and neighbors, some to Church members, and some to his colleagues in the history department at St. Cloud State University and to hers in the high school music department.

Only one tin was left undelivered. Paul suggested during supper that they present it to Erik and John Sorenson, elderly widowers living on a farm near Dassel, south of St. Cloud. She has been curious about these Sorensons. He has been talking about them for months now, and she welcomes the chance to meet them herself.

Besides, taking the cookies out to them will be as good a time-filler as anything—at least forty-five minutes drive time each way and probably another forty-five minutes talk time. The Sorenson brothers are great talkers, according to Paul, who has spent many hours with them while researching early farming practices in Meeker County.

She rinses the dishes and puts them in the dishwasher. "If you don't hurry, we won't get back for the service," she calls. She is referring to a Christmas Eve service some of her high school students will be singing in. She and Paul have never been to such a service before, but then, up until this year they have always had a family celebration to attend.

Paul comes into the kitchen now, freshly groomed and wearing aftershave that makes her think of lakes and pine trees—northern Minnesota in the summer, her favorite time of year. "We've got plenty of time," he says. "Besides, it won't be the end of the world if we miss it. I wouldn't mind spending Christmas Eve alone with you."

"We'll be alone whether or not we go to the service," she says. "For the first time since . . ."

Her voice cracks a little. "For the first time ever."

"That's not so bad, is it?"

"I miss Mom and Dad. I miss the kids."

He puts his arms around her. "JanaBeth and Curtis will be here tomorrow," he reminds her. "And the boys will call in the afternoon. They always do."

He doesn't mention her parents. They have been gone less than a year, killed in a car accident on a slick winter road, and she is still prone to tears. He hates it when she cries; it makes him feel helpless and uncomfortable. So she doesn't speak of her parents often, and she doesn't cry.

He fetches their coats from the closet and starts to put his on. She ducks into the bedroom and returns with a sack from Dayton's. "Your big present is already under the tree, but I saw this in the store the other day. I was going to wrap it tonight, but I want you to have it now."

He peeks into the sack. "A new hat!" he says, pleased. It's a driver's hat, much like the one he's worn for years now, only this time in a handsome blue-and-gray plaid. He puts it on and steps to the hall mirror. "I like it," he says after a moment's consideration. "It almost makes me look good."

She adjusts the hat slightly and kisses his smooth cheek. "You always look good to me."

The sun is very low in the sky as he shuts the kitchen door behind them. The temperature has dropped sharply from the fifteen-degree high of the afternoon, and the wind has picked up considerably. "It's going to be a cold one," Paul says as he helps her into the car.

He drives out of the city and heads south on Highway 15. The sky is royal blue at the horizon, deepening into inky blue-black over-head. It is sprinkled with stars; without the competition of city lights, they look large and low and are bright enough to make the snowy fields glow with a strange light. Not far from Dassel city limits, they turn onto a county road and shortly thereafter onto a dirt section of road. Soon they are far from the highway, passing through white fields marked now and then by a cluster of farm buildings watched over by tall silos.

"Here we are," Paul says finally. Set back from the road and bound on the north and west by a mature windbreak stands a two-story white farmhouse in good repair. The roofline of the porch is strung with colored lights, and through the big front window she can see the blinking lights of a Christmas tree.

"Aren't they awfully old to be stringing up lights?" she asks as they walk up to the front door.

"Yes. That's why they never take them down."

Their knock is answered by a stocky man with ruddy cheeks, pale blue eyes, and wispy gray hair. He wears a plaid shirt and dark work pants. "There you are, now," he says in the too-loud voice of the hearing-impaired. "It's about time you brought your wife to meet us. Come in, come in."

They step out of the cold into a Spartan living room lit by the Christmas tree and an old-fashioned floor lamp. Maggie notices there are only a few small packages underneath the tree; it seems a sadly meager lot, and she is glad they have come with the cookies.

Paul makes the introductions. "Erik, I'd like to introduce you to my wife, Maggie. Maggie, Erik Sorenson. And John," he adds as another blue-eyed, flannel-clad man, this one slightly stooped and frail looking, appears.

"Cold enough for ya?" John asks. It is the rhetorical question that passes for "hello" during Minnesota winters.

"It's nice to meet you both," Maggie says, shaking their hands. "You have a very fine-looking place."

The brothers beam with pride. "My son farms the land," says Erik. "We just take care of the house and a few pigs and chickens. Keeps us busy, ya know."

Maggie holds out the tin. "Here are the cookies we brought you."

"That's real nice of you," Erik bellows.

"You betcha," says John. "Let's go in the kitchen and have a few."

Entering the kitchen is like stepping into a time warp: the floor is of faded red and white linoleum tiles, and the appliances are right out of the 50s. John pulls a chair out from the well-used oak table and motions to Maggie to sit down. "I think I've got something here you might like," he says, and he holds out a plate covered with a shiny white mass. "Can I offer you some *lutefisk*?"

"Oh!" Embarrassed and flustered, she tries to hide her aversion to the lye-cured cod that is a Christmas delicacy among those of Scandinavian descent. "Ah, thank you, but I don't think . . ."

The Sorensons interrupt her with great gales of laughter. "It's a joke," says Erik, slapping his leg in mirth. John puts the plate away and asks, "How about some *lefse* with butter and sugar?"

"Wonderful," she says with relief.

While everyone eats, Erik and John tell Maggie stories of their growing-up years, years marked by never-ending struggle but blessed by a large family that worked, sang, and worshipped together. They tell of marriages, births, and deaths; of the August that a tornado wiped out their corn crop—the crop they had expected would pay for the big new tractor—and the hard times that followed. "But ya know, we just picked up and kept on going," says Erik. "We learned that from our parents."

When they finish their *lefse*, Paul thanks the brothers and says, "It's a bit of a drive back to St. Cloud. We'd probably better be on our way." With repeated thanks for the cookies, the Sorenson brothers escort him and Maggie to the door and send them on their way with shouts of "Merry Christmas" and "Drive careful, now."

A bitter wind catches at their coats and breaths as they dash to the car. Through chattering teeth Maggie says, "Coming here was a good idea. I'm glad you thought of it."

"How did you like the old boys?"

"They're sweet. And they seem so cheerful. Are they always like that?"

"I've never seen them any other way."

Paul turns out onto the road and begins the convoluted drive back to the highway. The car warms up nicely; Maggie leans back and closes her eyes, content to let him get them both home.

She is dozing comfortably when the car suddenly slides out of control. It throws her to one side, then tosses her forward as it flies off the road. Terror floods her and she thinks, *I'm going to die*. She sees her parents the instant before the car lands nose-down in the snowy barrow pit, flinging her head against the dashboard. The motor stops with a clunk.

For a moment there is nothing but stunned silence. She pushes herself upright and feels her head where it hit. Her fingers come away wet. A sob escapes.

"Maggie! Are you all right?" Paul asks.

"I think so," she says, but her voice is unsteady. "It's just my head."

"Let me see." He wipes her forehead with a tissue. "It's not too bad. I don't even think you'll need a stitch. "

"What about you?"

"I hit the steering wheel pretty hard, but I'm in one piece." He winces as he touches his breastbone. "At least, I think I am."

"What happened?"

"I hit a patch of ice. There wasn't anything I could do." He swears, smacking the steering wheel as punctuation. "You stay put. I'll go see how bad it is."

She tries to say okay, but what comes out is a cry followed by huge gulping sobs that shake her whole body.

"What's wrong?" He turns her toward him so he can look at her face. "Is there something else? Tell me!"

She can only shake her head.

Paul unbuckles his seat belt so he can put his arms around her. He holds her, giving her little pats on the back. After a while, he says, "This isn't helping anything. You'll give yourself a headache, is all."

Still she sobs. They are horrible sounds, even to her ears, and she wants to stop crying for him, but she can't.

Now he gives her shoulder a little shake. "Come on, Maggie! We're both okay, thank the Lord. There's nothing to cry about."

"I . . . have . . . to cry," she manages.

"Why? It's a stupid mess, but it's fixable. No use crying over spilt milk."

"It's not . . . fixable," she gasps between sobs.

"What do you mean?" For the first time there is fear in his voice. He needs her to answer; she wants to answer, but she can't.

Her tears are old tears, born of a grief as old as womankind. Grief for the loss of her little children with their bright eyes, sweet-smelling bodies, and tender, trusting hearts. Grief for the loss of parents who loved her no matter what, whose very presence on the earth was part of her self-definition.

Paul would think it silly that she misses the little ones that her children once were as much as she misses their adult companionship, now reduced in the case of the boys to a visit or two a year. He would think it a lack of faith that she aches for her parents, that loneliness is her constant companion, that meaning has been reduced to empty busy-ness. He wouldn't understand what courage it has taken for her to keep on going as Christmas approached, with its artificially orchestrated anticipation and its impossible burden of expectation. Even now, she hasn't meant to let go the tight grip she has had on her grief, but shock and the fear of death have dissolved all restraint.

Paul shakes her again, this time with gentle insistence. "Maggie, stop it," he says. "You're going to make yourself sick if you keep on like this." And later: "How can I help you if I don't know what's going on?"

She catches these words and almost chokes with bitter laughter. It breaks the cycle, and, after several shuddering breaths, she finds she can speak. "You don't really want to know."

"Yes, I do."

"No, you don't." She takes the tissue he offers and wipes her cheeks and nose. "Be honest with yourself. You never want to talk about how I feel, and you hate it when I cry. You're only here now because we're stuck."

"I'm here now because I want to be with you. Otherwise, I'd be out there trying to figure out how to get us out of this mess."

"Nice sentiment," she murmurs into the tissue.

"Don't you know I love you?"

"Do you really! Let's see: you love me when I'm happy. You love me when I don't rock the boat—"

"That's not true."

"Do you love me now?" She faces him, dried blood on her forehead, eyes puffed, and nose raw. "This is me," she says, jabbing her index finger into her breastbone. "Those tears you hate so much, they're me. The grief is me. The fact I don't know who I am anymore, that's me."

"I had no idea you were feeling like this," he says, his voice thick with emotion. He holds up a hand to forestall her rebuttal. "You're right. I didn't want to know. I can't stand it when you're in pain, because there's nothing I can do. I can't make it better."

"I'm not asking you to make it better. I just need you to care enough about me to be with me, no matter what. How can you say you love me if you aren't willing to take me the way I am—anger and pain and everything else?"

"Oh, Maggie."

"My whole life has changed, don't you understand that? I can't go back, but I don't know how to go forward. I don't feel anything except this huge empty loneliness."

"How can you feel lonely?" he asks. "There are people all around who care about you. All your music students. Your seminary students. Everyone at church. Those women friends of yours."

"But they're not family. It's family that's most important to me," she says, tears starting afresh. "Don't you ever miss the kids? And your own parents?"

"Sure, but it was time for the kids to get out on their own, and I knew when I accepted the teaching job here that I'd be two time zones away from my parents."

"So you manage by saying, That's just the way things are?"

"Pretty much," he says, nodding. "I guess that's why I like the old Sorenson boys. We have the same approach to life. The most important thing is to get out of bed every morning. The next is to find something to smile about."

"Are you telling me that you don't feel lonely or sad? Ever?"

"Of course I do, only I don't spend a lot of time thinking about it."

She regards him as if he were a stranger. "I don't understand you at all."

"Well, that makes two of us, because I don't understand you, either."

They stare at each other for a painfully long moment, then he pulls her awkwardly against his chest. "I may not understand you, but I love you. I'm sorry I haven't seen what's been going on with you. From now on, I'll listen to whatever you need to say. Honest, I will."

"I can cry when I need to?" When he doesn't immediately reply, she adds, "Forget it. That's asking too much."

"Cry all you want, only . . ."

"What?"

"Tell me if you want me to hold you, or if I'm just supposed to let you have at it."

She laughs softly. "Fair enough," she says, relaxing against him.

He gives her a squeeze. "Are you okay, now?" When she nods, he says, "Then I guess it's time for me to check out the damage."

With much pushing and mumbling under his breath, he manages to get his door open. She watches as he makes his way to the front of the car where he stands, considering, then slogs his way through the snow around the car. A few minutes later, he climbs back inside. Shaking with cold, he puts his gloved hands over his face and breathes into them to warm his cheeks and nose.

"Quick, start the car," she says. "We have to get you warmed up." To their relief, the motor starts easily. Before long, it is pumping warm air through the vents.

"It's not good," he says when he has stopped shaking. "The back wheels are in the air. There's no way we can get out of this mess by ourselves. I'll have to walk for help."

"You can't do that. You were only out there a few minutes, and look at how cold you are. Your ears are flaming red."

"That's my fault. I didn't put my earflaps down." He takes off his new hat and turns it over. "There aren't any," he says, unbelieving.

"I didn't even look to see if it had them," she says in dismay. "I liked the color of the plaid, so I bought it."

"Hey, no big deal," he says. "If you'll lend me your muffler, I'll tie it over my ears, put on my hat and be on my way."

"No! The first rule for situations like this is to stay with your car. You know that as well as I do."

"Maybe it's not as cold as you think." He turns on the radio and they listen to carols on WCCO until the local news at 6:55. "It's a cold Christmas Eve in the Twin Cities," the announcer says, "ten below zero on the thermometer with winds of twenty-five gusting to thirty-five. That adds up to a dangerous windchill, folks: thirty-five to sixty-five below zero. Unprotected skin will freeze in seconds in temperatures like that. It's even colder outside the metro area. So bundle up if you're on the way to church or a family party—*and drive carefully!*"

Paul turns off the radio. "Looks like we're going to be here for a while," he says. "But don't worry. Someone will come this way, sooner or later."

But Maggie is thinking of the great grid of section roads that crosses this sea of snowy fields. "I hope you're right," she says. "There must be a dozen different ways to get anywhere you want to go."

An hour later, they are still waiting. They have started the car twice more, but once it is turned off, the heat dissipates far too quickly. They are both shivering, and Maggie's toes are burning with cold again. "Can we have a little more heat?" she asks.

"We'd be in real trouble if I hadn't filled her up this afternoon," Paul says as he turns the motor on. "It's the first thing your dad taught me about winter driving in Minnesota: always drive off the top of the gas tank." Paul pauses, then adds, "He was a good man, Maggie. I miss him, too. I miss both of them."

"Thank you for saying that," she says softly. Later she says, "If we were at Mom and Dad's, we'd probably be reading the Christmas story from Luke about now."

Paul straightens up and intones, "And it came to pass that in the days of Caesar Augustus, all the world was sent to be taxed, every man into his own city."

"How much more of it can you remember?"

"Probably most of it, but not word for word." He clears his throat and starts from where he left off. Maggie fills in the gaps, and between them, they tell the story to its end.

"Now that we've done the Christmas story, it's time to sing carols," Paul says. He delivers a verse of "Joy to the World" in his energetic fashion. She has listened rather than joining in, so he insists that she sing a verse of another carol, solo.

Maggie knows he is trying to distract her from their situation, and she gratefully goes along, singing "I Heard the Bells on Christmas Day" in her rich soprano. He follows with "While Shepherds Watched Their Flocks." The edge of competition keeps them going for some time, through sacred songs and into the secular. He wins by topping her "We Need a Little Christmas" with "Chipmunk Christmas," which he sings in a funny high-pitched voice.

"I give up," she says, laughing.

"If I remember correctly, the next item of business is food," he says.

"I guess we're just going to have to use our imagination for that."

"Hey, don't we have one of those Cub Scout survival kits in the trunk?" Paul asks. He dashes to the back of the car, opens the trunk, and returns with a plastic Blue Bunny ice cream pail. He opens it and hands her a Hershey bar with almonds. She tears off the wrapper. Instead of being rich brown and glossy, the surface of the candy bar is dull with a whitish tinge.

"How old is this?" she asks.

"We've had the kit for half a dozen years, I'd say."

She hands the candy bar back to him. "I'll bet it's melted and solidified and frozen a kazillion times."

"At least that," he says. "Here's something you won't turn down." He has found two packets of Swiss Miss chocolate mix with marshmallows. He sets up the soup-can stove from the survival kit with a tea light underneath and has her scoop up some clean snow in the sec-ond can. Then he lights the small candle, and they watch as it glows and flickers, slowly melting the snow. It takes that long again to heat up the resulting water. When it's ready, she adds the hot chocolate mix, stirs it with a plastic spoon, and divides it between two paper cups.

"Merry Christmas," he says.

"Merry Christmas to you, too." The hot chocolate is delicious, and it feels wonderful to have something warm in her stomach, but she can't help but think of her mother's dining room table laden with holiday favorites: popcorn balls, fudge, fancy cookies, and the silver punch bowl full of some frothy concoction. What comfort there was in the sameness of that holiday ritual, what blessing in the presence of those who loved and understood her!

"Remember how thrilled I was when you got the teaching job in St. Cloud? Coming here meant we would be living near my mom and dad. All these years, I always thought we were the ones who benefited most from that. We had someone to call when we needed advice. Someone who fixed our favorite meal on birthdays. Someone to celebrate holidays with." She pauses, then says, "I've only just now realized that my parents got the benefit, too. We had them, but they had us."

"True," he says. "They never had to celebrate a Christmas alone."

"That's what I've been dreading for months now. Spending Christmas Eve alone."

"We didn't have to spend it alone. You could have asked someone at church."

"I tried. I mean, I sounded out a few people, but nobody invited us to come over. They probably thought JanaBeth and Curtis were driving up Christmas Eve."

"You could have told them they weren't."

"I didn't want to spend Christmas Eve with

someone, knowing we'd been asked out of pity."

"This is better?"

She laughs and cries at the same time, but her tears are no longer bitter. She feels the darkness begin to lift; in its place comes something as light and sweet and full of promise as the first warm breeze of spring.

His arms tighten around her. "I love you," he says, kissing the top of her scarved head. She bends her head to kiss his gloved hand. "I love you too." Their bodies soften into each other and their mingled breaths thicken the layer of frost on the windows.

* * *

They are asleep when a car roars by, so fast that before they can react all they can see are fading taillights.

"One of us is going to have to stay awake," Paul says grimly. "We can't let that happen again."

"What time is it," she asks.

"Past midnight. I thought for sure we would have been picked up hours ago." His face is grave. "It's getting dangerous, now."

"Paul," she says with quiet intensity. "I can't feel my toes."

"We've got less than a quarter of a tank left," he says, but he turns on the motor. "There's got to be something we can do to help keep ourselves warm."

"The plastic garbage sacks," she cries. He turns on the dome light so she can see to get the bags from the survival kit. "I think we're supposed to use them like sleeping bags," she says. "They'll help hold in the heat."

"Is there anything else?"

She holds up a little box. "Supposedly there's a thermal blanket in this," she says, handing it to him.

They pull the garbage sacks up over their feet and wrap the thin metallic-looking thermal blanket around their shoulders and up over their heads. Maggie's toes wake up burning, but it's a good sign: better than numbness. Paul blesses her in the name of the Child born on this night. Together, they pray for their safety, for others out in the bitter cold, for their children, for peace in the world.

Despite the fact that they have promised each other that they would stay awake, their new cocoons hold in the heat, and, comforted, they fall asleep again. They have been asleep a long time when they are awakened by glaring headlights piercing through the frosted windows. A voice yells, "Is anyone in there?"

"Paul, wake up!" Maggie cries, pulling the thermal blanket off her head. Paul fumbles at the window, then gives up and shoves the door open with feet still in the garbage sack. "Can you give us some help?" he calls.

Exclamations echo in the still, brittle air. Then the face of a worried young man appears. Before Maggie knows what's happening, he helps her out of the car and up into the front seat of a pickup truck with oversized tires. A young woman reaches out for her with a warm lap robe.

"Are you okay?" she asks anxiously.

Maggie nods. "Thanks to you, we will be. I'm Maggie."

"My name's Erin. That's my husband, Chad. How long you been stuck?"

Maggie checks the clock on the dashboard and calculates. "Almost nine hours."

"Nine hours! How awful."

"Thank heavens you stopped. Only one

other car has come this way, and it didn't even slow down," says Maggie.

"If I ever find out who that was, I'll give 'em what for," Erin says.

Chad climbs back into the truck. "Can you help us?" Maggie asks.

"Piece of cake," he says, maneuvering the truck around behind their car. "That little car of yours is nothing but plastic. Won't hardly have to rev my engine to pull you out."

It takes a while to get the cars chained together, but Chad is right. Their car offers only slight resistance before bouncing back up on the road. Erin gives a little shriek of delight, and she and Maggie hug each other. The men unhook the cars, and Chad empties his two-gallon gas can into their almost-empty tank. Finally they are ready to go. Chad helps Maggie out of the truck, saying, "You'll be all right now. The front is mashed in some, but the headlights are working."

"Thank you so much," she says. "I don't know what would have happened if you hadn't stopped." Paul shakes his hand and says, "Are you sure we can't give you something for your trouble?"

"No way," says Chad. "It's Christmas."

❈   ❈   ❈

It is 4:45 Christmas morning when Paul unlocks the back door; with an overwhelming sense of gratitude, Maggie walks into the warm kitchen they left almost exactly twelve hours before.

"Give me your coat and take off your boots," Paul says. "I want to take a look at those toes of yours." He squats down beside her and examines her bare toes one at a time. "They look fine," he says.

"They feel fine, too." she says. "And you?"

"I'm tough," he says with a grin. "Nothing bothers me."

Tears tremble in the corners of her eyes. "It's a miracle that we're here and that we're all right."

"Thank God." He pulls her to him for a quick, hard hug. Then he goes to hang up their coats. When he comes back for his hats, both of which are now lying on the kitchen table, she says, "I suppose you'll go back to wearing your old hat."

"I don't know. I think I like the new one."

Bone tired, she sits at the table, her head propped in her hands. "Yesterday, I couldn't wait for the kids to get here," she says. "Now, the last thing I want to think about is getting Christmas dinner on the table."

"It's a good thing you did all that cooking beforehand," he says.

She nods. Cranberry Jell-O and a yam-marshmallow casserole are in the refrigerator, and two pumpkin pies sit on the counter. But there is still the turkey to be cooked.

"What do you think about putting in the bird now?" she asks him. "I can set the oven a little lower than usual, and then we can sleep as long as we want to."

So they do what they have been doing Christmas mornings for almost thirty years. She puts water on to boil for the stuffing. He chops onions and celery in the Cuisinart. She sautés them and combines them with the moistened stuffing mix, while he takes the turkey out of its plastic bag and rinses it. He holds it just so to make it easy for her to insert the stuffing. Then he puts the turkey in the roaster, and she holds the oven door open while he slides the roaster in.

Finally, exhausted by cold and worry and

fitful sleep, they fall into bed. They lie pressed together spoon-style for warmth, his arm around her waist. Her still-cold feet touch his legs. She pulls them back quickly, but he says, "That's okay, you can warm them up on me."

"Thank you," she says. Awhile later, she murmurs, "This is nice."

"Um-hmm," he replies.

"JanaBeth will have a fit when she hears what happened."

"No doubt," he says, yawning. "But you know what? I'll tell her it was one of the best Christmas Eves I've ever had."

She smiles, deeply contented. She knows exactly what he means.

CARROLL HOFELING MORRIS is a copywriter and the author of several works of fiction and nonfiction. Carroll and her husband, Gary, are the parents of four children.

ANGEL

Emily Watts

WHY ME?"
It wasn't a question I usually asked the bishop, but I was so stunned that it just kind of popped out.

Bishop Williams chuckled. "We realized you hadn't had a chance to head up this little effort before," he said. "We thought you'd be a natural, especially with the music. Is there a problem?"

"Oh, no," I said. *Oh, yes,* I thought. But the problem, I realized, wasn't really the prospect of directing fifty-plus small children in a sacred event at the busiest season of the year. The problem wasn't the idea of following in the footsteps of the artistic, clever, committed women who generally put the Nativity play together for the annual ward Christmas party. The problem was Barney.

Barney Trulson was a sweet-faced little six-year-old with the smile of an angel and the manners of a gorilla. To the surprise of his parents, LuRene and Bud, who had been told they would never conceive a child, he showed up as a plus sign on the home pregnancy test kit just a couple of months shy of LuRene's fortieth birthday. It cost her a good chunk of her health to get him into the world, and once he was here she didn't seem to quite know what to do with him.

The moment he was able to walk, Barney was off at a dead run. Hardly a Sunday went by from the time he was a year old that Bud didn't have to chase him up the aisle in sacrament meeting. The year I played the organ, his favorite game was to run up one side of the chapel, cut across through the choir seats, and crawl down onto the organ pedals. I finally had to get my daughter Gloria to sit on the stand with me and run interference. Bud just wasn't fast enough.

Once I succumbed to a generous impulse and agreed to substitute two weeks for Barney's Primary teacher. The first week, I wore a dress with a black vinyl belt, the kind that doesn't have any holes but just threads through the buckle. I'm a tall woman, and when I hunched myself down into one of those little Primary chairs, the belt popped open. "Uh-oh," shouted Barney. "Better skinny up!" He grabbed the belt and swung it in a circle over his head like a lariat. When I reached for him, he hurled it to the front of the room. While I was retrieving and rebuckling my belt, he spit on my chair. This was all in the first five minutes. I played sick and made Gloria teach the class the second week.

Barney's behavior at the ward Christmas parties was legendary. When he was three years old, the woman directing the play convinced his parents that he was really too young to be in it. Barney consoled himself by unwrapping all the blocks that the Young Women had covered in Christmas paper for the centerpieces. Later he blew Santa's cover by shouting, "Hey, you're Jeffrey's dad!"—a fact that had escaped Jeffrey himself until that moment. He ate half of the candy cane "Santa" had hurriedly pushed into his hand, then smeared the other half all over his face and hands and Bishop Williams's slacks.

The year Barney was four, the director of the Nativity play was a costume designer for a local theater company. She whipped up a pile of little animal bonnets—donkeys, lambs, cows—and the children portrayed the friendly beasts in the stable on the night of Christ's birth. Not exactly scriptural, but cute as all get-out. Barney the lamb baaa-ed plaintively through the whole performance, sending the other children into uncontrollable giggling fits. The solemnity of the occasion was, to say the least, somewhat marred. At least they hadn't made him a donkey.

The next year, the woman in charge cut out and hand glittered large posterboard stars with holes in them for the children's faces to fit through. Barney missed being in the play because he was backstage picking off and eating every last speck of glitter from his star. LuRene just shrugged when they told her. "Doctor says anything smaller than a nickel will go right through him," she said. "And Sister Smoot used nontoxic glue."

What might Barney do this year, now that the Christmas challenge was mine? Beyond that worry, what would *I* do? I had little emotional energy and even less homemaking skill. Animal bonnets and glittered stars were way out of my reach. I obsessed, worried, prayed—and it finally came to me. The solution was relatively simple, in fact: All the extra girls would be angels, and the boys shepherds. Let the parents worry about the costumes. And if I slipped Barney into the back with a towel draped around his head, how much damage could he do, really? A few sweet Primary songs, a few verses from the Bible, and we'd call it good.

No sweat.

That Sunday I joined the Primary at the request of the chorister to help the children learn one of the songs I had specified for the program. She thought that hearing it sung as a solo would help them grasp the spirit of the piece more quickly. I had run through it a couple of times with the pianist on Saturday, and was kind of looking forward to sharing it with the children. It was one of my favorites, both musically and poetically.

"Boys and girls," the chorister said in that hearty voice all Primary leaders use to project above the post-sacrament-meeting din, "we have a *special* guest with us in our Primary today. Sister Blair is going to be our *special* helper this year for the Christmas play, and she's here to sing us a song and help us learn it *especially* well for our moms and dads. So please sit straight up in your chairs with your feet on the floor and use your *special* listening ears. Sister Blair?"

I stepped forward and surveyed the room. On the back row, several eleven-year-old boys were holding a contest to see who could tip his chair back the farthest on two legs without falling. Across the aisle, a trio of girls were leaning over a piece of paper, shaking with suppressed giggles. Younger children were slapping, poking, kicking, and making faces at each other. Here and there an earnest-faced child was sitting up stiffly, arms determinedly folded, a small island of reverence in the storm. It was grim—but it could have been worse. Barney was inexplicably, miraculously, blessedly absent.

Nodding at the pianist, I quavered into the first line of the song: "Stars were gleaming, shepherds dreaming, and the night was dark and chill." A few children looked my way to see what was going on. The girls in the back quickly ditched their paper and assumed angelic expressions. "Angels' story rang with glory; shepherds heard it on the hill," I went on, a little more bravely. The littler children stopping mauling each other. Even the bigger boys' chairs thumped down. I was rejoicing inwardly, reflecting on the power of music, as I came to my favorite part. "Ah, that singing, Hear it ringing," I sang. Outside the door, a strange noise vibrated in the hall. "Earthward winging," I sang, and the door opened a crack, unmuffling the noise to reveal it as a coyotelike howl. "Christmas bringing!" The howl swooped up and down the scale. The older boys guffawed; the girls and younger kids giggled. The chorister leaped for the door. "Hearken! We can hear it still!" I finished stoically. "Aaaaaoooooow," wailed Barney as the chorister hauled him into the room. She clamped her hand over his mouth and pleaded, "Boys and girls! Boys and girls!"

This woman clearly had had some experience with Barney. Locked in a death-grip against her bosom, he gave up struggling after only a few seconds. When she was sure he was ready to behave, she released him from the embrace and led him to a chair, steering him firmly with hands on both his shoulders. She pushed him—perhaps just a shade too vigorously—into a sitting position, smoothed her hair back into place, plastered on a smile, and came back to the front of the room.

"Wasn't that a beautiful song, boys and girls," she said. "Now Sister Blair is going to explain to you about your parts in the play." I did so. The response was one of quiet resignation, except from Barney.

"I wanna be an angel. My dad says lots of angels are boys. Angel Moroni was a boy."

Well, why not? Surely he couldn't do any more harm as an angel than as a shepherd. "Okay, Barney, you're an angel," I agreed.

"Yes!" he shouted. "I'm an angel! I'm gonna have wings this big!" He stretched his arms out as wide as they would go. "I'm gonna fly all over the whole gym!"

"Now, Barney," I rushed in, "you know that

angels really don't have wings. Angel Moroni doesn't have wings, does he?"

"Michael does. I saw it on the commercial for the movie," he insisted.

Thanks, Hollywood, I grumbled in my mind. Then, in a flash of inspiration, I suggested, "Why don't you ask your dad about it?" Bud Trulson was a stickler for doctrinal accuracy. It was his kid; let this be his battle.

The next few weeks were a blur of phone calls: Did I know anyone who had a boy's bathrobe? What did myrrh look like, exactly? Did the halo have to be above the child's head, or could tinsel just be pinned in her hair? Could a shepherd use a walking stick instead of a curved staff? Was Mary supposed to provide her own baby Jesus? By the time performance week arrived, I had become the acknowledged expert at the physical details of the Nativity. I could have stepped in for Cecil B. DeMille if he'd wanted to do a sequel to *The Ten Commandments.*

About half the calls were from LuRene Trulson.

"Barney says you told him he could have wings." This was an outright lie, and I think LuRene really knew it, but she had to try.

"Barney doesn't want to be the only boy angel. He wants you to assign some of the other boys to be angels too." I sympathized but told her I didn't think it was fair to make the other boys change.

"Barney wants to be a wise man instead." I refused—Barney had chosen his own role, and I thought he should be held accountable for his choice. Besides, the wise men's parts had already been assigned.

"Barney wants to bring his uncle's bugle to help him look more like Angel Moroni." A polite but nonnegotiable no.

We enjoyed these little interchanges right up to the Saturday-morning dress rehearsal, at which Barney arrived brandishing a glowing, three-foot-long, Star Wars light-saber.

"My dad says angels don't have wings," he informed me loftily, "but he said sometimes they carry a flaming sword."

"Now, Barney," I began.

"Prob'ly not on Christmas, though," he continued without missing a beat. "He says I gotta leave it home tonight. But Mom said I could bring it just for the practice today." Picturing the scene at the Trulson home, I decided that had been a reasonable compromise.

"All right, Barney," I said, ducking as he sliced through the air in front of him. "But if you so much as touch one of the other children with that, I'll have to take it away from you. Do you understand?"

He was all angel, wide blue eyes shining with the earnestness of his assent.

And he didn't actually touch anyone with the sword. He waved it within an inch of several faces. He knocked over a cup of punch with it. He lifted up the bottom of the Primary president's dress with it—only a few inches, thank goodness, before she whirled around and slapped it away. He backed into the newly decorated Christmas tree, too absorbed in an imaginary fencing bout to watch where he was going. But he was true to his word. And he knew all the words to all the songs and sang them out loudly, enthusiastically, beating time with his sword.

I was exhausted, emotionally and physically, by the end of the practice. By the time I had waved the last little cherub out the door, I was ready to collapse, which I did as soon as I got home to my bed. I fell into a deep and troubled sleep, in which angel choirs were singing and coyotes were howling in the background. Then the dream changed, and the angels were doing battle with demons, and in the front of the heavenly host was Barney, wielding his shining sword and urging the legions on. His eyes blazed with fierce joy, and he sang loudly as he slashed forward, fighting for the Good. And the darkness receded before his onslaught.

I woke up weeping.

That night, things didn't run exactly smoothly. "Mary" opted to bring a live baby Jesus who rolled out of the manger onto the floor of the stage and screamed until his mother bundled him away. The first wise man presented his gift of gold in a child's cash register that rang, "ka-ching!" as the drawer shot out. One of the shepherds lost the towel from his head and got shoved over when he stopped to pick it up. But the music was wonderful, and when Barney sang louder than the rest of the angels combined: "Ah, that singing! Hear it ringing, Earthward winging, Christmas bringing!" I wept for the second time that day.

He was a perfect angel after all.

EMILY WATTS is an associate editor at Deseret Book Company. She sings with the Utah Symphony Chorus, the audiences for which are never as harsh as a group of Primary children. She and her husband, Larry, live in Salt Lake City with their five angelic children.

FATHER CHRISTMAS

Arlen L. Card

BISHOP DON TREMAINE stood up from his prayer with Sister Jan Boothe. His throat was feeling a little tight. Jan Boothe's eyes ran with tears. She gave him a brave smile and said, "Thank you, Bishop. I won't disappoint you again."

"You haven't disappointed me, Sister Boothe," he replied. "This is what I'm here for. If things get difficult, don't hesitate to call."

He stepped out from behind his desk and shook her hand as he saw her to the door of his office. He could tell from her face and the way she carried herself that she was encouraged. They both knew there was much struggle left to come, but it was good to see hope back in her eyes. The atonement was such a precious thing.

When she had gone he closed the door, sighed, and settled into his chair. Then Bishop Tremaine removed a list from his battered book bag and studied it. Here were his unfortunates, his casualties, his grieving, and his wayward. Early in his tenure as bishop he'd learned how overwhelming this aspect of his mantle could be—at least if he tried to address these issues by himself. Counselors could help, but there were things he couldn't tell even them.

So he knelt again, and gave his burden to God. His prayer lasted almost half an hour, and as he arose his knees punished him for it. He grimaced and took his seat.

Following long habit, he settled into thoughts of those for whom he had just prayed, so the Lord could instruct him. One by one, as individuals, he considered each soul, each solution, each strategy. As he did so, familiar feelings of peace ratified some ideas, while others were replaced by entirely new ideas, accompanied by similar whisperings. In this way, many solutions for his Saints' problems were resolved. In fact, he was sure he'd been guided to some extent in behalf of each soul on his list.

Except for Jan Boothe.

Bishop Tremaine sighed wearily. Jan was most of the way through an illegitimate pregnancy. Only twenty-three now, Jan admitted freely that she had married too young, at a time when she was incapable of telling love from infatuation. Now she had three kids and a failed marriage, but it seemed she was still incapable of telling a good man from a predator. Seven-and-a-half months along, with birth-weight complications recently diagnosed, her doctor had ordered her to bed for eighteen hours out of every twenty-four. Therefore, effective two weeks earlier, she had found herself jobless and on ward welfare. She was humiliated. Sometimes it seemed unfair that such a sensitive, and basically good, young lady should be cursed with such bad judgment. Maybe she'd finally learned to say "no."

Maybe.

In the meantime, though, she hadn't said much about it. He knew she was agonizing over her lovely little six-year-old girl and four-year-old twin boys, all from her failed marriage, because she had no way to provide them a Christmas. And Christmas was only four days away, on Saturday. She hadn't asked for any Sub-for-Santa help. She was simply sharing the weight she bore with possibly the only man on the planet she felt she could trust. If the ward provided for her little ones' Christmas, he knew she would be at once relieved and mortified.

But there lay his dilemma: Should he come to the rescue and risk more humiliation for poor Sister Boothe, or let her try to work it out for herself and risk leaving her heartsick with disappointed children?

And tonight, the Spirit had spoken nothing of a solution.

Bishop Tremaine stood, winced at the cacophony of squeaks and creaks that the aging Bishop's Chair gave forth, and carefully slipped note pads and binders into his misshapen canvas book bag. Then he shut off his lights, locked his office door, and started home. As he walked out to his car, he thanked his lucky stars—no; he thanked his God—that he was successfully self-employed in a business that allowed flexible hours.

As he passed through the glass doors to the lonely parking lot, he thought of Jan Boothe and her fatherless children. Why did the Lord seem to be holding back on this one? He'd been praying for Sister Boothe for three weeks solid, and had included her family's needs in his fast, but no feelings, ideas, or intuition had come to direct or reassure him. *What have I missed here?*

As he started the engine on his four-year-old Camry, habit kicked in, and an unconscious checklist of events turned him back into Don Tremaine, ordinary human. Book bag wedged in front of passenger seat. Ignition. Pat Metheny tape into Alpine deck. Seat belt. Head back. Eyes closed. Drink in a few seconds of "First Circle." Thoughts turn to Debbie and the kids. Their images soothe and draw him. Eyes open. Reverse. Turn wheel. Forward. Sing along with Pat Metheny's band. Before he knew it, he'd pulled into his own driveway.

A tired Don Tremaine entered his kitchen and felt heaps of granite fall from his shoulders as Debbie arose from her chair with a beatific smile, set down her scissors, and embraced him.

* * *

On Wednesday it snowed as if another little ice age were commencing in earnest, and Don arose late to the instant realization that it was up to the high priests and elders to see to it that old Jed Kitchen, the Fosters, and the single sisters throughout the ward had passable driveways. School was still in session for the young men, so there would be no Aaronic Priesthood quorums to help.

Dodging between family members bustling to get on with another day, Don made quick work of breakfast, tossed on some coveralls, Sorrels, and a parka, and started out to do Jed's yard, since he lived just next door. On his way out, he had to play peacemaker for two different quarrels, one over bathroom rights, and the other over who got the Ding Dongs.

Finally, he made it out the door and grabbed his shovel. First, he had to clear a narrow walkway for his own family. The night had collected six inches of snow, but it was the powdery stuff that doesn't weigh anything, so the job took only five minutes.

Once at Jed's house, Don went straight to the top so he could work his way down to the street. He let his thoughts linger on Sister Boothe's situation, hoping that would open the door for the Spirit to counsel him. Long minutes passed with nothing but his same old round of thoughts and guesses. He knew God loved Sister Boothe; that was never in question. Don just couldn't understand why there was

such divine silence. Three houses away, around the corner, he could hear Gary Charnel's yard tractor growling good-naturedly as it moved snow with ease. Gary, he knew, would stop each plow swath within two inches of his property line and would go no further. Definitely, it was time to reactivate Brother Charnel.

The depressing thing about shoveling snow before it's stopped, thought Don, *is that by the time you get to the end of the double-wide driveway, the top of it doesn't even remember you were there.* Sure enough. A punishing twenty minutes later Don finished the bottom of Jed's drive only to turn around and see his work largely filled in. *Kind of like a bishop's work with troubled ward members—help fix one crisis, and as soon as you're done, you're faced with another.* Oh, well. He could always come back and shovel again later. He hurried home to join in family prayer before the kids left for school.

No sooner had they said amen than the phone rang. Don strode over and answered, "Good morning, this is Don Tremaine."

The brief pause was exactly the right length—Don knew instantly that it was a ward member in trouble. *Please, don't let it be morality again.*

"Bishop?" It was Jan Boothe, voice tremulous.

Bishop Tremaine answered, "What can I do for you, Sister Boothe?"

In response he heard the suppressed sounds of someone crying who didn't want to be doing it. "I'm sorry," she said, finally. "It's just that . . . the kids saw toy commercials this morning . . . you know . . . those new Disney things, and . . . started talking about which ones they were likely to get. Oh, Bishop, it just kills me to ask for it again, but I need your help. I can't let my kids wake up Christmas morning to nothing . . ." Muted snuffling sounds resumed. Bishop Tremaine had heard lots of fake tears and lots of real tears, and he knew these to be real. Jan Boothe wasn't freeloading; she was desperate.

"Don't you worry, Sister Boothe. We'll take care of you and your children. Let me change phones and I'll get some information from you so we can proceed." The Bishop set down the phone and turned to make his way into his studio.

"Jill, honey, could you hang this up for me when I holler?"

His lovely teenage daughter, just putting on her coat, indicated with a preoccupied smile that she would. At the sight of her, he thought, *How in the world did this magnificent creature erupt from my sorry genes?* He gave her shoulder a squeeze on the way past and hurried up the back steps into the room over the garage, all the way hoping that he could finish on the phone in time to see the rest of his kids off to school. *I'm five for five on incredible children,* he thought. *This really is a day of miracles.*

Shuffling aside a chaotic stack of half-used music paper—a project in progress—he picked up the receiver, covered it, and shouted, "Okay, Jill!"

"All right, Sister Boothe," he continued, "I just need to get from you a list of what you might need. How are you doing for holiday meals?"

He heard only faint line static in response.

"Sister Boothe?" He paused a beat. "Sister Boothe, are you there?"

He was just wondering how they'd gotten disconnected when Jan Boothe's voice, now overly calm, said simply, "Actually, Bishop, I do have a little something for the kids. I was just

overreacting. Sorry to have bothered you. We'll be fine. Really."

"Sister Boothe, are you sure?" he said, already knowing what her answer would be. "The Ward would be happy to help out."

"No thank you, Bishop. You've already been more than kind to me and the kids. Please don't mention this to anyone. Have a good holiday."

"Merry Christmas to you, Sister Boothe," he said, but she had already hung up.

Heavy of heart, Bishop Tremaine made his way down the stairs, sure that only Sister Boothe's mind had changed, not her situation. Back in the kitchen, he found Jill and Debbie leaning on the counter, heads close, whispering about something.

"Hey, beautiful girls. What's up?"

Mother looked at daughter, as if to say, "Go ahead."

Jill's eyes wandered as she said, "Well, Daddy—when you hollered for me to hang up the phone, I was sitting on the floor with one boot stuck half on and half off my foot. So I was a little slow hanging up the phone and I, uh, kind of overheard what Sister Boothe said. Dad, is she going to have a horrible Christmas?"

"Well, Jill, honey, I appreciate your concern—you've got a big heart, but technically you're not supposed to know about private matters of ward members. It's my fault for handling that phone call in a sloppy way, but I need to ask you not to breathe a word of this to anyone, and to . . . well . . . forget about it if you can. Honey, the Lord has a system in place to take care of needy members, so don't you worry."

"But, Daddy, she told you no. She said she'd be okay, but she won't."

"Sweetheart, the Lord will take care of her. I love your compassion for others, but this isn't to be your concern. I'm sorry I was careless. Please don't worry about Sister Boothe, honey, she'll be all right."

Jill gave him a yes-I'll-obey-but-get-a-clue look, scooped up her backpack, and headed for the door. "I love you, Dad and Mom."

Don and Debbie responded in kind.

Twenty minutes later all five children were gone to school—Debbie had driven the two youngest—and Don was left in a deafeningly empty house, as always a little uneasy that his children were in strangers' care for the next six or seven hours. That led his thoughts to Jan Boothe's little ones, and a certain basement apartment that Santa was likely to forget, and his heart ached in frustration until Debbie returned.

* * *

Thursday had dawned clear and sunny, and brittle cold was soon replaced with an encouraging feeling of cheer as steam rose from streets and driveways. As Don looked out his studio window down onto his actively thawing neighborhood, he realized that the first day of Christmas vacation for the kids was also the first day in a week without snow to shovel. *Lucky little people,* he thought.

He returned his gaze to the score paper in front of him. After two hours of work, it was still essentially blank. All he'd been able to do so far was lay out the format for this Deseret Book arrangement—pairs of woodwinds, five brass staves, three percussion staves, harp, vocals, and strings. Oh, yes, and measure numbers, too. But he had yet even to choose the best key, let alone write a note. Try as he might

to concentrate, his musicianship was being preempted by his office and calling. How do you help someone who needs help but won't allow it?

Don stood and stretched, took a deep breath, then paced along the perimeter of the studio. The difficulty was, if anything were done—by anyone—Sister Boothe would probably think he had started the ball rolling by telling the Relief Society President or something. He felt sure that any official help would be embarrassing to Sister Boothe. As a matter of fact, any help at all would be embarrassing to her, since she would have to stand there and face people who knew how dire her straits were. Alternatively, if help were given anonymously, without finding out from her what she needed and wanted, it might be so generic that it would feel impersonal. Hardly a Christmassy result. But maybe better than no help at all. *Father, why won't you guide me?*

* * *

That night, after an afternoon of witnessing Jill and the rest of the kids engaging in obviously conspiratorial behavior, Don finally pulled her aside, looked her square in the eye, and said, "Okay, Jill, sweetie. What are you up to?"

"Dad," she said, "I'll tell you when it's time, and not before." Then his barely-seventeen-year-old eldest daughter smiled, gave him a peck on the cheek, and breezed away down the hall. *I've just been manipulated by a master,* thought Don, astounded at how quickly these skills were handed down from mother to daughter without dilution.

* * *

At bedtime, as the Tremaine household gathered for prayer, Don could sense excitement in his children's demeanors. They were as giddy as if it were Christmas Eve, even though they were a day early.

"Wait, Dad," said Jill, as Don started to kneel. "Have a seat. Before prayer, we kids have a proposition for you and Mom."

He plopped into his worn chair without a word, as if, he realized with chagrin, Jill were the parent and he the child, ready to be instructed. *Way to take charge, Don,* he thought wryly. Debbie sat in her chair beside him, and the kids, smiles unsuppressible, formed an uneven semicircle around them on the floor.

Jill commenced, "As you know, I became aware of a family that isn't going to have much of a Christmas without help, and help—official help—is being refused."

The younger children nodded sagely. *I hope she didn't tell them who it is,* Don thought.

"This family," continued Jill, now really enjoying her spokeswoman status, "which shall remain anonymous for obvious *little* reasons [*Good girl,* thought Don] has children desperately in need of the most basic of life-sustaining holiday commodities . . ." Jill took a moment to make eye contact with each family member, then finished in a half-whisper, "*Toys!*"

She straightened, and everyone else followed suit. *Good grief,* Don realized, *fifteen seconds of oratory and she had us all leaning in to catch her every word! Who is this kid, really?* Jill stood, and started to gesture as she paced back and forth, "Now we all know how busy Santa is," the listening kids all nodded sagely, and Jill continued, "and has been forced for logistical reasons to give with economy—only one gift per child—lest he overtax his resources.

Therefore," she clapped her hands together in punctuation, "we cannot sit idly by and expect his offering alone to be sufficient for this anonymous family. So! The rest of the Tremaine children and I have devised a three-step program to alleviate the dire effects of this awful problem."

Jill now turned to Don and said, "I claim the right to proceed by rules of filibuster, meaning that no one may interrupt my presentation, not even one word, until I have finished and taken my seat. Can we expect constitutional behavior from the senior Tremaines?"

Don chuckled in spite of himself and exchanged glances with Debbie. *Heaven help the man she marries.* "Okay," both parents said in unison.

"Good," said Jill. "Step one is already complete. I have, entirely behind your back, phoned a particular individual who owns the apartment in which the anonymous family in question lives—"

"What?" six-year-old Evan tried to interrupt.

" . . . and we've arranged for surreptitious entry without the subjects' knowledge. Since the subjects live in a basement apartment in the very domicile which houses the landlord, said landlord has agreed to sneak you, late tomorrow evening, into the indoor stairway of said house with Christmas booty and a key to the dead bolt. The landlord will then phone down to the adult of the family, check to be sure the kiddies are all nestled snug in their beds, and invite said adult up for wassail and treats. Since the stairway opens into the living room of the apartment, you run no risk of awakening the anonymous tykes—if, that is, you don't bash things into walls like a clod."

While at first Don had been busy watching

and admiring his eldest daughter, now he began to thrill as Jill's idea took form for him.

Jill continued: "Therefore, step two is the clandestine delivery of Christmas loot to the subjects' apartment without compromising the secret of who's to blame. Should the adult subject be inclined to guess, the only connection she—or he—will have to this heinous act of holiday cheer will be the landlord. He can honestly say it wasn't him, and can threaten her with eviction if she tries to force our names out of him."

"What," Evan repeated in frustration, "is she saying?"

Jill turned to him, broke character, and said, "It's what we already discussed; I'm just saying it congressionally." Evan nodded.

"Step three," she continued, "is for us to sit back and enjoy the true Spirit of Christmas, in a way that no grinch can ever stop. Unless, that is, a grinch named Daddy says no."

She looked at him with earnest eyes.

"And if you say no, we'll impeach you and Mom can go find a real man." Then she grinned and curtsied.

Don loved her for what she'd thought up, but his practical side burst rudely forward to point out one obvious flaw. He said, "But Jill, honey, where will this 'Christmas booty' come from? Mom and I are spent out."

She beamed with joy, anticipation, and an infuriating air of superiority. Just like her mother. "Mr. Speaker of the Home, if I can show that the Committee for Youthful Christmas Cheer has a workable answer for that little objection, which does not involve raising your 'taxes,' will you *promise* we can do this?"

Still smiling up at his lovely daughter, Don's mind was flashing through the array of pos-

sible outcomes, needing to ensure that no offense would be given. *All I need to tell her yes is some feeling that it's okay with the Lord,* thought Don. No sooner had he thought this than he was flooded with a genuine, bona-fide, Doctrine-and-Covenants-section-nine burning in the bosom. It flared for several seconds—validating two weeks of prayer, thought, and fasting—and left him thrilled and breathless.

Jill, evidently taking his pause and his change in expression for a parental rejection, was starting to look crestfallen. Don hurriedly said, "Jill. Hey. The . . . um . . . Speaker wishes to respond to the proposal made by the Senator from the Northwest Bedroom."

She looked up from the floor to meet his eyes.

"Yes," Don said.

Jill's little hop and yelp of joy were so contagious that the whole family found themselves laughing. When the mood had calmed a bit, Jill said, "Okay, here's how it works. Do you remember the money we kids have been setting aside for this summer's trip to Disneyland?"

"Yes."

"Well, it's just souvenir money. We kids decided we don't need Mickey ears all that much. All together, that totals thirty-eight dollars and twenty cents. I told the kids that was a good start, but that it wasn't enough to give a good Christmas to three kids. Dad, we've talked about it, and all the kids understand, and we've agreed. We want you to give one of the gifts you have for each of us, a *nice* one, to our anonymous Christmas family. And for those of us too old for the gift to be appropriate for littler kids, we want you to take it back first thing in the morning for a refund. Then we'll spend the afternoon shopping and wrapping our hearts out."

Don Tremaine looked at his five children, feeling humbled: at Jill, with her woman's body and child's heart, at Stephen, eyes misty behind his glasses, at Julie and Jennifer, in different stages of awkward, yet noble as they held his gaze, and at Evan, who wasn't looking at him but nonetheless appeared lost in serious thought.

"Do each of you children understand what you'll be giving up?"

They indicated they did.

"And you really want to serve in this way?"

Again, they answered in the affirmative.

It was at this moment that Don realized his home felt just like the temple, and his heart was full.

Late that night, long after the children had gone to bed, Don and Debbie were sitting together in the family room, each finishing up the last of a day's busy work. They heard telltale sounds from the hallway, and seconds later Evan appeared at the doorway.

"Uh-oh, Mom," Don said, "looks like Evan's sleepwalking; I guess he needs tickle therapy or something."

Ignoring the implicit warning, Evan was obviously a man with a mission. "Daddy, would you come here for a minute?"

Don looked over at Debbie to see if she had anything to say, but she just smiled for him to go ahead. He set down his work and, while stepping over toys to cross the room, said, "Something got you worried, buddy? It's long since time for sleep."

"I know," Evan said as he led his father, by the hand, a few steps down the hallway. "Sorry, Dad."

Don knelt to be at eye level with his boy. "What is it, son?"

"Well . . . remember how I've been asking for a new bike?"

Don nodded.

"I asked Santa and I asked you, and I couldn't sleep 'cause I was thinking. I have my old bike. I can't change Santa's mind now, but if you got me a bike for Christmas, Jill says there's a kid my age, and he can have my new bike."

Don's throat got a little tight, and he said, "You're a very generous young man, Evan. That's the sort of thing Jesus would do."

"Just one thing . . ."

"Yeah, buddy?"

"If you got me a bike . . . can I see it before you take it tomorrow? Just so I can remember."

Don paused a moment, then said, "Yes, Evan. There is a new bike. And you can see it. Let's get your mom and we'll go take a look."

He called for Debbie to join them; then he took his six-year-old son by the hand and they went out into the garage. It was cold. Evan started shivering, but didn't say a word. Don opened the inside shed door, stepped in, and wheeled out a beautiful, shiny blue, grey, and green mountain bike. Evan's expression didn't change as he reached over, touched the near handlebar, stroked the seat, then knelt and looked over every square inch of it, shivering periodically.

At length, he stood. He looked up at Don and Debbie, who were standing together, then walked to them and gave them both a ferocious hug.

"Thanks for the great bike, Mom and Dad! We can give it away now."

Just as fiercely, Don and Debbie hugged their son back. Don's tears flowed warm in the quiet, cold garage. He looked down at Evan and found that he, too, was weeping, with a happy smile on his soft face.

* * *

"*Bishop found stalking single, pregnant ward member.*" Don grimaced as he imagined the headlines. He had been crouched in the pitch blackness at the bottom of the stairs for twenty minutes now, his back holding up an appliance box full of wrapped presents, his arm pinning a bike to the wall so it couldn't shift, and the door to Jan Boothe's living room six inches in front of his nose. Don was already starting to cramp, and he knew it was just a matter of time before gravity won.

It had been fifteen minutes since Brother Luther had called downstairs to invite Sister Boothe up for wassail. After that, the bishop had heard, from below, the door-muffled sounds of a young woman getting presentable at breakneck speed. Blessedly, her kids were sound sleepers, and none had awakened. Also blessedly, Brother Luther knew how to apply unfair pressure, because predictably, Jan Boothe's first reaction had been to demur. Bishop Tremaine smiled in the darkness. Now he knew who to call to head the next Friends of Scouting drive.

The sounds through the door suddenly stopped. A few seconds later, Randy Luther opened the upstairs door a crack and shout-whispered, "She's at the door, Bishop, so go on ahead. Remember, I'll stomp once on the floor, hard, when you need to disappear." As the door shut, Don could just hear Jan Boothe exchanging greetings with Sister Becky Luther. He reached out with his free hand, fumbled quietly for the lock, finally found it and, with a fair amount of effort, at last got that huge key into that tiny keyhole. He turned the key in the lock and opened the door into Jan Boothe's apartment.

Wasting no time, but always careful to be quiet, Don propped the bike in the doorway in as stable a pose as possible, then turned to wrestle with the box of gifts. Instantly half of his afflicted muscles sighed their relief as the other half cramped as if in rigor mortis. With gritted teeth, Don wrestled the behemoth box to the bottom of the stairs, then took two minutes to massage his knotted cramps into submission.

Don gave up trying to be the hero, and dragged (albeit as quietly as possible) the box of gifts across the living room carpet and next to a scraggly tree. Then he plopped down gently on the beat-up, stained couch to rest for another moment. As he rested, he examined the Boothe family Christmas tree. It was more yellow than green, which meant that it had sat out of water for long enough for the sap to fix and seal the trunk shut. But that had been Sister Boothe's only mistake, for the tree, though deceased, was alive with decorations not rich, but loved. There were gingerbread . . . things . . . with huge chunks missing—broken off or eaten. There was only one string of lights, but it had been artfully hung to show itself to maximum advantage, there seeming to be far more sparkling lights than there really were. Baubles and store-bought ornaments were few in number, mismatched, and showed chips and countless little fingerprints. Fully half the decorations were raggedly cut trees and snowflakes of ruled school paper, with bold crayon work for color.

There were no presents under the tree. Not one. But propped in the branches of the tree were three cards bearing, in neat block letters, the names Emily, Jonathan, and Joey.

Don stood, removed several pens from his pocket, selected one, and put the rest back. Swiftly, he removed eleven boxes of various sizes from the larger carton and laid them out on the floor in four piles. Then he proceeded, on the label of each package, to forge Jan Boothe's style of lettering as he dedicated three gifts to each member of the Boothe family, including Jan, except the eldest girl. Emily would be *opening* only two packages—the bike was unwrappable. That done, he then arranged the eleven gifts neatly under the tree.

Pausing to rest his back, Don glanced up again at the cards in the tree. He sat back on the floor and rubbed his eyes; it had been a long, busy day. With eyes closed, the sight of the three cards came again, unbidden, into his imagination, but this time they were scattered on a table, and he imagined he saw Jan Boothe writing on the last of the three:

My dear little Emily,

Merry Christmas to you. I'm so sorry that there's nothing for you to open, but the money situation is not good at all, and I had no choice. Grandma Lawlor will probably have something in the mail for you, but I'm afraid this year will mostly be a year for patience and a grown-up attitude. At least we'll be together.

Please know, my little girl, that I love you with all my heart.

Love, Mom

Don imagined he could see Sister Boothe at the table, stony faced—the face of someone so deep in disappointment that no tears will come. Then he saw her put each card in an envelope and begin to carefully letter her children's names on them.

He came to himself still sitting in front of Jan Boothe's tree, still staring at the cards. He wasn't sure whether this had been an impression from the Spirit, or if it had just been his imagination run amok. But if the cards contained the apologies he suspected them to contain, he didn't want to leave them there. They would belie the illusion he'd tried to create— that the gifts to the children were all from Sister Boothe herself. He stood up, gathered the cards from the tree, and left them face down on the mantel, where Jan could see them but the kids could not.

Don then turned back to the stairway to bring in the final gift. As he retrieved the waiting bicycle from the doorway, he whispered a prayer: *Father, please let these gifts, especially this one, be received with the same care and love that went into their giving.*

* * *

Don arrived home to find the kids in the family room, watching a video of a Grinch having his heart enlarged. They jumped up and flocked around him, clamoring for news of how it went.

"Not yet, guys," he said. "I've got to go get Mom first."

He left them waiting as he went to the bedroom, where Debbie, he knew, had been wrapping up a storm.

Sure enough, as he entered the room, Don saw all the gifts wrapped and neatly stacked on the bed. On the floor, amidst colorful paper scraps and ribbon ends, sat his dear Debbie, fast asleep. Her breath was coming in starts—near sobbing. Don gently shook her awake, then he leaned close and rubbed a tear from her cheek.

"Why so sad on Christmas Eve?"

After a pause, a half-whispered "Oh wow!" was all that Debbie could manage. She stood, and they held each other, Don patiently waiting for her to speak.

At length, voice muffled in his shoulder, she said, "I had a little daydream. I saw some things."

A familiar feeling began to form in his chest. "What things?"

"I . . . um . . . saw tomorrow morning, over at Jan's place."

His chest began to burn. He stayed silent, held her, and waited for her to move at her own speed.

"The Boothe kids, Joey and Jonathan, and Emily, unwrapped their gifts," she began. "They took turns, and each gift opened had everyone's attention. The kids kept saying things like, 'Mom, you remembered!' and 'This is exactly what I wanted!' It was as if we were guided on what we sent over, and each present was a little miracle for them . . . well, I guess for all of us." Debbie leaned back a little, smiled at Don through tear-heavy eyes, and went on.

"Oh, Don! That bike of Evan's . . ." She sighed and leaned in to his shoulder again. "All the gifts were opened, and little Emily just kept . . . staring . . . at that bike. She looked over at her mom, and Jan was trying hard to keep from crying, I could tell. Jan pointed to the tag on the handlebar. Emily reached out and turned it so she could read.

"Then she knelt by our little boy's bike . . ." Debbie's voice became tremulous, "and drank it in with her eyes, and touched it here and there, and then *hugged* it, and then . . ." Debbie stifled a sob, and continued, "Emily . . . um . . . sort of *launched* herself into Jan's arms—and there they were, crying and crying and crying . . ." Now Debbie was openly weeping,

and Don's heart felt like a furnace, and his nose burned. "Don, they just held each other and cried, and even the little boys cried, and . . . I can't describe what I felt . . ."

Don couldn't speak. He just nodded. And held her.

Debbie said, "Emily told her mom that she'd wanted a bike so bad, but didn't even ask because she knew there was no money. She said it was 'perfect.'"

* * *

That night in the Tremaine home, there was beauty, and peace. And there was a great deal of love. The children spoke in hushed tones, and their eyes sparkled. Don could see that Jill's generous idea had become, for each member of the family, a pivotal event—one that would last a lifetime. He looked over at his youngest child. Evan's eyes danced, and he just could not stop smiling. Don found, to his surprise, that he couldn't, either.

* * *

Christmas Day, in the afternoon, Don found that each member of his family was deeply involved in something, and he was left to himself. He realized that this would be a perfect time to sneak off to his office in the church and finish preparations for the next day's meetings. So he threw on a coat, grabbed his book bag, and hopped in the car for the three-block trek. As he turned the corner onto the street leading to the meetinghouse, he saw something that warmed him from head to toe, and left him grinning. Little Emily Boothe was fairly flying down the street towards him on a shiny blue, grey, and green mountain bike, her smile irrepressible, her eyes shining. Don memorized what he saw, so he could go back and discreetly report the gist of it—a reward for his family, especially Evan. And Jill.

I should have thought all this up, thought Don, with a twinge of regret. Then the thought came to him, *That's why you have a family, Don. It's okay for parents to learn from their children.*

Little Emily was behind him now, and he looked casually across at the Luther's house. A lone, bundled figure stood at the side of the house, watching the street. He realized it was Jan Boothe, watching her daughter. She looked over at him as he drove past. He waved. She waved in return—then slowly mouthed the words, Thank you.

He was still smiling his acknowledgement as he pulled into the church parking lot. *How in the world could she know?* But he'd seen enough of the hand of God in all of this to know better. He knew now, in a way he'd never known before, something of the deep love that his Father in Heaven held for His children.

A humble, joyful, Don Tremaine entered his office, knelt, and gave his heart to God.

ARLEN CARD is a freelance composer living in Orem, Utah. He composed, conducted, and produced the music for the LDS Church sesquicentennial musical, *Barefoot to Zion,* as well as for many Church films, including the 1993 conference feature *The Mountain of the Lord.* Additional credits include several features, numerous documentaries, and countless industrial/public-image pieces for corporations large and small. He recently won a "Telly" award for music he composed for the Living Scriptures, Inc., docudrama, *The Handcart Pioneers.* He enjoys being able to work at home, where he can spend more time with his wife/business-manager, Jennifer, and his four delightful children. "Father Christmas" is his first fiction publication.

THE BELL

Don L. Searle

THE WIDE CHRISTMAS BOWS on the trunks of the palm trees were a sickly red in the glare of the sodium vapor streetlights. The heavy ribbons fluttered occasionally in the early morning breeze across the park.

Probably scare the birds away. Those bows make about as much sense as that phony North Pole scene on the grass down in front of the civic center. Maybe the bright idea of some fool in the mayor's office—or the chamber of commerce—trying to make the snowbirds feel at home. Why in the world would those people want to think of snow in a place like this? They come down here so they can run around in their shirt sleeves two days before Christmas!

Tomorrow some of those snowbirds would be out here in the park in their shorts and straw hats playing shuffleboard, chess, or dominoes.

Steve wondered if Sam would be here.

Sam was the domino king. Nobody could beat him, and nobody played him a second time. But it was impossible to resist his friendly smile.

They had met one day when Steve walked through the park on his way from his job at the fire station to his car and stopped to watch a domino game. Sam had looked at the nameplate pinned to Steve's uniform shirt. "'Hasek.' Polish?"

"Yeah. My great-grandparents came to New York in 1910. My grandparents came down here in the '30s because they heard land was cheap along the Rio Grande and you could grow things all year long."

Sam had grinned and stuck out his hand. "Sam Jacobs, formerly your friendly Ford dealer of Lincoln, Nebraska, before I retired. My family came from Poland too. The name was Jacobowitz, originally."

Sam was not only friendly, he was a believer. He kept Hanukkah.

"Do you keep Christmas, Steve?" he had asked. "Any of the old country traditions?"

Steve had shaken his head negatively. "Don't know any of them." He had laughed, then nodded in the direction of the downtown stores a block away. "Can you hear the cash registers jingling from here? That's the tradition I keep. Seems like the things I buy my daughter get more expensive every year."

Sam's smile had faded away. "What about Jesus—the Christ child?"

"I don't know. I've got some real questions there. I mean, what the Bible says he taught would be a pretty good way to live. But a virgin mother? A real Son of God?" He had grimaced. "Besides, why are you asking *me*? You don't believe any of that."

"No." Sam had gazed off across the park for several seconds. "But what do *you* believe in, Steve? A man who doesn't believe in anything bigger than himself can get lost in life and wander for years."

But if what you believed in were only legends, what difference could they possibly make?

Steve stopped jogging and settled into his cool-down walk around the park. The only call tonight had been a minor fire in somebody's garage, quickly extinguished. But it had reminded him too much of another house fire, just last week, and thinking about that one had driven sleep from him. So he had given in to his sleeplessness, and now had seemed as good a time as any to squeeze in a little of his required physical conditioning. Jogging around the park, he was within earshot of the fire station, but he had carried a handheld radio just in case.

He looked up at the night sky as he walked. Maybe somewhere up there was a star—*the* star. Light years from earth. *Light years!* If it had shone exactly when the baby was born, then everything had to have been planned so that . . .

But why in some backwater spot in the Middle East in an era when he would never be able to tell his message to more than a few thousand people at most? Didn't people everywhere else deserve just as much to see and hear him?

Walking on water? Raising the dead? Knowing exactly what was in the mind and heart of a stranger he met by a well in a dusty little town? It was a stretch.

Maybe I used to believe, Steve thought, *or wanted to believe.* But that was before his parents had gotten a bitter divorce during his first year in junior high, before his own first marriage had come apart. It was before he had been in the Gulf War and seen what destruction the unchecked lust for power could cause, what evil people would do to each other in the name of national honor.

It was before the little girl in her burning bedroom five days ago.

He had prayed about each of those things—as much as he knew how to pray.

He had begged God in his own way to keep his mom and dad together, then not to let his first wife leave and take their little boy with her.

In Kuwait, he had asked in his heart, "Why?"

In the little girl's burning home last week,

he had screamed in his mind, "God, please help me get there in time!" But he had been too late.

Okay, maybe he didn't understand everything God had in mind for this world. But it was obvious from the lack of response to his prayers that *he* didn't fit into God's plans anywhere.

He glanced at his watch: 4:15. His shift would be over in a little less than three hours, about the time the sun came up. And this year it would be his turn to have the four days off that included Christmas Eve and Christmas. It would be only the second time in the five years since he and Lynne had gotten married that he would have the holidays off.

Lynne and her daughter, Amy, were the best things to happen in his life since he was a boy.

Steve walked along the row of palm trees on the edge of the park until he was even with the fire station, then turned to cross the street. Just before he stepped off the curb, something shiny in the grass caught his eye. He stooped to pick it up.

It was a bell—a little brass bell, the kind that stores sometimes put on Christmas packages or people sew on costumes. It was scratched, but the grass had cushioned it so that it had not been smashed by the feet of passersby. Steve held it by the tiny loop on top and shook it experimentally. Its tinkle could be clearly heard in the morning quiet of the park.

Back in the station house, he dropped the bell into the pocket of his uniform shirt before getting out of his running clothes to take a quick shower.

He dressed again and turned to catching up on some paperwork. The bell in his pocket jingled softly every so often, reminding him of . . . of what? What was it? The memory was close . . . almost there.

Seven—or maybe eight. His mom had usually dropped him off at the church on her way to do the weekly grocery shopping and picked him up on her way home. His folks had never been churchgoers themselves—maybe that had been part of their problem. Anyway, he must have been about eight when he was in Sister Flood's Sunday School class. Everybody at the church he had gone to when he was little had been "Brother" or "Sister" something. He couldn't remember any of the names now—except Sister Flood.

That Christmas season she had given each of the children in her class a small gold bell on a white ribbon. She had hung one around each of their necks, and to each child had said, "When you hear this bell, I want you to think of the angels' message when they came to the shepherds in the fields on the night Jesus was born—peace on earth, good will toward men." Then she had kissed each one, boy and girl, on the forehead, saying, "And I want you to remember that I will always love you."

Some part of him knew that Sister Flood always had loved him, and wherever she was now, she probably still did.

But he hadn't thought about her in years—probably had never told anyone about the bell. *No one could know about it, except . . .*

"Hasek—letter for you." Rich Cummings stood by the desk with a handful of yesterday's mail. He smiled as he held out a square, white envelope. "Looks like a Christmas card. Merry Christmas."

It *was* a card—plain, white, with the words *Thank You* embossed on the front in silver script. Inside there was a message written in black ink in a very neat hand.

"Thank you for giving me back my son. You cannot know how deeply grateful I am to you for saving his life when our house burned down last week.

"I know you were very upset that you could not save our daughter too. I saw you sitting by the fire engine with your head in your hands when they took us away to the hospital. You risked your life for her. You did everything you could, and I want to tell you how much I appreciate it, how much we all appreciate it.

"I don't know why, but I think God needs her to be with him now. We almost lost her when she was younger, and I promised him then that I would do anything if he would give us just a few more months with her, until she was seven. He gave us two more years, and I can only thank him for that.

"I know he sent you to be there for our son, and I'll always remember what you did."

It had been an instant choice, really—go for the younger child, the boy, immediately because there would be no second chance. Then when he had fought his way back for the girl and realized that he was too late, he had asked himself one of those questions for which there never was an answer: had he made the *right* choice?

She had been about nine, the same age as his stepdaughter, Amy. He had cried behind his face mask as he had carried the little girl out of the house.

Amy had been worried these past few days that he wasn't happy about Christmas. She loved this time of year. She and her mother had been making snowball cookies for the neighbors, and Amy liked taking a plate of cookies to the door and saying, "Merry Christmas, from all of us in our family." She had tried to get him to go along, but he wouldn't—he *couldn't*. Nor could he tell her about the little burned body he had cried over just days ago. Amy was young

yet. There would be years still for her to learn about death and hurt and why the world didn't always work the way she thought it should.

She had been little more than a baby when Lynne's first husband walked out on them. Amy had developed in her mind a picture of the perfect daddy, and Steve knew she wanted him to be that man—but he couldn't always do it. No one could. He tried anyway, knowing that he would probably disappoint her sometimes.

He looked again at the card in his hand. He would have to write and let this woman know that she had answered a question he thought was unanswerable.

Maybe two questions.

First the bell tonight, and now this. Maybe there was some way after all that he figured in God's plans—some way he just didn't recognize yet.

The bell continued to jingle softly from time to time while he worked, as though it were letting him know that its message could not be ignored. Finally, he reached into his pocket, pulled it out, rolled it around in his palm, then sat looking at it. He went to the supply cabinet, found the spool of white nylon string, and cut off a two-foot length. He threaded it through the loop on the bell, tied a knot to join the ends, and hung the bell around his neck.

It jingled lightly every time he moved, clearer and purer now that it was not muffled in his pocket.

When he walked out of the fire station at ten after seven, morning light was just touching the front of the stuccoed old resort hotel across the park, flanked by its palm trees with their outlandish red bow ties.

The park was empty. *Too bad Sam couldn't be here now. I'd tell him about the bell.*

The house was still quiet when he got home. In their bedroom, Lynne lay on her stomach, her long blonde hair partly across her face. He sat down lightly on the bed, touched her on the back, and began to massage her shoulders. She smiled and opened her eyes. "Mmm—feels good. How was your night?"

"Only one call—lots of time to think." He paused. "Honey, I was thinking it's time we ought to go to church."

She looked up at him in surprise. "Tonight?"

"No. At the church I went to when I was a kid—but I don't think they have services on Christmas Eve. Next Sunday."

"You know I've been wanting Amy to have a church," she said slowly. "And I wouldn't mind going along. But I thought you . . . "

"I thought so too. But a couple of things happened to make me think maybe I've been wrong."

"What?"

"This," he said, putting the card he had received on the nightstand. "And this." He held up the bell. "It reminded me of a woman I knew at the church a long time ago—Sister Flood. I'll tell you about her sometime."

Lynne smiled in the direction of the door-way. "Good morning, sweetheart."

Amy came and sat down by him on the bed, put an arm around his waist, and leaned against his side.

He put his arm around her shoulders. "Do you still have cookies to take to the people across the street?"

"Yes."

"Can I go with you?"

She hugged him. "Right after breakfast, okay?"

He took the bell from around his own neck and put the loop of string over her head.

She looked down at the bell. "Where did you get this? What's it for?"

"I found it. I used to have one like it when I was just a little younger than you." He took hold of the string and jingled the bell. "When you hear it, it's supposed to remind you of two things. The first is what the angels said to the shepherds—peace on earth, good will to men."

He kissed her on the forehead. "And the second is that I will always love you."

Don L. Searle, an editor for an LDS Church magazine, lives in West Valley City, Utah. He and his wife, Marie, have five children. His early elementary and high school years were spent in South Texas. He is indebted to his oldest daughter, Amy, for the gift of a small gold bell on a white ribbon, and to Sister Flood for the lasting memory of a teacher who cared deeply about each boy and girl in her class.

THE CHRISTMAS BEAR

Marilyn Brown

YOU MAY NOT REGARD this as a true story, but it is nevertheless as true as anything that echoes downwind from time. All of the characters—including the Christmas Bear—are chronicled in antique records engraved with words as authentic as the tales that were told by memory from one ancient storyteller to another ancient storyteller hunkered over their Christmas fires, warming their hands in flames while the winds howled in great waves outside the cold windows, making hollows of sound and great trumpets of thunder.

The story begins in Europe near A.D. 400 when the invading armies of Rome sacked helpless villages to take slaves and sell them to landowners abroad. One of their best customers was a wealthy nobleman in Spain by the name of Pandero.

Pandero owned thousands of acres of olive trees, miles and miles of farmland, and enormous herds of goats and lambs. He owned well over a thousand slaves and houses and fields in over eighty villages. He was so wealthy that he could host the very armies of Rome on his estate as they passed through. He needed only to speak a word, and his cooks would slaughter a thousand animals, spike them on spits, and roast them for feasts that lasted for several days.

Though he was a man of means, Pandero still managed to be a most vigilant father who considered that of all he owned, his most priceless possession was his beautiful little daughter, Koloma, her cheeks as fair as peaches, her curls as gleaming and dark as coils of black jade. As Koloma began to emerge from the nursery, Pandero observed her need for young friends. When she was eight years old he began to cast about to purchase a slave as her companion.

On one of Rome's visits to Pandero, he noticed that the captain of the army was in possession of a sixteen-year-old raven-haired girl from Sens, France, by the name of Maria. She was spirited and lovely, with high cheek bones and porcelain limbs. At first, the Roman captain would not hear of parting with her, but after a series of feasts, he agreed to sell her to Pandero for a great deal of money.

In only a few days Maria won the hearts of the Spanish courtiers and became the full-time guardian of the nobleman's child. Soon the two girls were seen everywhere in the castle together, the older girl hovering over the younger one— skipping with her in the corridors, gathering rocks with her in the courtyard, and finding birds' nests in the brushwood and sand.

Pandero rejoiced in his daughter's happiness. However, one day not long after he had remarked to his queen that their good fortune had been made complete with the addition of Maria to the court, he began to notice some rather strange behaviors in his daughter. At great feasts in the long hall, when the courtiers heaped food on their gold plates, Koloma drew a little earthen dish from her pocket and placed on it only a few pieces of fruit. When they served the glazed pork decorated in all of its splendor, swimming in honeyed yams with cinnamon and syrup, she humbly asked the servants to bring her their food, for she preferred simple gruel.

With growing concern the nobleman and

his wife watched her refuse the gilded clips and jewels for her hair and the garments of silk and fur. Wearing a simple woolen shawl, the girl often knelt on the cold floor of the castle with a brush doused in scrubwater, helping Maria and the other servants clean the stones. While she worked, she sang silver-noted songs of joy to someone no one recognized, but it was said his name was Jesus.

Alarmed, the master of the house demanded that his slave Maria visit with him in his chambers to answer questions he had concerning Koloma. "What is happening to my daughter?" he asked when she bowed low before him in the court. "She will not look upon the effects of this household. She will have none of our ceremonies nor their adornments—the fur capes, the silver tiaras. She will not eat the glazed meats, nor the sugared scones. And all that we have gathered for her good she seems to reject. It does not befit the behavior of a noblewoman—even a very young one."

Maria bent again before her master, trembling, for she was his slave, obliged to serve him as Koloma's companion. And she knew that her life depended upon his favors and approval. "She does not care for the riches of this world, good Master, but for the riches of heaven."

"And who is this Jesus?" he asked her. "What ideas have come into her head?"

Maria had never told him her treasured stories of Jesus. Now, although she trembled with uneasiness, she felt inspired that she must tell him of the Savior she had come to love.

"Jesus is the baby born in Bethlehem who came to make peace with all the world. He was born in a stable on a cold night, and the angels sang in the heavens at his birth. The wise men visited him from the east, and he grew to be the master of all love."

Though the father listened, he grew very restless. He walked back and forth in his tapestry caftan, tightening his fingers behind his back until his gold and ruby rings began to cut off his circulation. He had heard of these Christians, and he was uncomfortable with their creeds. "We cannot tolerate Christians in our province," he finally said. "They are put to death by the Romans. They are hunted by the neighboring armies. I had no idea you were a Christian. Please do not tell me you have filled her head with such nonsense and that already she professes to believe in these silly tales."

"But these tales are true, good master. He was God's son, an emissary for goodness and kindness. I have only told Koloma a few of these true stories. She loves them very much; she has chosen to be good and kind, to be humble like this Jesus about whom I have spoken many times."

In great distress, the master turned upon Maria and roared, "I wish you had not told my daughter about this Jesus, for he seems to have a terrible power over her. You have poisoned her mind, and we can no longer tolerate your presence here. Despite the time of year, the harsh weather, and the mountain snow, you must be driven from the castle immediately."

Tears welled in Maria's eyes, for she had grown to love the child Koloma. Backing away from the rugged nobleman, she felt the cold of the stone steps under her feet and drew her cloak around her shoulders. Pandero snapped his fingers and gave orders to his henchmen to give her time to gather a few of her things and then take her to the edge of their fields to be banned from the estate forever.

Maria shivered and cried quietly to herself.

But she did as the master told her. She went to her room to gather her clothes in a large traveling bag. On her way, however, she found little Koloma, weeping.

"I want to go with you," Koloma said. "I will not stay here if neither you nor Jesus can live here in this house. Please, Maria, take me with you."

Distressed, Maria dried the girl's tears and held her very close in her arms. Uncertain of the future, unsure she could find her way back to her native Sens in France, she was very hesitant to take the girl away from her wealthy home, from all that was comfortable and refined. But Koloma would have it no other way. "Please, Maria. God will protect us."

Such faith touched Maria's heart. Quickly she held open the large rucksack while Koloma climbed in. Then, carrying the bag over her shoulder, Maria struggled to the castle gate. Without lifting a hand to see how heavy the sack was, the henchman pushed Maria into the cart and drove her over the rough stony road through the fields. There he let her down, and she pulled the burlap bag with her and stood at the edge of the property looking out at the cold blue sun going down in the deep snow. She waited until the driver was out of sight before she whispered to the child, "You may get out now." And Koloma, her little face appearing white with a light of excitement, emerged from the sack and embraced Maria with joy.

For seven days and nights, eating only the crusts of bread Maria managed to take for the journey, the companions walked the cold roads, asking for help from neighboring farms when the sunlight rose. They often slept in haystacks, or in the barns if the farmhands seemed kind. God was with them. Wherever they went they told people the stories of Jesus.

Many had never heard of the Son of God who had died for them, who had shown them all a way to live that would change the world.

Eventually they found their way to Maria's town of Sens, France. Maria's family could not believe their good fortune that Maria had come back to them. And they were delighted to see that she had brought with her a little friend. Maria's mother made a cushion on the hearth for Koloma. She gave her a plump feather bed and a lace gown. "You must stay with us always," she cried. "We will love you as one of our own."

Maria and Koloma lived in peace and joy with the Christian families in Sens. But our story is not over, for you cannot imagine a father who loved his daughter as much as Koloma's father loved her without overturning every lump of earth, going to every length of difficulty to find her.

And that is what he did. He sent his emissaries into the countryside to ask if they had seen a dark-haired girl traveling with a child as beautiful as the sun, as golden as flowers. Eventually someone answered yes, and as the months crawled past more and more clues leading to the two girls became uncovered.

Finally, near the following Christmas holiday, while the winter wind began to howl in the barns and toss large flakes of snow out of the dark sky, a group of Roman soldiers straggled into a camp outside of Sens. It so happened that the captain of this group had been among the troops who had often camped at Pandero's estate in Spain this past summer. It also happened that he had been in touch with Koloma's father, who had declared that if anyone returned Maria to him they would receive a great reward. Pandero had begged the armies to recover Maria at all costs, even if they had to burn an entire city to the ground.

When the Roman soldiers marched into the town of Sens, the citizens scattered into their homes, terrified. They blew out the lamps in their windows, hoping the soldiers would think no one was there. But when the spies from the army scouted about, they finally found where Maria and Koloma were living with Maria's parents and brothers and sisters. Seated high on their quivering horses, they surrounded the house, horses prancing and men shouting, "Come out! Come out, you mongrels! We have come for Koloma. Get out, you beasts, or we shall kill the lot of you!"

Inside the house, the family prayed as they knew Jesus would have prayed. "Dear God, please at this Christmastime protect us if it be thy will." Miraculously—or perhaps the soldiers were just lazy—they stayed on their horses. Though they surrounded the house, not one of them climbed down from his saddle or attempted to come in.

When it grew very dark, Maria took Koloma by the hand and ran with her into the cold snow. They ran, hidden by the house and the ice-laden fence. Whenever they feared they had alarmed the soldier's horses, they stopped and huddled down in the snow.

In moments they were able to run away from the house and up into the hills near the cave that stood along the side of the mountain in the jagged rocks. As they drew close to the mountain, however, one of the soldiers lit a torch and dashed up the hill to see who was walking in the moonlight. In the bright light they could do nothing—he saw them.

"Go. Go quickly. God will protect you," Maria whispered to Koloma.

But Koloma did not want to leave her. "If you die, I will die too," she said. "We will die for Jesus."

"No, no, Koloma," Maria said in a stern voice. "You must *live* for Jesus." Maria's eyes were very bright and clear as she spoke, and Koloma did not argue with her. Reluctantly, she turned and ran up the mountain.

Maria stood still. She planted her feet in the snow and faced the soldier who, spurring his horse, rode to her with the torch high in his hand. When the light played on her face, she smiled at him.

"You're not the nobleman's daughter!" the solder exclaimed.

Maria did not answer. She stood very still and looked up to the sky, praising God in her heart and praying that Koloma would be safe.

Angry, with hatred burning in his breast, the soldier rode his horse forward upon Maria, and she fell into the snow under its hooves. "Where is she? Where is she?" The soldier screamed.

By now, the other soldiers had come to see what was happening. The Roman raised his horse on its hind legs again and again over the spot where Maria lay until her frail body was still. She did not make a sound in the blood-stained snow.

"The other girl has run up into the hills," the Roman shouted. "Go find her!"

They turned their horses swiftly toward the hills and forced the animals to trample through the deep snow. Carrying torches in their hands, they looked for the girl's footprints. When they found them, they followed them up deep crevices and into a maze of huge, dark rocks. The mountains loomed in ominous shadows before them, while thick clouds of snow now began to whirl out of the black sky.

"She's gone into this cave!" one of the soldiers shouted, and he took his torch to the mouth of a large hollow cave and waved it in front of him, peering into the black grotto and hoping to see the beautiful little girl who would fetch him a handsome reward. As the captain approached the cavern, he thrust the flaming light further and further forward into the smoky mist. Suddenly he shrank back in fear. Swimming in the murky haze he could see the reflection of the torch burst alive in two great brilliant and fierce eyes—the wild eyes of a huge bear!

Pulling the torch back quickly, the Roman soldier again played the light along the girl's steps in the snow. "I know she has gone into that cave," he murmured. "What has happened to her?"

As if in answer, the great head of the bear swung back and forth, back and forth. The ponderous flesh on his body swung rhythmically in the cavern's spare light against the black walls. The other soldiers, whose horses had come to the mountainside, pulled back quickly. The horses stamped their hooves, whinnied in fear, and began to prance nervously.

"Her tracks lead into that cave," the soldier's voice alarmed the others.

Just then the great furry beast stepped out of the mouth of the cave, his huge paws with heavy pads breaking through the snow's icy crust. He stood up and began to roar. His teeth dripped saliva as he roared and roared, his great head swinging upon his body as large as the mountainside itself, as great and magnificent as the sky.

The soldiers backed away. The horses backed unbidden down the hillside. Believing both girls to be dead—one to the hooves of their comrade's horse and one to the appetite of the big bear, they turned their animals around and swiftly rode back to the camp.

As soon as the soldiers were gone, Maria lifted her head out of the packed snow that had cushioned her, saved her life from the horse's blows. Though her tattered body was sorely bruised and several bones had been broken, she somehow dragged herself up the hill. When Koloma saw Maria, she shouted out with joy and fear for her friend's life. Running past the bear, she knelt by Maria's side and helped her crawl along the snow to the cave. As they moved slowly past the bear and through the entrance, Maria looked at the bear with a side glance.

"He won't hurt you so near to Christmastime," Koloma said. "He's a Christian bear."

It is told in this true story that the Christmas Bear watched over Koloma and Maria for several days while the Romans waited and watched, wondering where Maria had gone, wondering if Koloma were indeed dead. Not one soldier had the courage to face the bear in an attempt to enter the cave to find out for sure, and three days later, when the armies received orders to relocate, they gladly picked up their tents and left Sens, never to return.

No one in the village saw Maria and Koloma while the Romans were still camped. Some feared the soldiers had captured the girls to sell them as slaves. Maria's mother grieved more than anyone else for this second loss of her daughter, along with her little friend. She prepared for the celebration of Christmas Eve with a candle and a tearful prayer: "Dear God, please protect the girls, wherever they may be."

But when the Roman camp departed, the villagers were no longer afraid to come out of their houses. On Christmas morning, when the sun rose over the white hill, they looked up and could not believe their eyes. Coming down through the crevices of the mountain—wavering blurs stumbling on the rocks—their girls!

Maria's mother could not believe what she saw. She ran to them, laughing and crying with joy.

You may wonder what happened to the girls over time. They stayed in Sens, married, and had children of their own. Generation after generation, Maria and Koloma's children told the wonderful tale of the Christmas Bear by their firesides for centuries of Christmases. To tell the story well, their sons would rear up in mock anger to show the bear's powerful head swinging, his giant paws like padded pillows, the claws as sharp as nails. They would tell how Koloma and Maria became friends of the bear and climbed into his arms at night, cuddling against his huge massive fur. They would demonstrate how the bear would enfold the two girls in sleep with his great arms and legs while Maria healed and they awaited the soldiers' departure.

The soldiers were forever puzzled by the way Koloma and Maria disappeared. And when they reached Spain, none dared breathe a word to Pandero, for none was willing to admit that they had been defeated by a Christian bear.

MARILYN BROWN, the author of several Utah history novels—most recently *Statehood*—now writes musical comedies (*The Nutcracker, Midsummer Night's Dream*) for production in Springville's Villa Playhouse Theatre, which she and her husband Bill have owned and operated for two years. They have six children, twelve grandchildren, and live in Hobble Creek Canyon with the cats, raccoons, and squirrels.

GHOSTS

Michael Fillerup

THE JANITROL FURNACE that had kept them warm for eleven winters gave up the ghost late Friday afternoon, minutes after the last repair and parts shop had closed for the three-day weekend. Trapped in a veritable icebox, during a long, sleepless night Dale was forced to re-examine the wisdom of installing an attractive, eye-pleasing fireplace of malpais rock (his preference) instead of a utilitarian woodstove (hers). Thanks to his bullheadedness, aesthetics had overruled pragmatics, and he now found himself alone and without heat on Christmas Eve.

Last night the cold had grown so intense he was tempted to call the bishop for help, but his pride had overpowered his suffering. Besides, that would have been a bridge back.

What pride? he muttered to himself.

But he knew.

So had she.

Dale hooked a finger between two horizontal slats, drawing the lower one down a fraction, peered secretively outside, and grimaced: stars, zillions of them, shining like frozen tears. Clear skies meant another cold one. He could barely hear the mixed-and-matched voices of carolers rolling down the street like a slow ocean swell: Shirley Stedman's annual Christmas Eve block party. Dale had already closed the blinds and doused the outside lights to discourage any holiday do-gooders from paying him a charity visit, but for good measure, he quickly hit the family room light, leaving the house in inhospitable darkness. He waited by the front door until the chorus of "We Wish You a Merry Christmas" crescendoed and faded, then flicked the light back on, pulled the thermal blanket snugly around his neck and shoulders, and settled back on the velour sofa, close to the tiny space heater he had disinterred from the mini-junkyard in his basement. Ten seconds hadn't passed before he heard a loud and deliberate rapping at the front door.

Dale knew he couldn't ignore the visitor, because he'd just turned on the light. He tried waiting him out, but the knocker persisted until Dale reluctantly opened the door.

"Brother Watson! Mele-kaliki-maka!"

A tall, gangly Quixote-looking figure was ensconced on his doorstep.

"Excuse me?"

"Merry Christmas!"

Dale flipped on the outside light for a better look. It was Wayne Hampton, wearing faded blue jeans with frayed cuffs and a flaming red-and-orange aloha shirt. He was holding a coconut in one hand and a pineapple in the other. A white puff exploded from his lips with each breath. Just beyond the sahara of snow in his rolling front yard, Dale noticed several cars—Toyota Camrys, Honda Accords—parked in front of the Desmonds' home. Bundled up against the weather, couples bearing wrapped and ribboned packages were marching up the long, sloping driveway lit by twinkling lights and luminarias.

Dale had never liked Hampton. He didn't dislike him exactly, but he had never warmed up to the man. His looks were as odd as his mannerisms, with that stringy blond mustache and goatee dripping from his chin like Spanish moss, and a nose long enough to hang your hat on. He had an annoying habit of wheezing internally between words, as if breathing Darth

Vader–like through a box. Even more irritating was the way he would gaze at you with bulbous blue eyes and an overconfident grin that, in Dale's opinion, was totally unwarranted—the giant Adam's apple that jerked around as if a bird were trapped in his throat; the junky Rambler station wagon with the spare tire lashed on the roof rack; and the antique washers, dryers, and refrigerators rusting in his front yard, the lone eyesore in a neighborhood of small but neatly groomed cracker-box homes crowding the valley below. What right did he have to parade around with such beaming optimism? A new move-in to the ward, Wayne wasn't privy to Dale's recent history, which may have partly explained his unwitting obtrusiveness. Several times he had tried to make a home teaching visit, but Dale had adroitly averted each attempt.

"Thanks," Dale murmured, reluctantly accepting the two exotic edibles. "Well, Merry Christmas!" Smiling falsely, he started to close the door, but Wayne had edged into the entry like a cunning salesman. He noticed that the interior icebox effect was turning each breath, his and Wayne's, into a little cloud of cumulus. He reminded himself to breathe sparingly and discreetly lest he arouse Wayne's suspicion.

"Like I said, Mele-kaliki-maka!" Wayne blew on his reddened knuckles. "Mind if I come in for a minute?"

You already have, Dale thought, but it would be rude to say *Yes, I do mind,* especially tonight. Dale wondered, sourly, if this might be the answer to his earlier plea for help. If so, he wanted to repent and ask God to renege. *Lord,* he mused sarcastically, *I'll take my chances with the elements. Make this guy evaporate, pronto!*

"Sure," Dale conceded.

Wayne stepped into the middle of the

entryway, rubbing his bare hands briskly. "Boy, it's cold in here, too! Colder than out there, almost!"

"I left a window open earlier," Dale lied. "To get some fresh air."

Wayne's slanting blond brows twisted enigmatically as he took silent inventory: no tree, no twinkling lights, no colored bulbs, no advent calendar, no smiling paper mache reindeer pulling a fat little paper mache Santa across the window seat; no tinsel boas or miniature salt dough wise men peering down at the baby Jesus in a Popsicle stick manger. All of that disappeared when she did. Wayne motioned towards the bedsheets Dale had thumbtacked to the walls, creating a sagging curtain between the kitchen and the family room, a desperate (but surprisingly effective) attempt to contain the modest warmth generated by the space heater.

"New curtains?" he quipped.

Dale's smile came slowly, as if a razor blade were being drawn carefully across his face.

Wayne dropped to one Levied knee and placed his hand over the metal floor vent. "It's like ice! You sure your furnace is working?"

"Yeah, I think so. It was, anyway."

"Well, let's have a look!"

"That's okay, really. You don't—"

But Wayne was already striding down the hallway in his big clumsy snowboots, through the laundry room, and into the adjoining garage, with the intuitive foreknowledge of a cat burglar.

Wayne removed the louvered metal cover and genuflected before the silver furnace. He twisted a brass clasp, shutting off the corrugated fuel line, then switched it back. "Got a match?"

Reluctantly, Dale trudged inside and returned with a small box of wooden matches. Irritated at first, now Dale was flat-out angry. He'd spent all day in this subzero Antarctica he called his garage trying to breathe some fire into this idiotic machine he laughingly called a furnace. His nearest brush with luck occurred shortly after dark when, inexplicably, the furnace had issued three short, hard gasps before sputtering out for good. Dale had dropped to his knees on the concrete floor. He'd felt like bawling but instead offered a short, heartfelt plea for help.

Seconds later his hands had begun shaking like a diviner's, not from the fires of the Spirit but the cumulative wrath of the drop-dead cold. The arctic tremors had spread quickly throughout his body until he was convulsing like an epileptic. He'd staggered through the back door, down the hall, and into the bathroom, where he twisted on the faucet and plunged his phantom fingers under the hot water, tossing handfuls onto his face and throat, heedless of the volumes streaming down the front of his Gortex coat. When he finally paused to look, he'd flinched from the stranger staring back at him in the bathroom mirror: bulging brown Pekinese eyes; thin, stiff bangs, flattened by his ski cap; zinc oxide lips; bushy, twisted brows. Most alarming was the mouth, a deeply grooved frown that hooked down to the tip of his chin like a horseshoe. After thawing out in a hot bath, he'd layered himself in coat, sweater, thermal underwear, and ski cap, and then had curled up on the sofa chair with a thermal blanket, far from the malpais rock fireplace that was too stingy with its heat to even bother feeding firewood. And now, when he finally had a chance to get somewhat warm for the night, this church busybody was dragging him back out in the cold again for who knows how many more hours of freezing futility. Who did this knothead think he was, Merlin the Magician?

Dale handed him the box of matches, noting the red warning label on the panel, just above the fuel line: EXTREME DANGER! DO NOT ATTEMPT TO IGNITE THE PILOT WITH A MATCH OR OTHER OPEN FLAME!

"Well," Wayne said, "we've got gas. Now let's see—"

He struck a match and stretched it towards the parallel rows of metal tubes, near the igniter.

"Hey, you're not supposed to—"

There was a loud bolt, followed by a spooky whoosh as small blue flames bloomed along the metal tubes.

"Yep, we've got flame! Now let's see if we've got ignition."

Dale had to confess that the sudden appearance of fire, the promise of heat, momentarily filled him with a rush of warmth that had been absent in his home this holiday season, even with the furnace working. But his hopes were crushed when, inexplicably, Wayne switched off the gas, instantly killing the flame. Dale lunged for the offending hand. "What are you doing!"

"Let's have a look at that igniter."

He really didn't have a clue, did he? The rumors were true. Hampton wasn't playing with a full deck.

"Got a screwdriver?" Wayne asked, oblivious. "A flathead?"

Mumbling crossly, Dale ferreted through an old toolbox until he produced three flatheads of different sizes. Wayne rubbed his chin pensively before selecting the middle one. Dale looked over Wayne's bony shoulder as, arms

and elbows jerking and quirking, he performed minor surgery on the machine.

"Aren't you freezing in that shirt?" Dale asked.

"Nah!"

"I've got a coat if you'd—"

"Got it!" he said, withdrawing his head from the exposed belly of the machine. He held the part up to the bald bulb overhead, examining it like a scientist—a small square of metal with two short porcelain tubes set parallel to each other, and a stiff wire curving inward from each tube, like calipers. "Yep, this is the old model, all right. A real dinosaur. Let me see what I can drum up."

In a surprising feat of athleticism, Wayne snapped from his kneeling position to his feet, like those Cossack dancers in the *Nutcracker*. "Be right back! Don't go away!"

Wayne pressed the remote bar, and the garage door rattled open slowly and noisily. "You got some WD-40? You ought to grease those runners! Well, stay warm!"

The streetlights had cast a golden glaze on the snowy expanse, rendering the look of a desolate outer-space city. In the frigid semi-darkness of the garage, Dale watched the rangy figure trot off into the magical night—a little miffed, a little annoyed, a little amused, but mostly overwhelmed by an old sadness, and a nagging guilt.

* * *

His father had once said they were oddly, even tragically matched, like a pair of star-crossed lovers in a Greek myth: inextricably bound yet doomed to imminent disaster. In some ways Dale had spent most of his life trying to prove his father wrong. In other ways he seemed determined to fulfill the prophecy.

He first saw her late one afternoon as he was rushing out of the library en route to his five o'clock class. As the daily recording of the national anthem began blaring across the bucolic Brigham Young University campus, twenty thousand-plus clean-cut, bright-eyed students stood at robotlike attention: she alone had refused to stop. From the library steps, Dale watched curiously as the young iconoclast in paisley skirt, sandals, and macrame shawl slalomed around the obedient bystanders cluttering the cement walkway. One of them, a towering, blue-eyed Aryan, hollered at her in righteous indignation, "Hey! Stop for the anthem!"

She never broke stride, never looked back. "I will when Nixon does!" she hollered over her shoulder.

It was the spring of 1972. Watergate was nothing more than a swank hotel in downtown Washington.

To further ruffle the feathers of the self-anointed Patriot Police, she committed another unpardonable by veering off of the concrete path and marching defiantly across the middle of the lawn, a collective gasp trailing behind her.

The instant the music stopped, Dale lit out after her: up a flight of stairs, across an expansive parking lot crammed with economy cars and station wagons, and up a residential side street lined with winter-stripped elm trees that pierced the blue sky like giant pitchforks. She turned left on one street and right on another that gradually ascended into a little universe of box homes cluttering the foothills of the mighty Wasatch. A slight winter chill still lingered in the April air, but bits of spring green

and gold had begun to bleed through the massive white wall that sheltered the little university town from the rest of the planet.

Dale believed in spiritual promptings, to a point. Since returning from his mission in Argentina almost two years ago, he had dated dozens of marriage-minded mannequins, and in every case the Spirit had ordered him to bail out—sometimes in a front-seat whisper, other times with a clarion call. He didn't know if the Spirit or lame curiosity had directed him to follow this unusual young woman to her residence, nor, at the moment, did he really care.

She turned into a short, narrow driveway leading to a small brick home where two tricycles and a host of Fisher Price toys were scattered across a dormant lawn. He cleared his throat: "So, what's wrong with Nixon?"

She turned. He was expecting something, or someone, quite different: cast-iron jaw, sledgehammer chin, maybe a little hair bristling her upper lip, tougher eyes, a scar on the cheek perhaps—or a tattoo of a knife, a flower, a hammer and sickle. A peace sign. Something.

Lightly freckled, her face looked soft, gentle, Madonna-like. An angel's.

But her tongue cut like a razor: "He's a crook! They'll put him behind bars! Mark my words!"

"Is—is this—is this your house?" Dale found himself stuttering, and he never stuttered.

"I rent a room in the Dungeon."

"The Dungeon?"

"The basement. It's cheap. Twenty a month for a bed, a bathroom, a hot plate, and a refrigerator. What more do you need?"

Dale nodded. *Sure. Right. What more?*

Dale knew he didn't believe in love at first sight, but she must have. How else could

someone like her have fallen so wholly and instantly for someone like him? They were the Owl and the Pussycat.

"I'm Dale," he said.

She smiled. "Hello, Dale. I'm Verna. How long have you been back?"

In the spring of 1973 Richard M. Nixon resigned from the presidency in disgrace. Six months later Dale and Verna were sealed for time and all eternity in the Salt Lake Temple.

Verna liked to think it was a storybook romance, but in fact Dale's parents, multigenerational members of the Mormon aristocracy in Mesa, Arizona, had opposed the union. Yes, she was intelligent, ambitious, hardworking, all the more admirable for having pulled herself up by the bootstraps, defying genetics and genealogy to put herself through school, but . . . This is life, his father, the stately, silver-haired surgeon had argued, not the movies. She had no lineage, or at best a broken one, and a dubious past. She was still wet from her baptism, for pity's sake. There was more, much more, to consider in a marriage. She's not just going to be your wife but the mother of your children and our grandchildren

All of his life, Dale, the firstborn of seven, had obediently jumped through the requisite hoops: Eagle Scout, Seminary, mission, and now temple marriage.

"So what's wrong with that?" he said.

"You're making your bed, you're going to have to sleep in it."

"As long as she's in it, I'm okay."

His father couldn't believe he'd said that. Neither could Dale.

"Don't, Dale. I know what you're thinking, but the novelty will wear off and you'll regret it. She's like nailing jelly to the wall."

"I like jelly," Dale said. "Jam, too."

"What's that girl done to you? You never talked like that before."

Hordes of Dale's aunts, uncles, cousins, and shirttail relatives attended the sealing ceremony. On Verna's side, a half brother hobbled into the reception wearing mangy brown hair to his shoulders and a thrift store suit.

After graduating that spring, they drove across the country in his old Ford Pinto, resurrecting it once with baling wire and again with the power of prayer, to attend law school in Baltimore, conveniently distant from relatives of either tribe.

Their first Christmas was celebrated in a tiny apartment with a bedroom so small they had to shuffle sideways to get around the queen mattress on the floor. Too broke to buy a Christmas tree, she constructed a hearth out of cardboard boxes, painting the bricks red, the mortar gray, with golden flames wavering in the grate. At a yard sale she bought a string of twenty Chinese lights for a dollar and strung them around the perimeter. On Christmas Eve they shared a simple dinner, half of it from cans. Alternating verses, they read the scriptural account of the nativity and sang a few carols. Dale was accustomed to a vast Christmas Eve gathering of family and friends, complete with baked ham and turkey and candied yams and egg nog flowing like a river, an all-night ceremony of conversation and song. But their evening was still young, barely eight o'clock, and they had already exhausted their itinerary. All that remained was their modest gift exchange.

She opened hers first, a pocketbook of Shakespeare's sonnets, thanking him profusely. Her gift to him was a soft bundle about the size of a small pillow, swaddled in butcher paper she had decorated with Crayola markers: a solitary star shining above the domed silhouette of Bethlehem. Unwrapping it, he looked at her oddly and forced a smile. It was a heavy wool scarf, the ugliest plaid affair he had ever seen. "Thanks," he said. "This is—it's really neat."

They sat at the little kitchen table with the warped Formica veneer trying so hard to appear happy. But the bright-eyed baby face that had greeted her that first day in the foothills of Provo sagged with sadness.

"What's the matter?" she asked, leaning across the table and stroking his forearm. "It's Christmas!"

"I'm fine," he said, but his smile was an anchor waiting to be dropped.

"You look so sad."

"I'm fine."

"You miss your family, don't you?"

"No."

"Yes, you do. I would if I . . ."

"If you what?" he asked a little more sharply than he'd intended.

"If I had a nice family like yours."

"Look, I don't miss them, okay?" He waited a moment for his anger or frustration or whatever was eating him to subside. "And I'm sorry for barking at you like that."

"You don't bark. Dogs bark."

"Oh, I don't? Then what do I do?"

"You kind of scowl—maybe like an alley cat when you take his food away."

"An alley cat, hunh?"

"Yeah. An alley cat."

Then he turned the tables on her. "I'm sorry, Verna."

"Sorry about what?"

"This. I didn't mean for it to be like this."

"Like what?"

"This!" he shouted, and she winced, looking guilty, like she felt she was the cause, as his arm swung out and around, encircling the entire apartment—the cramped kitchen, the paint-peeling walls, the cheap plastic dishes, the tiny ground-level windows buried under snow.

He would remember her expression at that moment and carry it with him for the next twenty years. Although he didn't fully appreciate it at the time—wouldn't until it was too late—really, at that moment he realized that she absolutely adored him. It wasn't the puppy dog admiration that had trailed him through his letterman days in high school, but something altogether different. He had wondered, at that moment, if he could ever possibly love her as deeply as she appeared to love him.

He waited for her to say the obvious: "Hey, cheer up! We have a home, food, a nice soft bed. The snow's falling but it's warm. I have you." But she had other plans.

"Aren't you going to try it on?" she asked.

"Sure," he said, slowly unfolding the pathetic piece of cloth. Hidden inside he found a collection of objects: toothbrush, toothpaste, a bar of soap, a hand towel, three packages of trail mix.

"Are we going camping?" he asked sourly. "This looks like a survival kit."

"It is a survival kit!" she said. Popping up, she reached across the table and grabbed his arm. "Let's go!"

He gazed around the cramped apartment incredulously. "Go where?"

"Come on!" she said, tossing him his down jacket. "And don't forget your survival kit!"

As she led him up the dark stairwell to the ground floor, he pressed her for details: Where are we headed? What's going on?

She remained elusive. "It's important," she

replied, "for families to establish Christmas traditions."

"I agree. Now would you mind telling me about ours?"

She smiled. "Trust me," she said, and they stepped out into the frigid night. The snow had stopped falling but the wind had stiffened, tugging curtly at the hem of her overcoat. As they began marching briskly down the city sidewalk, banked with dirty, cindered snow, like rows of rotting teeth, she instructed him to read the note taped to the tube of toothpaste. Reluctantly, he did: *Please deliver to someone less fortunate before the clock strikes twelve on Christmas Eve. If you fail, you'll turn into a mistletoe and spend the rest of forever hanging from a rafter watching happy young couples kiss passionately in broad daylight. Good luck and God bless.*

He stared at her oddly, uncertain whether to laugh or cry. What on earth had he gotten himself into? They were so totally, absolutely different. Maybe his father had been right. Nailing jelly to the wall.

She blew him a kiss. "Smile," she whispered. "It's painless."

They hadn't gone half a block before they found an old black man in a threadbare windbreaker curled up asleep in a metal grate, trying to garner some subterranean heat. Dale quickly surveyed the igneous moonscape that was the old man's face, his prickly-pear chin, his mouth hanging open like a caught fish. A green ski cap covered his head, and his stubby fingers poked through his mittens like bloated worms. Dale knelt down, gently lifted the man's head, and placed the bundle underneath it. Rising, he gazed down the street to where a handful of colored lights were blinking on the grim storefronts, barred and locked for the

night. For a moment he thought he could hear carolers belting out a hearty Christmas tune, but the distant screaming of a siren instantly chased away any holiday illusions tinkering in his head. Dale removed his down jacket and placed it tenderly over the old man. Then he turned to go, quickly, embarrassed.

As they hurried back to their apartment in silence, she hooked her arm around his waist and leaned her head on his shoulder. "I love you," she whispered.

He didn't answer her that night. He knew she was right, one hundred percent right. He also knew that that would be their eventual downfall.

"Next year," she panted, trying to keep pace with him, "you get to make the kit and I get to do the honors."

Such was the birth of their Christmas Eve ritual. Each year they alternated roles, one person creating the kit, the other delivering it. During their law school days, when they lived downtown, it was quite easy to find a needy soul. But as Dale's practice flourished and they found themselves moving farther and farther west and higher and higher up the hill, their search for worthy recipients became more of an annual odyssey. Their survival kits grew bigger and more elaborate as well, until they found themselves purchasing Alpine backpacks from R.E.I. and stuffing them with dome tents, mess kits, sub-zero sleeping bags, and a week's supply of food. But they were always faithful to their tradition, even when they returned late from a Christmas Eve party or the year he contracted a nasty virus that staked him to his bed for a week. Even the year he broke her heart.

Last year was the first year in twenty they had missed their Christmas Eve ritual. He'd sat up all night in the sofa chair waiting for her, hoping, praying at one point, that God in His infinite mercy would peer into his ravaged heart, part the veil, and allow her to pass through for a few moments to offer a bit of comfort to a lonely man groping through middle age. In retrospect, he'd longed to see her not so much to perform their private ceremony but to talk, to apologize, to tell her the many things he couldn't because it had happened instantly, so fast. An hour would have been heaven, but all he really needed was four seconds. Four words. "Thank you. I'm sorry." Make it seven. "I love you." Eight. "Always." Eight seconds. Anything.

In retrospect, it had been a silly, naive, childish hope—a Christmas wish far beyond the permissible pale. Death would have been the next best alternative—death and reunion. But taking his own life now would have jeopardized theirs together in the hereafter: there was that much religion left in him, or fear. So while he didn't actively seek death out, he'd taken no precautions to avoid it. He recalled late one night as he was meandering down the cul-de-sac, a big, black pickup truck swept around the corner of a merging side street, tires screaming, engine roaring, headlights speeding towards him like a pair of Nolan Ryan fast-balls. Instead of diving for safety, Dale walked calmly towards the speeding fireballs, unflinching, wearing a smile that probably unnerved the teenaged driver even more than the impromptu game of chicken. The driver managed to swerve around him, hollering a string of obscenities as he passed. At that point Dale had realized deliverance was a distant country, and many miles remained in his journey. Lonely miles.

* * *

He was awakened by a loud yet intimate rapping at the front door. Groggily, he cast aside the thermal blanket, rising slowly from the sofa, like a drunk in a rowboat on rough waters, and trudged across the family room. Pushing open the French doors, Dale confronted an invisible wall of ice. The oak bannisters, the Tewa pottery occupying the antique nightstand, the walnut coatrack, the chandelier, the framed portrait of the prophet—everything in the entryway looked cold, sterile, cryogenically bound. It reminded him of that frozen country manor in *Dr. Zhivago*. A thin layer of ice framed the vertical window, beside the door. He placed his finger tentatively in the lower right-hand corner and scratched, confirming his fears: the plague had crept inside. It began squeezing his bare scalp and mercilessly pinching his ears and the tip of his nose. Each breath blossomed ash-white before his eyes. There was a cold, creepy presence, as if the Ghost of Christmas Future had moved in for the night.

Dale yanked open the heavy oak door.

"Come in! Come in! You must be freezing!"

Wayne's mouth arched into a big clownlike smile. "Not too bad." He was still wearing his aloha shirt, his bare arms pebbled with goose bumps, the thick blond hairs levitating from the chill. He was holding a cigar box overflowing with assorted metal parts, wires, tubes—a micro junkyard.

Wayne stepped eagerly into the frigid entry, his free hand buried deeply in the pocket of his faded blue jeans.

"What time is it?" Dale glanced at his wristwatch. "Eleven-thirty—hey, you didn't walk all that way, did you?"

Wayne shrugged. "It wasn't that far."

Dale silently chastised himself for being so

inhospitable, so focused on his own suffering that he failed to see or feel the ailments of others. Verna would have been disappointed in him—not angry or ashamed, but disappointed. She would never have turned someone out the night before Christmas, or any other night. She was always bringing strangers home, rescuing them from the camps and shelters and freeway on-ramps, the Will Work for Food folks. One night she brought home a mangy couple she'd seen stumbling across the railroad tracks. Their clothes were ragged and reeked of urine. Dale greeted them guardedly in their majestic entry, then pulled Verna aside. "What are you doing? Are you nuts?"

"They need a bath."

"I can smell that!"

"And a place to sleep."

"Sleep? We can't—they can't—"

"How can we say no?"

"We don't know anything about these people!"

"So let's get to know them."

She smiled at him, fluttered her eyelashes, not mockingly but flirtingly, and whispered, "'Inasmuch as ye have done it unto the least of these' . . ."

"Come—come in here," Dale said, directing Wayne into the family room and seating him next to the space heater. He placed the thermal blanket over his shoulders, Indian style. "You want some hot cocoa?" Dale was already moving towards the kitchen counter.

"Yes. Yes, that would be nice." Wayne's lips looked pale, dangerously blue.

Dale popped open a cupboard and rummaged around until he located the box of Carnation hot chocolate mix. He tore open two small packages, emptied each into a mug, filled the mugs with water, and placed them in the microwave. He punched several buttons on the control panel. The machine purred softly as he scanned the refrigerator for snacks: cheese, carrot sticks, lettuce, cranberry juice, a half loaf of twelve-grain bread. Verna's vegetarian tendencies had gradually prevailed over the years.

"Are you hungry?" he asked. "Will you eat a grilled cheese sandwich?"

"Wonderful! That would be great!"

Wayne seemed genuinely pleased, which eased some of Dale's guilt. He was not yet ready to admit that perhaps it even made him feel good as well.

Dale cut several strips of Wisconsin cheddar, slathered Shedd's Spread on four slices of twelve-grain, and placed the sandwiches in a frying pan, checking them periodically. The microwave bleeped. He quickly removed the two mugs, stirring the chocolate froth bubbling darkly on top until it formed a rich, smooth blend. He offered the bigger mug to Wayne, whose face was beginning to appear less stiff and contracted and more its saggy old self.

"Thanks," he said, sipping loudly. "This is great! Wonderful!"

Dale retrieved the two grilled cheese sandwiches, and the two men sat side by side on the sofa and ate.

"You should have asked me for a ride," Dale said.

Wayne sipped slowly, smiled. "You should have offered."

"True."

Wayne wolfed down his sandwich and began licking his greasy fingertips.

"Let me get you a napkin," Dale said, rising. "Want another? There's plenty?"

"No, no! I'm fine."

When Dale returned, Wayne was sitting on the carpet, leaning back against the sofa, his legs crossed Indian style, crowding the penurious warmth of the space heater. Dale sat beside him on the floor.

"So what made you come here tonight?" Dale asked. "And don't say you were prompted by the Spirit. I used to be a bishop. I know the script."

"And all the tricks, too, I'll bet."

"All of them. So tell me, the bishop put you up to it, didn't he? Or old Brother Wyman. He's always trying to light a fire under the high priests."

Dale was bantering, trying to thaw the ice that he himself had hardened. Wayne peered thoughtfully into his mug, as if he were reading tea leaves. "I guess I just didn't want to be alone tonight." He looked up, but this time his face cracked like plaster from his effort to smile. "I wanted some company. I thought you might want some too."

Dale nodded cautiously. It was one thing to share food and shelter; it was something else to assume associations.

"Yeah," he said, "I lost my Cheryl five years ago."

My Cheryl? It sounded so intimate, so endearing, so—human? Odd, or perhaps indicative, that he had never regarded Wayne in a married state, or any other state. He tried to picture Wayne and his wife. A watery image from American Gothic formed in his mind.

"It's hard," Wayne said. "Isn't it?"

Hard? Which part? Before or after? Giving, receiving, or taking away? Dale recalled fights that seemed so picayune now—sandbox quarrels over infertility, adoption, vacations, his second marriage to racquetball, hers to whatever cause was en vogue at the time: save the rain forest, save the spotted owl, walk for hunger. What should have been mere asterisks to an otherwise beautifully told tale had been blown grotesquely out of proportion in his memory, like dismal caricatures. His grief, he realized, was grounded less in loss than in regret, little things he had and hadn't said or done; wishing he could graciously tape over this or that part of their life story.

In retrospect, he had secretly hoped that over the years she would grow out of her idiosyncrasies. But while he had climbed the ladder socially and professionally, she had moved laterally, if at all. She still wore funky broad-brimmed hats to church and long paisley skirts to her ankles. The "Hippie Lady," the church kids called her behind her back. When they moved into their dream house, a gabled Victorian manor in the La Plata Mountains, just outside of Durango, it annoyed him that she didn't seem to fully appreciate his hard-earned bounty. When she joked about "large and spacious buildings" and too many rooms to clean, he took it personally.

The day after he was called to serve as bishop, he took her out to lunch for a heart-to-heart. He was looking so handsome and professional in his three-piece suit, like a junior General Authority. He ordered ahi Hawaiian-style, her favorite, and they sat in an intimate little booth overlooking the canyon, talking casually. Towards the end of the meal, he mentioned his new calling.

"Oh, you'll be wonderful!" she said. "You always are! I just know it!"

Twenty years and she still adored him, somehow had managed to overlook his moodiness and after-cracker fits, his exacting insistence that the dishes be stacked just so.

Not just for him, he explained. But also for her, the mother of the ward now. Setting an example was so important, especially to the youth. Avoiding even the appearance of evil.

"So who's evil?" she asked, batting her eyes seductively. She still wore no makeup except for a touch of blue under her eyes. It was beginning to show now, her cosmetic indifference, and all those years of loitering in the sun without protection. Little webs were engraved on her cheeks and grooves spread from the corners of her eyes like spokes from a wheel. Still, she hooked her foot around his, tugging it gently, teasingly.

"No one's evil," he said. "That's not what I meant. I think you need to be—look, will you knock it off for a minute? Can't you be serious for once? I think you need to be, oh, a little more fashion conscious, that's all."

She was silent for what had seemed like a short lifetime.

"Verna?"

"You really want me to do this, don't you? I mean, it means a lot to you, doesn't it?"

"Yes. Yes it does." And then he had said the one thing that she could never forgive. "My church career—"

"Okay," she said, dabbing the corners of her lips with her napkin. "Okay, I can do that."

She asked for the check, although he paid the bill. They kissed and parted company: he drove back to the office in his Lexus, while she zoomed off to the mall in her little Subaru where, in her words, recorded in her journal: *I strolled into Dillard's like I had money and knew what to do with it, and I bought out the store: dress suits, heels, three-piece drop-dead showcase stuff.*

He was thirty-nine that summer; she was thirty-eight. They would share three more years together, more or less.

He was trying to recall how it had gone that October morning, who had cast the first stone? Was it him, mumbling something about her half brother's devil-may-care ship-without-a-rudder existence, how he was brave and adventurous with the macho stuff of the world, but in the spiritual wilderness of commitment and sacrifice, he was a total washout. Or had she started it, sensing his annoyance, beating him to the draw: "Of course you don't want to! It's spur-of-the-moment, unplanned, unscheduled, unapproved by sixteen committees and four show-of-hands!"

It went back and forth like that, childishly, thoughtlessly, and then cruelly: "And most of all, it just might be fun, heaven forbid! Just because you're afraid of your own shadow doesn't mean you have to lock the rest of the world in a box!"

Contrary to her accusations, Dale's fear of flying wasn't entirely irrational. Shortly after his eighth birthday, his Uncle Lenny and favorite cousin, Chris, were flying down to attend Dale's baptism when, for reasons Dale would never truly understand, the Cessna suddenly dipped and tucked, and what had at first appeared to be a simple sky trick ended up a tragic pillar of smoke and fire on the chaparral-studded hills of southern California. Dale and his father had watched from the runway where they had arrived right on schedule for the landing.

"You're not going up in that tinker toy plane with your half-cocked half brother. End of discussion!"

At that moment she had mentally drawn a line in the sand. No more knuckling under—she'd even used that phrase: "And I suppose you expect me to knuckle under again?"

Afterwards came a dark period of second guessing: if he hadn't been so insistent, dictatorial, pigheaded, maybe she would have relented. Or if he'd agreed to join her. Maybe she was just testing him to see. If he'd gone with her, things would have run smoothly. No gasping engine, no twirling free fall, no smoke and fire. At worst, they would have died together. But why did she have to ride the stupid plane to begin with? Why didn't he just grab her by the arm and say "No! No you will not go!" Why didn't he back off for once? If he'd just let her see the worry in his eyes. If he'd told her about his cousin Chris and Uncle Lenny. No, he had to have it his way, always his. He was the priesthood holder; he was the boss. But it wasn't even that: no one could have lorded it over her by virtue of the priesthood or any other -hood. No one could have unless she allowed them to. And why had she allowed him all those years?

As a bishop he used to wonder how some of his most staunch Latter-day Saints could lose their faith in what appeared to be a relatively short time. Now he knew. The words of comfort and logic he used to shower on others (adversity is part of life . . . the refiner's fire . . . if God answered all of our prayers all of the time . . . Mortality is the twinkling of an eye, and we'll be united eternally . . .) rang hollow. At best, God seemed coolly indifferent; at worst, sadistically ironic.

"Well, you know what they say?" Wayne was hunkered up by the sofa now, cradling the cigar box of junk in his arm.

"What's that?" Dale asked. He was still sitting on the floor Indian style, close to the space heater.

"It's always hardest on the one who stays behind." Wayne hopped to his feet and began marching down the hall.

"Hey, where are you going?"

"Work to do!"

Three hours later, the two men were kneeling side by side in the freezing garage, not in joint prayer but in a desperate effort to work a miracle in the cold belly of the furnace. The cigar box was almost empty, the misfired parts forming an altar to futility on the cold concrete floor. Dale's hands were tucked under his armpits, and he was rocking slowly back and forth, trying to generate some warmth, as Wayne jerryrigged yet another old igniter with a pair of needlenose pliers. Both men were wearing down jackets and ski caps that Dale had salvaged from the basement. Although they were in no grave danger yet, the bitter cold had lowered their defenses, and like doomed men in a rowboat or trapped in a Himalayan blizzard, they began sharing confidences. At one point Dale asked Wayne about his wife. "Do you ever get over it?"

Wayne withdrew his head from inside the furnace and smiled sadly. "Nope."

"That's encouraging."

"It does get better, though. The first year was awful. At first I'd look around and see her everywhere: as a twenty-year-old in faded blue jeans strolling to the post office, at thirty-five checking out the vegetables at Safeway. One day at the mall I saw her from behind. Twenty-four or twenty-five, streaked blonde hair past her waist and cheerleader curves. I picked up the pace, began weaving through the Saturday crowd. When I finally caught up to her, she was standing in line at the Sears charge card place. I reached out and put my hand on her shoulder and gave it a little squeeze, in a certain way, like I used to do. She looked back with a split-second smile, as if she were expecting me, but in that moment my Cheryl disappeared, and I was looking at a total stranger, although all I remember now is her mouth, this big giant pit with red around it and the awful sound coming out, like a broken siren, and then a thousand rent-a-cops, potbellied old guys in uniforms, reaching for their guns like it was their first time ever, and the woman still screaming like a siren, and I'm standing smack there in the middle while the rest of the store's crowding around to watch. And there's a dozen folks from church or work or the neighborhood, folks you really know, you know. And next thing they're putting cuffs on me, and I'm standing there with my eyes closed, wishing, praying that everyone else has theirs closed too, hoping they can't see me because I can't see them. But it was never the same after that. The bishop, when I explained it, he said he understood, things like that happen, no harm done really, but I really ought to be more careful from now on—you know how people are about things like that nowadays. I said yes, yes, of course, I'll do that, bishop, I will. But it wasn't another week before I was released as Blazer Scout leader and made secretary to the high priests. You just get so lonely sometimes, you know what I mean?"

Dale nodded. "So, have you got any plans tonight?"

Wayne reburied his head in the machine. "Fixing your furnace, I guess. Give me that flathead, will you?"

Dale handed him the tool. "Why don't you spend the night here?"

Wayne's elbows jerked and pulled as he inserted the jerryrigged igniter. "Okay, give me some gas."

Dale twisted the brass clasp.

"Power?"

Dale inserted the plug into the outlet and turned the pilot knob to "on." Dale's heart soared as he heard three quick clicks, like ticking teeth. A thread of laser-blue began writhing as if it were being tortured. Then nothing.

Dale's shoulders collapsed. "No!"

Wayne calmly removed the igniter and with the pliers twisted one of the wires inward a fraction of an inch. "Amazing what a teeny tiny little adjustment can do."

As he reinstalled the igniter, Dale watched from behind.

"You never give up, do you?"

"Nope."

"Do you think you'll ever remarry?"

"Nope. Do you?"

"I don't know. Maybe. Do you think that's wrong?"

"Nope."

"You just don't want to remarry? You said you were lonely."

"I try to keep busy."

"You know something? I think my wife would have really liked you."

Wincing, Wayne tightened the last screw. "Why do you think that?"

"I don't know. She just would. And believe me, that's a compliment."

"I believe you. Gimme some gas, please."

Dale turned the fuel valve and twisted the pilot knob: he heard the ticking teeth; the blue thread wriggled like a worm on fire.

"Come on," Wayne muttered, tapping the screwdriver against the metal frame. "Come on."

The furnace issued a deep, consumptive breath. There was a moment's silence, and the cold belly belched blue flames. It was a modest show of pyrotechnics, but to Dale's cold yearning it bore sheer wizardry, as if Prometheus had just pulled off a cross-cultural whammy, stealing fire from the Norse gods. He gazed admiringly at the gawky Quixote man, the midnight nightmare who had become a miracle worker. "You did it," he whispered.

As blue flames bloomed along the metal tubes, Dale listened for the first warm breath to puff through the interior vents. And for just a moment, he thought he heard a jubilant shout from within, as if a dear old friend had been magically raised from the dead.

MICHAEL FILLERUP is the author of *Visions and Other Stories* and a novel, *Beyond the River*. He lives with his wife, Rebecca, and their four children in Flagstaff, Arizona.

THE HOPE CHEST

Eileen G. Kump

IT WAS NOT A NEW GAME, the game of sacrifice at Christmas. Others had done it. People we knew had given generously and even gone without themselves, but it had always looked too hard. It meant that Julie, who was only four years old and who had already begun to be very, very good, would not receive a doll for Christmas. I watched our children, an astonished spectator.

The older children hovered around Julie, their foreheads furrowed. Poor Julie! In their excitement, they had forgotten about her.

Robert, twelve, and always the first of our children to feel sympathy, spoke first, spelling slowly. "*J-u-l-i-e* still believes in *S-a-n-t-a C-l-a-u-s*. If we let her play, she won't get a *d-o-l-l*."

"Play? I want to play." Whatever the game was, Julie always begged to be included.

"It isn't exactly a game, Julie," said Rachel.

"You're too little," said Linda, age ten.

"I want to play. Please let me play."

"She won't understand!" Robert pleaded. "She won't!"

* * *

Rachel, sixteen, had placed herself in charge. I knew that she was now the commander in chief. She would see this sacrifice through and her marching song would keep the younger children going. She explained to Julie that we were going to give Christmas presents to another family we didn't even know. "And," she said, "to be really true, we are not going to get any gifts ourselves. We're giving them up to make some poor children happy."

Julie looked amazed, but she adored her big sister.

"Is that okay?" asked Rachel.

"Okay," said Julie.

"How will you feel when Susie comes over with a new doll and you don't have one?

"I *want* to play."

"All right. You can play. We'll all play."

* * *

Christmas was two months away, but excitement, like a gigantic balloon, filled the house. The children were cheerful and secretive with each other. When I suggested later that maybe we could give without giving up, Rachel was patient with me. "Mother, don't you see that we have to go without our own presents too? We have to really sacrifice. We have to."

In the days that followed I often wished the children had given us a chance to persuade them. If they had, I might also have convinced myself that they could do this. After all, it was my fault.

I had run into an old friend downtown who, of all things, was Christmas shopping in October.

"Already?" I gasped, and was quickly swept into a cynical look at the entire season. "Christmas is such a trying time," I began.

"Oh my, yes," said my friend. "I just struggled through snoopy September—and it's no easy thing trying to find out what people want! Now it's the middle of October already, and I can't find a thing on my list that I can afford. In November I'll panic and end up buy-ing all the wrong things so I can spend December recuperating!"

We both laughed, but even as I said, "I know what you mean," I really didn't, and at supper I told the children that as I had driven home I was sure that my own Christmases had been beautiful, especially the ones with them, but that in spite of all this, I wondered if Christmas had ever been quite true. Somehow, I told them, there must be a way to find out. Would giving to a needy family help? When Rachel suggested to me later that we give up our own gifts as well, she made it sound easy—even necessary. Perhaps that was the answer. Could they see it through? Could I bear to watch?

Rachel, gifted, her piano teacher said, would give up the desired metronome. "I think it would be neat to sacrifice." Robert was memorizing every country in the world for social studies, his only hope of an A. "Ah, what's so special about a sixteen-inch laminated world globe? The world was flat a long time before it was round."

Linda frowned. Not that she wasn't willing, but she had refined her sacrifice into a philosophical dilemma. Which gift would she give up because she couldn't have both, and which would she give up so that someone else could have a merry Christmas? Julie, uncomprehending but willing, would make do with last year's doll.

* * *

As the days passed under gray skies, bringing morning frost as thick as new snow, as November unfolded, white and biting, I warmed toward sacrifice. Roy and the children went about buying gifts for that other family.

Main Street became a sea of light. Carols flowed from the old tabernacle tower into the cold air. They flowed to me, and I sang as I sewed for someone else's children and baked twice as many cookies as usual. My own would at least have all they could eat.

I became obsessed with the rightness of our adventure and perhaps would have been able to follow it through with certainty if I had not gone downtown with Roy one crisp glowing evening a few days before Christmas. The stroll had become a ritual for just the two of us while our children decorated the tree. Among a few remaining toys on haphazard display, I saw the doll.

"Oh!"

"What's the matter?"

"Oh, Roy, isn't it pretty?"

He put his arm around my shoulders. "We already have a doll for their little girl."

"I know—I—I was thinking of Julie. I was thinking of our own little girl, and I suddenly realized how bleak, how—"

He kept me beside him as we walked on. "I understand, believe me. I've thought of our own every time we've come shopping. But you underestimate them. They can do this."

I was not listening. The doll had curls the color of butter. They were not made of glossy imitation strands that would soon snarl but had been drawn there. They reminded me of my own childhood dolls, dolls with painted swirls of golden hair that quietly faded but never tangled.

I could see the doll in Julie's arms and with each step was torn between the rightness of giving to the poor and the sadness of not giving to our own. Why, I didn't even know that other family! They were sizes and ages and they were wanting, but what did they need? Rachel needed a metronome. Robert needed a world globe because he needed to succeed. Amy had waited with much beyond ten-year-old patience for the year that meant a bicycle. Oh, the radio had been a sudden fancy, but even that was a need because a serious child needed to be fanciful.

* * *

That night I lay awake. The balloon of excitement that filled our house soared for the children, bright and buoyant. For me, it had acquired an invisible leak and was losing air with each passing day. I got out of bed and went downstairs where that other family's gifts surrounded our Christmas tree. As I turned on the lights, their glowing colors almost sang to me: *Joy to the world! Peace on earth!* We looked so prosperous. And we were! Why invite disappointment? Couldn't we give without giving up? Christmas was supposed to make us happy too!

Suddenly, I could not go through with this adventure, and I knew what to do. On Christmas morning the children could feel not only the warmth of giving to that other family but the surprise, the true surprise, of seeing unexpected presents! Of seeing their unselfishness rewarded! Why not buy for them after all? Their hearts had already given, and the heart was the thing. Surely Roy would agree with me. Tomorrow we would buy them at least something.

* * *

I closed my eyes and saw the doll propped under our tree. Dolls and Christmas belonged together. To think I had almost forgotten that! I invited a memory, a memory of my last doll, the one I had pretended not to want because my friends wanted ice skates and books. They said we were too old for dolls, but my beloved parents knew better. A few months later, I left my Christmas doll out in the rain. The cloth body matted. The sweet face blistered. Of course I saved the doll, but I never played with it again. Soon I really was too old, and years later I gave the doll to Rachel, who wore it out lovingly. But my Christmas memory was of a blistered as well as a beautiful doll.

Other memories awoke in my mind. There was the silly Christmas I had the mumps and got exactly what I asked for, prayed for, peeked into drawers and closets for, and then was too miserable to enjoy. In those days all the kids had a store-bought snowsuit, except me. That Christmas morning my parents coaxed me to come and see what was hanging by the tree, but I wouldn't do it because my jaw hurt. Why did I remember that morning when I wanted to bring back something happy? A few days later I must have put on my new snowsuit and run out into the snow, but that silly mumps memory had lingered, and I realized that even though my parents understood mumps, they had struggled to afford what I just had to have—and on Christmas morning I had disappointed them.

Why *these* memories? My first Christmas with Roy, the package that looked extravagant and mysterious and turned out to be a saucepan.

One Christmas, forever tender to memory's touch, I tried not to remember. I had felt all grown up at sixteen. I was too tall, freckled, and skinny but hopeful. It was the year my girl-friends and I spent guessing how long it would be until we got married, the year the world came to an end every time the phone rang for

somebody else. I had wanted a real cedar chest with a shining surface, a waterfall lid, embellished corners, and insides that smelled like the canyon. A place for hope and embroidered pillowcases. I had wanted it more than I had ever wanted anything, but it cost too much. I knew that. I tried not to talk about it, and when I did I felt mean and ungrateful.

That was the December when, every night after supper, my father went back to the school where he taught social studies. None of us asked why. Christmas was a time for mysteries. And I did not worry when Dad and Mom didn't ask me what else I dreamed of. It would be fun to have a surprise, and I would be happy for their sakes no matter what.

* * *

When I walked into the living room that Christmas morning, the first thing I saw was not presents but the expression on my father's face. He was watching me, and he had never looked happier. My heart jumped. Was it possible?

Then I saw the hope chest. It had a shallow lid with square corners. It was dark brown, obviously homemade, and it smelled like paint. I hurried to lift the lid as if with pleasure but really to see if there wasn't something inside, something to help me over this moment. The chest was empty. I hugged my dad and ran my fingers along the brown surfaces, but of course it was too late. I knew my face had betrayed me. My heart shouted, "Smile! Be grateful. Can't you see the love that has gone into this gift?" But I knew without looking at him that the joy I had seen on my father's face was not there now. The pain had already been inflicted. I added to it a few years later when I took my own money and bought a cedar chest with a waterfall lid and fancy corners, and into it moved my romantic dreams.

As I lay remembering, I created in my mind a scene I had never considered: my school-teacher father turned awkward carpenter, slowly building a hope chest in the junior high shop room for his oldest daughter—sawing, sanding, hammering, humming, maybe allowing a few tears over the little girl suddenly a young lady thinking about a trousseau. He must have wished I would stay little a while longer, but he had put time and love into making my dream toward womanhood and romance come true.

Now I was the mother of a sixteen-year-old daughter who wanted a metronome and a four-year-old whose doll was worn out, and I knew that I must let them feel their sacrifice through. A gift was no assurance of happiness. Even the most meaningful gift did not necessarily make a day merry. Giving it up might.

Pain and Christmas. An odd pair. But in my memories they went together, belonged together. Why had pain and Christmas seemed so contradictory anyway? Christ's glorious birth, a time for angels to sing, had been after all but a beginning. Ultimately, he was "a man of sorrows, and acquainted with grief."

* * *

Grandma sent her usual Christmas box of sleeping socks for Roy and me, mittens for the children, and candied popcorn for everyone. By noon Christmas Day the house was a jungle of orange peelings and peanut shells. I kept an inquisitive eye on the children and was astounded. Over and over again, they recreated what must be happening in a humble home somewhere in another part of town, recreated everything down to what a two-year-old tries to say when he sees his own red truck.

I tensed when friends burst in with "Where's the loot?" But how easily Rachel and Robert and Linda explained. Soon even their young guests were enjoying that other Christmas somewhere and predicting it as if each were Santa Claus himself. Julie—still amazed—had only a bad moment or two. She hadn't expected a new doll but the surprise of her playmates when they discovered she didn't have one was hard for her. Of course, with a little nudging from Rachel, they took turns being the daddy.

"Mother," said Rachel as we straightened the living room that evening, "Can we sacrifice again next year? That was fun." I smiled. I didn't know what to say. Another true Christmas would be too hard. But I knew that this Christmas would be added to my memories of Christmases past and that because of it the pain in remembering others had diminished.

Eileen G. Kump lives with her husband, Ferrell, in St. Joseph, Missouri. They are the parents of four children. She is the author of one book of short stories, *Bread and Milk and Other Stories,* and numerous other published articles and short stories. She taught in the English Department at Brigham Young University for six years. She is currently a homemaker, volunteer in adult literacy, and grateful grandmother.

"YOU BETTER WATCH OUT!"

Jennifer Pritchett

HERE I AM, a grown adult, and I'm afraid of Santa Claus. I thought I was over it long ago. But today I was walking through the mall with my daughter, and the Santa Claus just outside Mervyn's winked at me. And I realized it's still there—the fear.

It's just the beginning of the Christmas season, and the stores are bringing out all their lights and tinsel and Styrofoam snowflakes. Outside Mervyn's they have set up what amounts to a winter palace, with giant be-ribboned boxes as big as refrigerators, mechanical reindeer who walk in place pulling a sleigh, and brightly dressed, though somewhat diabolical-looking elves. Set back among this holiday wonderland are three wide steps, covered with a gold-fringed carpet, that lead to a huge, velvet-covered armchair. Here Santa sat, waiting for helpless children to be perched on his knee, and winked at me. And I felt like running away.

* * *

When I was a little girl I was scared to death of Santa Claus. After all, I reasoned, who in their right mind wouldn't be? He'd corner you in drugstores and outside of Hallmark's and make you tell him how you were and what you were doing and what you hoped to get for Christmas. He was nosy and intrusive, watching you all the time and sneaking into your house at night once a year to reward your deeds. Just think of the words to the song, how he sees us when we're sleeping, and knows when we're awake, how he knows if we've been bad or good—so you'd better be good for goodness sake! Be good or what? What would he do to you? For me, there was always something threatening about that song. And Santa Claus was someone "out there" who always knew when I did something wrong.

My dad knew I was scared of Santa and used to make the most of it. He'd get that look he gets when he spins a ridiculous tale, his eyes bright, half-smiling and half-filled with a look of mock innocence. "You know, Nat," he'd say—that's his special nickname for Natalie—"when Santa comes down the chimney on Christmas Eve he wants to know if you're really, truly asleep, and not just pretending. He'll quietly sneak to where you're sleeping to find out. If you're awake, you'll only barely be able to hear the padded footsteps of his soft black boots. Then he'll come right up to you, and he'll move his face closer and closer to yours until it's almost touching. And if you wake up and open your eyes his face will be close—this close!" he'd say and thrust his face right up against my nose, "and he'll be staring you right in the eyes!"

"Dad!" I'd say accusingly, trying not to laugh. "That's terrible!" I knew he was teasing me. But something about his story haunted me, and when Christmas Eve finally came around, the feeling would linger and I was afraid to go to bed. I didn't want to tell my brothers and sisters, because I knew they'd make fun of me. And I was even more ashamed to tell my dad, because I didn't want him to know I almost believed him.

I was therefore left on Christmas Eve lying in my bed, afraid to be found awake—in which case I had no idea what the jolly old fellow would do to me—and too afraid to fall asleep for fear I'd awake with Santa's face pressed close, his piercing blue eyes staring into mine. So I'd lie awake for hours, sometimes pretending to be asleep, sometimes afraid to pretend, my ears straining for the sound of his faint bells, hearing only the softness of falling snow or the ringing silence of an icy night sky.

My father had his own reasons to be cautious of Santa. When he was a boy, his Uncle Ace told him if he'd hold his hand straight up in the air all night, Santa would leave a candy cane in it. "I heard the old man say it himself," Ace confided. "I heard him downstairs and sneaked out of bed to the upstairs railing. He was telling one of his elves. He was laughing, saying all the children had to do was leave their arm straight in the air all night, but none of them ever makes it. Not one."

Ace was a tease too—and Dad knew it—but what if this was true? Dad knew he had to try. It wasn't just the candy cane he wanted. It was the challenge of being the first to get one. So when my grandma came in to my dad's room that Christmas Eve night, she found my dad's arm stiffened in a salute to the ceiling. After she politely inquired what in the world he was doing, she scolded him for believing such nonsense, saying that Santa had a place for depositing candy canes, which place is your Christmas stocking. My dad, nevertheless, ventured to act on faith and fell asleep—he is positive to this day—with his arm straight in the air. When he awoke Christmas morning, to his dismay his empty fist clutched nothing; there was not a candy cane to be found.

Now there is always the possibility (as Uncle Ace pointed out) that he lowered his arm in a weak moment of his fitful slumber, but then again there is the possibility that Santa let him down. I learned from that story that Old Father Christmas may have more sides to him than we are generally led to believe.

Anyway, I'd seen for myself how Santa treated children who were afraid of him. Luckily for me, my parents never made me sit on Santa's lap. But I'd walk by the long lines of children waiting to see him. He was always over-boisterous—over-jolly, if you know what I mean. He'd "ho ho," and hug kids he'd never met before and press his face way too close to theirs. I'd seen more than one child burst into tears, and when they'd cry and call for their mother, Santa would usually just laugh like it was all a big joke. I was always grateful my parents never subjected me to such a harrowing experience. But one year at the ward Christmas party my mother decided maybe I was just a little too shy.

Our ward Christmas party was always a blustering, tinselly successful event. That year, we had just enjoyed the usual dinner of sliced ham, dried-out twice-baked potatoes, and those green beans that are really rubbery and squeak if you squish them between your teeth just right. After dinner we watched the annual Christmas program, in which Sister Duffy sang "O, Holy Night." Sister Duffy weighs more than three hundred pounds and wears what my mother calls flowing gowns and lots of shiny jewelry. Then Tiffany, Tami, Tara, and Tasha Tanner tap-danced to the tunes "Up on the Housetop," "Frosty the Snowman," "Jingle Bells," "Santa Claus Is Coming to Town," and several other Christmas favorites. To top off the evening—an appearance of Santa Claus himself!

The big moment arrived when Santa entered, ringing his jingle bells and adjusting his beard. Some of the wiser children hung back, but most were delighted. "Santa, Santa!" they shouted and began swarming about him. The bishop announced that the children must form a line and that Santa would sit on the stage and hand out our Christmas presents. He had a brown paper lunch bag for each child, filled with an orange, two candy canes, seven unshelled peanuts, and some red and green salt water taffy. Looking back, the temptation seems meager, but at the time I wanted my Christmas present just as much as any of the other kids. I just didn't want to go get it. I watched as all the Primary children from ages four to eleven clamored into line.

Just then Alex Payne walked by. Alex was my nemesis. He's the one who was always rational on the playground when I was feeling emotional. He's the one who always raised his hand with the answer one millisecond before I could. He's the one who asked Becky Larson—Becky Larson of all people!—when we got to pick partners for the school square dance. Alex Payne would never be so irrational as to be afraid of Santa Claus.

"Hey, Natalie. Why aren't you getting in line?" he asked, instinctively sensing a little opening for him to make trouble.

"Why do you care?" I responded crossly.

"Geez, I was just asking," he said. "No need to be crabby about it." Then he got a look of something between skepticism and inspiration. "You're not afraid of *Santa Claus,* are you?" He stressed the words *Santa Claus* to emphasize how utterly ridiculous that would be.

"No."

"Well, then why don't you go get your candy?"

There was no readily apparent answer to this, but I thought fast. "I'm waiting for the line to get shorter," I explained.

"Yeah, right." With an all-knowing look, he turned and headed off toward the stage.

Now I didn't want to be outdone by Alex Payne, but after all that was *Santa Claus* up there on that stage. My heart started to rush out of control, and I wondered if I was going to faint. At that very moment my mother called me to her side.

"Look at the kids up there, honey," she said. "They just walk by and Santa hands them their bag. They don't have to sit on his lap or anything. It doesn't look like they even have to talk to him."

She was right. There were too many kids. All Santa had time for, with the help of Mrs. Claus, was to hand them each a bag of candy and let them go by.

"If you go up there and get your candy," my mom continued, "you'll probably just have to say 'Merry Christmas' to him. Just 'Merry Christmas' and then walk on by. Maybe you'd be okay, walking up there, just saying 'Merry Christmas' and that's all. I think you'd be okay. What do you think?" She smiled; her eyes were very kind. Maybe she was right, I thought. It would be a huge step, a very brave thing, but maybe . . . I watched the other kids file by the busy Santa, Mrs. Claus replenishing his stack of brown paper bags out of a big box. Just then I saw that Alex had made his way to the front of the line. I saw him take his bag of candy. Then he turned, caught my eye, and grinned at me. An all-knowing, triumphant grin. That was it: I decided to get in line.

Once I got there, the line suddenly seemed to slow. Here I was, through my own choice, headed straight to my doom, and I couldn't even get there. I waited. I started to wonder if this was such a good idea. My fingers were squeezed tightly against nothing. I began to fidget. Suddenly it seemed like I'd been standing there for hours . . . like I'd been standing there forever . . . like there had never been a time when I hadn't been standing there. I noticed how the wood pieces of the floor were fit together and how shiny the finish looked under the hot lights of the stage. Then there were only four or five kids ahead of me. I strained to hear what Santa was saying to them, but I couldn't make anything out. Then it was the turn of the boy right in front of me. I watched his black-and-white Nikes as he walked confidently up to Santa Claus.

Santa smiled. He handed the boy his sack. He said, "Merry Christmas, Merry Christmas," and the boy moved on.

I breathed out. Mom was right; I'd be okay. I slowly ventured forward.

When I got within reach of Santa I stopped. He had his back turned, reaching for my bag of candy. It seemed like his back was turned a very long time, and I started to feel nervous. Was he out of bags? Would he tell me I had to leave? Maybe he would ask me my name or what I wanted for Christmas or why I even thought I deserved anything. What would I say? What was I doing here? No candy was worth this. Or maybe . . . maybe he wasn't getting candy at all. What did he have hidden behind him? Was it always just *toys* he carried in that huge bag of his? Maybe he would turn around and yell at me. Maybe he'd stand up and tell everyone in the ward all the things I'd done wrong that year and my bishop would ask my family to leave and I'd get kicked out of Primary and—

Santa turned around. He had a brown bag in his hand, that's all. He didn't speak, and nei-

ther did I. I just stared at him. I needed to get out of there, but I didn't know how. I forgot what I was supposed to do. For a fleeting moment it occurred to me that I should say "Merry Christmas," but I couldn't. I couldn't say anything. Santa looked puzzled. Then he was saying something to me, I think, but I wasn't sure. I just kept staring, my eyes locked into one position. Finally he said, "Merry Christmas." Something in his Merry Christmas jogged my mind, and I automatically reached forward to take the bag of candy he held in front of me.

Now, I'm not exactly sure what happened next. Maybe Santa didn't like the fact that I hadn't smiled at him or said anything nice. Maybe he expected me to say "Merry Christmas." Maybe he was bored by the long line of Primary kids, or maybe it bothered him that I had just kept staring at him and then reached for my prize. Maybe he thought he was being funny. Or maybe, just maybe, what I thought was true—that Santa Claus is a mean old man.

Whatever it was, Santa Claus did an unthinkable thing. As I reached for my bag of candy, he snatched it away and held it out of my reach. I paused; I felt lightheaded; it was hard to breathe. My mother had said it would be okay. It wasn't. Then I did the only thing there was to do: I reached for it again. Again Santa snatched it away. I looked in his face and I saw a wry, wicked smile.

Now I may only have been a little girl, and it may only have been a ward party. And it's true that Santa's beard needed an awful lot of adjusting that night. But when I saw that smile—that careful, smug, saucy, triumphant, little smile of enjoyment—I *knew* that every scary, mean thing I had ever been told or imagined about Santa was true. In that moment I was trapped on the lap of an old man I did not know, and he was questioning me. In that moment I was my dad with his hand reached hopefully upward—empty. In that moment I was lying in my bed, pretending to be asleep, and I could feel Santa closing in on me, could hear his silver shoe buckles jingle as they rustled against his boots. And I knew if I opened my eyes, he'd be there as I'd always feared. But he'd be smiling.

* * *

So here I was, all these years later, with a daughter of my own, and I was still afraid of Santa Claus. This was ridiculous!

I stopped and looked down at my little girl in her tiny white sneakers and denim overalls. She looked back up at me, all soft brown curls and innocence. "Sweetheart, do you want to go see Santa Claus?" I asked confidently, hiding my own feelings. Her eyes widened, her hand squeezed mine even tighter, and she shook her head a definite no.

"Are you sure? It will be all right, honey."

She shook her head more vigorously. "No, I don't want to! He's scary!"

I smiled and leaned down to my daughter and whispered, "It's okay. Mommy didn't used to like him either."

JENNIFER PRITCHETT is an editorial assistant at Deseret Book Company. She and her husband, Bruce, live in Kaysville, Utah.

WISDOM

Donald S. Smurthwaite

I HAVE SEEN THIS ROAD before but never traveled on it. Next to me, my guide squirms with excitement. "Turn here," he says, so I slow the car and follow his instruction. "It isn't far now," he says in his high, fluttery voice, so out of place coming from a man his size.

The road is graveled and dips into a swale. Across the way, I see a small house standing next to a grove of maple trees. "Is that it? Is that your house, Ben?"

Ben Drummond nods. We're only a quarter-mile from the county road we just turned off of, but already it seems we are a world apart.

The house is now clearly in view. It is painted a dull olive color and reminds me of August leaves, their fresh green sheen fading from too many days in the summer sun. The old house's roofline sags, the shingles at the top pitching upward at awkward angles. It was probably a farm home once, the only residence in the area, long before the county road was turned into a four-lane highway to accommodate the traffic bound for the new community college a mile away.

"Straight ahead?"

"Yes," Ben says, smiling, his pale, watery eyes staring at the house. A minute later we pull in front of it. "We're here," he says. "This is a nice house. It's good inside."

Why I'm here is still a mystery. I only know that Ben wanted to show me something. He provided few details. He was persistent. "Come to my house. I have something to show you," he would say each day at the office. Finally, I relented and offered to take him home one day after work. "But I can't stay, Ben. I have plans for the evening."

He was appeased. "That's okay. I have something to show you."

We get out of the car, the early autumn light slanting through the trees, backlighting leaves of soft brown, gold, and crimson. I expect to walk up to the house, but Ben motions me toward the garage. We walk together. He fumbles with an old rusty latch, then pulls back on the door. I step inside, squinting as my eyes adjust. The smell is one of musty newsprint and papers. Ben stands beside me. In the dim light, I can see a wide smile on his face. Inside, I make out stacks of newspapers, magazines, old books, and pamphlets. I don't know what to say.

"This is a library," Ben says simply. "My library. In a garage."

"Where did you get all these things?"

His eyes flutter and seem to circle, like a marble twirling about in a bowl. "I save them. Some of the papers are twenty years old."

"Why, Ben? Couldn't you recycle these and earn some money?"

He looks at me patiently, benevolently. "I could, but I don't want to. I want these for wisdom."

"Wisdom?" Only his earnestness prevents me from laughing.

"Yes, Paul. Wisdom," he says firmly.

I press no further. I learned a long time ago not to argue with him. He always wins and my ego can tolerate only so much bruising.

"Okay, Ben. Wisdom it is." A wind from the north ruffles the leaves and drops a few more to the ground. "Do you want to show me your home now?"

Ben works at Fitch and Rathdrum, an accounting firm. I am one of the partners there. Ben pushes the mail cart around the office and does other odd jobs. Ben is my best friend at Fitch and Rathdrum.

He is mentally retarded.

And on the drive across town to my home, I think about old farm homes under peeling layers of paint—and about driving by too quickly to recognize that something good is underneath.

*   *   *

Ben came to work for us early in the summer. The office mail delivery was a mess, and we needed someone to cut and paste stories from magazines and newspapers and circulate them around the building. Our administrative assistant, Kristina, got in touch with a local community group and inquired about sending someone who would be reliable. Ben appeared two days later, a little nervous, dressed in baggy slacks and a shirt that was at least a size too large, even for him. He had an old striped tie on and obviously had been coached about the importance of this interview. Kristina and I quizzed him about the job. "Can you do this kind of work?" "Are you organized?" "Will you always be at work?" Anxiously, Ben smiled and answered the questions in the same way: "I think so." "I am." "I will be." We asked him to leave for a few minutes, and, after some debate, decided to offer him the job on a thirty-day trial basis. Kristina called Ben back in.

"Welcome to Fitch and Rathdrum, Ben. You'll be part of our team," I said, extending my hand. His eyes darted to me, then back to Kristina. "It means we want you to come and work for us," I said gently. "Can you start on Monday?"

He let out a long sigh of air, and his shoulders slumped with relief. "I was tired of making brooms," he said.

Later, after Ben left, Kristina and I met in the hallway and congratulated ourselves on the decision we made.

"I have a good feeling about that young man," she confided. "He seems very sweet." I nodded in agreement.

We hired Ben at the minimum wage.

* * *

At first, Ben was quiet as he made his office rounds. He delivered the mail, and the clippings appeared faithfully. He had a knack of spotting an article of interest. We gave him a list of key words, and he rarely missed a story. About six weeks after he began work, I came into my office unexpectedly after a conference call with a client. Ben was bent over, hands on knees, staring at a photo on my desk. It was almost a comical scene.

He didn't move as I entered. He only stared, his face no more than six inches away from the photo. I coughed, a signal to let him know he wasn't alone. He didn't move for another few seconds. Finally, I spoke.

"Good morning, Ben. That's my family."

"I thought so," he said, glancing at me. "Why do you and the other boys have on ties? And the girls have on dresses. You're outside, by a tree."

"I don't know. I guess it was a formal photo. So we got dressed up."

"I see," said Ben, which is something he says often, usually at moments when I'm uncertain that he sees or understands anything at all.

"How about you? What is your family like?"

"I live with my sister and her boy. My mom died, and I haven't seen my dad in a long time. Since the funeral." Ben has long, wispy hair, and a scraggly beard. And the eyes, watery and moving, seemingly on an endless search. He hunched down in front of the photo again. "I want a picture taken by a tree someday. I want my boys to have on ties. My wife will be pretty, like yours."

I didn't know what to say, watching him, almost motionless, looking at a picture of people who were strangers.

"I hope you can meet them sometime," I finally uttered.

Late that night, after a long high council meeting, I walked into my home, where everyone was asleep. I took off my suit coat and laid it quietly on the foot of the bed. I crept along the hallway, outside of the bedrooms where my children dreamt. One by one, I pulled their blankets close to their chins and softly kissed them good night. I said a quick and quiet prayer at each bedside. It had been a long time since I had done this. Too long, I realized. When I came back into the hallway, I clicked off the light that had been left on for me. And there in the darkness, I said aloud two words to no one but myself.

"I see."

* * *

Ben and I are friends. Fast and true, we look for each other every day. I now know what he likes: movies, chocolate, sports, and anything he can read. His reading is urgent. Somewhere someone told him he would never be smart and Ben believed it. In absence of knowledge, Ben has chosen to pursue wisdom. He must be wise, he must find wisdom—it is his way to fit in a world filled with people he holds smarter. Wisdom, he must think, comes from books and magazines and old faded brochures, which is why a garage is transformed into a library. Why begrudge him? The world needs more wisdom. The world needs more Ben Drummonds.

* * *

A Wednesday in November, gray, drizzly, with a wind that cuts. The beauty of autumn is gone; most leaves fell long ago when temperatures plunged into the teens three nights in a row. The remaining leaves are shriveled and gray. It seems years ago since that warm fall day when Ben coaxed me to his home and let me see his library from which he hoped to extract wisdom.

Ben appears in my doorway, coat on, ready for what has become our midweek ritual.

"What day is it, Ben?"

"Wednesday."

"Must be close to lunch. What kind of a day is it?"

He pauses. "A hamburger day."

"Hamburgers it will be, then. Cheap hamburgers or expensive hamburgers?"

"Cheap hamburgers." Ben does not hesitate.

"With fries?"

"With fries. And a chocolate milk shake, too."

"You buy or I buy?"

"You buy."

"You're a hard man, Ben Drummond. Maybe you should be the accountant."

"Maybe."

"Let's go, before I change my mind."

I grab my coat, looking forward to my weekly lunch with Ben. It is the one time of the week when I can be myself, only myself. We stop at the reception desk on the way out.

"Diane, our beloved Ms. Holladay, Master Benjamin and I are going to lunch. It may be an extended lunch, due to the difficulty of finding a good greasy hamburger. If we do not return, do not call the authorities. We are safe. It means we have merely reached hamburger nirvana and we are extending our experience. We will also be keeping a sharp eye for young ladies interested in Mr. Drummond. He is, as you are keenly aware, young, handsome, and very eligible."

Ben blushes, and his eyes seem to dance and spin more than usual.

Diane nods solemnly. "I will cover for you with the other partners, and should any of our founders, by strange coincidence, notice you are gone, I will not let on as to your whereabouts."

"Thank you, oh, noble Lady Diane."

Late in the afternoon, when the greasy hamburgers are long gone, Diane stops me on my way to a meeting with a client. "What you're doing for Ben is wonderful," she says. "His whole face brightens when he is around you. I think he has himself a hero."

I feel uneasy, for reasons I can't explain. "Maybe it's the other way around," I say.

* * *

Thanksgiving Day. Outside, a lead-gray endless cloud covers the valley. A wind, cold and unforgiving, whips through the bare trees.

Inside, the sight is different—warm creamy light, the fragrance of baked turkey, homemade bread, cranberry, and spice. A pale yellow blaze hisses and spits in the fireplace. My family gathers around our dining table as darkness encircles outside. My wife, Lauren, brings in the platter with the turkey. I look at my family. The boys are dressed in slacks, shirts, and ties. Lauren and Amber are in dresses. Tradition in our home dictates that we get dressed up for Thanksgiving dinner, although the grumbling from our older children has increased of late. It seems right, though, that on a day of giving supreme thanks, we show our respect in all ways.

I pause before offering the prayer. I think of the picture on my desk at work. I think of Ben Drummond, and I hope that somewhere he is sitting down to a good dinner with family and close friends, secure and warm, a tie hanging down the front of a clean white shirt.

I hope that he is surrounded by wisdom and kindness this day.

* * *

Early December. Christmas lights seem to twinkle on every street and corner. Trees grace the front windows of many homes. Throngs of people crowd the stores, jostling, packages underarm, children tired and anxious. Bing Crosby and Karen Carpenter slip onto the airways. And in the offices of Fitch and Rathdrum, the tinny, scratchy sound of vinyl records on an old portable phonograph player float through the hallways. We are home to a Christmas elf, this one large and jovial. Ben darts through our hallways, a Santa hat limp on his head.

"Merry Christmas, Paul."

"Merry Christmas to you, too, Ben. I bet this is your favorite time of the year, right?"

He looks pleased. "It is. How did you know?"

"A lucky guess. I enjoy the music coming from the mail room."

"Good. I like Christmas music. Is it too loud?"

"No, I think it's just right." He smiles happily and rumbles to another office with his mail cart.

That afternoon, in a staff meeting, a young accountant named Ross, someone who will be very good at his job one day, looks at the partners, clears his throat, and wonders aloud if Christmas music in the office is "professional."

There is a heavy, awkward silence. Then I hear myself saying, "I have no problem with a message of peace on earth and goodwill to all being played on a phonograph." The young accountant shrinks in his chair.

Jerry Rathdrum, tall, white-haired, founder of the firm thirty years ago, says, "Anything else on that issue? The spirit of Christmas, then, lives on in our office. Let us proceed."

* * *

Christmas is ten days away. The first heavy snow struck yesterday, a Sunday, six inches, and now an arctic cold front has moved in, preserving our city in fluffy white. Ben takes the bus to work, and I hope he doesn't have to wait long outside in the icy temperatures. I know exactly when he should arrive, at 9:07, and wander to the front door at that time. "Just to make sure," I say to myself.

A large figure ambles through the doorway. He is dressed in a bulky coat, the Santa hat still in place. He breathes heavily, his cheeks red from the raw cold. He carries a blue canvas bag with him.

"Good morning, Ben."

"Hello, Paul."

"What's in the bag? A big lunch?"

"No," he says, with a furtive smile, his eyes washy and pale. "Christmas gifts. For everyone. I made them." He reaches into his bag and retrieves in one large hand three or four small packages, clumsily wrapped in bright Christmas paper.

"See?"

I nod. "Yes. They look very nice, Ben."

Late in the afternoon, when a conference on health-care packages is over, I come back to my office. A small package sits squarely on my desk, with an inexpensive Christmas card. Ben has stopped by. I pick up the package, which feels like a tree ornament. I open the card to see a star shining brightly over a nativity scene. Inside, beneath the printed message, is a note, scrawled in Ben's hand. "Thanks for being my friend. You do a lot for me. Ben." Below that, in another color of ink, in bold, dark letters, Ben has written an address, followed by the words, "Be there. 7:00. Wednesday, PLEASE."

* * *

"I guess you can go. The older kids have mutual, but I can get them there," Lauren says as we plot out the evening transportation plan. "I'll do a little shopping and then pick them up at 8:30. Sounds important to Ben."

"He doesn't ask much. This and the time he wanted to show me all his books and newspapers. That and some greasy hamburgers is about all. I know whatever it is, it means a lot to him."

"It's okay, Paul. I'll take care of the kids."

"I think I'll take the gift to Ben tonight. One less thing to do. I won't have to take it into the office that way."

"Set, then?"

"I think so. Be careful driving. It was slick on the way home."

Gray, big-bellied clouds moved over the valley at midmorning. Three more inches of snow fell, and the wind blew all afternoon. Little snowdrifts were mounding all around town. "Be careful," I repeat. "Take the good car."

Just before seven, we bundle up, Lauren and the kids going one way, I another. For the tenth time, I wonder about Ben's note and its urgent message.

I back out of the driveway, the tire scrunching and squeaking on the new snow. Since it is Ben whom I am going to meet, I push in a tape of Christmas music and smile at the thought of him in the saggy Santa hat. I turn the car heater up, fumble for the address, and begin my drive. The snow has stopped. In the backseat of the car is Ben's gift, a cassette boom box, wrapped in dark green paper with a red bow affixed. It is meant to replace his old phonograph.

I'm unsure of what is at the address, which is actually just the intersection of two streets. It is in a residential area, I think. For a moment, resentment works its way into my thoughts. Ben can be insistent. Don't I do enough for him? Is he taking advantage of me? A retarded man, and I am at his beck and call.

I look at the little package Ben gave me, unopened. No. Ben is a friend. Above all, Ben is a friend. A man who gathers books and newspapers, who reads them in a complicated search for wisdom that even I do not understand.

The neighborhood is unfamiliar. On the right side of the street, in a small opening, is a city park. Cars are everywhere. I pull to the curb and stop, bundle my coat closer to me, and set off for the far side of the park.

The night has by now become clear, and overhead, stars shine. The wind is almost still, yet the cold pierces. I see more people as I walk away from my car. From the other side of the park, bright lights sparkle. I see hay bales and hear the bleat of a lamb. I move closer. A man and a woman kneel, a small wooden cradle in front of them. Shepherds watch in silence. And there on the side of the manger farthest from me, still and stately, dressed in elaborate robes, staffs in hands and a look of supreme serenity, are the wise men.

Ben stands in the middle.

The fresh snow. The silence. The sublime dignity of each person in the living nativity. It is perfect. Bethlehem and 2,000 years ago are close by. And for no reason at all, and many good reasons together, I find myself staring at Ben and my eyes welling with tears. It all makes sense—the old garage stuffed with books and magazines, his talk of wisdom, the scene before me now.

I cannot leave. Someone mentions that the living nativity will last about an hour. I stay the whole time, watching Ben and the others, watch as they stand so still, except for an occasional tremor brought by the cold.

There is movement. It is time for the living nativity to end. I walk up to Ben, who seems reluctant to leave. He looks at the manger, into the cradle, where a doll lies.

"Hello, Ben."

He turns. "I knew you would come."

"I'm glad I did. Thanks for inviting me."

He takes a step closer and looks at me intently. "I am a wise man, Paul. I do this thing for Him."

"I know, Ben. I know."

I glance at the cradle. I am startled to see a real baby lying there, sweetly, bundled. *This cannot be explained,* I think wildly. *What is happening?* I look at Ben. He smiles again, munificently, his eyes clear and focused. "I see," he says. I turn back to the cradle. A young couple is reaching for the baby. "We wanted to put him in there for a moment," the father says. "Just for a moment. It seemed right," he says. "It's silly but it means something to us." Wisdom, I think, is everywhere. He picks up his infant son and walks away in the darkness.

"I am a wise man," Ben repeats.

*   *   *

Ben read about the call for participants in the living nativity in one of his newspapers. He went to the meeting, he told me, not wanting to be anything but a wise man. Someone there, forever unknown but forever kind, selected Ben to be one of the wise men.

Ben came to our home for Christmas Eve dinner. He seemed to enjoy the boom box, which I decided not to give him until then. We hung his little ornament, a star carved of cedar, on our tree where it will occupy a place of honor for many Christmases to come. The best memory of all that Christmas is Ben holding our seven-year-old son on his knee as we sang carols while Lauren strummed her guitar.

For days I struggle with questions. *What do I make of this? Where is the meaning?* At last I think I have an answer. I think the meaning is this: I am a man who keeps track of things, who counts money, who tries to save people money. I am a man who calculates and looks for the best of deals. I am a man of business, yes, but also a father and a husband, a man called a good Church member. I look for chances to serve others, but I am selective about it. Those chances must fall in places where I am comfortable. I play golf in the summer and take long and too expensive vacations. We invested well and have enough money. Our children will be able to go to college. I worry too much about taxes and driving a car that is more than five years old. We have a beautiful home and a yard that is the envy of the neighborhood in May. That is my life in a nutshell. Am I hard on myself? Maybe yes, and perhaps not.

And Ben? Ben seeks wisdom.

I think I will seek wisdom too.

DONALD S. SMURTHWAITE works in marketing and public information for a federal agency in Boise, Idaho. He and his wife, Shannon, are the parents of four children. Donald has published two novels and many short stories. In his spare time last year, he claims to have watched part of a basketball game.

CHINA DOLL

Margaret Blair Young

MY BEST FRIEND has a doll collection like Fort Knox has gold. Her room is a tribute to Madame Alexander, no lie. Me, I have two Barbies ("Jewel Magic" and "Bridal Wonder"), one "Tattoodles," and one "Baby Twinkles," whose hair I cut when I was five and was bent on becoming a punk beautician. The style she wears these long years later I call "Short-cut Straw." One of her blue eyes is stuck half open. I used to love her when life was as simple as a haircut. I suppose that's why I've never managed to give her up during thrift store drives.

As of this past Christmas, I also have a porcelain doll, which my dad makes me keep locked up in the china cabinet, top shelf. I get to look at her and say, "Nice eyelashes, nice ringlets," but no actual contact is permitted because she's "so extremely fragile" (Dad talking).

I don't mind having a doll just for my eyes; I'm glad for any half-decent gift from my dad. I mean, you should see the other presents he's given me since Mom's death. The first Christmas after, when I was twelve, he handed me an unwrapped pad of sketching paper and a set of calligraphy pens. He beamed like he was God's own shiny Band-Aid. Of course, he took the pens back the following Tuesday because he was sure I would poke my eye out with one of those mean points. He got me some nice, safe, pastel chalk instead, but did not approve of the sunset I chalked up on my wall. He made me wash it off with pine-scented Lysol, which leaves walls and hands virtually spotless and kills thousands of germs while it cleans. (I find that unspeakably reassuring.)

Dad thinks pine-scented Lysol smells like a forest. I think it smells like a hospital pretending "this here's a camp out—nobody's sick—just smell them pine trees."

The second Christmas after Mom crashed on (I think "passed on" is like pine-scented Lysol: "this here's a flower show—nobody's dead—just smell them carnations as you pass on to the roses"), Dad got me a chest of drawers and a lovely, navy blue, plastic garbage can.

I cannot describe to you how thrilling it is for a young woman to have her very own garbage can. Not only can you use it to hold crumpled papers (as in love letters you will never send to Joey Jarren), you can pretend it's an echo canyon. Or you can climb inside it and be a jack-in-the-box, which is something most thirteen-year-olds don't do nearly enough. You can sneak some Liquid Paper from your dad's desk and paint constellations on it—which he will not approve of, because he needs all his Liquid Paper to cover future mistakes (he still uses his black Royal typewriter), and besides that, you shouldn't go into his study because it's private and if a person's privacy can't be respected in his own darn house *then what's the world coming to anyway?* (But he will say all of this in a soft, sugary voice, and his nearly bald head will glow like a 20-watt bulb and the wire-rimmed glasses he's worn since he was seventeen will reflect your extremely sorry face, and when you say you'll never do it again he'll put his arm around your shoulders and pull you into the forgiving scent of his Brut cologne. He'll whisper like they're his dying words, "It's okay, kiddo.")

The year before last, the great Santa Pop bestowed upon me a safety helmet. No bike, no skateboard, just a safety helmet. This (need you ask?) was nearly as thrilling as the trash bin.

Why the safety helmet? Because I am on my high school diving team.

Is the connection between helmets and diving a tad unclear to you?

Let me describe a good dive: You launch yourself into the air and for one brilliant moment you're beyond gravity, suspended flying above blue water, and the board is just a shimmering white vibration beneath you, like static. Then you point yourself down. The best divers get enough height that they miss the board by a calculated hair. Sometimes, a diver hits board before water. Some years back, in state competition, a Hillcrest diver broke her nose on a swan and still kept her feet pointed all the way into the pool.

So Dad, on a rare excursion from work, sees me do a one-and-a-half and decides I'm within an inch of a concussion. He is absolutely serious that I should wear a safety helmet when I dive.

Can you picture it? Say you're a judge of the high school swimming-diving meet. Say this kid gets called to the board. She starts her confident walk, nods towards you as if to say, "Yes, I shall be performing now." Then she pulls out a safety helmet from somewhere behind her and straps it to her head. Are you going to say, "Now there's a careful child—how wonderful! We should all be like that!" Or will you say, "Who's the klutz?" Are you going to peacefully watch her execute her one-and-a-half, or are you cringing the whole time, listening for the crack of helmet against board? And have you ever seen a helmeted diver make a clean entry into the water? We're talking mathematical impossibility. Maybe if Dad had thought to build a pointy little pyramid on top of the helmet, I could have put it to some use. I see real marketing possibilities in pointy helmets for divers. Gold-leafed ones, like Siamese dancers wear. Actually, you could just superglue a tepee of calligraphy pens to the helmet—that should work. You could market them babies in *Paranoid Parents' Journal of Near Misses and Coming Catastrophes* and become rich beyond the dreams of cross-eyed horses.

Did I mention the helmet was hot pink? No lie.

So did I wear it to my diving meets out of respect for my father?

Are you kidding? It was pointless.

So did I lie about it?

Not exactly. I'd wear it for two seconds every morning when I had a meet, then tell Dad at supper, "That helmet fits so snugly! Thank you so much for that incredible helmet! I love that hot pink helmet, Dad! Makes me feel so *safe!*" He could interpret it however he wanted. We didn't generally pursue the conversation. We don't, generally.

Then along comes Patricia. (Read: I'd love to be your stepmom, dear.) She and my bald pop start doing dinner and G-rated movies. Once a month or so, she makes us dinner, usually tacos or enchiladas, since she's one of those happy, plump Mexican women who fits her mouth to English words like they're pastries. Her hair is chin-length salt and pepper, and she has these cool wrinkles that curve up from her eyes. She looks like she's laughed herself into middle age.

So after Patricia makes her way over the border and into Dad's social life, I wake up on Christmas morning, and "Away in the Manger" is playing on the tape player. In the front room

there's a Christmas tree all lit up—we don't usually do the tree thing—and it has little donkey ornaments made out of clothespins hanging from every branch. A donkey tree. Just what I always wanted but never knew I did until there it was. And Dad hands me a box wrapped in actual Christmas wrap with a bunch of Santa heads and holly, and I'm thinking "Sensible shoes, right?" Then I open it and it's a brown-eyed, brown-haired doll, and Dad's eyes are fired up even more than mine. Even though he makes me put her on the shelf, behind glass, five minutes later.

"You like your doll?" Patricia asks me a week afterwards.

I say, "Yeah!" like the word could jab exclamation points into the air.

"She was the most beautiful one."

Then I know who suggested that gift to my dad. Without Patricia's help, he probably would have bought me a truly eye-catching smoke alarm. I say, "Thank you, Patricia" (pronounced "Pat-ree-cee-ah").

"You miss your mother?" she says.

This is not a subject everyone brings up like the weather. I swallow my shock and answer vaguely, "Sure."

"She was the most beautiful one too."

"She was pretty." I'm smiling a Barbie smile—it's everything but real. I'm distancing fast.

"Like her daughter is." (Read: Invasion. D day. Mind if I climb into your heart? Mind if I sail along your bloodstream?)

I tell her I look more like my dad, because my face is round and my hair is blonde and Mom was a skinny redhead. Though I do have her brown eyes.

"Your doll, she is an angel, you know," says Patricia. "She has wings."

"I noticed that." I swear I do not intend to sound mean as I add, "I guess angels have wings in Mexico. They drop them by the time they hit Utah. Mormon angels don't need wings."

"I am Mormon too." Which I already know, duh. My dad converted her on his mission a century ago.

I start to say, "Duh," but manage to draw it into a change of subject: "Duh Forty-niners lucked out with Steve Young, don't you think?"

She isn't buying. "Your memories of her are very close."

Then BAM, I'm tearing. I tell her I need to go potty (yes, that's how we say it in our house), and I stay in the bathroom for an hour, flushing TP and tears down the john.

I am not actually a teary person.

My memories of her are close. But the memory of the day she crashed on keeps knocking down the prettier ones like a quick-shot weed.

In her wedding album, she's posed in an alcove on the outside of the Salt Lake Temple, next to those big wood doors. She's decked out in lace and satin, her red hair completely veiled, the headpiece making a sparkly triangle on her forehead, pointing to her nose like it's her best feature and she wants everyone to notice it on her wedding day. My hairy, young dad is on the stairs just beneath her. Her arms are spread like she's set to dive into his embrace. They both look worn-out from laughter.

On the way to the hospital the day she died, all I said—over and over—was, "Please. Please. Please." I don't know who I was talking to.

Once she made a cake that ended up with a big bump on either side and a ditch in the middle. Dad started to tell her about how important it was to distribute the baking powder evenly, and she said, "Ron, there's nothing wrong with this cake. It's just female, is all."

Dad didn't cry—not that I saw. He involved himself in the funeral plans, went into detail on who should give the eulogy and why the Relief Society sisters should not sing "Though Deepening Trials" because Mom always thought that was such a depressing hymn and it reminded her of ironing ("Press on, press on!") but they should sing "There Is Sunshine in My Soul Today." Which they did.

She always commented on the hymns. She told me that when she was a little girl, she thought the chorus of "Dearest Children, God Is Near You" said not "Cherish virtue" but "Cherries hurt you." She thought her own mother would burn in hell one Sunday because she served cherries for dessert after they had sung that very hymn in church. And she thought the Primary song, "Up Up in the Sky" was talking about a puppy dog in the sky. A little collie with purple wings. A pup in the sky where the little birds fly. And when she started laughing, she hardly ever stopped until she was crying too and her face was as red as one of those forbidden cherries.

The day she died is a still photo in my mind. The funeral is flowers. Pink roses, mostly, but sometimes they have no color at all when I let myself remember.

Patricia didn't pursue her invasion during dinner. She talked about how Mexicans celebrate Christmas, how January something-or-other is their big day, when the kings suppos-edly bring their gifts to the Christ child. I asked polite questions while I ate my tamales. I glanced at my out-of-reach doll.

She dropped the little bomb while I was helping her do the dishes. She said, "Your father and I are getting a little bit serious" (pronounced "leetle beet").

I grunted courteously.

She said, "You mind?"

I said, "I've always been obedient."

"I mean, you mind I love your father?"

Oh. The "L" word. What I said was, "No, no, I don't mind." But I'm thinking, "How could you love such a bald person? You ever heard how risky intercultural marriages are? Whatever happened to safe love? You expect me to call you Mommy?"

"I will not try to replace her." Like she was reading my thoughts.

I gave another grunt, even more courteous than the first one.

"I will be your friend," she said.

"Don't expect too much."

"I don't."

"And don't expect my father to turn into Romeo."

"No," she said.

Wiping the cups dry, I managed, "Does he love you?"

My peripheral vision took in her pleased and serious nod.

Gee, I'm thinking, how swell for you. What's he going to give you for your wedding? A hand-painted mop? A year's supply of Endust? My mother's wedding album?

"But he loves *you*," she said, "even more. Worries so much for you. He lost the person who was his whole heart—lost her for this life, which is a long time. He worries he could lose you too. Worries you could break your head on the diving board."

"Did he tell you about giving me the helmet?" No eye contact.

"He knows it was a stupid gift."

"He knows that?" I let myself look at her.

"I told him so. I said to him, 'That was a pretty dumbest thing to give your only daughter.'"

"I don't wear it."

"He knows that too."

Then I was grinning despite myself. I said, "Thanks, Pat-ree-cee-ah."

"In the temple," she whispered, "we do proxy work. We take someone else's name on us. We act for them, on behalf of them."

I don't know if she expected me to gasp or what.

"I will not take your mother's name," she said.

I gave her an "As if!" look, no words.

"But maybe I can do some proxy work for her, no? Maybe you can feel her love through me? Leetle beet?"

I do not answer. I dry the glass serving bowl and stand on tiptoe to fit it into its place on the top shelf. I'm holding it with both hands, my arms stretched up like I'm setting to launch myself into a one-and-a-half. I look at my reflection in the glass, and I see my mother's eyes. My mom and I, we're gazing at each other, both of us set to dive. Patricia is just a blur behind us. And Dad is opening his terrified arms somewhere I can't see. He's saying, "Please. Please. Please."

Margaret Blair Young is on the Brigham Young University English Department faculty. She has published two short story collections and two novels. Her forthcoming novel, *Dear Stone,* was presented as a play in the BYU 1996–97 theatre season. She and her husband, Bruce, and their four children live in Provo, Utah.

CHRISTMAS WITHOUT LIZA

Lee G. Cantwell

IT WAS HARD FOR the Andersons to think about celebrating Christmas without Liza at home. She was the Christmas Girl, the Twenty-fifth of December Birthday Kid, the Snow Queen, the Frost Fairy, and had a hundred other titles that Mark Anderson had conjured up over the years to honor his firstborn.

He had made up his mind to avoid the tendency of families to overlook December birthdays, especially those that fell on or near Christmas Day. A Christmas child might find among her presents under the tree one marked Happy Birthday, and Christmas dinner in that home might include a cake with candles, but the powerful Christmas rituals so overshadowed those token efforts at remembrance that their impact was blurred if not completely lost in the excitement of the greatest holiday of the year. Mark was determined that this would not happen to Liza.

Liza never tired of hearing her dad tell the story of how she was born on Christmas Day. He told it differently every year, and every year when he was finished, her mom would give the same knowing smile and say, "Yes, that's just how it happened."

The only part of the story the kids knew to be true was that their parents had been living in Portland, Oregon, at the time. The rest was a mythical, ever-changing tale that became more incredible with each telling.

Every Christmas Eve, the Andersons sat around the dinner table and did their best to remember all the versions of Liza's birth that Mark had told over the years. Some were short and funny, some elaborate and fantastic, always they were entertaining—at least to the Andersons. Paul and Garth were only three and four years younger than Liza, so they knew the stories almost as well as she did. Michael, the baby, at age six began correcting his older brothers and sister when they made a mistake in the retelling of a story, and sometimes he even reminded them of one they had overlooked.

When they had told every version they could remember and were finished eating, Mark would clear his throat loudly to get the attention of the family. "I have a confession to make," he would say, looking down at his plate in mock contrition. He glanced up briefly so all could see the expression of humility on his face and the light of true repentance in his eyes. "I lied all those other times. I'm finally ready to tell you the real story about how Liza was born on Christmas Day."

Then Mark would put his arm around Liza or take her hand and spin yet another unlikely yarn about the circumstances surrounding her birth. Sometimes he would say she was born at Emmanuel Hospital during the worst snowstorm in thirty years; sometimes at St. Vincent's Hospital when black ice had turned all the roads in the city into skating rinks; sometimes in a taxicab with Mark himself performing the delivery; sometimes on a Portland Rapid Transit bus with a midwife, who just happened to be a fellow passenger, presiding. Mark always varied the exact moment of her birth—five seconds after midnight on the twenty-fourth, or exactly at high noon on Christmas Day, or just as the clock was about to strike announcing that Christmas Day was at an end—always specific, always dramatic, always different than in stories he had told previously.

Garth had an infectious laugh that he had difficulty suppressing. He giggled and snorted through the entire story every year, even when Mark feigned hurt feelings at his son's lack of respect. Paul pretended to be completely taken in, looking up at his father with an unblinking stare that affected total trust and belief in a father who would rather die than stretch the truth.

After confirming Mark's story, Sara would disappear for a few moments and return carrying a cake decorated with lighted candles. Then Paul turned off the lights and everybody began to sing the birthday song. At first they sang in unison, then in sweet harmony, then one of the boys pretended to hit a sour note, another would follow his lead, and by the time they got to "Happy Birthday to You," the angelic family choir had degenerated into a cacophony of discordant notes that ended in laughter. Sara served the cake and then Liza opened the only gifts that were opened that night, her birthday presents. Everybody pitched in with the cleanup, and when the last dish was put away, Liza's birthday party was officially over. They devoted the rest of the evening to the celebration of Christmas.

The family loved to gather in the living room by the lighted tree and sing Christmas carols from memory. Both of the older boys were tenors, Mark was a deep bass, Sara sang alto, and Liza and Michael carried the melody. The Andersons didn't fool around when they were singing Christmas carols. They sang as if they were in a recording studio, and their harmony improved year by year.

The carol singing created just the right mood for Sara's reading of Luke's account of the Savior's birth. Actually, she quoted the verses from memory, though she sat with the Bible open on her knees and a penlight in her hand just in case. Each year Mark came up with a Christmas message that expanded the family's understanding of the true meaning of that sacred holiday. Mark had a wonderful sense of humor, but he had a spiritual side too. He loved the Savior, and it showed as he talked to his little family on Christmas Eve.

By the time they turned the lights back on, the boys were suddenly hungry again and set about making popcorn and hot chocolate. As they cracked nuts and passed plates of homemade candy they remembered other Christmases.

Mark would usually start things off. "Now remember, Paul, when I call 'Christmas morning' tomorrow, it really will be Christmas morning!"

Paul was always hard to wake. It usually took two or three calls to get him going. Mark had tried some creative calls like: "Paul, the house is on fire," and "Paul, you won the Reader's Digest Sweepstakes." One Sunday in July, Mark got him up promptly by calling softly, "Paul, Christmas morning. Everybody's waiting to open the presents." Paul leaped out of bed and found himself blinking at the rosebushes blooming outside his bedroom window. It only worked that one time, but Mark continued to try it again and again.

Sara would give Liza a suspicious look and say, "So, what did you think of your Christmas presents this year, Liza?"

One year Liza had opened all her presents two days before Christmas and then carefully rewrapped them and put them back under the tree. She felt so guilty on Christmas morning pretending to be surprised that she ended up confessing to the whole family.

A word, a look, a fragment of a sentence, and Christmas images from the past came rushing back: "Do you really want to wear your ski boots to church, Garth?" "Don't burn the toast, Michael." "Mom, are you sure there are no presents still hiding in the trunk of the car?"

The Andersons were always together as a family on Christmas Eve, even the year that Mark had a heart attack in mid-December. He was still in the hospital, but the family came and spent the evening with him. They left nothing out of their traditional celebration, but they had to compress things a bit because the doctor had insisted they not stay longer than an hour. Mark cried and hugged each one of them before they left that night. He whispered in Liza's ear, "When you wake Paul tomorrow morning, tell him it's the Fourth of July."

Mark Anderson died a week later in the ICU of the hospital after a second heart attack. Liza was haunted by the thought that maybe something could have been done to save him. Perhaps to find the answers to her questions, but more likely because she was a born caregiver, Liza became a nurse.

After Mark's death, the family had a full year to recover before having to celebrate Christmas without him. All through the holidays, they did their best to maintain the family traditions that had become so precious to them. About December fifteenth, they started calling Liza by the pet names their father had used. On Christmas Eve, they celebrated her birthday as they always had. They even insisted that Sara tell them the story of Liza's birth. "C'mon, Mom, tell us how it really happened,"

they urged. "Were any of those stories Dad told us true?" Sara resisted briefly and then gave in.

She started out in a matter-of-fact manner, stating the circumstances as she remembered them. "As I recall, we were living in an upstairs apartment in northeast Portland. Dr. Brown was my obstetrician; he was a bald, grandfatherly man who wore glasses. He examined me on the twenty-third of December and told me not to plan on another tax deduction that year. He estimated my date of delivery to be about the sixth of January." Sara droned on, purposely summoning up boring details that would give her account the taste and texture of reality.

When everyone, including Liza, seemed properly hooked, she expanded the tale into one that rivaled the most outrageous that Mark had ever mined from his very fertile and overactive imagination. She led them carefully into believing that she and Mark, with Dr. Brown's blessing, had decided to drive to Bend, Oregon, early on Christmas morning to spend the week between the holidays with friends.

Their credulity began to waver as she described the icy highway on the slopes of Mt. Hood, where they went into a spin on a patch of ice that involved three complete rotations of the car and a near splash into the Zig Zag River. By the time a member of the ski patrol at Timberline Lodge (who happened to be a senior medical student) delivered Liza, they were grinning. When the driver of a snowplow who came into the lodge for a bowl of soup and offered to take them to the nearest hospital turned out to be Mark's long lost cousin Stanley from Cedar City, they were roaring.

They gave their mother a standing ovation as she bowed her head humbly in recognition of the honor. "Dad would be proud of you,

Mom," Paul said as he struggled for breath. They continued laughing, but Sara's and Liza's eyes filled with tears as they thought about Mark and how he would have loved to be there that night.

This year Liza wouldn't be with them. She was a new employee at Providence Hospital in Portland, the city where she had been born twenty-one years before. Only nurses with seniority rated Christmas Eve off. "No Liza, no birthday party," Sara announced when she put down the phone from talking long-distance to Liza in mid-December, but Paul resisted. "We've never had a Christmas without celebrating Liza's birthday, and I don't think we should start now. We'll call her at the hospital after dinner and each one of us can get on an extension. We'll sing her the rowdiest version of 'Happy Birthday' ever, and I'll blow out the candles on the cake."

They each picked up an extension, called Liza right back, and told her what they planned. She was to arrange to be on a break at exactly eight o'clock on Christmas Eve, standing by the telephone ready to receive their call. They would light the cake first, then dial the number. When she answered the phone they would turn out the lights, describe the cake to her, and then sing her the birthday song. For almost a full minute, they heard nothing on the other end of the line except some soft coughing sounds that they all recognized. When Liza finally spoke again, she was laughing and crying at the same time. "You're crazy, you know, all of you; Mom included. But if you're serious, I think I can get the use of a private office here at the hospital for a few minutes that night."

"Can you hear us?" Michael wanted to know. "Can you hear all of us?"

"I can hear you fine," Liza whispered. She hesitated and then continued, "Dad would be very proud of you."

On Christmas Eve, while they were helping prepare the birthday dinner, Paul and Garth began pretending that Liza was really there with them.

"Michael, go get Liza to help us make the gravy," Paul called out. "She always does the best job. I think she's down in the bathroom fussing with her hair."

"Yes, go get the Snow Queen," Garth laughed. "Just because she's the December Birthday Kid doesn't excuse her from the kitchen chores."

Michael looked a bit bewildered at first, but he soon got into the spirit of things. "Hey, Liza," he yelled down the stairwell. He called a second time and then ran down the stairs and off in the direction of her room. When he came back a few moments later, he said, "She's not in her room. She must be taking a bath."

They continued to talk about her, calling her Santa's Little Hostess, the Sultana of the Snowdrifts, the Siren of Slush, the Ice Princess, the Silver Belle, and dozens of other names they remembered from previous Christmases or made up on the spot.

They had all of Liza's favorite dishes: roast prime rib, honey-cured ham, sliced yams swimming in marshmallows, cranberry Jell-O filled with nuts and other crunchies, hot rolls, homemade frozen raspberry jam, and sparkling cider. They told all the old stories about Liza's Christmas birth and tried to laugh just as heartily as they had in other years, but Sara refused to tell a new story—she just wasn't up to it. "It's almost eight o'clock," she said. "I think I'd better light the cake so we can call Liza on time."

The cake was Christmas red, four layers, with creamy white icing between each layer and covering the top. Garth calculated the circumference of the cake, divided by twenty-one, and made a tiny indentation in the icing where each red candle should be placed. Michael insisted on pushing the red candles into the indentations, and everybody agreed that he had done a perfect job. In the center of the cake, Sara had written in bright Christmas green: "Happy Birthday to Our Liza."

"When you tell Liza how the cake looks, don't forget to tell her I put in the candles," Michael said.

They lit the candles and then hurried to the four telephone extensions. Paul was in the kitchen next to the cake. When they were all in place, he turned out the kitchen lights and began pressing the buttons on the lighted dial of the telephone, speaking the memorized numbers as he went: "Area code 503 . . ."

The doorbell rang. "Oh, nuts!" Paul muttered under his breath. Who could be dropping by at eight o'clock on Christmas Eve. He looked at the cake. The candles were burning in earnest. If he answered the door and had to talk to someone for even a couple of minutes, the candles would burn down to sputtering red splotches on the top of that beautiful cake. "The lights are out," he mumbled. "Maybe they'll just leave the plate of cookies, or whatever, on the doorstep and go away." It rang a second time. *They're not going to leave,* he thought. *What if it's somebody who wants to stay and visit? What will Liza think? She'll be sitting there by the phone, waiting for us to call. If they stay even ten or fifteen minutes, Liza's break will be over, and everything will be spoiled.*

The doorbell rang a third time. Paul heard his mother walking toward the front door. He quickly blew out the candles and hid the cake in the only place he could think of, the freezer compartment of the refrigerator. There was just room for it next to the frozen vegetables. "Nuts! Double nuts!" He hissed as he headed toward the front door.

Garth and Michael were there ahead of him, and Sara was just opening the door when Paul turned the corner. Sara forced a smile and swung the door wide. There, framed in the doorway, stood Liza and a tall, handsome guy with a sheepish look on his face.

Michael shouted, "Liza!" and leaped into her arms. They would have rolled down the front steps if the tall, handsome guy hadn't grabbed them.

Paul and Garth hurried out to help them all into the house while Sara stood helpless and smiling with tears rolling down her cheeks.

"This is Rick Stevens," Liza managed after she had properly hugged and kissed everyone. "He just drove me from the parking lot at Providence Hospital to our front door in—" she glanced at her wristwatch, "twelve hours and sixteen minutes."

Garth looked at Paul and raised his eyebrows slightly. Liza had mentioned Rick a couple of times when she was talking with the family on the telephone, but when they asked about him, she described him as "just a friend." Sara took their coats, waved them into the living room, and sent the boys for their luggage. When they returned they noticed Liza and her "friend" holding hands as they talked to Mike and Sara. Paul confirmed Garth's suspicions with a nod.

"Rick's a surgeon," Liza said proudly.

Rick corrected her. "Actually I'm a first-year surgical resident, low man on the totem pole, just like Liza is on the nursing staff."

"We were both supposed to work tonight, a twelve-hour shift," Liza laughed.

"Then the head resident got a Christmas card from his old football coach."

"A Christmas card!" Garth echoed.

" . . . and two tickets to the Rose Bowl Game," Liza added. "Their team is playing in Pasadena on New Year's Day, and the head resident was scheduled to work that day. He asked Rick to switch schedules with him, and Rick agreed if I could be off too."

"I knew how much Liza wanted to be here tonight, so I decided to drive her down. She said I was crazy, that we'd never make it. She predicted we'd get caught in a snowstorm and spend Christmas in Pendleton."

"Instead, it worked out perfectly. Rick picked me up just as I got off my shift, and we headed up the Columbia Gorge in a rainstorm. I was sure it would turn to snow or, worse, to ice. Instead we drove out of the rain just east of Hood River. I changed my clothes at a gas station in The Dalles while Rick filled the tank. From there on in the road was dry as popcorn, even through the Blue Mountains. We took turns driving and sleeping, so we're not even tired—well, maybe a little. Now where's my birthday cake?"

Paul rescued the cake from the freezer, and Sara replaced the half-burned candles with new ones while the boys heated up some leftovers for Rick and Liza. They insisted on initiating Rick into the complete Anderson Christmas Eve routine. While the two of them ate, the rest of the family sat around the table and made him listen to every wild story of Liza's birth they could think of. Sara outdid herself with a brand new one to add to the collection. Rick joined in on the off-key version of the birthday song, and Sara smiled as she noticed that his discordant notes were in the bass range.

After Liza opened her birthday presents, they went into the living room and sang carols. With Rick singing bass, they sounded like the old days. Nobody wanted to stop, so it was nearly eleven o'clock when Sara finally began:

"And it came to pass in those days, that there went out a decree from Caesar Augustus that all the world should be taxed . . ."

LEE G. CANTWELL, a retired dentist, is now serving a Church-service mission with his wife, Karen, at BYU—Hawaii. He and Karen have two sons, two daughters, and seven grandchildren. He has published two novels and several articles in the LDS market.

ANGEL VOICES

Sharon Downing Jarvis

CHRISTMAS WASN'T STARTING out too well. Mom had been working overtime nearly every day and would come home tired and frustrated that she hadn't had time to shop or bake or even send any cards to let people know our new address. I tried to keep up on the laundry and put together something to feed the boys for supper, but at twelve-longing-for-thirteen I was no great shakes as a cook, and I'm afraid I ordered pizza more often than our budget or our nutritional level should have allowed. Jimmy and Josh never complained, though, even when Mom made them eat carrot sticks as a sort of after-the-fact salad when she got home. Pizza was worth it, in their minds.

"So, Mom—when're we gonna put up a tree? Can we get a flocked one?" I asked, sprawled at the kitchen table where yet another cardboard box announced the presence of dinner. Mom hung up her coat and kicked off damp boots, wriggling her toes and standing on one foot and then the other as she reached to try to warm the toes with her hand.

"Oh, Cassie—I don't know. No, we can't get a flocked tree. We're going to have to put up the artificial one this year. I can't—I hate to keep saying I can't afford this and that, but you have to realize, honey, things—"

"I *know!*" I interrupted, anticipating her next words. "Things are *different* this year." I hated myself for the mocking, whiny tone in my voice, but I couldn't seem to keep it out. Mom looked at me for a long, silent moment,

during which I glared rebelliously back at her, though inside I wanted to apologize, and to cry, and to have her hold and comfort me.

"Yes, Cass," she said quietly. "Things are very different. And we all have to make adjustments, whether we like it or not. But Christmas can still be fun."

I sighed. "So where is the stupid tree anyway?"

"If you'll remember, it's actually a rather nice tree, and it's downstairs in our storage unit. Give me a chance to eat a bite and thaw my feet, and we'll go bring it up."

I pushed the box toward her. "There's the pizza."

"So I see." She opened the refrigerator and poked around.

"We're out of carrots, if that's what you're looking for."

"And milk?"

"The boys drank it after school." Well, and so had I, and my friend Amber had had a glass, too. But I didn't mention that.

"What are the boys doing?"

"Nintendo."

Mom set out a carton of cottage cheese and a can of pears, then went to check on my brothers.

"Hi, Mom!" Josh said, and Jimmy squealed, "Mom-mee!" as he tackled her around the middle. I had to admit, their greetings were far more welcoming than mine had been. The truth was, I was feeling perverse and out of sorts, and the coming of the Christmas season hadn't helped. It had, in fact, made things worse, pointing up the differences between this year and last. Last year, we had had two trees—a big, fresh one in the living room, fragrant and glowing with pink lights and pink and gold ornaments to go with the rose and cream decor, and the artificial tree down in the family room, hung with multicolored lights and ornaments that we had made and collected over the years—Styrofoam gingerbread men, little framed pictures of Josh and myself from school, and strings of plastic popcorn and Lifesavers that Jimmy used to cry and reach for, thinking they could be eaten. But that was when we'd had a house—and a dad. Now Dad was gone—living somewhere in Indiana with his new wife—and we had moved to a two-bedroom apartment in the city, closer to Mom's job.

The apartment was kind of nice, I had to admit. The bedrooms were pretty big, and Mom let me put up my posters and have my stereo in the one we shared, but it wasn't the same as having my own room—and a whole house and yard to rattle around in and find a place to be alone when I wanted. I think I missed the house almost more than I missed Dad, and I missed him a lot. I didn't understand exactly what had gone wrong between my parents, because they had never fought or even had serious discussions in front of us. Whenever Dad said something that Mom didn't like, or that hurt her feelings, she just got very quiet, as she did with me, and sometimes disappeared for an hour or two, coming back when she could be cheerful again. But at Christmas, I guess they both always made a special effort to make it nice for us. We would play games together, go sledding or ice skating, and always, on Christmas Eve, read the Christmas story together from the Bible. I can't remember Mom and Dad giving each other much in the way of presents—maybe a box of chocolates and a tie—but there were always several gifts for each of us—things we had

asked for, or needed—and stockings full of our favorite goodies and other little surprises.

Though Christmas had always been a pleasant time, it had always held, for me, a slight edge of disappointment. I guess I expected too much, though I don't think it had to do with presents. Santa always seemed to bring the items I wanted most—and if he didn't, then my grandparents or Aunt Jenny or Uncle Bruce somehow came through for me, so I had no complaints in that department. There was something else—some indefinable thing—that was missing. I wanted there to be magic in the season! Somehow, the sight of twinkling lights and the singing of familiar songs, some merry and some haunting, awakened in me a longing for something I couldn't even name. How is it that the sight of colored lights on shrubs, muted to glowing pastel pools through a layer of snow, could have the power to bring a lump to my throat? Even the familiar words of the Bible story intensified my yearning. I wanted to *be there in Bethlehem*—to hear the cattle lowing and the soft cries of the newborn Baby. I wanted to see the wise men kneeling in awe before the young Child, presenting their exotic and costly gifts. I wanted to know the fragrance of frankincense. I wanted to be on the hillside with the shepherds. I wanted the angels to sing to *me!*

I *didn't* want to traipse down to the storage area in the basement of our building and drag up our artificial tree and our collection of childish, handmade decorations. No magic there. Mom put together the stand for the tree, then leaned back with a sigh.

"Tell you what," she said. "I'm so tired tonight I don't think I can face putting this whole thing together. All I feel up to is a hot shower and bed. Cassie, why don't you kids do it tomorrow after school? You remember how, don't you? You just match the colored stickers on the branches to the same color on the trunk, and start from the bottom. Josh can fluff the branches out first, and Jimmy can hand them to you, and you put them in. Okay? That'd be a big help. Then we'll decorate it together when I get home."

"Yeah, sure," I responded. "If you're not *too tired*, again."

"You know what, Cassie? I think you must be really tired, too. That's the only excuse for the way you're behaving. In fact, I want you in bed in ten minutes."

"Mom, I'm not tired! I wanted to watch—"

"No, indeed. No TV tonight. And no more Nintendo either, guys. Cassie, I mean it. You go to bed now. I'll tuck the boys in." Mom's voice had gone into her I've-had-enough mode, and I knew there was no arguing with her. I knew too that I had brought it on myself with my whining and sniping.

"Thanks a lot, Cass," Josh said, throwing me a resentful look. "Now we all have to go to bed early, just because of you."

"Just like me," said Jimmy cheerfully. He knew it was his bedtime anyway, and for once he wouldn't be the only one excluded from the evening's activities.

Mom smiled at him. "Get your jammies on, guys, brush your teeth, and I'll read you a story."

"A Christmas story?" asked Jimmy.

"Sure."

"I hate Christmas," I offered, as my parting shot. "It always promises more than it delivers."

"Goodnight, Miss Grinch," Mom said. "I hope you'll feel better in the morning."

I lay in the semidarkness of the bedroom and turned toward the wall, listening against my will to the familiar cadences of Mom's voice reading a story I knew by heart and had always loved. Then I heard Jimmy's five-year-old voice saying a prayer, including "Please bless Daddy to come home safe, and please help Cassie to like Christmas again." Dumb kid. Couldn't he figure out that Daddy wasn't away on a business trip? He'd been told many times that Daddy wouldn't be coming back. But probably, like Josh and myself, he just kept wishing it would happen.

When Mom came in from her shower, smelling sweetly of soap and deodorant, she sat down on the edge of my bed. I opened my eyes wide to prove I wasn't sleepy after all.

"You know, Cass—you're at an age when it's easy to be really critical of everything and everybody, especially when things aren't going the way you'd like them to. But as you grow, you'll learn that most situations—and most people—give back to you about what you give to them. That's true of friends, and parents, and little brothers—and even of Christmas. If you'll jump in and do whatever you can to make the season meaningful and pleasant for others, you'll find yourself enjoying it more. The more you give, the more you'll receive. And you know I'm not talking about presents. I'm talking about relationships. They're what's most important, at Christmas or anytime."

"Then I guess you didn't give much to your relationship with Daddy, did you? Because you're sure not getting much back!" I could have bitten off the tongue that uttered such wounding words the moment I'd said them, but there they were, hanging in the darkness between us.

Mom was silent for a moment, then she whispered, "Maybe you're right."

I closed my eyes tight against the tears that

wanted to come, and willed myself to sleep, to make this awful evening be over. Sometime later, I awoke to hear soft, stifled sobs from across the room. I was shocked; Mom had never cried in front of us, even when she explained about the divorce and the sale of our house. Had I thought she had no feelings? And was she crying now because of the divorce, or because her only daughter was being such a thoughtless beast? I wanted to fling off my covers and go hug her and apologize, but I held back, not wanting to intrude on her private grief. Silently I promised to do better—to be better. For the first time, it occurred to me that I wasn't the only one who might be missing the privilege of having my own room, my own privacy. Where could Mom go, at work or at home, to be alone with her feelings?

I made an effort, the next day, to be nicer to my brothers, and to do a little extra cleaning around the apartment. We started working on the tree, but right away we ran into snags. The red stickers on the branches tended toward orange, and the orange stickers, higher on the tree, were definitely reddish looking. Josh was certain that the orange-stickered branches went on first, at the bottom. I disagreed, pointing out that the red-stickered ones were longer, and anybody with half a brain knew that the longest ones went at the bottom of the tree. Josh, who seemed to be in much the same mood I had exhibited the day before, stubbornly insisted that it was the other way around, and I was just being mean and bossy. He put the orange-stickered branches in place, and I promptly removed them. Josh started crying and flailing at me with the stickery branches, and Jimmy started crying in response to our fighting, so I threw up my hands and said, "Okay, dork—go ahead and do

it your way! But don't blame me when it looks stupid."

"It won't," he declared. "I know how it's s'posed to go."

I shrugged. "Go for it."

It was wrong, of course. But I refused to have a thing to do with it, even when Josh had to drag a kitchen chair over to put the top on the tree and nearly fell getting it into place. The topmost branch was bent to one side, and no self-respecting angel or star could have made its home there.

Josh stood back to admire his work.

"See?" I demanded rudely. "It looks dumb."

"I like it like that," he said, and slammed the door to his and Jimmy's room.

Mom was home earlier than usual that afternoon, her arms laden with sacks, her cheeks pink with cold. "I finally got some time off to shop. Now, don't snoop," she warned softly, swooping across the room to stash her bounty in the back of the utility closet. "And don't let the J-team know where this stuff is. As soon as I get it wrapped, I'll put it somewhere else."

"I have absolutely no interest in snooping," I said, my almost-a-teenager voice indicating that I'd grown beyond all that. "Also, have a look at the wonderful tree. And can I just say that it's all Josh's doing? He hit me when I tried to do it right."

Mom paused and frowned as she took in the tree. Then she covered her mouth as if to try to hold back the smile that insisted on forming. "It looks like a pear!" she said, her voice dissolving in a giggle. It had been so long since I'd heard Mom giggle that I stared at her in surprise. Was this the woman who had sobbed quietly in the night? I looked again at the travesty of a tree. She was right—it was pear-shaped, and the bent twig at the top looked like a stem.

"Well," I said slowly, "then all we need is to find a partridge to put in it, and we'll be all set." Mom's giggle erupted again, and I heard mine joining it, and we laughed till our sides hurt. Jimmy and Josh heard us and came running in. Jimmy danced around in pure glee to see us laughing instead of snapping at each other, but Josh's expression became darker by the second.

"Don't laugh at my tree!" he yelled. "That's how I like it."

"Oh, Joshy, I love your tree," Mom said, drawing him into her arms. "I wouldn't change a thing. We'll just get busy and decorate it, okay?"

"Then what're you laughing at?"

"Cassie made a joke about a Christmas song, that's all, and it tickled my funny bone. How was school?"

"We had a party, and it was the last day. We're out till next year!"

"Hey, that's right! And I only have to work Monday, then I'll be off for the rest of the holidays, too. We'll find all kinds of fun things to do, won't we?"

"Like movies? and skating?" Jimmy asked.

"Yes, and driving around to find the best Christmas lights, and playing in the snow at the park, and coming home when we're cold to have hot cocoa and play games or do puzzles."

"Oh, yay," I said with a marked lack of enthusiasm.

"And one day Cass and I will have a Mom-and-daughter day out," she continued. "We'll have lunch somewhere nice and look through all the stores we want—maybe buy something at the after-Christmas sales. I'll bet we could

even find a movie that we'd like but the boys wouldn't."

"Okay," I said reluctantly, then reached to pick up the ringing phone. It was Grandma Thomas, Mom's mother, and she sounded excited. I passed the phone to Mom and listened as she got excited too. By the time the call was over, I knew she had committed us to something.

"Well, team, guess what? Christmas is going to be even more exciting than we thought," she began. "Grandma says Aunt Jenny's flying home from Germany for Christmas, and she wants us to come too! I haven't seen Jenny for over four years. Jimmy, you were just a baby the last time I saw my sister—Josh was younger than you are now, and Cassie was only eight. Oh, it'll seem so good to be home again for Christmas, and Jenny there too!"

I had a vague but good memory of Aunt Jenny, who was younger than Mom. I remembered long, wavy brown hair and a rich laugh. I also knew that she always sent nice presents from Germany, where her husband was stationed with the Air Force.

"So when are we leaving?" I asked, trying to stamp out the little flicker of resentment I felt at not having been consulted in this decision.

"I'm not sure. I have to call the airlines and see if there's any chance we can get tickets. Grandma's going to send me some money to help with the expense, but it's so late now that we may have to drive."

"How long does that take?" Josh asked.

"A good fourteen hours, if the roads are clear. We could do it in one day if we start early."

As it turned out, we left on the twenty-third, we drove—and we didn't get a very early start—and the roads were definitely not clear.

Anticipating this, Mom had made reservations for us at a really nice motel, one with an indoor pool and hot tub and a play area for kids. She swam a few laps in the pool and then soaked in the hot tub, watching the huge snowflakes drift by outside the window. When we were all relaxed, we went back to our room, ordered in sandwiches, and watched Christmas shows on the TV until we fell asleep. So far, so good, I thought drowsily. If the rest of the trip worked out as well as the first day, I wouldn't complain—though I hadn't been too thrilled at the idea of not being around to do stuff with my friends over the holidays.

Things changed the very next morning. The farther west we drove, the more snow we encountered and fewer and fewer cars appeared on the interstate, though it seemed there were plenty of huge semi trucks to roar past us, blinding us momentarily with the sprays of slush they threw up. For a while, we poked along behind a snowplow, but it turned off at an exit to a small town and we were on our own. We sang songs, then listened to the radio when Josh and Jimmy quieted down. I knew Mom was listening nervously for weather reports and I found myself doing the same, almost wishing I were still as young and carefree as my brothers, who trusted Mom implicitly to take care of them in every situation and never doubted that she could meet any challenge. As it was, I was old enough to recognize that she was human, and vulnerable—and that I was not much help. The fourteen-hour trip had already taken eighteen—and we still had over 150 miles to go. An early blue dusk had fallen, and all I could see between swipes of the wiper blades was an unending supply of snowflakes being hurled at our headlights. When a highway patrolman stopped us just west of Twin Falls and asked where we were headed, I knew things were serious.

"Word is that we're probably going to be closing the freeway, ma'am. This storm is packing a lot more punch than we expected it to, and we can't keep ahead of it. How far do you folks have to go?"

"We're headed to my mother's house, just the other side of Boise. For Christmas," she added, as if that made a difference.

"Well, word isn't official yet, but my advice would be to pull off at the next exit where services are available and see if you can't get a place to stay over. Chances are conditions will improve by morning, and you can still spend part of Christmas with your mom. Take care, now." He headed back to his patrol car.

Mom sighed deeply, and looked across at me. "Oh, dear," she said. "I don't know what to do. I really think we can make it, if they just don't close the road on us."

I wrinkled my nose. "I don't want to spend Christmas Eve in a motel. I mean, last night was fun, but—"

"I hear you."

"Mom, what did that policeman want?" Josh asked. "Were we speeding or something?"

"No, honey. He just warned us that the roads are snowy and dangerous."

"Well, duh—we know that!"

"So, what're we going to do?" I asked. "I vote we keep going."

"I guess we will, for the moment, at least," Mom said. "We'll just take it exit by exit and see how far we can get."

We passed a couple of exits, and then our car made the decision for us.

"Look at this, Cass," Mom said in a low voice, pointing to a gauge on the dash. "We're overheating. We're going to have to pull off and find out why."

I couldn't argue with that. I nodded glumly and looked at our map. "Okay, the next town is . . . um . . . Glenns Ferry, I think. Or Mountain Home, beyond that. Mountain Home is bigger."

"I'd like to go for bigger, but I'm going to have to opt for closer."

We crept along, both of us searching through the relentless snow for the exit sign, while Josh and Jimmy tussled in the backseat. By the time we spotted the sign for Glenns Ferry, a red warning signal that had been coming on intermittently shone steadily, and Mom had turned off the heater and radio just in case they were stressing the engine. We eased onto the off-ramp, straining to see some lights, preferably those of an open service station, through the snow.

"Cassie, say a prayer."

"You mean right now?"

"What better time?"

"Um—right. Um—Dear God, please help us find somebody to help us fix our car, so we can get to Grandma's for Christmas. And please help us be safe. Amen."

"Where're we going, now?" Jimmy demanded. "I need to go to the bathroom."

"We're hoping to find one pretty soon," Mom said. "Are you boys getting cold? Wrap up in your blankets back there. Cassie, do you see any service station signs?"

"All I see is snow. And smoke, or something. Mom, it's coming out of our car!"

"I'm going to have to stop, if I can just see a place to pull over and not get stuck."

When she braked, the engine died, and having lost power to both brakes and steering, the car pretty much found its own way to the side of the road and was stopped by a big drift of snow that cushioned us from exchanging damage with a rural mailbox on a fence post. Clouds of smoke or steam poured from under our hood, and a peculiar odor filled the car.

"Mom, is the car on fire?" Josh asked in alarm.

"I don't think so, honey. I think we've probably got a broken hose, or something." Mom turned on our flasher lights and sat staring straight ahead, her hand covering her mouth. I stared at her, feeling my eyes widen with fear. If she had shown any signs of panic in that moment, I'm sure I would have become hysterical. Instead, she turned with a small, wry smile and sang softly, "Oh, the weather outside is frightful . . . "

"And our car is not delightful," I added shakily. We sang through one chorus, making up words that fit our situation, trying to banish the fear and disappointment that threatened to overwhelm us along with the early darkness of this Christmas Eve. We were getting cold, especially after we had bundled Jimmy out of the car and over behind a snowbank to relieve his bladder. When the headlights of another vehicle suddenly lighted the inside of our car from behind, we all jumped and turned around eagerly.

It was then that the magic began. The man who waded through the snow to peer in at us had a white beard—not wavy and flowing like a store Santa's, but neatly trimmed—and the woman who followed closely behind him wore a red parka with a fur-lined hood. I could hear Jimmy from the back seat, saying, "It's them! Look, Josh—it's Mr. and Mrs. Santa Claus!" and Josh saying, "Stop hitting me, it is not!"

"You folks stalled here, ma'am?" he was asking Mom, who nodded, and stiffly got out of the car to explain the situation. It was difficult to hear the conversation over Jimmy and Josh, but I did catch the woman's high, clear voice insisting that it was no trouble at all, so I assumed we were getting some kind of help and gave a deep sigh of relief.

"Come on, team—we're going up to these good people's house to use their phone," Mom said, opening the door to get her purse and us. "This is their mailbox we almost took down."

We piled out into the snow and then into the back of some kind of sport utility wagon, which plowed and ground its way up a snowy lane toward the cheeriest sight I had seen all day—a large log house with sparkling Christmas lights strung across the front porch. Mr. and Mrs. Santa—or Dean and Connie Richardson, as they introduced themselves—chatted cheerfully with Mom as if they had always known her and asked us our names and ages in a way that sounded like they really wanted to know.

They ushered us into their huge living room and apologized that it wasn't warmer, because they'd been away all day. Mr. Richardson started a fire in the fireplace and turned on the lights on their tree, which was so tall it almost touched the highest point of their vaulted ceiling. It was a deep foresty green, and tiny multicolored lights twinkled and sparkled in its mysterious depths. I couldn't resist going over to sniff a branch, and, as I expected, a rich resinous piney smell spoke to me of Christmas. I caught Mom's eye. "Now, that's a tree," I said softly, and she nodded.

Mr. Richardson was on the phone, making several quick calls that apparently didn't get the responses he had hoped, because he was frowning and shaking his head as he turned to Mom.

"Can't get a promise out of anybody to look at your car till day after tomorrow," he said, "although Hank Pritchard says he can probably come out and tow it tomorrow afternoon, after his Christmas dinner. If he's awake, that is," he added with a chuckle.

"I hate to ask anybody to work on Christmas," Mom said. "Is there a motel in town, and any way to get there? I don't suppose there's a taxi?"

Mrs. Richardson spoke. "Now, Barbara, what do you need a motel for? Here we are—the two of us rattling around in this big old house where we raised nine children, and not a one of them expected here tonight! We've got plenty of room for all of you and then some. Cable TV and a VCR, too," she added, winking toward us. "And homemade cookies and no grandkids here to feed them to on Christmas Eve."

"Yeah, Mom," Josh added. "Let's stay here!"

Mom looked like she might cry. "I . . . how can we impose on you folks, on Christmas Eve, of all times, and—"

"What better time? And it is no imposition," said Dean Richardson, putting an arm around his wife's shoulders. "There's room in our inn. Besides," he added, "unless you want to take these kids and hike several miles through this storm to find a motel that's probably full anyway and might, if you're lucky, let you sleep in the lobby, I'm afraid you don't have a lot of choice! As for us, it seems right and natural to have kids around the place at Christmastime, and we don't expect any of our grandkids in till a couple of days after—so you'd be brightening things up for us, too."

Mom gave in. "What can I say? You're so kind to offer, and we're so glad to be here. Thank you."

She called Grandma and explained where we were, and Mr. Richardson invited us kids to go out to the barn with him where he milked—not cows, but three anxious nanny goats—while we sat in the straw and played with a litter of frisky kittens. I breathed in the pleasant-unpleasant mix of odors in the warm barn and thought of the Bethlehem stable. It wasn't hard to imagine Mary and the baby Jesus resting against the straw while Joseph kept watch over them and their donkey munched and drowsed in the background. I said as much to Mr. Richardson, who looked back at me with interest.

"I've often thought the same thing myself," he said with a smile. "It's not too bad a place to be on Christmas Eve, is it?"

Back in the kitchen, Mrs. Richardson had warmed a big pot of stew for our supper. We ate it with thick slices of homemade bread and glasses of cold goat's milk, which to my surprise tasted good. Then she brought out a selection of Christmas cookies that made Josh's and Jimmy's eyes light up with greedy anticipation. I chose a frosted gingerbread boy. There must have been a dozen varieties on the plate. Mom commented on this, to which Mrs. Richardson said, "It's a tradition with us. I've been making and freezing cookies now for a month. I mail a box to the grandchildren who can't get here and send some home with those who come."

After dinner, we sat around the fireplace with the lights turned low so that the tree lights looked brighter, and Mr. Richardson asked if we minded hearing the Christmas story read.

"That's one of our traditions, too," Mom assured him, and we all listened in sleepy contentment to the familiar words. When Mr. Richardson finished and laid his Bible aside,

Mom leaned over and picked it up curiously. It was small but very thick, and bound in brown leather. "Are you folks . . . LDS?" she asked, looking at the gold print on the binding.

"We sure are," Mr. Richardson said warmly.

"I used to go to the LDS Church with my friends when I was a teenager. In fact, I was baptized."

"You were?" I heard myself asking. I had never heard of this before.

Mom nodded, smiling slightly. "It seems so long ago. I've forgotten a lot about the doctrine, but I remember the good feelings I had—and all the nice people at church."

"Why didn't you keep going?" I asked, fascinated with this new aspect of my mother.

"Well, your grandma didn't like me to, and then we moved to Boise and I got busy with school and met your dad. He'd been brought up Protestant, as I had. It was easier not to insist, and I just sort of drifted away. But I've always kept a soft spot in my heart for the Church."

Mrs. Richardson smiled at her. "Ever considered going back?"

Mom took a deep breath. "It's something to think about, now that we're on our own. I know I'd like the children to have some solid spiritual training."

"The gospel's brought our family a lot of joy," Mrs. Richardson said. "Kept us close together, working for a common cause. Our four boys served missions, and six of the nine kids have married in the temple."

"For time and eternity?" Mom asked softly. "I remember that concept. It sounded so wonderful."

"It is wonderful," Mr. Richardson said, smiling at his wife. "I heartily recommend it, along with the rest of the teachings. Barbara, we know this is Christ's true, restored Church, Connie and I—and we're hoping to serve a mission ourselves before long. I'll tell you, it'd be a source of tremendous strength in your life, as well as the greatest blessing your kids could have, if you could see your way clear to make it a part of your lives again. They'd enjoy Primary and Mutual—that'd be Young Women for Cassie here."

"Right, Young Women—that's what I used to go to with my friends. And—and sacrament meeting. Did I remember it right?"

"Sure did."

"I wonder—I'll have to look up the Church when we get home. See when the meetings are."

"You'll be glad you did," Mrs. Richardson put in, looking at Jimmy and Josh, who were close to sleep on the hearth rug. "Shall I just go tuck these boys in? I'll give them Mark and Cory's room, so they'll be together. And Cassie, how about you? Are you sleepy, yet, or do you want to stay up and listen to the grown-ups talk?"

"I want to stay up—but I'm kind of tired. Is there a room ready for me?"

"There sure is. I'll give you Shellie's room. She'll be flying in from Seattle in a couple of days, and I've already put fresh sheets on her bed. Why don't you carry your little brother?"

I picked up Jimmy, who curled his legs around my waist and laid his head on my shoulder, and carried him up the broad staircase after Mrs. Richardson, who led Josh.

"I'll be up in a few minutes," Mom called after us, but I could tell she was glad to have the chance to keep talking to Mr. Richardson. We deposited the boys in twin beds. I pulled off Jimmy's shoes and clothes, down to his underwear, and covered him with the soft comforter. He was asleep before I even finished. Josh hurriedly undressed and jumped into his bed while our hostess was putting out towels in the adjoining bathroom.

"Cass," he asked worriedly, "What about Santa? How's he going to find us, here?"

"No problem," I told him. "He never misses. He'll either come here or at Grandma's."

"Oh. Well, that's good, 'cause Jim was scared he wouldn't find us."

I grinned at him. "Right," I said knowingly. "Sleep well, brat."

He grinned back. "Okay, rat."

Shellie's room was smaller, but cozy, with a poster bed and tons of dolls and photographs of guys. A counted cross-stitch sampler hung above the bed. It said, "I can follow God's plan for me." I wondered if God really had a plan for each of us. Did he have one for me? Was it part of his plan that we were here, tonight? Did he send the storm or make our car konk out? I wasn't sure exactly how God worked or if everything that happened was his will. I went to the window and peeked out through the blinds. The snow wasn't falling as heavily as before. The yard looked like a Christmas card, with evergreen branches drooping like arms too tired from holding up their white burden. I wandered back through the room, out the door, and onto the landing, which was wide enough to make a little reading area with a loaded bookcase and two soft chairs. I curled up in one of the chairs, from which I could see down into the living room and hear some of the conversation. Mr. Richardson was talking about somebody named Joseph Smith, and Mom was asking questions in an animated voice. She sounded young. It was weird. I guess I dozed off in the chair, because I woke suddenly to the sound of a growling engine outside and wondered sleepily why someone was running a lawn mower in the winter. Then the engine died, and the front door opened to a man's voice calling cheerfully, "Merry Christmas! Where's the cocoa and cookies? Oops—sorry—didn't know you had company!"

I blinked and peered through the railing at the tall man who pulled off gloves and shrugged out of a parka.

"Barbara, this is our son Neil, who lives down the road—within snowmobiling distance," Mr. Richardson said. "Neil, Barbara Andrews. Barbara and her kids were stranded when their car blew a hose or something down by the mailbox."

"Just when you were on your way somewhere for Christmas? That's a bummer," he said, coming forward to shake Mom's hand. "I saw the car—wondered whose it was."

"Well, if we had to stall, I can tell you we picked the best possible place," Mom said. "Your folks have been so gracious to take us in on Christmas Eve, of all times. They've fed us royally and turned a bad experience into a wonderful one."

"Yep, they're pretty terrific. I've always been glad I had the good sense to pick them for parents." He winked in his mother's direction, then sat down in a rocking chair, his long legs stretched toward the fire. "I finally finished my reports, and thought, 'Now, where would I most want to be on Christmas Eve?' Then I remembered Mom's cookies, and I knew I had to help keep the old tradition alive."

"I'll make cocoa. Who wants some?" his mother said, standing up.

"We all do," said Mr. Richardson. "But I think we've got a job for Neil before we feed him, don't you, Mother?"

"What's that?"

"Well, I'm sure Barbara'd like her luggage out of her car, and what about this emptiness under the tree? Doesn't look right. I'll bet she's got some presents for those kids stashed in her trunk, too. Here you go, son—why don't you take Barbara down to get what she needs before her car gets completely covered and frozen in?" He tossed a set of keys to Neil, who bounded up and got into his parka again, apparently delighted to be of service.

"Oh, thank you so much," Mom was saying. "I didn't want to trouble you folks, but—"

"No trouble at all," Neil replied, smiling at her. "Can't have Christmas without Santa. How old are your kids, Barbara?"

I only heard part of Mom's reply as they went out into the night. Mrs. Richardson came to stand almost under me, folded her arms, and looked at her husband, who was tuning in some Christmas music on the radio.

"What?" he asked innocently, responding to her look.

"I think you're thinking what I'm thinking," she replied softly.

"Stranger things have happened," he said, going to give her a hug. "After all, the Lord works in mysterious ways, his wonders to perform. But he expects us to do our part too." He sighed. "Goodness knows, Neil needs someone. It's been two years since Janet died, and I don't think he's dated a soul, do you?"

Mrs. Richardson shrugged. "No one I know of. And I can't honestly think of anyone around here who'd be suitable. They really are a sweet little family, aren't they? He could help Barbara back into activity, and those precious children . . ."

"Well, mustn't count our chickens, sweetheart. Barbara may have other plans."

No, she doesn't! I wanted to shout from my perch on the landing. *She's lonesome and sad, and we miss our dad, and I know even if the boys don't that he's not coming back. And Neil seems nice, and you'd be neat to have for grandparents, and . . .* I stopped short, realizing suddenly that I'd been listening to things that weren't meant for me to hear, which wasn't very nice of me considering how good these folks were being. But I couldn't be too sorry, either, because I liked what I'd heard! I crept back toward Shellie's bedroom with the sound of a choir singing "O Holy Night" following me. "He knows our need," the choir sang, and I thought, *Maybe he really does!*

"Fall on your knees," the choir commanded. "O hear the angel voices!" A thrill swept through me as I got into my borrowed bed on this most magical and amazing Christmas Eve. At last the angels were singing to me.

SHARON DOWNING JARVIS, a former high school English teacher, grew up in the southern states, where she was converted to the LDS Church at the age of seventeen. She has been writing stories since she was seven, and finally became serious about publishing her work in 1992, when her novel *The Kaleidoscope Season* appeared, followed by *The Healing Place* in 1994. She and her husband, Wayne, reside in Orem, Utah, where Sharon teaches piano and continues to write and to research her southern roots. They are the parents of two grown children, Andy and Camille.

CHRISTMAS OFFERINGS

Jay A. Parry

THIS IS NO SANITIZED hospital setting. No soft bed with electronic controls. I am kneeling in matted straw in a close cave, the only light a flickering fire that casts moving shadows against the walls. Just the three of us there— laboring mother, anxious father, and, inexplicably, me. No animals, either, despite all the pictures and stories, though I can smell them and hear them shuffling and breathing in the dark outside.

Soundlessly her water breaks; later I see the blood; still later at the birth I can see the baby's spirit shining through translucent skin. The place is thick with the feel of holiness.

This was my dream, but it felt so real each time that I was shocked by the strangeness of reality when I awoke.

It started when I learned my wife, Mary, was pregnant again. Twice before she'd carried a baby, and twice the baby had come forth early, too early to survive, our thrill over the budding life giving way to disappointment and grief.

"I'm pregnant again," she announced on a warm night in mid-May.

"Can we bear it?"

"Have to try. Keep trying," she said. She smiled at me like she'd never known a moment's pain or disappointment in her life.

"You're a marvel. You keep reminding me why I love you so much."

She never miscarried smoothly, the life passing into death in a quick release. No, it was always a struggle, a mighty struggle, with true labor and a terrible pushing against something so small it hardly seemed to be there at all.

"There's more," she said. "It's due on Christmas Eve."

I took in a silent breath. A Christmas gift. From the One who suffered more than we can imagine to give his own gift.

It seemed uncanny that her name was Mary, preparing to give birth on Christmas Eve—if we could get the seed to grow and flourish in the quiet cave of her womb. What I haven't said yet is that my name is Joseph. Well, my middle name is. New acquaintances always laugh when we tell them we're Joseph and Mary.

"You're putting us on."

"No, we're really quite serious."

"No, really, this is a joke, right?"

"No, really, it's no joke."

Finally we'd come clean. "Okay, she's Mary and I'm Alan Joseph."

Still, here we were, Joseph (almost) and Mary looking toward a precious birth at Christmastime.

The night she told me these things was the night the dreams started.

The third night it happened I woke up feeling confused. Why did I keep dreaming that I was present at the birth of the Savior? What did that have to do with our own hopes and desires? Was it just my unspoken anxieties finding an outlet? Or was there maybe some deeper meaning?

Again and again I entered the cave, always feeling that I didn't quite belong but knowing that I must be there. And again and again I awakened trying to make sense of it all.

In the third month the doctor put Mary to bed. "I know we've tried this before and it didn't seem to help much. But we want to keep this one, don't we, and I know you're willing to try whatever is necessary."

She agreed, with all her heart. I think she would have allowed herself to be immobilized with straps if we had thought it would help.

In previous years she had stayed down pretty well—until someone needed her help. She never complained much to friends or neighbors in the ward, so people didn't know not to ask.

"Mary, Sister Jenkins fell and bruised her hip. Do you think you could go sit with her today?"

"Mary, I'm sure by now you've heard about the tragedy with Susie Stanger. Both her parents at once—what a heartbreak. There's going to be a real crowd at the funeral. Since you're not working we thought you'd be able to come over and help serve at the luncheon. Oh, and could we drop by a bag of potatoes for you to scallop? You're such a dear."

"Mary, we need to double up on your visiting teaching assignments for the school year while the young student sisters are so busy."

I told her to say no, even talked to the bishop and asked him to spread the word, discreetly of course. Mary's a private person, didn't want to make a big deal out of it. And sometimes she tried to say no. But she's a server and a giver, not a taker. She'd stay down, then get up, then back down, then up, then the miscarriage.

"This time's got to be different, honey," I said. "No exceptions. I know it's hard to stay down. But you've got to."

"That's what I've been thinking. We've got to make this work."

In one dream I was waiting inside the cave before Mary (the first Mary) and her Joseph even arrived. I saw myself lead the animals outside so the young parents-to-be could have more room, more privacy. I like the Thomas Hardy poem about the oxen kneeling in the straw to give honor to the new king. But even more I liked the idea of the baby being born in a reverent solitude. My part was small, but maybe it was important.

As always, before I awakened, I saw the birth—the water, the blood, the spirit.

That was the recurring motif—the water and blood and spirit of birth. That was Mary's gift to the world. She gave her very self to give her baby to a wicked world.

Before my mission I went in to see my bishop. My heart was pounding and my palms were sweaty. Maybe that sounds like a cliché, but still it's a good description of how I felt. He met me at the door.

"Alan, good to see you. Not too long before you're nineteen. Still on track for a mission?"

He closed the door behind us and motioned for me to have a seat. I could tell from the grave look in his eyes that he *knew*. He knew why I was there.

"Actually, Bishop, well, you know, sometimes people mess up a little."

I had messed up more than a little, though not enough to keep me from going on a mission. I was pretty sure of that. But still I had to clear it up, and I didn't like it one bit. And what if the bishop held me back? I knew that had happened to friends, though I suspected their sins were darker than mine. But who could say?

I'm telling you this because I sense I need to be more honest about my feelings about the birth of the baby Jesus and the sacrifice of his mother. She didn't offer her very life in the birthing process just so her baby could bless a wicked world. She gave that gift for *me,* so that he could give his greater gift to me. Because I

am one of those natural men King Benjamin talked about, though I try to be good. Not wicked, really. Actually I'm pretty honorable. I stay pretty worthy—could be much worse. But have I had a change of heart? Was I renewed in Christ? Have I been born again?

I was trying, but the world kept butting into my life.

That's one reason the cave was so important. I needed that baby to be born even more than I needed our own baby. I longed for a little child to love, to expand our family. But I needed a Savior.

My Mary stayed down for two months, and the doctor was quite proud of her. "You're doing better than ever. The baby's thriving. But don't quit quite yet. Check back with me in another month, and we'll see if you can then get up for some gentle activity."

She liked her doctor. She liked his manner. He talked to her like she was a person. "That's not something you can learn in medical school," she said to me as we slowly walked back to the car that day.

"I'll bet some of them unlearn it there, though," I said. "The bedside manner of some of those guys makes me wish *they'd* go home to bed instead."

She went home and went back to bed. She stayed there faithfully day after day. "This time we're going to make it," she said. "I can feel it in my bones."

Joseph tenderly took his just-born child in his arms and wrapped him in clean white linen they'd brought with them, wiping his face clean as he did. *They're prepared,* I thought. They knew it was going to happen here, in this place, at this time. They're ready for it. It was part of a grand timetable that had been set in place aeons before, and they knew it.

Mary gave some of her blood and water for the baby. Just as the baby would give blood—and water and spirit—for me.

Those were the real gifts, after all.

My Mary had only one week to go before her next doctor's appointment. I came home from work, calling at the door, yelling the same thing I did every day since she'd been put to bed: "Honey, I'm home! What's cookin'?"

It was a little joke between us. Mary liked to cook well enough, but I'd taken on the duty since she wasn't supposed to be up. So I knew nothing was cooking—but still I hollered at the door.

There was no answer. She wasn't at home anywhere. Not on the couch, in the bedroom, anywhere. And no note.

I sat on the couch and tried to read the paper. I couldn't concentrate. I tried to watch the early evening news. But my mind kept darting around at where she might be, what might be happening. Finally I got up and called her sister, who lived forty miles away in a neighboring town. Ally didn't know anything. I made some supper and set up the TV tray I served Mary on. I called the doctor's emergency number. The answering service reassured me that Mary had made no contact.

She came home a little after seven, looking exhausted—and glowing.

"Where have you been? Do you know how worried—"

She raised a hand to quiet me. "Sister Whitaker (our Relief Society president) needed some help with Sister Ohlmeyer. Oh, Alan, you should see her. She's really gone downhill since I saw her last. I don't know if you know, but I used to go over there every Tuesday to read to her and help her, but I can't believe how much she's deteriorated. Sister Whitaker needed to find a couple of sisters to go over to give her her bath. One can't do it alone anymore. She couldn't find anyone. Finally she called me. 'Are you up and about yet?' she says. 'Or still being careful?' I said I could come help. 'Are you sure?' she asks. 'I don't want you risking anything.' I thought I could handle it. I'm feeling strong and the baby seems fine."

I made her go to bed, saying I wanted her to rest, but she couldn't stop talking. I brought her the supper on the tray, nothing fancy but I hoped nourishing. Finally she settled down. It had been too long since she'd been able to give of herself. She was exulting in the sweet joy of her service. It was a simple offering, the kind of thing she'd done dozens of times before. But helping to lift and cleanse Sister Ohlmeyer's frail body was renewing to her. She had a hard time getting to sleep, but when she did she slept more deeply than normal.

I worried into the night.

Somehow I was on top of the cave. Joseph was gone, but Mary was there, right by my side. Rising above us on the cave's dome, like a defiant, angry gesture, was a rough, heavy pole, with another pole set crosswise on it. The baby wasn't there, but Jesus was, the matured Jesus, and I thought of Mary's offering, and his infinitely greater one—of blood and water and spirit.

Finally I understood.

That's what he was asking of me. That I yield myself to be born of him and the Spirit, no matter the cost. He wanted me to give a replica of the gift he gave, a gift of myself in heart and being. As he hung there with arms stretched out like he'd promised so often in the scriptures—arms stretched out to bless all the day long—I knew he was inviting me to partake of his pain and his glory, with the grace of his help.

Mary woke me early, saying she was cramping. We called the doctor without delay. We'd been through this drill before. He was at the hospital before we got there. No wonder she likes him. They put her in a wheelchair and gave her a shot to relax her. They put her in an antiseptic room, in a bed with electronic controls. There were no animals in the room, and I knew there were none outside either. But Mary was offering herself to the process of life and death, as she had the day before in helping Sister Ohlmeyer.

The baby was born later that morning, at 10:09 the nurse's record said, too tiny to take even one breath. It was a boy. They let me stay in the room with Mary the whole time. I saw the blood and what looked like water. We couldn't sense the baby's spirit. But there was another Spirit in the room, and that helped.

The sacrament that Sunday was quiet and sober. I thought of my dreams, of the tense hours in Mercy Hospital the Tuesday before, and of the long and hopeful months as we had tried to protect and preserve the life of this baby. I couldn't be upset at Mary for serving. I was having a hard time figuring out whether she was a little foolish or innocently selfless, but I couldn't be angry at her. We'd just try again.

But all through the sacrament meeting that day I couldn't stop thinking about the birth I was supposed to come to, the one where I truly would come unto Christ, withholding nothing, sacrificing everything, and partake of the power and blessing of his atonement to be changed. I thought of my visit to the bishop's office all those years before, and the birth process that began. And I began to think that the birth celebration of Christ at Christmas

was nothing less than incomplete if it celebrated only his birth.

I'm not sure when the dreams stopped. Long before Christmas. But on Christmas Eve that year I finally told Mary about them, and about the weight that had been pulling at me for most of the year. "I need to be clear of this," I said. "I want to feel joy again." I knew what I had to do—but how?

"The only way out is through," she said. She flashed me that smile I told you about. I began to think that in all her goodness she might know something I didn't know—not book learning or scripture knowledge, but a knowing that comes from feeling and being.

The following year we celebrated Christmas with our infant son, whom we had named Christian, hoping he would take a hint. Our family has continued to grow, and Mary's body has learned to carry those precious vessels to term.

As I rejoice at the blessedness of those children, I always think of Mary and Joseph and Jesus, and the dream scenes I saw in the cave that's called a stable. I think of the blood she gave then (to make his mortal life possible), and the blood he gave later (to make our spiritual life possible), and the water and spirit that were poured out for our sakes. And then I think of my own poor offering, now given with a true heart, my daily Christmas gift to him. And of the joy I've found.

JAY A. PARRY is an associate editor for Deseret Book Company and is the author or coauthor of more than two dozen books. He lives in Salt Lake City with his wife, Vicki; they are the parents of seven children.

Between the Nails

Kristen Randle

O KAY, IT'S NOT AS IF I never do anything for my family. But here's my mother saying, "At least could you put these lights up on the new room!" as if I hadn't already gotten down about fifty boxes of decorations for her. As if I didn't spend about four hours two Saturdays ago stringing lights through all the shrubbery out in front.

And tonight it's freezing. This means I'm going to have to go out in the garage, get out that filthy ladder, and climb up practically on the roof to hang these things. Which would be nasty enough if it was just normally cold—but the way it is out there tonight, I'm going to have to find my ski gloves and my thermals to do this. And I'm going to be late to the play.

But it's not like I can say no when she puts it like that—like she's had to do everything herself. Which is probably true. Dad never really does that much—I doubt he even has a clue how much there is to do. Not that he's not willing to be supportive. But the fact is, maybe she's just trying to do too much. Well, that goes without saying—she probably has always done too much. But it was different when we were little; when everything was so new.

In those days she would make, like, five different kinds of cookies every year. Those little white, powdered sugar balls other people call Russian Tea Cakes—but my dad calls Reindeer Drops—and these molded candy cane ones you put crushed peppermint on, and this kind you slice off a roll, which turns out to be hard because they've got chunks of gum drops in them, chunks that can only be made by somebody with hot scissors and a lot of time to kill.

And sugar cookies. Not the kind you're probably thinking of, the fat ones with all the icing. The kind we make are from my great-grandmother's recipe, thin and crisp, green and red and yellow, trees and stars and camels. My mother used to flour the whole dining room table, put aprons on everybody, and then roll out the dough over and over again while we cut stars right out of the middle, just where we'd end up wasting the most space.

We'd cut, then she'd try to recut so she could actually detach the cookies from the table; we'd get these stars with three or four edges to them, as if somebody'd feathered them on purpose. She'd line them up on the cookie sheet, row after row, and then we'd sand them with sprinkles. She had every kind of sprinkles from colored sugar and thousands of tiny colored balls to the big silver BB things you're not really supposed to eat. And most of it, of course, ended up on the table or between the cookies.

We have pictures of this, years and years of them—all of us leaning across the table, flour and whatever all over us, garlands and lights in the background. The one thing you can't get into the pictures is the Tabernacle Choir's *Holly and the Ivy,* which has always been the official sugar cookie music. But I remember that, too. I would remember it all, even without the pictures.

I'm thinking about that as I go mincing through this half-hearted snow. I get to the garage and find out it's locked. Like I carry keys with me all the time. So I have to go back and get the keys, and my ears are already frozen.

She used to make a triple recipe of those

sugar cookies because that's what her mom did. But it always took us about three weeks to work through all that dough, and now she says cookies have too much fat in them anyway. So this year, she made half recipes of everything—except she gave up completely on the gumdrops. Which is understandable.

But I helped. On the sugar cookie day, I got home in time to help. There are pictures of me leaning over my little brother, Jacky, helping him get the right feathered effect on his stars. It's not like I wasn't there.

It's just, I have a life now. I have band concerts to play and friends—and church—I mean, are you supposed to skip church to stay home and address Christmas cards to people you don't even know? When I put it like that, *she* can't say no.

And like tonight. Some of my closest friends are in this play. Not only is this the last night, but there happen to be some people in it who are, like, not exactly friends yet, but who I think are pretty interesting, and we're all supposed to go to Carousel afterwards for ice cream. Okay, so maybe this isn't earth-shakingly important, but it's important to me.

There are just things I want to do, things I have to do. Not bad things—there isn't a thing my friends and I do that my parents would really worry about. Probably. Well, most of the time—there's no anticipating momentary stupidity. Still, we never do anything immoral; sometimes we're just sillier than life, is all.

Do you have any idea how cold a metal ladder can be in subzero weather? Try carrying one across a yard the size of Montana. So my dad put this new room on the side of the house. It's kind of cool, all shingled on the outside and with these big windows. He and my brother and my mom did a lot of the work

themselves. And I helped. As much as I could—they were always doing stuff when I was at school or at lessons or something.

But this is the only place on the house that hasn't been encrusted with lights. Neither of my parents came from exterior-lighting families. It was like, "We don't *do* lights." But then, after my parents had been married about two years, they looked around and realized that outside lights were not necessarily a moral issue, more like a financial one, and that they could put lights on their house without shame. So now, on a foggy night, small aircraft use our house for a landmark.

The trick with setting up a ladder against the wall of a house is to not put it through a window. Especially not through the window that happens to be framing the Christmas tree. Which is what I am right now trying very hard not to do.

So, if I tell you we have over fourteen hundred lights—both the big ones and those little tiny ones—on the trees and the house outside, you'd really want to know how many lights my mother puts on the tree itself. It takes her an entire day. You can't just drape them around like garlands, you have to wrap every branch, every twig on every branch, every *molecule* on every branch. She actually had to cut back because our trees were drying out and dying after about a week and a half. Picture a tree with a couple thousand lights and no needles.

It takes another day to put on the ornaments. We have about three hundred of those, mostly handmade. Some of them are old—there are a couple of felt birds my mom made when she was about twelve, and there are some with my Grandad's signature on them dated 1967, and that's really old.

In fact, my parents have this Christmas

party every year; it's always been basically the same people, and they each have to make a tree ornament, and then they play this wild game where they end up stealing ornaments from each other. It gets very loud. But some of the stuff they bring is incredible. It's the perfect party for my mom, because she's into making little tiny stuff. And so our tree has all these, like, little surprises hanging all over it—little sculptures made out of clay or silver wire or fabric or wood or beads—the smaller the better. It's an incredible looking tree with all those lights and all that stuff. But it takes a million years to get the whole thing set up. Which is the problem. Because nobody but my mom has a million years to spend on it.

So, what you don't want to do when you're hanging lights outside, by the way—those big, pinched-egg shaped lights like the ones I just pulled out of this box—you don't want to just drag the string around or let it drop so that it hits the ground. Those lights blow up if you breathe on them. They just pop and then there's next to nothing left. Then you have to dig them out of the sockets, which means you have to take your gloves off, which is miserable enough. But then you have to take hold of this jagged bit of glass that's still sticking up, and talk the whole thing into letting you unscrew it. Meanwhile, your fingers are totally falling off. As in right now, when my hands are so cold, I can't even feel when I'm blowing on them.

Which is too bad, because with my gloves on I'm not going to be able to hang these things on the nails Dad stuck under the rain gutter, which means I'm going to have to do the rest of this bare-handed, and I'm already starting to form icicles where my breath is condensing all over my scarf. I hate doing this.

Christmas is supposed to be this magic time when things just happen. You're supposed to walk into a room and be amazed—candles and greenery, things that shimmer, boxes full of potential energy, bows of a thousand colors, secrets, mounds of treats that are rich beyond dreams—every time the doorbell rings it could be something wonderful, someone you love but hardly ever see, standing there ruddy-cheeked and blowing on their hands, chins buried in their parkas, maybe wanting you to come away, to go and do something or see something.

But here I am, hanging on this ladder, trying not to feel how cold the metal is where it's pressing against my jeans. But it's always cold like this—I can remember going numb, taking plates around to the neighbors, which we have done every year since I can remember. It used to be plates of the cookies we made, but, like I say, we don't really do that so much anymore, so my mom has to find other things to fill the plates now. And, of course, she does a certain amount of stressing over this. Guilt, I think. Like she is personally responsible to make sure that every person we know feels happy at Christmas. Which means about twenty-three plates, if she limits herself to our street. And you couldn't possibly take something store-bought.

We used to go around delivering as a family, hitting all our neighbors in one marathon evening the way the Mannings do it with the scones they make. But we can't ever find a time when we're all home at once, so now Mom makes the plates up and then shoves them into our hands, two at a time, whenever she can catch anybody to do it. I mean, it does get done. I've delivered several myself this very year in that formless time between home-from-school and later.

The best part of this is coming home to hot chocolate. You may be freezing to death, your fingers and nose and ears may be falling off, but it's worth it when somebody gives you a mug of chocolate and you get to sit in front of the fire until you thaw out. That's the one time I seem to be able to hold still. Then I can actually smell the tree.

The only thing I can smell at the moment is ice.

Really, all I had to do was plug this string into the one my brother put over my parents' window. It wasn't that hard. The tricky part was getting the cord between the nails in the corner. Now, I just have to run the string down the roofline without getting any of the bulbs stuck in the joins of the ladder.

You can see the top of the Christmas tree from up here. Kind of a weird perspective, looking down through the window this way. Like, you're looking into the room past the angel on the tree. There aren't very many ornaments on this side, but the lights are everywhere and the tree shines like you'd expect from something with an angel sitting on it. And there's somebody moving around in there, but I can't see them very well; the closer I get to look, the more my breath clouds up the glass.

I hang about a foot of cord on the nails, and then I have to get down and shift the ladder, which still has clumps of mud on it from the building last summer. And the ground slopes here, so I'm messing with this heavy thing, trying to get it to sit straight. Which it won't. But I'm climbing it anyway, the rain gutter groaning under the end of the ladder, because I've got to get this done and get out of here.

So, I get the cord through the first set of nails, then I've got to, like, thread the lights under the ladder to get them to the other nails, so now I've got my cheek resting against this gross ladder while I'm groping around underneath it with both hands. And when I straighten up again, I can reach the other nails—and maybe one more set if I lean out really far and don't end up on the ground with the ladder in my lap.

While I'm leaning out here, I get this glimpse of my little brother. At first, I think he's messing with the presents. But then I realize he's just sitting there on the floor in front of the tree. I can see about half of him. And before the window fogs up, I can see his face, turned up sort of, the lights reflecting in his eyes like he's got all the colors of the world in there. He's just this little guy, and to him everything's a mystery. You can tell him the story of baby Jesus, and he worries. You can tell him about the angels and the sheep, and he gets scared. But then, he puts it all together looking at that wooden carousel on the dining room table, the one with Mary and Joseph holding the baby, and all the sheep and angels and camels and stuff going around them, and he loves it. And I'm thinking maybe the Baby had to be kind of like he is, warm and solid when you hold him, kind of sweet, the kind of kid who nestles into you and makes you feel like a human being.

And while I'm watching, my mother comes in. She does the unthinkable; she hands my brother a little mug—hot chocolate in the study on the carpet. Then she sits down beside him, and they are both looking up at the tree. They don't see me until I clear the glass, rubbing it dry with the end of my scarf. Then my mother laughs and points and my brother's face shines at me and they're laughing. And I'm laughing, which doesn't make any sense at all, considering my situation out here.

Then my mother points at my brother's mug. I can see the marshmallows now, the little kind, and she points at me and raises her eyebrows. Like, she's telling me I can come in now. I glance over, figuring out how many more times I'm going to have to move this ladder before I'm finished. And then I think about how cool the house is going to look when the lights are actually finished. Then I look at her and shake my head—I'm still smiling—and I kind of wave my hand. Yes, I'm coming in, and yes, I want chocolate. But just give me a minute.

There's only a little left to do.

KRISTEN RANDLE is an aging kid who lives with her fine husband and wild children on the banks of a Utah river. She finds that time goes by altogether too quickly in the case of the children and the wear and tear on her own face. She has written several novels, some published by Bookcraft, others by companies east of the Mississippi, as well as a number of children's song collections, one of which was published by Deseret Book. She will probably keep writing—as much as family, church, and the business of making music will allow.

THE CHRISTMAS ERRAND

Annette Paxman Bowen

NO ONE SHOULD HAVE to make a cross-country move the week before Christmas—especially with a sick baby. But my husband was in the navy, and when the navy says move, you move.

We were living in Pensacola, Florida, where my husband, Chad, had just completed his training as a navy flight surgeon, and we had our first assignment: San Diego, California, where Chad was to report on January third. The one bright spot: we'd have the chance to spend Christmas with our families back in Utah, if we could get there in time.

Florida had been a place of warm sunshine, new friends, and thrilling experiences as Chad began his training as a jet pilot. But our six months there were also a time of trouble and grief.

We had been in Pensacola just a few weeks when our first child, only four months old, stopped growing. At a routine check-up, the doctors were alarmed by his height and weight and came up with the terribly ambiguous diagnosis: Failure to Thrive.

When I heard this news, I felt like someone had grabbed my heart, wrenching it continuously. I inhaled deeply, feeling oxygen-deprived. In fact, for the next four weeks, I don't think I took one easy breath. I certainly didn't sleep well. And I felt as though I went through the routines of daily life in a grey haze of worry and concern. A woman in a grocery store asked me my baby's age, guessing he was two months old, and I felt a sense of panic and paranoia that lasted for days.

What could cause tiny Bradford James—BJ, we called him—to stop growing? I was horrified by the possibilities, and my doctor-husband knew all too many frightening disorders that could affect an infant's development. We fasted and knelt in prayer together, pleading with God to help our son grow normally, and if that wasn't God's will, to help us understand and handle the situation with faith.

The next month passed as a never-ending series of doctor's appointments and lab tests. BJ was strapped, poked, stuck, prodded, observed, and monitored. Feeling terrified by the possibilities, and so desperately far away from beloved friends and family and support, we continued our desperate prayers and coddled this precious—and tiny—boy. I remember sitting outside a hospital lab as they ran yet another test for a deadly disease (this time it was for cystic fibrosis), with tears slipping silently down my cheeks as I hugged my child, all the while trying to will him to *fail* this test. Thankfully, after a month of appointments, and a trying trip to Houston, Texas, for special pediatric consultations, no such diseases were diagnosed. When he was five months old, tiny BJ began growing and gaining weight, ever so slowly, and we were left with the gratifying knowledge that many terrifying options had been ruled out; yet we still had no sure answers as to why he was so small and was growing so slowly.

As Chad and I planned for our trip home to Utah, then on to California, we decided that it would be wise for me to fly to Salt Lake City with BJ, sparing us both the long cross-country drive in our small and aging station wagon. I was emotionally spent and I just wanted to go *home;* and we didn't want to risk

BJ catching a cold in a drafty car. Then, after Christmas, the three of us would complete the trip to San Diego together. Unfortunately, we could find neither a driver nor a passenger for our car, which left to Chad the exhausting task of getting the car from Florida to Utah, alone.

So, after prematurely stripping our tree of its Christmas decorations and packing up our apartment, an exhausted Chad climbed into our stuffed car and started the long drive west. I spent a final Florida night with neighbors, who took me and baby BJ to the airport early the next morning.

The long flight to Salt Lake City was awful. We had to change planes several times and had an extra-long layover in Denver. Still, I was grateful that BJ and I were not making the journey in a car. The poor little guy had a cold, which plugged his ears each time we took off or landed, causing him terrible discomfort. I did my best to help him to suck on a bottle in an attempt to open his little ear passages. I held him, rocked him, sang to him, and bounced him, trying to comfort him and all the time being acutely aware of the other passengers around me who glared at me as my son fussed. By the time we reached Denver, I was nearly wiped out.

As the plane landed, BJ threw up all over me.

In the airport, I quickly located a lounge and changed my son's clothing. Because I had a change of clothes for my son, I thought I had prepared well for the trip, but I had not anticipated needing a change of clothes for me. In the women's room, I tried to clean up my shirt and sweater—while holding my cranky son and silently wishing for some kind soul, some stranger, *anybody* to offer help for just a minute. I think I would have accepted help from anyone short of a convicted ax murderer. Yet no offer was made, and I just couldn't bring myself to ask total strangers for help.

During the final leg of the flight—again holding, bouncing, and comforting my little boy with his aching ears—I counted the minutes until I could be with my family, with someone who could take the baby for me, who cared about him—and about me. And I looked forward to the opportunity to take a shower and get into clean clothes. I really felt sorry for those who had to sit close to the bouncing babbling boy and his odiferous mother in seats 28 A and B, but we couldn't exactly crack a window and let in some fresh air.

At the airport gate in Salt Lake City, I was surprised to be met by Chad's teenage brother. After responding with an honest and spontaneous, "Oh, yuck!" to the sight of my shirt and sweater, he explained that he'd offered to make the drive from Provo to Salt Lake International to fetch me and BJ, and my mother and Chad's mother had been thrilled to have him meet me, since they were in the middle of a multitude of holiday activities and plans. I didn't tell him how disappointed I was to be greeted by only one person instead of the loving multitude I had envisioned, and he didn't tell me how disgusted he was by my appearance—and smell. But there was certainly no handing off a sick little guy to this sixteen-year-old.

Thankfully, BJ fell asleep in the car during the drive from Salt Lake to Provo. I was equally exhausted, but I wanted to visit with my brother-in-law, whom I loved dearly and had honestly missed.

At last, after what felt like days instead of hours since we had left Florida earlier that morning, we pulled into the driveway of my childhood home. Tears swamped my eyes as I saw the Christmas tree lights through the windows and anticipated the long-awaited welcome inside the warm kitchen where I had grown up.

I was not disappointed by this welcome: as soon as we stepped through the back door, I was engulfed in hugs, tender greetings, and the overwhelming comfort of being with people who loved me. BJ was kissed and hugged and passed from sister to sister to grandma to grandpa, and at last whisked off to be bathed and changed. Meanwhile, I collapsed into a kitchen chair and burst into tears.

My mother was baking gingerbread cookies, filling the kitchen with sweet spices. As I tearfully told her about the trip home, the most recent medical appointments and the still unanswered concerns about my baby, plus my anxiety over Chad's solo drive across the country, my mother listened and sympathized as she rolled out gingerbread men and women, deftly dropping cinnamon hearts and currants into their dough-bodies to make eyes, noses, mouths and buttons. Sitting in the familiar kitchen with my mother, sharing my emotional load with her, watching her lovely hands working the cookie dough—all this brought great comfort and a feeling of safety I hadn't felt in a long time. I didn't want to budge from the spot. Ever. So many times during the past months, I had sat outside a doctor's office or a laboratory, holding my little son while awaiting test results, and I had yearned to have someone familiar near me. The relief of my mother's presence brought more tender tears.

A sour smell from my soiled clothes suddenly reminded me that I needed to shower and change, so when Mom suggested that we had whole days ahead to talk and that I would feel better when I was cleaned up, I dragged away from the comfort of that kitchen and climbed the steep back stairs to my old room, here to find that my thoughtful father had already carried my suitcases up to my room and had left them, conveniently opened, on my old bed. And there, safely and soundly asleep in the crib that had been moved in anticipation of his arrival, lay my tiny son, sweetly breathing the high-desert air of Utah. Home.

When I emerged from the shower, the sun was drooping in the late afternoon sky, and BJ was still sleeping. My college-age sister, Kellie, was busy in her room, so I stopped by to thank her for tending him. "You must be exhausted," Kellie said.

"I am," I confirmed. "Oh, it's so good to be here," I sighed.

"It's nice to have you home for a while," Kellie smiled. "Mom said to tell you she's got a little errand for you to run when you have a minute."

I was surprised by this announcement. An errand? Didn't Mom understand how tired I was? That my body's clock was set three hours ahead of Utah time? That after I had supper and a family visit, I would be more than ready to head to bed?

"What does she have in mind?" I asked Kellie.

"There's no telling. You know Mom. She's got a list of Christmas projects as long as her arm. She's in her final countdown. Becky and Spencer will be arriving any time now, and then tomorrow is Christmas Eve."

Christmas Eve. That morning I had awakened very early in Florida, over two thousand miles away, and now I was in Utah, and the next day was Christmas Eve. I wondered where Chad was by then and hoped he'd make it home by tomorrow night in time to hang the stockings. Then I tried to send a telepathic message for him to call me, call me, call me.

Just then, Mom called my name. "Will you keep an ear out for the baby?" I asked Kellie, as I turned toward the stairs.

"Sure. That's one of my assignments for this evening, according to Mom," Kellie grinned. "I'm supposed to give you a break."

This simple announcement brought tears again and I choked out a thanks. No one had given me a break in a long, long time.

When I descended the stairs into the kitchen, Mom turned and lifted a piece of paper from the kitchen counter. "Lindsey, honey, I'm wondering if you'd mind walking over to Sears and buying some things for me. By the time you get back, Becky, Spencer, and little Jason should be here, and we'll set the table for supper."

She handed me the paper and I read a simple list: Boy, 6; Girl, 5; Girl, 3; Boy, 2; Baby Girl, 7 months.

"What do you want me to buy?" I asked.

"Pajamas. Sears has those warm blanket-sleepers on sale, and I'd like you to buy a pair for each of these children."

I smiled. This was a classic Mom idea and errand. "So, who are the kids?"

Mom turned back to the stove, stirring a pot of homemade soup. "Oh, they're some children in the ward. Their father is in school at BYU, and their mother is a very hardworking nurse. I often sit behind them at church. They're a darling family, but poor as church mice. The children remind me of you kids when you were little."

"And Dad was still in law school and you were a nurse," I added. "I guess you can relate."

Mom chuckled. "Oh, yes, I can relate." Then she wiped her hands on her apron and handed me her Sears charge card. "I think they'll let you use my card. Just call me if there's a problem."

I knew Dad had graduated from the University of Utah law school with four children by his side. The *Tribune* had run a picture of him and Mom and my four older siblings. I'd seen it in the family scrapbooks. I was child number five, followed by my two younger sisters, numbers six and seven. As I went to find a coat, I wondered how my parents had survived the challenge of graduate school with four little bodies to clothe and feed and love. I was exhausted caring for one little boy, and my husband had already completed much of his professional training.

When I stepped out into the cold air, I debated going back inside and asking for the car keys. Sears was only a few blocks away, but it was *freezing,* and my body was still acclimated to Florida temperatures. The sidewalks were glistening with ice, and I did not relish the idea of slipping and sliding my way to Sears. However, I did not want to face my mother with a wimpy request to drive instead of walk, so I buttoned my coat and carefully descended the front stairs.

It was now dark outside, with a beautiful cobalt sky. Christmas lights blinked and gleamed from the houses along our street. Patchy snow covered the neighborhood lawns. As I walked and slipped down the block, I thought of my good neighbors inside their houses. I could not keep myself from smiling as grand memories of growing up on this street popped up and played across my mind. As I reached the second block, I reminisced over the countless walking trips I'd made toward downtown to do Christmas shopping. As a little girl, I'd headed toward Pay Less and Woolworth's and had managed to buy seven Christmas

presents for under five dollars. As a teen, I'd worked at Clark's, a prestigious downtown store, during the busy holiday season and had loved walking to work wearing a Victorian Christmas costume; I had loved even more carefully selecting rather elegant gifts for my family, using my extra income. Now, here I was, a mother myself, and I was heading out Christmas shopping again—this time for someone else's children, using my generous mother's credit card.

I wondered about this family in my old childhood ward. It was mostly a student congregation now with a few retired folks thrown in—newlyweds and nearly-deads, we used to call them. Would this family know where these pajamas came from after we wrapped them and slipped them quietly onto their porch? Would they suspect that they came from my parents? I knew my mother well enough to know that these gifts would be delivered anonymously.

I pushed the heavy glass door open and stepped into the store's bright inside. The heat felt good. Christmas music played over the store's system. The layout of the store had changed again, as it had multiple times as I grew up. I wandered through the departments until I found children's clothing. Sure enough, there was a counter filled with bright blanket-sleepers, on sale. I pulled Mother's list from my pocket and began matching sizes and colors to the list. Pastel pink for the baby girl. Yellow for the two-year-old boy. Hot pink for the three-year-old girl. Purple for the five-year-old girl. And then I was stumped. The sizes stopped at size five. Realizing that Mom would definitely want each child to have new pajamas, I found another rack and selected some blue pajamas with cars printed on the warm flannel for the oldest boy.

When I presented my selections and Mom's charge card to the clerk, she said, "Oh, new pajamas! We always had new pajamas on Christmas Eve when I was a little girl. Is that a tradition in your family?"

I shook my head, no. Then I remembered that Chad had once said that he had always unwrapped new pajamas on Christmas Eve when he was a child, so I impulsively selected another blanket-sleeper for BJ: red, for Christmas Eve; size nine months. I prayed that he'd grow into it in the coming months. I had the clerk ring this purchase separately, and paid for these pajamas with cash.

On the way home, I whistled Christmas carols. I slid across ice patches as I had when I was a kid, taking a run at them and then gliding. I wondered again about this family of five little children and tried to put myself in the mother's shoes: husband still in school; living in an apartment; working hard to provide food, shelter, clothing, and enough love for everyone. She would be moved by my mother's thoughtfulness.

Then I started counting my own blessings. My husband and I were headed toward another grand adventure in San Diego. My son was finally growing and gaining weight. We lived in a great country and had enjoyed being in a distant corner of the United States for a while. We were blessed with wonderful families, who loved and cared and prayed for us. We had been comforted and sustained by that love and those prayers. And, best of all, for this short, sweet, precious Christmastime, we would be fortunate enough to be with them.

As I reached our driveway, I stopped there on the sidewalk, hugging the bulky bag of warm pajamas, and took in the sight of the home I loved so dearly. Inside, my son was being cared for by my sister, Kellie. My father was undoubtedly in the kitchen helping my mother with final dinner preparations. Another sister, Brittany, was probably wrapping gifts in the family room. I realized that another car was parked in the driveway: my older sister Becky had arrived with her husband and son, and they were surely engaged in getting their suitcases settled and their Christmas gifts placed under the tree. In the middle of this whirlwind of holiday activities would be my mother, the person who made Christmas happen in our home. My mother, the wise woman who had sent me out on a walk through the crisp December air on a secret Christmas errand to buy pajamas for children I had never met, knowing full well it could only do me good.

I realized just then, as I stood there outside my home, that my mother had already given me the best possible Christmas present—one that I needed, one that I would remember for a long, long time. She had showed me the way to turn my heart away from myself and my own concerns by thinking of and serving others. In doing so, she had given me the precious gift of joy. It was a simple lesson learned at an important time.

* * *

It has been twenty years since I purchased those warm pajamas for those five little children in Provo. I've purchased plenty of Christmas pajamas since then: annually for my own children—to continue my husband's family tradition of opening brightly wrapped packages containing new pajamas on Christmas Eve—and often for others' children.

BJ, my tiny infant son, has grown into a healthy, energetic, enthusiastic young man, who has returned to the deep South to serve as a missionary. My husband, Chad, arrived safely in Provo late, late on that distant Christmas Eve. I am still as happy to see him each time he walks through our door as I was on that blessed night. My mother and father are still performing acts of quiet service for those around them, and they still care for their large and ever-growing family with the same love and wisdom that they shared with me when I landed, exhausted and self-concerned, at their kitchen table.

I doubt that my mother remembers that Christmas errand she assigned to me all those years ago, but I have never forgotten it. For the past twenty years, I have made sure that my children have been assigned similar Christmas errands. They know the joy of selecting and wrapping gifts for strangers, of running through cold December nights to drop packages anonymously on doorsteps, and of returning to the warmth and comfort and safety of home. Whenever I find myself feeling a bit sorry for myself and my circumstances—no matter what the time of year—I remember that Christmas errand, and I turn my heart outward. And I often walk out the door to perform some secret act of service, continuing my mother's legacy of love, unselfishness, and joy.

Annette Paxman Bowen loves holidays, friends, quilts, books, laughter, good food, a stimulating conversation, and the ever-changing skies of the Northwest. She and her husband, Dr. J. Scott Bowen, are the parents of three sons. She has authored three books and articles for dozens of national magazines.

THE ANGEL OF THE BATHTUB

Leslie Beaton Hedley

RACHEL STRUGGLED to reach past her pregnant belly to the cloth that floated just beyond her fingertips. The baby was crying—she'd got splashed in the face again. Her four-year-old sister, unconcerned, continued slapping the water, watching the drops fly upward.

"Katy, stop that," Rachel warned weakly. She was so tired she could hardly hold her head up. Baby Jennifer continued to cry. Little Susan was crying now too, whether in sympathy or because she too had water in her eyes, Rachel didn't know.

"Look, Mommy! My dolly's an angel! Glory in ex-punchis day-o!" Katy cried, flying her dripping doll over Susan's head with a speed that seemed more characteristic of the *Star Ship Enterprise* than an angel. Susan screamed in indignation. The baby continued to cry.

Slowly Rachel knelt at the side of the tub where her three daughters splashed and shrieked. She fished out the elusive washcloth and wiped the little girls' faces. Then, still kneeling, she lay her head on the cool side of the bathtub. *Only for a moment,* she told herself. *I'll just rest here a moment.*

Rachel savoured the respite from her too-busy day. It was so good to put her head down, to stop wondering where each child was and what she was up to. She was too soon jolted from her reverie as Katy shrieked again, then a small tidal wave drenched Rachel from the shoulders up. Water trickled down the back of her neck and made her T-shirt stick to her uncomfortably.

If only I were not so tired, Rachel thought, *I would pull Katy out of the tub.* If she were not so tired she could discipline her. But she dared not lift her voice for fear she would shatter into bits and end up screaming at her daughter. In a few seconds, she wearily sat up, grabbed a towel, and began mopping her face.

The rough towel felt good, and Rachel buried her face in it, muffling the shouts and cries of the girls in the tub. She moaned softly, and the towel absorbed welling tears of frustration.

However would she manage to get them all clean and into bed? Her body craved sleep undeniably. Rachel could lay down right here in this puddle, in this racket, and fall sound asleep, she knew it. But there was still so much to be done—the bathroom was a swamp of wet towels and leaking bath toys, and the living room and kitchen weren't much better. If only Jim were home.

But he wouldn't be back for three more days, and then they would be getting the Christmas tree and finishing the shopping— they still hadn't bought each other anything. *Only five days until Christmas,* Rachel thought, *and look at my house. Look at me.* She lowered the towel again and caught sight of herself in the mirror, eight months pregnant, with wet ropes of hair hanging to her shoulders and black mascara smudged around her eyes. She had wanted to get a haircut before Jim came home, but how would she ever find the time?

Above the shouting voices of her daughters, Rachel thought she heard another sound. She struggled unsuccessfully to rise to her feet. "Hello!" a woman's voice called. "Rachel?"

In the mirror, Rachel's blue eyes grew wide with panic. Oh no! Who could possibly be here now? Now, of all times! She hurriedly wiped the streaked makeup from her face and tried to pull a comb through her uncooperative hair. At that moment, there was a knock at the bathroom door.

"Hello, Rachel. It's Donna. I hope you don't mind. I rang the bell, but there was no answer. I thought since the door was open, and I'm sort of in a hurry I'd . . . well, I'm just dropping off a little Christmas treat. I'll leave it on the table."

Rachel sighed with relief. She forced what she hoped was a breezy reply. "Sure, Donna. I'm tied up in here. I'll see you later. And thanks for thinking of me!" She was fairly certain her voice hadn't given her away.

Donna Rowen cleared a space on the cluttered kitchen table and set down the plate of cookies she and her kids had made. She turned to leave. There were still two more sisters to visit tonight, and it was already 8:30. Hmm— 8:30 and Rachel's kids were still up! Well, it sounded like they were having fun in there anyway, judging from all the noise.

As she reached out to grab the doorknob, Donna looked about her at the dishevelled living room and paused. Earlier that day she had explained to her children that Christmas was a time for helping others. "That's why we're making cookies," she told them. "To give people an unexpected treat."

Now, as she stood in Rachel Halvorson's front entry, Donna pondered her gift of service that night. A plate of cookies. She heard again Rachel's tired words: "Thanks for thinking of me!"

Donna slipped out of her ski jacket and hung it in the closet. As she did so she picked up two other little jackets and hung them on hooks. It only took a few moments to sort the jumble of boots by the door and put them in pairs. She smiled as she quickly bustled about the living room, grabbing baby toys and empty bottles, stacking picture books and magazines. It didn't take long to put the room to rights. Donna snapped on the kitchen radio. Christmas carols filled the air.

"O tidings of comfort and joy, comfort and joy . . ."

A little girl's wail rent the peace. "Mommy, Katy splashed Baby Jen again! And she splashed me too! Mommy! Mommeeee!" There was no reply from Rachel.

Donna's smile faded. Her children were older now, her youngest nine. But memories of bedtimes past flooded back to her as if borne on Katie's splash. Tired mother, tired children—by the time everyone got to bed there had usually been at least one major battle and several minor skirmishes. Donna remembered barely staying awake through her children's prayers and almost crawling into bed when they were done, limp with exhaustion and unwilling to face the thought that she would have to get up and do it all over again the next day.

"An unexpected treat" at that time would not have been a plate of cookies or even a tidy living room. Donna hesitated, then strode toward the bathroom, rolling her sleeves up as she walked.

The knock startled Rachel. "Rachel, Donna again." She had to raise her voice over the baby's crying. "Could I come in?"

Rachel glanced wildly about her. Frantically she began gathering damp towels and sopping up the water on the floor. What would Donna think of this mess, of the children? "Uh, sure, Donna! Come on in," Rachel called.

Donna with the perfect family, Rachel thought. *Donna with the clean house and the two cars and the sensible hair. What on earth could she possibly want? She wasn't going to give her the monthly message now, was she? Why now of all times?*

Donna opened the door to see Rachel kneeling on the floor, half soaked, a big smile on her face. A smile that did not match her empty eyes.

"Rachel, I was wondering . . . It's been so long since I had a chance to bathe a little girl— would you mind?" Not waiting for a reply, Donna knelt on the wet towel at Rachel's side. She plunged her arms into the tub up to her elbows. Next she found the cloth and began to play a game of peek with Jennifer. The baby stopped crying and stared at Donna with fascination. A slow smile wreathed her face.

Donna turned to Rachel's oldest, Katy. "Have you already washed your hair? Good girl. Then how about helping Susan wash hers? Do you think you're big enough?" Seeing Katy's quick, mischievous smile, Donna added, "And no dumping water over her head, either!" Katy sighed but nodded. Donna continued cheerily, "I'll rinse. Here, put out your hand and I'll give you some shampoo."

Donna Rowen, it seemed, knew songs for everything. Anything Katy could think of, Sister Rowen knew a song about. Or she could make one up, with sometimes hilarious results. Laughter filled the cramped room, sparkling like drops of water. They switched to "Rudolph," then "Jingle Bells." Five voices rose over the splashes and echoed from the tiled walls—Donna's rich alto, the girls' high bird-song, and Rachel's tremulous soprano.

Over the top of Susan's newly washed head, Donna and Rachel exchanged a smile. Traces of mascara ringed Rachel's eyes, but the small lines in the center of her forehead had disappeared.

"Okay, assembly line time! How about you dry 'em and I'll comb their hair?" Donna asked. Rachel, feeling lighter than she had in weeks, hoisted herself up and fetched a stack of clean towels. The three girls were bundled and dried, then combed and cuddled. Nightgowns were found and wriggled into.

Donna asked if she could read a story. It had been such a long time, she explained abashedly, since she'd read anyone a real Christmas story. Would that be okay with Katy? Katy agreed and so *The Night before Christmas* was read dramatically, with flourishes and whispers and great sweeping gestures. As Donna read, Katy and Susan giggled, seemingly entranced. Jennifer drank her bottle contentedly, watching from Rachel's lap. Small rosy faces and damp, clinging curls emanated the scent of soap and childhood, and at last the girls' eyelids began to droop. Rachel cast Donna a grateful glance and set about tucking the children into bed. Donna heard murmured prayers from down the hall and found herself unexpectedly blinking back tears. She jumped to her feet and hurried into the kitchen.

Later, she spoke over her shoulder as Rachel entered. "I saw some hot chocolate mix here on the counter, so I made some for both of us. And I brought cookies. Go on, sit down!"

Rachel sat. "Oh, look, my counter is green! I'd forgotten what it looked like," Rachel grinned at her unexpected guest. It felt good. She grew serious again. "You shouldn't be doing this, though."

Donna took a quick swipe at the counters with the dishrag.

"I can manage," Rachel protested.

Donna folded the cloth and laid it beside the sink. She sat down across from Rachel and wrapped her hands around the warm mug in front of her. She took a drink of hot chocolate. Finally she spoke, looking into Rachel's face.

"Listen," Donna said. "I know that. I know you can manage. I guess all of us manage, somehow. But sometimes . . . well, sometimes it's nice to let someone else do it, even for an hour. I remember what it was like—I'm not *that* old," she laughed. "Now," Donna pulled another chair closer to Rachel. "Put your feet up. Go on."

Rachel did as she was instructed. She wiggled her toes, and felt her shoulders relax. A sigh of contentment welled up from within her tired, laden body.

"This has truly been an unexpected treat," Donna smiled. "And I thank you. Well, go on and have a cookie!" she urged. "Made with you in mind."

Rachel leaned back in her chair and closed her eyes. She curved her hand around the warmth of the mug and listened as Donna stood and moved about the kitchen, singing softly to the radio.

" . . . the world in sol-emn still-ness lay to hear the a-an-gels sing."

Rachel smiled and took a cookie from the plate. *Five days until Christmas,* she thought, *just five precious days.*

LESLIE BEATON HEDLEY has published two novels with Deseret Book, *Twelve Sisters* and *Zoe's Gift.* She is currently working on a third. Leslie lives in Calgary, Canada, with her husband, David, and four children, and is far too busy.

CELEBRATING BIRTHDAYS

Mary Ellen Edmunds

'TWAS THE WEEK before Christmas, 1989, and I couldn't seem to get into the swing of things. I don't know what was wrong, but I just hadn't gotten the spirit of the season yet. I hadn't even bought any presents, let alone get them wrapped.

Part of it was what happened every year. My birthday was the same day as His—the 25th of December. Most years it kind of got swallowed up in Christmas, and I guess I have to admit that there had been times when I'd wished I'd been born in July or May and could have had kind of a solo birthday celebration with considerably more focus on me. This was to be my eighteenth birthday. It felt significant. I'd be graduating from high school soon and making big decisions and plans for the future. But everyone was focusing on Christmas, not my birthday.

So I wasn't feeling too thrilled about anything. I was just hoping that with a week to go I'd start feeling much more excited about everything. Then Mimi called. That's not her real name, but I've called her that since she made me go with her to *La Boheme* when I was in junior high. She said it would change my mind about opera. She was wrong, but I appreciated the effort.

Her real name is Marilyn, and she's a lot older than I am. Not as old as my dad, but almost. She's sort of like an aunt, but mostly like a friend. We've always been able to *talk*. You know what I mean. You get talking and you forget about age. In fact, mostly you can't tell how old she is until you get close to her face and see the lines from all the grinning, squinting, frowning, and pulling faces.

She asked what I was doing, and I said "nothing." Even if I'd been doing a little something, I think I'd have said "nothing" because she was using a certain tone of voice that sounded like something big was in the wind. She said, "Wanna have some fun?" Sure! I liked the feeling of anticipation with such an invitation.

She pulled up in front of our place around 5:30. It was already getting dark. She gave me a birthday card and then said "Let's go!" Even before I got in the car I could feel the excitement. I didn't have a clue as to what was going to happen, but all of Marilyn's grinning wrinkles were "on duty."

She said, "How about if we pray before we start on our adventure?" That meant we needed help with whatever was going to happen, and I felt something familiar in the region of my heart. She offered the prayer. She said a lot of neat stuff about the season and the Christmas spirit and my birthday and all. Then she asked Heavenly Father to help us find someone who needed us, and she started to cry. I didn't know quite how to handle this. What were we going to be doing?

Then she told me as much as she could. Someone had given her five crisp new $100 bills. She showed them to me. Wow—there was Ben, smiling kind of like Mona Lisa, without showing his teeth. Five times. The bills looked almost unreal.

I was curious about where they came from, but Mimi couldn't tell me much except that they weren't from John Beresford Tipton, "The Millionaire." Someone had given her these

$100 bills to give away, and the only restriction was that those who received them couldn't know where they came from.

This was our job, our responsibility—to give them away. As I look back on it now, eight years later, it strikes me as interesting that neither of us even thought or talked of what it would be like to keep one for each of us—or maybe even to split one and have $50 each. There was too much joy on the way, and we had to do what we had to do.

We discussed where and how we might find someone who really needed $100, knowing that almost anyone in the world could surely find something for which they could use extra money.

I knew of a family with a lot of challenges, and I told Mimi a lot about them and she agreed they could probably use some extra help. So we put a "Ben" in an Avon sack she happened to have in her car (which sure smelled good, by the way) and drove a block or so away from the home where my friends lived. We walked through the snow, and I was thinking how quiet it was. And I can't really explain it, but it was as if I could hear Christmas music even though there wasn't any. I felt so good all over. I wasn't cold at all.

Sandra answered the door, and we told her we had come to sing to her, that it was our assignment. We were giggling a bit because we were feeling so happy. Sandra was *very* surprised. We did sing, but I'm sure she was happy we hadn't sung more than one verse of anything. Sandra was a somewhat discouraged mother of five children whom I'd met on one of my baby-sitting adventures.

And then we handed her the Avon sack and told her not to open it until she was alone in her room and it was 10:00 P.M. We were in such a jolly mood by this time that we were explaining to her about the "big hand" and the "little hand" so she could tell when it was exactly 10:00. Such a deal!

We were just making up the "rules" as we went along, making the whole thing quite elaborate. Sandra had *no* idea what was in the sack and got laughing too. We told her that if she felt especially thankful or happy or whatever when she opened the sack, she didn't need to do anything except be grateful. We reminded her she knew Whom to thank for surprises (a.k.a. blessings). And we let her know several times that we were acting only as messenger-deliverers, not as the givers of whatever was in the sack.

This was *great.* One down, four to go, and I was already as happy as I'd been in a long, long time. I was wondering about that thing in the scriptures somewhere, the place where it says you feel better when you give than you do when you receive. I was getting a fine dose of whatever that meant.

We headed back for the car laughing and humming and talking about the look on Sandra's face and the feeling in our hearts. Then we talked about what to do next.

We thought we might find someone who had great need if we went to a local discount food store. Many who shopped there were young families trying to get through college on next-to-nothing. We knew there weren't many with a huge food budget who would frequent that store, so that's where we decided to go next.

We felt like spies or detectives or perhaps employees of Perry Mason. I guess we weren't sure exactly who we were looking for, but we felt like we'd *know.* So we started wandering up and down the aisles, watching people. We may have felt more conspicuous than we actually were. We didn't have a shopping cart or anything. Just four more brand new copies of the Ben Bill and a desire to give them away.

We found her near the canned soups—a young mother with her little child. We watched her for a while as she carefully shopped, and then we looked at each other and I tried to grin just like Mimi did when something had "clicked."

The few things the young mother had in her basket looked like necessities. No "frills." We whispered our observations and made our decision. This young mother was about to receive a big Christmas surprise. Show time!

Mimi approached her and asked, "Could we talk to you for a few minutes?" We were strangers, and who can imagine what kind of expression we had on our faces at this point. She further convinced us she was "the one" as she cheerfully and sweetly said "Sure!"—as if to say "How can I help you?" Later Mimi said, "She probably even does her visiting teaching regularly and cheerfully."

Mimi said something like "We've been watching you, and we apologize for that. But we prayed we could find someone who needed a special Christmas gift." And of course Mimi started to cry. Right there in the soup aisle of a busy food store. She can't seem to help it. It's her thing.

The woman was puzzled, still having absolutely no idea what we were up to or why we wanted to talk to her. Mimi told her that someone had shared some money to give away, and she handed the woman an envelope with a $100 bill in it.

Still looking puzzled, the young mother looked in the envelope. There it was. The smiling Ben looking out at her and the little note that said "Merry Christmas." She lost it and started crying. Now both of them had lost it, and I didn't know what to do. But, oh, I felt *good* inside!

She said—kind of whispered, kind of sobbed—"Oh, *thank you!* We can *really* use this! You have *no idea*. We've been praying too . . . " It felt so *good!* We both hugged her as she headed for the checkstand, trying to stop her tears.

We kept walking around the store for a while, feeling as good as I think you can feel as an earthling. This was fantastic. We went out in the parking lot and made fools of ourselves, dancing and jumping around, squealing with joy and giving each other "high fives" as we rejoiced in an amazing way.

We drove around, laughing and sharing and feeling not just close to each other but close to Something Else, to Someone Else. I was going to say it was something magical, but maybe it was about the most natural thing ever—the joy of *giving*. Yes, it was someone else's money, but I guess almost everything we give really belongs to God and not us. We're always kind of like instruments.

The next idea we got was to stop at a little gas station near the cemetery. We watched two cars and a pickup come and go and didn't feel like it was the right person yet. Then he drove up. He was in some "old person" car like a fifteen-year-old Buick or an Oldsmobile. I can't tell the difference—it could have been a Chevrolet. But you know the kind—four doors and a huge trunk, and it had probably been 200,000 miles. So had the man who got out, I think. He was old. I'm thinking now that he may not have looked that old to Mimi, since she was much closer to his unknown age than I was, but to me he was old. He moved slowly. He had a heavy coat on. I didn't see his wife at first because she was a little person—hardly showed over the headrest from where I was half hidden near a cinder block wall. But she was there.

We looked at each other and we knew. I'll tell you that it kind of made a lump in my throat when he only got $5 worth of unleaded regular and went up to the little window thing and paid in cash. We whispered that he probably didn't have enough to fill the thing. It probably had a fifty-gallon tank, too.

So we went up to him as he was coming back to the car and wished him a Merry Christmas. He smiled at that and said, "And the same to you, ladies." No one had ever called me a lady before, and I was still seventeen. But it seemed like a polite thing for him to say. I wasn't upset or anything.

Mimi was so social about then. "Is this your wife?" "Yes, this is Mildred. I'm Stan." I don't know why he trusted us, but he seemed to. You don't find that enough these days. Maybe we had some kind of glow after what we'd already been through that night.

Out came one of the envelopes we'd fixed. Mimi had told me I could hand it to him and say anything I wanted to. "We want you to have whatever's in this envelope. We want you to have it for Christmas. You and Mildred—you and your wife. You can probably fill up your car three or four times with what's in here. We can't tell you who it's from. Maybe Santa for all I know. But Merry Christmas!"

Maybe I should have practiced, or maybe I should have had a script or something, because Mr. Stan just looked at me with a sort of weird expression as if I were an alien or a teenager or I don't know what. Then he got some tears in his eyes. Why does this always seem to happen to people who are over forty or fifty? He really

did—he got tears in his eyes. His "thank you" wasn't too strong, but I heard it anyway. I felt it too. Oh, I really could feel it.

And away we went, waving and smiling and wanting to jump the cinder block wall on the way back to the car. I thought that if I did it—and I could have easily—Mimi might try too, and she'd obviously not make it and might hurt herself, and we still had two Bens to give away. We got in the car and talked for a while, and then we headed south. Stan and Mildred were still there at the gas station, sitting in their big car.

Our next stop was at a laundromat—one of those almost-all-night places. By now it was about 8:45 at night, and there were only three people in there. We didn't go in right away. We "cased the joint," which is the way I put it.

One woman in there had two boys with her, probably her sons. I'm not good at guessing ages, but I'd say the kids were maybe in first and third grade. They were running around, and she was hollering at them. Sort of. She was reading some kind of magazine—one of those with lots of coupons, pictures of food, and smiling people with perfect teeth. I'm probably not the only one who's ever worn braces and noticed other peoples' teeth.

The woman was smoking. I don't think that's a good idea, and I told Mimi I thought we ought to save the money for nonsmokers. She didn't say anything—just kept watching and thinking. After a while, I got to feeling bad about what I'd said. I can't say why—I just felt bad, like it wasn't a kind thing to say. I changed my mind. Mimi still hadn't said anything. So I said, "I've changed my mind. I think this woman needs the money."

It was still a little while before Mimi said anything. Then she said, "Know what I think? I think you're right. I think she needs the money, and I also think she needs a break. I wonder how long it's been since something unexpectedly *good* happened to her."

When we went in and sat by her, she glanced up briefly but didn't seem to pay much attention. That was strange, because of all the places where we could have landed, we were right by her. "In her face." Mimi said, "Ready for Christmas?" The woman looked up at her and kind of blew us off. Really. It was not a pretty sight. But I didn't feel mad or anything. I just waited. I know there have been times when I wasn't in a particularly good mood, and I've been ticked off if anyone around me was too happy right then. And the two of us were *way* happy by this time.

Mimi said something like, "We're sorry to interrupt you, but would you mind if we surprised you in a big way right now?" I have *no idea* what this woman thought we might do. Or what *she* might have been thinking *she* wanted to do. I'm here to tell you I think it could have gone either way. She could have called to one of the other people in there. "Call 911!" She could have told us to get lost.

Instead she kind of slumped and said, "What do you want? What are you selling?" Mimi piped right up, "We're not selling anything—aren't you glad? Besides, it's against the law in here." The way she said it made the woman smile just a little bit. It didn't last but a nanosecond, but I saw it.

"Okay, what's the deal. Are you on some kind of a scavenger hunt or something?" "No—we're here because it's *Christmas!*" I think it's great that such a simple phrase can be used to cover a multitude of kindness. "We have an assignment to give you this envelope and wish you a very Merry Christmas. And we really mean it—have a wonderful Christmas!"

She didn't say anything. She just watched us walk out of the laundromat. I could feel her eyes on my back.

We had parked quite a ways away. When we got to the car and looked back, she was just looking in the envelope like it wasn't real. She jumped up, ran to the door, and hollered, "Who are you?" Mimi hollered back, "We're elves! Merry Christmas! We love you!" And off we went, feeling even better, even happier. Mimi said, "Have you ever heard about 'the least of these'?" I said I hadn't. She said she'd tell me what she meant later.

We had one left. And we had one more store between where we were and my place. It was a grocery store, and it was kind of crowded. We parked over in a corner of the parking lot and walked in. We decided we'd take a while choosing our last "victim." It was kind of hard to see our supplies of $100 bills coming to an end.

So in we went, and we began to wander around, watching the people. We'd talk to each other quietly, giving what I thought were very hilarious observations. I think we were in such a happy mood that we'd gotten too silly. We were out of control, and we were loving it.

And then we saw them. A young couple. We were both impressed that they were there together. They had their baby with them, pushing him around in the cart. We liked the feeling we had as we followed them, trying not to be too obvious. They weren't in a hurry. They might even have been enjoying this week-before-Christmas shopping trip.

We noticed that they were carefully choosing what they were going to purchase. We got the feeling they had to count every penny. Maybe we were making that up, but I think it was true. They had a list and everything. They had probably eaten before coming. All those things they tell you to do so that you don't turn into an impulsive buyer and get more than you need.

We went away from them for a while so we could talk about them without them or anyone else hearing. We kept walking as if looking for something, but we were making a Big Decision. We both felt good about this young couple and decided for sure they were the ones. So we went outside and waited for them to check out and come out in the parking lot.

Here they came. They didn't have enough to need the cart. The mom had the child and the dad had a few plastic bags of stuff. We walked up to them and handed them a box we had fixed. In it we had two candy canes, the $100 bill, and a note saying we had been given an assignment by Santa to give this box to them and to wish them a very Merry Christmas.

That is *so fun*—just watching the look on their faces and wondering what they'd do when they find out what's in the box or the envelope or whatever. I was becoming *hooked* on this feeling! We walked away, leaving them looking very puzzled, standing by a "not new" pickup truck with a child car seat thing in it.

I peeked back as we walked away to hide. I was reporting everything as I kind of walked backwards. The wife, who was the first to see what was in the box, looked up at her husband with a very amazed "Honey?" I could hear that, but I couldn't hear anything after that. We got to where we could hide and then we just watched.

This time I cried too. Not hard, but I cried. It was as if the *real* Christmas feeling had come to me. I felt like a little child, and yet I felt a newer, deeper understanding of what the season should really feel like and what it should mean. No *wonder* the angels sang, and no wonder the wise men and shepherds rejoiced.

I was thinking and feeling so many things as we watched what happened next. The guy put the groceries in the back of the truck and then they got in the cab, put the baby in the seat, started the engine, and then just sat there. We were wishing we could hear what they were saying, but maybe they weren't saying anything at all. Maybe they were crying too. I think there was probably no way they could have been even half as happy as *we* were.

After quite a while, like maybe almost five minutes, they leaned over and hugged each other and then drove away slowly. We did the same thing. We hugged each other, and we drove away slowly.

We didn't say a whole lot on the way to my home. It was one of those times when we didn't need to. Much, much more had happened than giving away $500. The "joy to the world!" feeling had come into my heart big time. It came. Into my soul and into my days came the spirit of Christmas. The *real* one. Love's pure light. Oh, yes—He *is* love's pure light, and He is the light of my season and my life. The reason for a season of giving and peace and goodwill. Happy birthday to Him and to me.

From that night until now I have approached Christmas and "our birthdays" in a very different way.

Mary Ellen Edmunds, a former member of the Relief Society General Board, has taught nursing at Brigham Young University. She is the author of two books, *Love Is a Verb* and *Thoughts for a Bad Hair Day*.

DANCE OF
COURAGE

Lee Nelson

I KNOW THY WORKS, *that thou art neither cold nor hot: . . . because thou art lukewarm, and neither cold nor hot, I will spue thee out of my mouth" (Revelation 3:15–16).*

When Olympic decathlon champion Bob Richards presented his assembly at Clayton Valley High School in the East Bay Area of Northern California just before Christmas in 1959, I was in the front row. Bob's photo was on every Wheaties box in the world at a time when Wheaties had a market share in double digits. Every morning at breakfast millions of kids would read about Bob's Olympic exploits and the character traits that made him successful. Bob was more of a role model for kids than United States president Dwight D. Eisenhower.

After telling some funny stories about the Olympic games and breakfast cereals, Bob delivered an emotional and persuasive sermon on goal setting. Along with a lot of shouting and arm waving, he told us that if we set goals and worked hard, like he did, we could do or have anything we wanted. It seemed to me he was saying any kid with polio could play professional baseball. Any poor kid from a broken home could have a million dollars if that's what he wanted.

If someone had turned out the lights so we could ask questions while keeping our identity secret, I would have asked Mr. Richards if goal setting could make it possible for a young man with average looks and below average athletic ability to date the prettiest girls in the high school. I mean, here I was a senior in high school, surrounded daily by what I thought were the prettiest women on the face of the planet, and they didn't even know I existed.

I was smart enough to notice how these girls seemed to flock around the athletes, particularly the stars. I had just been cut from the basketball team even though I could shoot better than most of the regular players, at least I thought I could. But I weighed in at 140 pounds and was three or four inches under six feet—not exactly the kind of specimen the coaches drooled over. So I was cut every year.

As a freshman I had tried to wrestle because they had weight classes for the little guys, but when I came home from practice with sores on my ears, my mother talked me into quitting before I got cauliflower ears.

Part of the problem was that my parents, thinking I was very bright, had started me in kindergarten when I was four years old, making it difficult for me to compete in athletics with boys who were taller, stronger, and more mature than I was—a situation that persisted though all my school years. It wasn't until my senior year that I started catching up, but by then it seemed almost too late.

Nor was I a straight A student in school either. I got A's in physics, algebra, and other classes that had tests with lots of problems. I could solve problems. But I did poorly in the more subjective classes where teachers expected attention and participation in the classroom—history, sociology, English, political science, and the like.

The problem was that school interfered with my personal reading program. By the time I reached my junior year I had read every dog and horse story in the school and public libraries. I had read everything Ernest

Hemingway, John Steinbeck, and Jack London had written. It was nothing for me to check out six books on a Monday and read them all by the following Monday. In school I tried to have a seat in the back of the classroom, making it easier to hide the book I was reading inside a school textbook. I thought I was fooling the teacher, but when report cards came out I realized I hadn't fooled anyone; nonetheless, my personal reading was an addiction and I did not stop.

I read nonfiction too, like the time in junior high school when a father of one of my friends discovered we were playing poker for pennies. He joined the game in an effort to teach us a lesson about the evils of gambling. After winning our money he thought we wouldn't want to play anymore. Instead I went to the library and found the classic book on poker by Hoyle. The saying "according to Hoyle" originates with his analysis of poker. The book was wonderful, introducing me to applied probability theory and the psychology of bluffing.

A few weeks later my friends and I lured the well-meaning father into a second poker game. We won our money back, plus a lot more. And cured that father of trying to teach us lessons on the evils of gambling. We were obsessed with the game for a few months, then realizing that there was more to life than playing cards, we decided to limit our poker to one grand game every New Year's Eve.

With the winter holidays approaching, and therefore the prospects of another all-night poker game, I had checked out Hoyle again and had the book in my hand during the Richards assembly.

As the decathlon winner talked about long-range goals I thought about mine. Particularly I remembered a recent career counseling ses-sion with my school counselor. He laughed when I told him that ever since I was three years old I had wanted to be a cowboy. He said I needed to grow up and get serious about my life. Nobody who was a senior in high school wanted to be a cowboy.

Both of my grandfathers had been success-ful cattlemen, so I wondered what was wrong with wanting to follow in their footsteps. The counselor said I needed to pick something more realistic. "Isn't there anything else you want to be?" he asked.

"Well, there is," I said, hesitating, not want-ing to be laughed at again. At this period in my life the two things I liked best were horses and girls. It seemed sensible to have a career involv-ing the things you liked best.

"If I can't be a cowboy, I'd like to help beau-tify the world," I ventured.

"That's more like it," he said with gusto.

"I'd like to be a hairdresser," I responded, encouraged by his newfound enthusiasm.

The counselor gulped, but didn't say any-thing.

Had he encouraged me to keep talking, I would have told him how I had trouble estab-lishing and maintaining relationships with the many beautiful girls in the school. When I did get a date, my hands dripped with sweat, I couldn't think of anything to say, and my stomach was too tied up in knots to eat pizza. I just thought if I was unable to enjoy the com-pany of these beautiful girls on a personal level, maybe I could do it on a professional level—hence, hairdresser.

But the counselor didn't encourage me to keep talking. He gulped again, still saying noth-ing, then scribbled "cowboy/hairdresser" on the top of my career guidance folder. Next, he made an appointment for me with the school psychologist, but I didn't go.

Anyway, the Bob Richards sermon was convincing. He promised that if you wrote down your goal, any goal, developed a plan for achieving it, and worked hard, it would happen.

I decided to test his promise. The Christmas preference dance was two weeks away. The girls asked the boys to this one, and I had not been asked. I wrote down on a piece of paper that my goal was to get asked by one of the popular and beautiful girls to the Christmas dance.

Writing down the goal was easy, but devising a plan was not. How do you plan what someone else will do? After all, the girl had to ask me. Instead of working on the plan, I started writing down the names of the girls whom I would like to go to the dance with.

Barbara Roe was first. She lived down the street from me. We had been in some of the same classes since first grade. She had long black hair and large brown eyes with a sad, sexy look. She always wore short skirts and sat next to me in English class. When she wiggled her knee back and forth, I could not hear what the teacher was saying.

Next was Billy Holdaway. She drove an old car. She had shoulder-length brown hair, sharp facial features, a perfect complexion, and a perfect figure. A slightly crooked nose was the only thing that could prevent her from hiring on as a New York model. She was the best dancer in the school, and I figured I was the worst. She had an outgoing personality and was very friendly, even to me.

Without a lot of thought I wrote down the name of my Spanish teacher, Miss Bozantine. She was single, in her mid-twenties, and loved horses. Sometimes she would tell us stories about horses she had owned. Now that was my kind of woman, and she would fit perfectly into my dreams of becoming a cowboy. I had daydreams of me and Miss Bozantine going on romantic horseback rides. She had medium-length blonde hair that she usually wore in a pony tail, a few freckles, and what her face lacked in natural beauty she made up for with a happy countenance and a perfect figure. But as I thought about it, even though there might be a chance to go on a horseback ride with her, there was no way we could go to a school dance, not without her losing her job. I crossed her off the list.

There were some other names that I will not mention here, but the one I underlined and circled was Rita Romero, a Mexican girl who without question was one of the most beautiful females ever to walk on this planet—jet black hair, big brown eyes, a creamy olive complexion, perfect in every way. She was somewhat shy and reserved, but that only added to the mystery. She was never loud or mean.

About once a week when we would pass in the halls, Rita would look at me and say hi. I would say hi back, my heart pounding in my throat, my palms sweating. No other words had ever been exchanged between us. I think *hi* was my favorite word in the English language, because Rita always said that when she looked at me. Her desirability was best described by my friend Dave, who claimed he would donate a piece of his brain to medical research if he could go on one date with Rita Romero.

And Rita was available. She had just broken up with Buddy Savage and had given him his ring back. Buddy was about six foot two inches tall and weighed about 180 pounds. He played forward on the basketball team and linebacker on the football team. He had blue eyes and wavy black hair. The girls thought he was handsome. But he was a bully, always cutting in front of someone in the lunch line or ordering some little guy in the locker room to fetch him a towel or a bar of soap—if the little guy didn't want to get pounded into something roughly the size of a tennis shoe. Buddy would never say hi to kids whom he didn't think were his equal. The only time he had ever been friendly to me was when he wanted me to show him my answers during an algebra test. I refused.

Everybody knew Buddy was upset when Rita gave him his ring back. I loved her for it. Now I could make my move, but how?

It was easy writing down the goal and the names of the girls whom I wanted to ask me to the Christmas dance, but the question that haunted me was how to make a plan that might work. Richards said nothing was impossible, but it seemed to me that I might as well be trying out for a professional basketball team after being cut by the high school team. I wished I could have five minutes alone with Richards. In his speech it had all sounded so easy and automatic.

Nonetheless, I was good at solving problems, if you'll remember, and as I continued to wrestle with this one, a possible plan of attack began to evolve. I had read Dale Carnegie's book, *How to Win Friends and Influence People*. He claimed the shortest distance to a person's heart was with sincere flattery. I could start calling the girls on the list, showering them with compliments about how smart and beautiful they were. After three or four days, if none responded and asked me to the dance, I could pick out the one who had warmed up to me the most and offer her a thousand dollars if she would ask me. (I had a good after-school job at a grocery store and had managed to save a little over two thousand dollars.)

While the plan seemed workable, the idea of buying my way into the dance with flattery and money left a sour taste in my mouth. I ran the idea past my friend Syd, who thought I was nuts.

"How much would you pay to go to the Christmas dance with Rita Romero?" I asked.

"Maybe a hundred bucks if I knew she would kiss me," he said without having to think about it.

"Rita's not like that," I said in disgust.

"So?"

"I want something better than that," I said.

"What could be better than kissing Rita Romero?" he asked, obviously puzzled.

"Having a girl like Rita *fall in love* with you," I said.

"You want to get married to the girl and you haven't even gone out with her yet?"

"No, not yet. I just think it would be nice to be in love with someone who loved you back, instead of always having crushes on girls who don't even know you are alive."

"I don't think you can get anyone to fall in love with you by paying them money," Syd said, wisely. I decided the money thing was a bad idea. I had to find a better plan.

As I analyzed the situation at school, the love potion that seemed to attract the most desirable girls was masculinity, as expressed in physical strength and athletic ability. The ball players, runners, swimmers, wrestlers, and fighters were noticed most by the girls. Being on the honor role, president of the German club, captain of the debate team, or having a part-time job where you earned more than the teachers didn't seem to be things girls noticed.

I needed to do something macho, but since

I had already been cut from the basketball team, participation in athletics seemed out of the question, especially since the Christmas dance was only two weeks away.

While I was thinking along these lines, an outrageous plan popped into my mind, so outrageous and daring that just thinking about it brought a surge of adrenaline into my heart and made me feel sick to my stomach.

I decided to slug it out with Buddy Savage. Buddy was a bully, and not very smart. It would be easy to lure him into a fight. He was the superjock at 180 pounds and I was the 140 pound algebra ace. No challenge. He would enjoy beating me up.

I had a theory about fighting. When a little guy gets in a fight with a big guy, the little guy always wins, even if the big guy beats him up, because everybody will think the big guy is a bully—the little guy becomes a hero because he had the courage to fight someone bigger than himself. If the little guy happens to win, then he becomes a king—like David after whipping Goliath. It amazed me that the school bullies didn't realize that they couldn't win in a fight with a little guy. Everybody hates a bully. Everybody loves the little guy who will stand up to a bully. It doesn't matter who gets beat up, the little guy always wins.

I knew there was no way I could whip Buddy Savage in a fair fight. But I also knew that if I could muster the courage to slug it out with the bully, I would become a hero of the kids who had been pushed around by Buddy, and hopefully some of that feeling would rub off on the girls on my list.

I knew further that if I planned the fight in the middle of the quad where the students gathered during the lunch hour, there would be plenty of teachers around to break it up

before he had a chance to kill me. There was no doubt in my mind that once the fight started he would indeed try to kill me.

I also knew Buddy could hurt me—crack ribs, break my nose, and black my eyes—if I was lucky. At worst he might break my neck or crack my head on the cement.

Still, I wanted to go ahead. Pain and possible serious injury were better than what I perceived to be the average mediocrity of my existence. Half the kids in the school, including most of the attractive girls, didn't even know my name. It was time for a change.

The problem was that I was not a fighter. In the course of getting through school I had been challenged to fight on a number of occasions, usually on the playground. What started out as a philosophy that "discretion is the better part of valor" became a pattern. I routinely backed down from fights, even when I had a chance of winning. I would be the first to admit that there are better ways to solve problems than by fighting, but it's one thing to let wisdom guide your decision about fighting, and quite another when cowardice sets the course. I hated being called chicken when backing down from a playground challenge. Again, it was time for a change.

I was old enough and wise enough to realize that if I was ever to amount to anything, or accomplish anything in life, I had to overcome my fear of fighting and bullies. Taking on Buddy Savage would do that, and maybe get me an invitation to the Christmas dance too. Kill two birds with one stone.

That night I filled my Dad's army duffle bag with old clothes, hung it from a rafter in the garage, slipped on a borrowed pair of boxing gloves, and began punching the bag, pretending it was Buddy Savage. I hit it until my arms felt like rubber, but that didn't relieve my growing sense of panic.

During the night, since I couldn't sleep anyway, I raided the medicine cabinet, assembling a handful of various pain medications, including half a dozen aspirin. I decided to take the pills about a half hour before the fight, believing I would be less inclined to chicken out if I didn't feel any pain when Buddy started pounding on me.

I picked the lunch hour as my time of reckoning. My plan was to walk by him after we had eaten, turn towards him without warning, and slug him in the nose. Blows to the nose are supposed to be very painful, so I hoped my blow would stun him sufficiently to allow me to get in five or six additional blows before he started hitting back. About that time the teachers would show up to pull us apart. I would become the hero of the little guys and pretty girls, and Buddy would be suspended from the basketball team, a common penalty for athletes who got in fights at school.

At the end of my last morning class I gulped down a couple of pain pills and headed for the cafeteria. I figured on eating light to decrease the chance of throwing up during the fight. My plan was set and I was determined to follow through. Today my life would move forever from the realm of mediocre and average.

But something happened on the way to the cafeteria necessitating a change in plans. Buddy was standing outside the cafeteria door, holding Rita by the arm, trying to tell her something while she tried to pull away. She could not pull free of the bully's grasp.

On the way to the cafeteria I had passed Billy, Barbara, and several other girls on my list. Miss Bozantine had drawn lunch duty and was standing nearby, a silver whistle hanging on a chain around her neck. The plan was unfolding better than I had dreamed possible. The only thing left to do was to walk up to Buddy and whack him on the nose.

Instead, I stopped and started to talk.

"I think Rita would like you to leave her alone," I said to Buddy. He turned to look at me, a look of disbelief on his face.

"If you don't disappear in three seconds, I'm making your face into hamburger," he snarled, still holding on to Rita's arm.

"If you don't mind, I prefer sausage," I laughed. I had read somewhere that the hyenas in Africa laugh because they are afraid. That's what I was doing.

He let go of Rita's arm and cocked his arm like he was going to smash my face. I willed my fist to double up and hit him, but my arm wouldn't move, only my mouth.

"You've already proven yourself to be the biggest bully in the school," I squeaked. "I'm not about to let you enhance that reputation any further at my expense."

As he stepped forward to hit me, I instinctively turned and ran into the lunchroom. As I did so, he begun clucking his tongue like a mother hen and calling me chicken.

I had no rebuttal. Once again I had played the coward. I was indeed a chicken. I had failed to grasp the opportunity to pull myself out of a life I hated. I was ashamed. Fear had stopped me from following through on a plan that might have changed my life.

With my head down, I walked to the counter and picked up a lunch tray, thinking how high school had been a miserable time of failure for me. I figured it was time to gather my things and head out to Nevada to get a job as a cowboy. I would lose myself on some remote ten-million-acre ranch where nobody would ever hear from me again.

As I moved away from the counter, my tray loaded with food that I didn't intend to eat and probably couldn't eat, I headed for the least-crowded table so I could eat alone. The biggest open space was across the table from a red-haired retarded girl named Tina. She had had some kind of paralyzing disease that had left big braces on her legs and had slurred her speech. Her eyes were slightly crossed. Some of the boys would imitate the funny way she walked, but never when she could see them.

While the students were generally kind to Tina, none had befriended her. She probably didn't belong in a public school, but her parents insisted on her having a normal education.

"Hi," I said in a subdued voice, taking a seat across from her. She looked up but didn't say anything, at least not right away. I started picking at my food.

"Why did you sit by me?" she asked. It was obvious she was unschooled in the social graces. She should have asked if I thought it was a nice day, or if I thought the basketball team was going to win its game that week.

I didn't want to tell her the truth, that I had just backed down from a fight with the school bully and didn't want to sit with my regular friends.

"You were alone, so I figured you could use a friend," I lied.

"Are you my friend?" she asked. For a girl that people thought was retarded, she sure knew how to ask uncomfortable questions.

"Sure," I said, without much enthusiasm.

"I didn't believe Mom when she said if I kept going to school, someday I would find a friend," she said matter-of-factly.

"When you go home today, tell your mom you have a friend. He gets A's in algebra and is heading out to Nevada to be a cowboy."

"A real cowboy?" she asked, her eyes getting big. "You ride horses and rope cows?"

"That's why I'm going to Nevada," I said, seriously. "Someday I'll let you ride my horse."

"Wow," she said.

"Thanks for having lunch with me," I said. "I've got to go out to the parking lot." As I started to get up, I suddenly noticed every eye in the cafeteria was looking at me and Tina.

Take a good look, I wanted to say. *In fact, why don't you take a picture—it lasts longer.*

"Thank you for having lunch with me," Tina said, a quality of sincerity in her voice I hadn't noticed earlier.

"You're welcome."

"Thank you for being my friend," she said. For the first time, I looked at her face, into her eyes. There was a tear on her cheek. I realized that behind the braces, slurred speech, and crossed eyes was a heart that yearned and ached as much as mine, perhaps more. I felt like a selfish jerk, realizing my problems were nothing compared to the suffering this girl had to endure. I reached out and patted her on the arm, then headed for the door, figuring my actions of the last half hour would keep the gossip mill going for a long time.

No sooner had I left the cafeteria than Syd caught up with me, demanding to know if I had accepted Tina's invitation to go to the Christmas dance. He said that's what everybody in the cafeteria was talking about.

"Sure, why not?" I lied as I continued towards my car.

Getting inside and closing the door, it took about five minutes to decide once and for all what I was going to do. No more school. No more California. In the morning I would drive to Nevada to get a job as a cowboy. This place was history as far as I was concerned.

Getting out of the car, I headed towards the building on the far side of the quad to get my personal belongings out of my locker. I didn't plan on checking out or saying good-bye to anybody. I was just leaving, forever.

As I approached the quad I could hear loud laughter. I could see the backs of many students, crowded in a circle, looking at something inside. I could not see what was happening, but amidst the laughter, I thought I could hear a cry of distress. The voice sounded familiar. Tina.

I pushed through the circle of people. An ugly cat-and-mouse game was taking place, Tina trying to hit Buddy with her purse as he danced about. Her swing was slow, and she had trouble moving with leg braces, so he had no trouble avoiding her. She lurched awkwardly towards him, swinging her purse with all her might, then fell to the ground. Clumsily, she got to her feet and repeated the process once again. She was crying. He was laughing, and so were many of the students forming the circle.

I glanced at some of the faces, unable to comprehend how anyone could laugh at something so cruel.

My chicken heart was pounding as Buddy danced backwards towards my place at the edge of the circle. The memories of my cowardly retreats were replaced with a savage rage that could not be denied. Tina's torment would not last another second as long as I was alive to do something about it.

If I had had a baseball bat, I would've broken it over the bully's head right then and there. Instead I stuck out my foot and tripped him. As his hands went back to catch himself

from falling hard on the cement, I flew upon him, my right fist smashing his lip over his two front teeth, my left fist catching the front of his nose head on, spraying both of us with blood. Tucking my chin, I continued to swing as hard and fast and furious as I could.

It didn't take Buddy long to get his knees under him and start hitting back. Somewhere in the distance I could hear Miss Bozantine blowing her whistle. A powerful blow to the chest took my wind away. I thought I could feel a rib crack. Suddenly he was upon me, now in a wild rage too, showering me with a hundred blows. As I tried to knee him in the groin, all went black.

The next thing I remember was trying to turn my head away from the smelling salts. I was on a cot in the nurse's office. Buddy was across the room on another cot, holding a cold towel on his still bleeding nose and lip.

Mr. Smith, the assistant principal, was standing between us, his arms folded, a stern look on his face.

"All I want to know is who threw the first blow," Smith said.

"He did," Buddy whined.

"Is that true?" Smith asked, turning to me.

"I'd like to explain what—" I started to say, but was cut off.

"All I want to know is who threw the first blow, nothing else. Is that clear?"

"Yes sir," I said, in mock respect. "The truth is that Tina attempted to throw the first blow with her purse."

"Answer my question," he yelled.

"Okay. I threw the first five blows, and I'm glad I did."

Smith excused Buddy so the nurse could take him to the hospital for some stitches.

Smith told me I was expelled from school

for two weeks, one week for starting the fight, and another for my uncooperative attitude.

"Furthermore, you are banned from extra-curricular activities, ball games, assemblies, and dances." The poor guy thought he was dispensing strong medicine, when in reality none of it mattered because in the morning I was headed to Nevada. And if he thought I had any desire to go to another one of those stupid Bob Richards assemblies he was crazy. As far as I was concerned Bob Richards was an idiot. His goal-setting garbage didn't work. At least it hadn't for me.

"You'll have to tell Tina you can't go with her to the Christmas dance," Smith continued. If my ribs had not been so sore I would have laughed. Less than an hour after having lunch with Tina, false rumors of her asking me to the dance had spread clear to the principal's office. Amazing.

But none of it mattered. I was off to Nevada, this time knowing at least that I was no longer a coward. I felt good, really good.

My parents were pretty upset that night when I announced I was going to Nevada. I had rolled up a big cowboy bedroll, about forty pounds of canvas and blankets. I had packed my chaps, spurs, silk scarves, some horse train-ing books, shirts, and jeans.

"But it's almost Christmas," my father protested. "You might as well wait until after the holidays. They won't be hiring until spring, anyway."

"I have plenty of money to hold me over. Besides, it's time for me to go," I said, agreeing to stay one more day so we could have a farewell dinner with some of my friends.

The next night Syd was the first to arrive at the dinner, announcing that Rita and Billy and some of the other girls had invited Tina to eat lunch with them at school that day. I felt good about that, really good.

We were about to sit down to dinner when Mother called me to the phone. The teasing look on her face told me this was no ordinary call.

"Hello," I said.

"Hi, this is Rita."

I couldn't believe Rita Romero was calling me. I couldn't think of anything to say.

"How are you feeling?" she asked.

"Ribs will be sore for a couple of weeks. But I'm fine."

"I talked to Tina at lunch today," she said.

"I know. Syd told me about it."

"When I asked her about going to the Christmas dance with you, she said she hadn't asked you."

"The truth finally gets out."

"It's amazing how fast false rumors can spread."

"It is."

"I suppose," she continued, carefully, "since everybody thought you were going with Tina, nobody else has asked you to the dance."

"That's right."

"Would you like to go with me?"

I almost dropped the phone. If Bob Richards had been in the room I would have kissed him. I had tested his theory on goal set-ting, and it had worked.

"I can't. Mr. Smith expelled me from school activities."

"The student council had a meeting with the principal this afternoon. Your expulsion has been revoked."

"Then I will go to the dance with you, Rita."

"How would you feel about inviting Tina to come with us?" she asked.

"With those steel braces and that big purse,

she ought to make a good chaperon," I responded, without a lot of enthusiasm.

"I feel really bad about how the kids have treated her," Rita ventured. "Even though she can't dance, I know she would enjoy going with us. She says you are her best friend."

"On one condition," I said, boldly. "That when we go home after the dance, I can drop her off first so you and I can spend some time alone."

"I would like that," she said.

"Really?"

"Absolutely."

"Then it's a date."

When I returned to the dinner table, I announced that my move to Nevada had been postponed until after the holidays. No sooner had my friends begun giving me advice on how to successfully woo Rita Romero than the phone rang again. When Mother picked up the receiver, she gave me that same teasing look.

"Hello," I said.

"Hi, this is Billy."

When she started telling me about learning that Tina had not asked me to the Christmas dance, I told her I had had a similar conversation a few minutes earlier.

"Did Rita ask you to the dance?" Billy demanded.

"Yep, but if you were planning to ask me too, I'd sure take a rain check."

"Last time I saw you at a dance," Billy said, recovering quickly, "you looked pretty clumsy."

"I've never been much of a dancer," I confessed.

"Dances are more fun if you know how to dance. I'm the best dancer in the school. Would you like me to drop by after school for a few days and give you some lessons?"

"Sure. Should we start tomorrow?"

"See you after school."

When I returned to the table, I announced that the move to Nevada might have to be postponed until spring.

Later on that evening, Mother called me to the phone with that same teasing voice for the third time. Before leaving my room I tossed the big bedroll into the back of my closet. Cowboying would have to wait until long after the Christmas dance.

LEE NELSON is a writer and inventor living on a small farm in central Utah. He has written 25 books and hundreds of articles and stories. Lee is known for his authentic research, which includes killing a buffalo with a bow and arrow from the back of a galloping horse—a research project for his *Storm Testament* series historical novels. Lee's hobbies include team roping and horse packing. Every spring he takes fans on wilderness horseback treks through some of the wild country he uses as background in his stories.

Lee was in the first graduating class (1960) of Clayton Valley High School in Concord, California, where this story takes place. The story is based on actual events, though some of the names have been changed or forgotten.

Leah Monson Unawares

Randall L. Hall

6:19. ONLY ELEVEN MINUTES now until 6:30. Leah Monson fussed with the cookies, rearranging them for at least the seventh time and placing the small, red and green napkins at just the right angle. Then she pulled back the drapes and looked outside. It was still snowing.

Walking to the back of the Relief Society room, she turned on the slide projector one more time and adjusted the focus again. She felt in her pocket. There, carefully wrapped, was the spare bulb. Two minutes later she was at the window again. Still snowing. Perhaps, she thought with sudden anxiety, she had put the wrong day or time on the flyer. Quickly she walked down the hallway of the church to the bulletin board in the foyer and reread her note.

Please come and share an hour of Christmas spirit reviewing Leah Monson's recent trip to the Holy Land—A few, brief slides and comments accompanied by light refreshments. Sunday evening, December 25th, in the Relief Society room at 6:30 P.M.

She had purposely set the time late enough so most of the holiday activities would be over and early enough so families could bring their children, and she had made an extra two batches of cookies using real cream and real butter, something she never did for herself. Leah checked the clock again: 6:31. "Well," she said with a dutiful smile, "I'm sure the snow will cause some delay."

Leah was nearing sixty, rather short and round with a well-lined face that seemed laden with anxiety, and small blue eyes that never quite seemed to focus behind her glasses.

She looked at the clock once more: 6:33. Then, pulling back the curtains, she took one more hurried peek outside. Nothing but snow falling past the lights in the parking lot. Suddenly very tired, she arranged herself in a padded maroon chair near the front of the room and closed her eyes. Taking care not to dwell on her solitude, she thought back to her tour in Israel . . . the people had been so kind . . . the Sea of Galilee . . . Jerusalem, Jerusalem . . . the Garden Tomb . . . Leah felt her body slump into comfort.

* * *

"Leah, Leah?"

She heard her name being called. Shimon, the tour guide? Startled, she opened her eyes and looked up. Then she remembered.

"Have you already shown your slides?"

"No," she replied, sitting up straight, her head slowly clearing.

"Oh good, we'd love to see them."

He was a white-haired gentleman, not especially tall, but slender with a pleasing, light-filled countenance. Behind him stood a woman whose face was radiant and whose hair was equally white. They looked familiar but she could not place them. Perhaps, she thought, they were the older couple who had recently moved into the Morgan place.

Feeling herself redden, she stood. "Excuse me," she said much louder than she needed to, "I must have dozed off."

"An easy thing to do in such pleasant

quietness," the woman said in a voice wrapped with understanding.

Leah glanced quickly at the clock. 6:53.

"It's so late," she said, "perhaps we should begin. Those who come later will just have to see what they see." Then, sensing she spoke a bit harshly, she added, "but at least they'll be here for the refreshments."

The couple smiled. The man's sympathetic nod was reassuring.

Leah moved toward the projector, then stopped. Turning, she asked timidly, "Would either of you be willing to offer an opening prayer?"

The woman smiled, nodded, and stood. Leah bowed her head, and the woman began. As the woman prayed, Leah could not help glancing toward the front of the room where she stood. Somehow Leah knew that truly this was prayer, natural and sublime, spoken with reverence and an intimacy that seemed to bring heaven and earth together. With a slight twinge of guilt Leah closed her eyes and bathed in the spirit of the prayer. "Amen," she echoed at the end. She just sat there for a few seconds, refreshed and serene. Standing, she turned the lights off and the projector on. Pop. The room went dark, but Leah stayed calm. Turning on the light and smiling proudly she said, "Luckily I brought another bulb."

She took it carefully from her pocket and slowly unwrapped the tissue paper she had wrapped around it. She turned the projector slightly with one hand and fumbled with the latch to the compartment where the burned-out bulb was. It was stuck. She pulled harder and felt the projector falling. Grabbing it quickly with both hands, she secured it just in time to hear the unmistakable shattering of the extra bulb on the table.

Kneeling down, Leah bit her lower lip to keep from crying as she picked up the pieces. At least, she thought bravely, there were the cookies.

Suddenly the older gentleman was kneeling near the projector. "Let me see," he said almost to himself, "sometimes these bulbs get loose enough to stop working." He took out a clean white handkerchief from his pocket and slowly turned the bulb tightly into its socket. Leah could see no movement at all. Oh well, she thought to herself, they'll probably be glad that—

Her lamentation was cut short by the projector clicking on, with a steady beam of light focused on the screen at the front of the room.

"There," the man said, smiling. He sat down near his wife, waiting for the slides.

Leah wiped a tear from her eye and began. "Here's the airport in Tel Aviv. I took some slides of the airport and the plane in New York but I didn't really think that anyone would be interested in seeing that, especially when the flyer said slides about the Holy Land. That's why this first slide is taken just after we'd landed. It was a warm day and I didn't even realize that Jerusalem wasn't the capital of Israel. I just sort of thought that it would be and I was rather surprised to find that Tel Aviv . . .

" . . . that's the Shepherds' field. I had no idea how close Bethlehem was to Jerusalem. I could almost imagine the star appearing above us. It changed my feelings about Christmas . . .

" . . . and this is the Sea of Galilee, so deep blue and refreshing. I was about to say *cold* but somehow that word doesn't fit. I even talked myself into going swimming there the evening we stayed in Tiberias and the water was cold, not like the Mediterranean. But *refreshing* seems to be the best word. I'm sure the Savior felt that way about it."

"Yes," the woman replied confidently.

"This slide shows our group standing on the Mount of Beatitudes. It was a very calm place and beautiful. I tried to picture myself listening to the words of the Sermon on the Mount. And there, you see that lady in the pink blouse? She was from Phoenix, Arizona. Shirley McQuire. She lost her husband two years ago in a construction accident. We got so we could almost smile about her losing a husband and me not being able to find one. I was a little surprised at Nazareth, it was such a small place.

" . . . and at first I was a little disappointed with the River Jordan. It really wasn't a very big river. Of course it's hard to say exactly what it looked like at the time of the Savior . . ."

"I'm guessing much the same," the gentleman said kindly, "with a bit more vegetation on its banks."

"Perhaps," Leah conceded. "Anyway, I came to love the feeling that it had, a serenity about it. There was even one time when . . .

" . . . and as we came up over the hill from Bethany and saw the city for the first time, I started weeping. Of course, I know it looks much different now but still—Jerusalem. How I wished I could sing, 'Jerusalem, Jerusalem!'" Leah dropped her voice and added confidentially, "The Holy City, you know."

The old gentleman sighed. "The Holy City," he repeated, his voice full of sorrow, heaviness, and praise.

Leah looked toward him. "You've been there?"

The man half turned and smiled. "Yes and no."

"Well, for me it was marvelous. It's like it

has a presence or something. And I remember thinking of what is yet to happen there."

Leah paused and took a deep breath.

The projector clicked and whirred, and a new slide appeared on the screen.

"The Garden Tomb," was all Leah could say. Slowly she went through half a dozen slides of the tomb without speaking. The quietness in the room was warm and sure and healing.

She lingered in silence for just a moment longer and wiped her eyes dry; then she turned the lights on and the projector to cool. "Thank you so much for coming," she said, her heart full and pleased.

She looked at the clock on the wall: 8:42. "Oh my," Leah thought, walking quickly to the table at the front of the room. "I've baked some cookies. Would you please have some?" Leah motioned toward several trays on the table.

"Why thank you," the woman replied, accepting Leah's invitation.

It was then Leah remembered. The salt. She had meant to go next door and get some. How impossible to be completely out of something like salt. But then the phone call from Margaret Hansen wishing her a merry Christmas. And well, she hadn't thought about it until that very moment and now over one hundred saltless cookies sat on the table before them.

Leah felt a chill spreading from the inside as the woman slowly touched each plate as if deciding which of the three kinds to take.

She picked up a green napkin and took two cookies, as did her husband. Leah watched as they took a bite and smiled. She forced a smile as well and kept watching, waiting.

But they seemed to enjoy the cookies.

"Almost heavenly!" said the woman, smiling graciously.

"Delicious," her husband added.

Leah reached slowly for one herself. She nibbled at first, then took a full bite. They were rich and moist and yes, delicious. Leah smiled. The warmth came back into the room for her.

"Well, we must be going," the woman said. "Thank you for a most enjoyable evening. Merry Christmas."

"Yes, thank you so very much," the gentleman said. "Some wonderful slides and wonderful feelings. It must have been a marvelous time for you."

"Yes," said Leah, reaching for another cookie, "it was something I'll remember forever. Thank you again for coming. Merry Christmas."

The couple smiled and left the room.

"Oh dear," Leah thought as soon as they had gone, "I should have offered them some of the cookies to take home." She picked up one of the trays and bustled down the hallway but they were already out of sight. "Oh well, the neighbors will be happy," she thought.

Slowly Leah turned off the projector, put it in its case, and put away the screen. She placed the cookies in their Tupperware containers and turned off the lights. Carefully she made her way down the hall singing softly, "O little town of Bethlehem . . ."

She stood for a moment at the door in the foyer, buttoning her coat and looking out over the four or five inches of new snow that lay undisturbed on the sidewalks like a quilt of peace. "I'm glad I remembered my boots," Leah thought to herself as she walked carefully to her car, and placed the projector and cookies in the trunk.

The car started on the first try. Leah smiled. It had been a good evening, and they had been such a warm, receptive couple. Nice to have people like that in town, she thought as she made her way across the deserted parking lot, into the quiet Christmas night.

RANDALL L. HALL was born in Logan, Utah, served a mission in Brazil, and later received his masters degree in American Literature from Brigham Young University. He has worked for the LDS Church Educational System for over twenty years and is currently the CES Area Director for the Utah Valley South Area. He and his wife, Lloya, live in Orem and are the parents of eleven children. His previous publications include a novel (*Cory Davidson*), a book of poetry (*Mosaic*), and poems and stories in various periodicals and collections.

THE NORMAN ROCKWELL CHRISTMAS FEAST

Kathryn H. Kidd

GRANNY VAN PEEBLES was a funny old lady. She was the best bubble-gum bubble-blower I've ever seen, and she had an ancient convertible Volkswagen beetle that she washed and waxed every Saturday morning. Believe me, I was the envy of all the kids in the neighborhood. All *their* grandmothers did was watch soap operas and bake cookies. *My* grandmother got a traffic ticket for playing chicken at a stoplight with an off-duty police officer, which was infinitely more cool.

She was so young at heart that everyone thought she'd live forever, but she keeled over dead at a grocery store checkout line one Saturday afternoon, deeply engrossed in the cover story of the *Weekly World News*. My cousin Becca Rae was standing in the line with her, and she said Granny was laughing so hard about the headline ("World Ends Next Week!") that she scared the baby in the cart ahead of them into a crying fit. The last thing Granny ever said was "*Their* world may be ending next week, but this one sure as shootin' isn't." Then she dropped in the aisle like a brick, with the pages of the tabloid newspaper fluttering around her like hungry pigeons.

Grandpa decided to give Granny's powder-blue convertible bug to the first of his grandkids who completed an honorable mission. That promises to be a story in itself, but it hasn't ended yet, so I won't get into it here. The other big decision he made, after Granny was firmly planted under the sod of the Murray City Cemetery, was that he was going to continue the family tradition of Christmas dinner, even without Granny there. After all, a party's a party. When the light of the party goes out, you can cancel the party, or you can pull out the candles and carry on. Our family has always been of the candle-lighting kind, and I'm grateful for that.

Christmas dinner at the Van Peebles table was always a hectic affair. My dad was the third of four kids, and each of those kids had a passel of children of his own. My Aunt Lloydene is still popping out babies like kernels of microwave popcorn, although I'll wager to say that the kernels who are popping up now aren't in the running for the Volkswagen convertible.

Not only are the Van Peebleses prolific, but they're also as chummy as puppies in a litter. Back when Granny was alive, every last kid and grandkid showed up at that Christmas dinner every year. Without her sitting at the head of the table, we were going to be down to twenty-seven men, women, and children, plus Houdini, the family dog. Granny's presence would be missed, but the house would still be packed to the windowsills without her.

After Grandpa determined to continue the family tradition, there was one big decision he had to make—whether to continue serving the kind of Christmas dinner that was traditional in our family or to make some editorial changes. Naturally, he broached the subject with me. I like to think I'm Grandpa's favorite, being named after him and all. I know Granny always said he liked me best, but when I overheard her telling my cousin Marlon that *he* was

Grandpa's personal favorite, I realized she might have been stretching the truth.

Grandpa drove me down to Snelgrove's, which was a habit of his after he picked me up from a dentist's appointment. He ordered a banana split instead of his customary chocolate soda, so I thought he might have something on his mind. Chocolate sodas are desserts, but Grandpa always said that because banana splits have bananas in them, they're serious food. I was glad to see he was taking care of himself, nutritionally speaking, now that Granny was out of the picture.

"Tell me, Teancum," he said, "what do you think of Christmas dinner?"

"There's nothing to think about. It just *is*."

He took a large bite of banana with chocolate sauce on it, chewing slowly. When he swallowed, his Adam's apple bounced like a Ping-Pong ball. "I'm not talking about the dinner in general. I want to know what you think about the food."

Now it was my turn to concentrate on the ice cream in front of me, as I tried to judge how much of the truth Grandpa wanted to hear. Because although I'd never put much thought into Christmas dinner as a social event, every Van Peebles child, grandchild, and in-law had thought a whole lot about what Granny put on the table.

Hands down, Christmas dinner was the worst mishmash of garbage we put in our stomachs all year. The food was as prefab as one of those trailers you see being hauled down the highway in pieces, ready to be stapled together when it reaches its final destination. Although we all looked forward to Christmas dinner because we enjoyed the traditional hubbub of the reunion, Mom always carried an oversized handbag with her on Christmas Day.

It was full of bottles of Maalox and Rolaids and Tums. As new products came on the market, Mom would add rolls of Tempo or bottles of Tagamet or Pepcid AC to the inventory. On Christmas Day, half the people at the dinner visited Mom more than once, either for protection before the meal or for solace after it.

In fact, Houdini the dog got his name after the first Christmas dinner he attended. His name started out as Fred. But when a snowstorm drove him indoors when I was eleven, we each discovered independently that Fred had a talent for disposing of Granny's Christmas concoctions. That dog would eat anything. Uncle Harvey said that even Houdini couldn't make rabbits disappear as fast as Fred could eat a piece of Granny's peanut butter pie. Granny, instead of being insulted, changed Fred's name to Houdini on the spot. From then on, Houdini was as indispensable to Christmas dinner as the supplies Mom hid in her purse.

Truth be told, any change in the menu of our Christmas dinner could only be an improvement. I would have said that without hesitation while Granny was alive, but I didn't say that now because I didn't want to speak ill of the dead.

Without waiting for me to decide between truth and prevarication, Grandpa bailed me out. "What I'm asking is, how attached are you to pressed turkey roll? If I change the menu, are people gonna be upset?"

There was nothing to do but to tell the truth. "Let me tell you a secret, Grandpa. Have you ever seen that picture hanging in Aunt Lloydene's dining room?"

He snorted. "Your Aunt Lloydene doesn't *have* a dining room: She has a Tupperware inventory room. But yeah, I think I know the picture you mean. The Norman Rockwell one."

"That's it, Grandpa—the one where that huge family sits around the table with the turkey on it. That's my dream. I want a Norman Rockwell Christmas."

Grandpa raised his eyebrows and waited for me to continue.

"What I want is a Christmas dinner that has real food in it. I want mashed potatoes that come from potatoes instead of from flakes. I want stuffing that doesn't taste like it came out of a box. And a turkey that's shaped like a turkey, with wings and legs and a wishbone, and pieces that are either white meat or dark meat, but not both white meat and dark meat squashed together by a machine in the Armour plant."

"I think that can be arranged," said Grandpa.

But I was so caught up in my reverie that I kept right on trying to convince him. "It wouldn't be so hard, Grandpa. Aunt DarNell would be tickled if you'd ask her to bring a real turkey, and you'd have the rest of 'em fighting over who got to make the pies. Mom could make real mashed potatoes if you asked her. There's gotta be a recipe somewhere."

Grandpa put down his spoon before his ice cream was even finished. He lifted his water glass, checked it for floaters, and drained the glass in a big gulp. If I'd thought about it, I would have known that was a bad sign. Whenever Grandpa was ready to rope somebody into one of his grand and terrible schemes, he fortified himself with a big glass of water. But I was too distracted by my dream of a Norman Rockwell Christmas to realize how much trouble I was in. I'd never told anybody about my wish, and now that I'd finally talked about it, I didn't want the opportunity to go to waste.

Then he opened his mouth, and I forgot all about Norman Rockwell. "Actually, Teancum, I've never been big on that covered dish stuff. I was thinking you and I could do the dinner. It's just food. How much trouble could it be?"

"I can fix hot dogs," I said. "If you want hot dogs, I'm your man. That's all I know how to cook."

"You don't need to know how to cook," he said. "They've got cookbooks for that. Besides, I'm going to do the real cooking. All I need is somebody to show up a few minutes before dinner and help me put the stuff on the table. It's just go-fer work. Are you up for it?"

"I'll be your go-fer," I said, and my fate was sealed. In my excitement over getting a bona fide Norman Rockwell dinner, I didn't even think to have Grandpa sign a release that would relieve me of any liability if the meal was an unmitigated disaster.

On Christmas afternoon, Mom and Dad finally tore the twins away from their Christmas presents long enough to march us over to Grandpa's house. We arrived after Aunt Lloydene and her group, which meant that Uncle Willard already had possession of the remote control. He lowered the volume long enough to wrinkle his nose in my direction.

"Pee-yew. I think a muskrat died in here."

"Nope," said Dad. "Tea's wearing eau-de-skunk. His *girl*friend gave it to him."

I still wasn't ready to admit that Cookie and I were an item, so I gave Dad a dirty look and hied my kolob to the kitchen. There I was greeted by the most glorious gastronomical vision I ever hope to see. There, by actual count, were twenty-seven of the tiniest turkeys God ever created, stuffed and baked to perfection. There was a mountain of steaming, boiled potatoes, waiting to be mashed and buttered.

There was a big bowl of homemade cranberry sauce, and a tureen full of soup that smelled like heaven itself. I opened the refrigerator to find three Jell-O molds that were full of the most Christmassy red Jell-O salads I'd ever seen. This kitchen had come a long way since Grandma and Dow Chemical had presented us with Christmas dinner last year. As much as I missed Grandma, I realized there may be some advantages to life without her.

"This is just like the dinner in the picture, Grandpa," I said. "How'd you do it?"

"I was a cook in the Navy. You know that."

"I thought you washed dishes in the Navy."

"Same difference. I was in the kitchen. There's not a big stretch between cleaning up after the cooks and doing the cooking yourself. Grab yourself an apron. You have work to do."

I pulled an apron over my head and tied it on. "How'd you shrink those turkeys?"

"Those are Rock Cornish hens," he said. "They taste just like turkey, only everybody gets one. Think of it, Teancum: a wishbone on every plate. Today, everybody's wish comes true."

I didn't need a wishbone—I already had my wish. I'd always suspected there was more in the world than Stove Top stuffing. Today I was finally going to find out what it was.

We couldn't fit around one dinner table to say the prayer, so we congregated in the living room. Uncle Willard muted the television long enough for Aunt DarNell to thank the Lord for our bounteous feast. She went on longer than it had taken me to set the tables, carried away by the aroma of the first real Christmas dinner most of us had ever smelled. The amens resounded, as the descendants of Teancum and Minnie Van Peebles ran, crawled, or were carried to their respective dining chairs.

"Something's missing," said Uncle Harvey, pushing back his chair. "We forgot Houdini."

"We don't need Houdini today," said Grandpa. "Feeding this food to a dog would be casting pearls before swine."

"Pearls before *canine*," Uncle Harvey corrected, and he guffawed loud and long. Uncle Harvey always laughed the hardest at his own jokes. But he pulled his chair back up to the dinner table, sans the dog. Christmas dinner seemed lonely without Houdini begging under the table.

Napkins were lowered with a flourish into waiting laps. Then the procession began. I carried the soup tureen from table to table, as Grandpa ladled out hearty portions of the thick greenish liquid. Reverently, everyone waited, spoons poised, until Grandpa and I were seated and the chef took the first bite.

"Aah!" said Grandpa.

"Aah!" echoed his twenty-six joyous descendants. Grandpa beamed, and I puffed out my chest with the pride of being part of such a glorious repast.

"This is the finest soup I've ever tasted," said my cousin Willardina. Willardina has always been a boot licker, but for once she was speaking the truth. My cousin Boynton, the pickiest eater in our family, was the first one to hold up his bowl for seconds.

It was Cousin Fanny who brought the celebration to a dead halt. Until today, Fanny had been the finest cook our family had ever produced. She won ribbons in her home economic classes and everything, so everyone had looked up to her as the family authority. She took a sip of soup and then another, making little kissy noises over her spoon as she tried to distinguish the constituent ingredients. "I taste the peppercorns," she said. "And the cayenne, and the Worcestershire sauce, and the lemon, and

the garlic. I just can't place the base. Is it chicken?"

"Nope," said Grandpa. "It's turtle."

"Turtle?" squeaked my cousin Barbie. "We're eating *turtles?* Oh, *yukko!*"

Boynton laughed and chanted, "We're eating Ralphie. We're eating Ralphie."

"Who in tarnation is Ralphie?" asked Grandpa.

Aunt Edna gave him a murderous look. "Ralphie's the box turtle we gave Pearline for Christmas," she said. Pearline theatrically jumped up from the table and burst into tears. She ran from the room, sobbing. "Go look after your sister, Boynton," said Aunt Edna. "If you're going to tease her like that, you have to pay the consequences."

No sooner had Boynton hopped up to help Pearline than my cousin Minnie jumped up and ran pell-mell to the bathroom. "Minnie's going to barf again," shouted Boynton gleefully, jumping out of her way so they wouldn't collide in the hallway. Minnie always threw up at the slightest provocation, just to be sociable. She did a great job of it this time, judging by the sound of her performance. The moment Minnie barfed, the soup course was over for everyone.

"Do you have any other surprises?" Aunt Edna hissed, once Pearline had composed herself and Minnie had swished out her mouth with Listerine.

"I'm full of surprises," said Grandpa, "but unless somebody got mollusks for Christmas, we should be okay." Nobody even gave him a courtesy laugh, and Grandpa settled back into his chair, wounded at the injustice of it all. But nobody comforted Grandpa; everyone turned his attention to the mounds of food before us, more interested in the dinner than we were in the cook.

Uncle Parris dug a spoonful of stuffing from the cavity of his Rock Cornish hen and popped it in his mouth. He spat it right back onto his plate. "Yuck! What's this garbage?" Aunt Edna gave him a withering look but he ignored her, poking at a gray gelatinous glob with his fork. "There was a piece of lung in my Stove Top," he reported.

Aunt Edna leaned over for a look at the quivering mass on Uncle Harvey's plate. "That's a lung, all right," she concurred. "Whose lung *is* it?"

"Maybe it's a *turtle* lung," said Boynton, and Cousin Pearline burst into tears again. Aunt Edna banished him from the table, and Grandpa's Christmas dinner suffered its first defection.

Grandpa waited until Boynton had parked himself in front of the television and the hubbub of his departure had died down. "That's not a lung," he said, "and it's not Stove Top." By now he was exasperated, and his voice wheezed in annoyance. "That's eggplant-oyster stuffing, entirely homemade. Haven't you ever seen oysters? What kind of barbarians did I raise, anyway?"

"Nobody in our family eats oysters," said Aunt Edna.

"How do you know?" asked Grandpa. "You've never tasted 'em."

"Nor will I," said Aunt Edna. She stayed at the table, but she pushed her plate away. My cousins Barbie and Willardina and Marlon pushed their plates away too. Five descendants were down, with twenty-one still to go.

"At least we've got Jell-O," said Cousin Thos. "There's *always* room for Jell-O." He took a huge wedge of a Jell-O mold and shoveled a forkful into his gullet. His eyes bugged, and he whisked the napkin from his lap. Out came the Jell-O. Thos left the room to rinse out his mouth, and when he returned, he joined Boynton in front of the television set.

Fanny took a tentative taste, smacking the Jell-O around her palate like a taster at the king's table. "This is tomato aspic," she said. "It's got tomato juice and horseradish and onions in it. I think those little squirmy things are shrimp."

"I don't want onion Jell-O!" shrieked my brother Nephi. "This is the grodiest dinner I've ever tasted." With that, he threw his napkin across the table and went to the kitchen. He banged around in cupboards and the refrigerator, apparently looking for edible sustenance.

Uncle Harvey pushed his chair out and faked a yawn. "I'm going to get a breath of air," he said. He trotted to the door and opened it, drawing air into his lungs conspicuously. He was too discreet to call, "Here, fella," loudly enough for any human to hear it, but Houdini had dog ears, and he bounded inside with a bark of joy.

I took the first bite of mashed potatoes. Being Grandpa's favorite grandson and all, I refrained from spitting them out on the table, but they were the nastiest mashed potatoes I'd ever put in my mouth. "What'd you put in these potatoes?" I asked, trying to keep my voice casual.

"Who said those were potatoes?" asked Grandpa. "Those are pureed turnips. They'll put hair on your chest."

"I don't *want* hair on my chest," whined Becca Rae. She threw down her napkin and exited the table, and the eighteen people she left behind gave her envious looks.

I made a whistling sound in the back of my mouth, and Houdini's ears perked right up. He scampered across the room and parked next to my left elbow. When nobody was looking, I scooped up my pureed turnips and threw them

on the floor in a lump. Houdini sniffed and then looked up at me with an aggrieved expression. Then, without taking a bite of my turnips, he wandered around the table to see what Aunt Lloydene had to offer. Aunt Lloydene tossed some unidentified item to Houdini and then looked up in surprise. "Well, I'll be," said Uncle Willard. "Even Houdini can't make *that* stuff disappear." Then he whispered under his breath, "Traitor!"

A slamming sound came from the kitchen. My brother Lehi left the table to investigate. Soon he reappeared. "What was that puffy thing in the oven?" he asked.

"That's our dessert," said Grandpa. "It's a raspberry souffle."

"I think it's a raspberry *pancake*," said Lehi. "Nephi opened the oven to look at it, and when he shut the door the whole thing went flat." Grandpa leaped so quickly from his chair that Lehi threw himself against the wall for protection. "He didn't do it on purpose, Grandpa. It went flat all by itself."

The party broke up about that time, seeing as how none of us wanted to stick around and listen to a grown man cry. Making as little fuss as we could, we grabbed our coats and scarves and sneaked away, leaving Grandpa to mourn his ruined masterpiece of a dinner. He and Houdini had food enough to last a month, if he could convince the dog to eat it. The last thing I heard him say, as I pulled the door shut behind us, was, "They didn't even taste my cranberry chutney."

We were still standing on Grandpa's front walk when Mom dug through her purse and passed around Tums for everyone. Not that we'd actually eaten anything to disagree with us, but she medicated us the way you get rabies shots after you have a close encounter with a bat—just in case. While we were chewing the wintergreen-flavored lozenges, my cousin Barbie said, "I sure am hungry." The rest of us had to admit she had a point.

We were downright lucky that the local McDonald's was open on Christmas afternoon. The whole family went there after we escaped Grandpa's house, drowning our sorrows in Big Macs and gigantic orders of fries. Aunt Edna and Uncle Parris treated us all, and it was the best Christmas gift I ever got from that neck of the family.

We were attacking our Christmas feast when Aunt Lloydene choked. I thought a hunk of bacon-double-cheese had gone down the wrong pipe, and I had my hand raised to slap her on the back when I caught sight of the thing that had caused her to lose her breath. There, idling at the drive-up window, was a powder-blue Volkswagen convertible bug.

"It can't be," I said.

"Of course it is," said Uncle Harvey. "Either that passenger is the ugliest woman I've ever seen, or Houdini's riding shotgun in the front seat."

We invited Grandpa inside to share Christmas dinner with us, and once he got over his embarrassment at being caught at McDonald's, he thought that was a good idea. He unwrapped Houdini's Big Mac and left it on the ground outside. Houdini gobbled it up and begged through the window for more.

It was only as I polished off my apple turnover that I looked at the situation with new eyes. As I sat there watching Cousin Boynton pulling Barbie's pigtails and seeing my brother Moroni smear his face with special sauce, I realized that the thing I'd always admired about that Norman Rockwell picture wasn't the turkey shaped like a turkey, or the mountains of

potatoes that weren't made from flakes. It was the people in that picture—the kids with freckles and crooked teeth, and the adults with love in their faces—that made Christmas dinner so important. No matter what our family ate, we'd had that treasure all along.

Although Grandpa never admitted it, the family theorized that his beautiful Christmas dinner ended up as compost around the rose bushes in his backyard. When we learned in the spring that all his roses had mysteriously died during the winter, Grandpa's pureed turnips and his eggplant-oyster stuffing were the only poisons any of us could name that were strong enough to do the job.

By the next Christmas, I was in the mission field, and my companion and I were invited to eat dinner at the home of some recent converts. The spread that Sister Brandon provided was like manna from heaven. It tasted every bit as good as I had always imagined the turkey dinner in Aunt Lloydene's Norman Rockwell picture would taste, but it wasn't my Norman Rockwell Christmas dinner. I'd had my Norman Rockwell feast the year before—not in the family dining room, but gathered with a loving family under the neon shadow of the golden arches.

KATHRYN H. KIDD is the author of several books of Mormon fiction, among them *Paradise Vue* and *Return to Paradise,* and has also co-authored the science fiction book *Lovelock* with Orson Scott Card. She and her husband, Clark, are members of the Algonkian Ward in the Warrenton Virginia Stake, and are ordinance workers in the Washington D.C. Temple. For the record, her culinary tastes run to eggplant-oyster stuffing and cranberry chutney, and she never dines under the golden arches.

A Mighty Fine Christmas Message

Alma J. Yates

It was a good message, boy," Bill called to me as I climbed out of his ancient, army-green Plymouth and pulled my coat around me to ward off the icy night. Bill stared down the street into the darkness, his cracked, calloused, grease-stained hands clasping the steering wheel. It was always hard for me to know what Bill was thinking. All his secrets were locked behind the browned, leathery face topped by his graying, short-cropped hair. "I'd sure like to know the scriptures like you, boy," he muttered, shaking his head. "But," he added with resignation, "I figure I'm too old for all that now." He cleared his throat and a hoarse chuckle rumbled in his chest. "I could tell you plenty about diesel engines—I've worked on them for over fifty years—but I never had much time for the Bible and that sort of thing. Yeah," he added with a sigh, "it was a mighty fine message, boy."

I coughed nervously into my fist and muttered a good night. I didn't ever know what to say around Bill. I'd known him all my life—at least I had lived down the street from him—and yet, I still didn't know what to do with myself when he was around.

Slamming the car door, I started up the front walk. I glanced about me. The porch light was encased in a misty haze of snow. I ducked my head further into my collar and leaned against the white wintery onslaught.

"Well, Daniel, you're back early," Dad greeted me. I pulled my coat off and shook the melting snow from it. "How'd it go?" Dad asked.

I shrugged. "Same as usual," I grumbled, dropping down on the sofa and closing my eyes.

"How's Sister Rencher?"

"She says she feels a lot better. At least she can get up and around with her walker." For a while both of us were quiet, and then I said, as much to myself as to Dad, "Well, there's one advantage of home teaching with Bill. When he's not in a talkative mood, which is most of the time, we can visit all three widows in about thirty minutes. That must be some kind of record."

There was a rustle of paper and I opened my eyes. Dad had dropped the newspaper he had been reading into his lap and was staring at me. "What's wrong with Bill?" he asked.

I heaved a sigh. "Nothing. I guess. That is if you don't mind doing everything yourself," I added sarcastically. "All he ever does is show up and beep his horn. The second Wednesday of every month. There are some things that never change—Bill's beeping horn is one of them. No appointment. We're just supposed to know. But all the rest is my job. I do the talking, give the lesson, everything."

I heaved a sigh. "Why does Bill home teach anyway?" I asked, suddenly curious.

"What's that?"

I shrugged and shifted my weight. "Well, ever since the bishop assigned me to Bill three months ago, I've wondered why he even goes. Has Bill ever gone to church?"

Dad dropped his paper on the floor. "He used to go some. Before his wife, Tillie, had her stroke. But even then he always seemed more at home in his garage dressed in a pair of dirty coveralls with grease to his elbows."

"I can believe it," I grinned. "He always smells like an old engine. He's never able to get all the grease off his hands." I hesitated. "Bill smokes, doesn't he?"

Dad looked over at me and shrugged. "I've never seen him."

"You don't have to see him. All you've got to do is look at his yellow-stained fingers. And he sucks those gross green lozenges to kill the smell. That's why I can't understand Bishop Clark letting him home teach."

"Those three widows never complain."

"But a home teacher's supposed to set an example. And don't tell me this is my chance to get Bill active. You and I both know that's not ever going to happen."

"I suppose the Lord knows that home teaching is one place where Bill can do some good," Dad answered somberly.

"Do some good?" I gasped. "But he's totally inactive."

"You can learn something from Bill."

"I don't want to be a diesel mechanic."

"Maybe you can learn something about the gospel."

"From Bill?" I asked incredulously. "I'll bet he's never read a scripture in his life."

"I don't think you know Bill. When he stands before the Lord, I doubt the Lord will be looking at his greasy hands and tobacco-stained fingers." Dad cleared his throat and changed the subject. "Can you take your brother's paper route again in the morning? He still has that bad sore throat and cough."

The next morning I was up a little before five, tossing bundles of the *Herald* onto the back seat of the car. During the night the snow had stopped and the world was buried under its wet cottony mass. I glanced down the driveway and wondered if I should take a few minutes to push some of the snow away before pulling out. Blowing on my numb fingertips and stomping the snow from my feet, I shook my head. I didn't have time, I reasoned. And I was sure I could get out without getting stuck.

The first stop I made was at Sister Rencher's. With most people I didn't make the effort to set the paper inside the front door. I just tossed it in the general direction of the porch. But with Sister Rencher I made an exception because it was so hard for her to get around. I snatched a paper off the back seat, stepped from the car, and sprinted for the front steps. I stopped at the end of the walk and stared in disbelief. The front walk and steps were swept completely clean. I glanced at my watch—5:15 A.M. "Boy, somebody's sure been up early this morning," I muttered, hurrying up the clean walk and setting the paper inside the storm door. "Maybe Sister Rencher can get around with that walker better than I thought," I grinned.

"That was quick," Dad called to me as I burst in from the cold ninety minutes later. He was just putting on his coat and stuffing papers into his briefcase before heading out of the door for work.

"There's a ton of snow out there," I remarked. "It must have snowed another four inches after we went to bed."

"I guess you cleaned off the walks and driveway," Dad joked.

"What did you want me to do, get up at three o'clock?" I grinned back. "I was lucky to get the papers delivered. But somebody was sure up early. Sister Rencher's walks were clean as spring."

Dad smiled. "What about Sister Hatch's and Sister Ballard's?"

"Dad, I was delivering papers, not home teaching. I don't go over that way."

The following Tuesday, a week before Christmas, I was in my room getting ready for a Young Adult Christmas party. We were going caroling and then to Tracie Heath's for food and fun. As I pulled on my heaviest socks and stomped my feet into my moon boots, a car horn began beeping out on the street. I ignored it until Mom called down the hall, "Daniel, were you going home teaching tonight?"

"Tonight? No, I've got a Young Adult caroling party."

"Looks like Bill's out front waiting for you."

"Bill?" I gasped, coming down the hall. "We've already done our home teaching this month. You sure it's him?"

"That's his black Ford truck, isn't it?"

I rubbed the steam from the kitchen window and peered out. It was Bill's truck all right. I thought his '63 green Plymouth was ancient. His black Ford was an antique, something from the early '50s. "If anybody thinks I'm going with him tonight—" I glared out through the window again. "What does he think I do, just sit around waiting for him to pick me up to—"

"Daniel," Mom cut me short, "you don't even know what he wants."

"Mom, I'm almost late."

"Just tell him. Surely he'll understand that you had other plans."

Grumbling to myself, I stepped out into the icy evening in my shirt sleeves and trotted out to the black Ford. Bill opened the door and leaned across the seat to talk to me.

"Did we have an appointment tonight?" I asked before he could speak, flapping my arms and shuffling my feet against the biting cold.

"Christmas is next week," was Bill's simple explanation as he rubbed the bristle on his chin. "I have a couple of things for the ladies," he added. "Would you like to come?"

"I have a Young Adult party. I didn't know we'd planned anything."

"It should take only a minute," Bill said. "You'd better grab a coat, though." He chuckled. "This old truck ain't got much of a heater. But I had to bring it instead of the Plymouth." He nodded his head toward the back. "Got a little something extra for Vivian Rencher."

I glanced in the back of the truck. A bulky object lay under a ragged canvas tarp.

"I'll get you back for your party," Bill went on when he saw my hesitation.

"Did you have an appointment?" Mom asked as I banged the front door and went for my coat.

"No," I sighed, "but that doesn't make much difference to Bill. And I'm going to freeze in that black heap of his. No heater and the door on my side doesn't close. Dang! Of all nights!"

Bill and I didn't speak as we drove to Sister Ballard's place. And, as I expected, I almost froze.

When we stopped in front of Sister Ballard's place, Bill grabbed a brown paper sack from under the seat and the two of us started up the walk to the front door. I knocked once and, almost immediately, Sister Ballard pulled the door open and peered out at us. It was a moment before she focused, and then a huge smile burst upon her face and she pushed the storm door open and greeted us cheerfully, "I wondered if you'd come tonight. Well, come in."

We took our usual places on the worn couch with the afghan draped over it. Before Sister Ballard could drop into her chair in front of us, Bill held out the brown paper sack and announced gruffly, "Some walnuts. Off my tree."

"Why, thank you, Bill. I used your last ones at Thanksgiving. I guard them all year. I keep them in the freezer to keep them fresh."

"They're shelled and cleaned and everything," Bill added, looking down at his rough, cracked hands. He rubbed them together and I could hear the dry chaffing sound. I studied them for a moment, remembering the message I'd given last month on the Word of Wisdom. Though the Word of Wisdom had been only a small part of the First Presidency message that month, I'd hammered pretty heavy on it. I really hadn't needed to, not for the sisters. I suppose it had been a cruel attempt on my part to dig at Bill's bad habit.

"Why, Bill," Sister Ballard exclaimed, bringing me back to the present, "there must be five pounds of shelled nuts here."

Bill shrugged self-consciously and pulled on his nose.

"It must have taken hours to do all this work. Thank you so very much."

Bill wasn't one to accept praise or compliments very well. Any fuss over him seemed to make him nervous, self-conscious, and tight-lipped. His only escape was to turn the focus to someone else. He jerked out his red handkerchief, blew his nose, and then to my surprise announced, "The boy's got a Christmas message for you."

Startled, I glanced over at Bill, who began rubbing his hands on his pants and tapping his right foot. I wanted to protest, but any protest at this stage would have been futile. With no further notice or preparation, the only thing that seemed appropriate was the Christmas story.

When I finished my choppy Christmas account, having forgotten some parts and mixed up others, I ducked my head, my ears and neck bright with embarrassed confusion. Bill pushed himself to his feet and said, "That was a mighty fine Christmas message, boy." He coughed and added, "The boy can say a prayer before we go."

Sister Ballard nodded her consent and I prayed. As we were leaving, Bill stopped by Sister Ballard's wood burning stove as though remembering something. Turning back to Sister Ballard, he asked, "Them deacons did bring you your load of wood, didn't they?" She smiled and nodded. "And it's split, ain't it?"

Sister Ballard hesitated. "Oh, I can take care of that fine."

"You mean they didn't split it?" Bill burst out, almost angry.

"Don't worry about it, Bill. I can manage fine. I don't use the stove that much anyway. Bishop Clark keeps telling me I shouldn't fuss with my stove, that I should just turn on the furnace. I do most of the time, but on cold nights I surely do enjoy putting my feet up next to that warmth—"

"But they didn't split the wood?" Bill broke in.

"Oh, the neighbor boy comes over sometimes and—"

"Me and the boy will split the wood," Bill cut in. "I got my ax in the truck if the boy can borrow yours."

I couldn't believe that Bill was really offering to split wood. Tonight! I had my good clothes on. And if we split wood, I'd never make it over to Tracie's place before everyone left to go caroling. But Bill was already halfway to the truck.

A few minutes later the two of us were in Sister Ballard's backyard splitting wood in the dim yellow light from a weak bulb on the back porch.

"What good's a bag of nuts?" Bill muttered as he swung his ax furiously. "She can't get warm with a bag of nuts, can she? I shouldn't ought to've forgotten. I usually don't forget, boy. I usually check up better. I knew something wasn't right, but I didn't know what. Then I saw that cold stove. She usually has a little fire going in it. That ain't much to ask for. These widows need taking care of. A sack of nuts and all the talk about angels and shepherds and mangers is fine, but on cold nights Martha Ballard likes wood to burn."

I stopped chopping and stared over at Bill. I forgot my good clothes, my cold hands, my wet feet. I studied Bill for a moment, this time looking past his chapped, cracked, stained hands. When I resumed chopping, the caroling party seemed so insignificant.

Thirty minutes later all the wood was split and piled next to the back door. As we were leaving, Bill warned Sister Ballard, "Now don't you go splitting no more wood. There's them that can do it for you, that should do it for you."

Sister Hatch seemed to be waiting for us. She opened the door after the first ring, her face lighted up with a smile. She grabbed my arm and pulled me inside. "I just knew this was the night," she laughed, pumping Bill's hand and leading us both into her living room. "I even have hot chocolate and fruitcake."

"These're for you," Bill said, holding out another sack of walnuts.

"Oh, Bill," she gasped as she took the sack,

opened it tenderly, and peered inside. "You never forget, do you, Bill?"

Bill's nervous agitation started again, so he jabbed a thumb in my direction and said hoarsely, "The boy's got a Christmas message, then we've got to be on our way. The boy's got a party."

Our last stop was Sister Rencher's. The door opened before I even had a chance to knock, and Sister Rencher, grinning and hobbling along with her metal walker in front of her, welcomed us inside. Once more Bill went through his ritual with the walnuts. He and Sister Rencher chatted about the weather, her new great-grandson, and the horrible condition of the city streets. I was rapidly reviewing the Christmas story in my mind, getting ready for the moment when Bill would turn the time to me. Suddenly Bill stood and said, looking at the floor, "I've got a little something else for you." Turning to me he asked, "Want to help, boy? You can hold the door for me." Bill went to the truck, tore the canvas tarp off some kind of chair, dragged the chair from the truck bed, and brought it up the walk. He staggered into the house, lugging a huge oak rocking chair, crafted and polished to near perfection. He set it down gently in the middle of the room, stepped back, and smiled proudly. Sister Rencher just stared, unable to speak. She looked first at the chair, then at Bill, and finally back at the chair.

"When your other one broke last spring," Bill explained shyly, "I figured I'd make you another one. I used to make them all the time, you know, my daddy being a carpenter and all. I don't figure this one will break on you. It's not like them store-bought things."

Bill was finished. The smile disappeared, his

words dried up, and he dropped down on the couch beside me.

Slowly Sister Rencher pulled herself to her feet and crept over to the rocking chair. She touched its smooth, hard glossy finish with the tips of her fingers. She pushed on its high back, and it began to rock rhythmically. Slowly she eased her frail body into its comforting, curved-wood grasp, and leaned her gray head against its solid back. For a moment she sat very still; then she began to rock, ever so slowly, and as she rocked a smile came to her lips and huge crystal tears welled up in her eyes. "Thank you, Bill," she whispered. "Oh, how I've missed my other one. But this," she added, touching the curved arms, "this would put my old one to shame."

Bill coughed and announced suddenly, "The boy's got a bit of a Christmas message for you."

"Let's have a prayer first," Sister Rencher suggested.

"The boy can pray, too."

"I'll pray tonight, Bill," Sister Rencher said softly.

The three of us bowed our heads, and, as Sister Rencher prayed, I understood so well why Bill Hayward had never been released as a home teacher.

"And, Father in Heaven," Sister Rencher prayed, "I thank thee so very, very much for Bill and his kindness. I thank thee for the many times he's pushed the snow, raked the leaves, tilled and weeded the garden, and cared for my every need. He has truly been an instrument in thine hands. Oh, Father in Heaven, please bless and keep this great man."

As soon as the *amens* were said, Bill nervously turned and stammered, "The boy's got a mighty fine message for you."

For a moment I couldn't speak. I had a lump as big as my fist in my throat, but it wasn't the lump that stopped me. My mind went blank. I, who had thought I knew the scriptures so well, especially compared to someone like Bill Hayward, couldn't seem to remember anything—not even the Christmas story, at least not well enough to give it right then. The thing that did come to mind was a strange, strange parable. And it wasn't even one that had anything to do with Christmas—or so I thought.

I wet my lips and rubbed my hands on my pant legs. "I guess I'd like to explain what Christmas means to me," I stammered hesitantly. "At least what it means tonight." I looked down at my hands. They were clean. The nails were clipped, the palms devoid of callouses. "There were two men that went to the temple to pray, one a Pharisee and the other a publican," I began. "The Pharisee was clean and educated and thought himself so very wise. The publican was a laborer, with dirty, calloused hands. Both men went to the temple to pray, and the Pharisee . . ."

When we reached my home, Bill clasped the steering wheel and stared down into the blackness beyond the piercing glare of the headlights. "It was a mighty fine message, boy," he said. "But I don't ever recall hearing the part of the Christmas story you gave at Vivian Rencher's, you know about the two fellows going to the temple." He paused. "I'm not even sure I figured out the meaning. I guess that's what happens when a fellow studies diesel engines more than the scriptures."

"Oh, but I think you do know the scriptures, Bill," I answered quietly. I turned to Bill and held out my hand. I had shaken hands with Bill before but never unless he had offered his first. "Thanks, Bill," I said huskily. "Thanks for your message," I continued, shaking his rough hand. "It was a mighty fine message."

ALMA J. YATES is the author of six novels, *The Miracle of Miss Willie; Horse Thieves; The Inner Storm; Ghosts in the Baker Mine; No More Strangers, PLEASE!;* and *Nick.* He is also the author of numerous short stories and articles that have appeared in the *Friend,* the *New Era,* and the *Ensign.* He is a school administrator in Snowflake, Arizona, where he lives with his wife, Nicki, and their seven sons and one daughter. "A Mighty Fine Christmas Message" first appeared in the December 1989 issue of the *New Era.*